TRANSPACIFIC
FIELD OF DREAMS

TRANSPACIFIC FIELD OF DREAMS

HOW BASEBALL LINKED THE UNITED STATES AND JAPAN IN PEACE AND WAR

SAYURI GUTHRIE-SHIMIZU

THE UNIVERSITY OF
NORTH CAROLINA PRESS
CHAPEL HILL

© 2012 The University of North Carolina Press
All rights reserved
Set in Merlo and Aller types by Tseng Information Systems, Inc.
Manufactured in the United States of America

The paper in this book meets the guidelines for permanence and durability of the Committee on Production Guidelines for Book Longevity of the Council on Library Resources.

The University of North Carolina Press has been a member of the Green Press Initiative since 2003.

Library of Congress Cataloging-in-Publication Data
Guthrie-Shimizu, Sayuri.
Transpacific field of dreams : how baseball linked the United States and Japan in peace and war / Sayuri Guthrie-Shimizu.
    p. cm.
Includes bibliographical references and index.
ISBN 978-0-8078-3562-3 (cloth : alk. paper)
1. Baseball—Political aspects—United States. 2. Baseball—Political aspects—Japan. 3. United States—Foreign relations—Japan.
4. Japan—Foreign relations—United States. I. Title.
GV863.A1G87 2012
796.357—dc23
2011044953

Portions of this book appeared earlier, in somewhat different form, as "For Love of the Game: Baseball in Early U.S.-Japanese Encounters and the Rise of a Transnational Sporting Fraternity," *Diplomatic History* 28, no. 5 (2004): 637–62; and "Baseball in U.S.-Japanese Relations: A Vehicle of Soft Power in Historical Perspective," in *Soft Power Superpowers: Cultural and National Assets of Japan and the United States*, ed. Yasushi Watanabe and David L. McConnell (Armonk, NY: M. E. Sharpe, 2008). Reprinted here with permission.

16 15 14   5 4 3 2

For 220 and 284,

in memory of victims of the

2011 Tōhoku earthquakes

and tsunami

CONTENTS

Acknowledgments ix

Introduction 1

CHAPTER 1.
   Pacific Crossings 11

CHAPTER 2.
   Colonial Baseball 40

CHAPTER 3.
   Leagues of Their Own 75

CHAPTER 4.
   The Business of Baseball 109

CHAPTER 5.
   Empires of Fun and Games 140

CHAPTER 6.
   Spartan Leagues 171

CHAPTER 7.
   A Field of New Dreams 198

CHAPTER 8.
   The Search for Postwar Order 224

Epilogue 241

Notes 245

Selected Bibliography 285

Index 305

A section of illustrations follows page 170.

ACKNOWLEDGMENTS

Writing this book was a long journey, and I have, as most long-distance travelers do, accumulated debts of gratitude to countless individuals and organizations along the way. First, I would like to thank the following institutions for their financial support: Michigan State University's Intramural Research Grant Program (IRGP) made possible a semester of full-time research and writing; the Social Science Research Council / Japan Foundation Center for Global Partnership and the Japan Foundation's Short-Term Research Fellowship funded earlier stages of research in Japan; travel grants provided by the Northeast Council of the Association for Asian Studies and the University of Maryland Center for Historical Studies were indispensable to visits to archival collections within the United States. Archivists and librarians who have assisted me in the course of my archival odyssey are too numerous to list in full here, but I would like to acknowledge some of them by way of expressing my deep appreciation for their support and expertise. David Kelly of the Library of Congress, Julia Gardner of the University of Chicago Library Special Collections, Akiko Ogawa and Reiko Yamane of the Japanese Baseball Hall of Fame Museum and Library, Eiko Sakaguchi of the Prange Collection, Tokiko Bazzell of the University of Hawaii Hamilton Library, and Miruko Atsuta of the Japanese Foreign Ministry Archives unstintingly shared their fount of knowledge about the records I needed to consult. Frank Baldwin, Frank Costigliola, Itsuki Kurashina, Bill Lannen, Michael Lewis, Patrick Miller, Masako Notoji, Steven Riess, Cecilia Samonte, Takuya Sasaki, Kristin Stapleton, Koji Terachi, Takuya Toda-Ozaki, and Hiroshi Yoneyama provided me with venues for presenting my preliminary research and receiving valuable feedback from informed audiences.

Many colleagues generously shared their own work in progress or their time by reading and critiquing my earlier drafts, and some of them directed my attention to scholarship I overlooked that was relevant to my project. These generous souls and comrades in the community of scholars include Toyomi Asano, E. Taylor Atkins, Eiichiro Azuma, Thomas Blackwood, Philip Block, Robert Bonner, Sandra Collins, Matthew Connelly, John Coogan, Mark Dyreson, Maureen Flanagan, Gerald Gems, Dan Gilbert, Laura Hein, Masaru Ikei, Richard Isomaki, Kohei Kawashima, William Kelly, Barbara Keys, Hidemasa Kokaze, Fumitaka Kurosawa, Barak Kushner, Peter Levine, Michael Lewis, Mary Lui, William Marshall, Adam McKeown, Hiromi Monobe, Emer O'Dwyer, Manako Ogawa, Michael Stamm, David Stowe, Yasuko Takezawa, William Tsutsui, Matthew Wittmann, Yūjin Yaguchi, Louise Young, and Thomas Zeiler. To this list I must add the two anonymous reviewers for the University of North Carolina Press. They read my manuscript with ineffable care and offered truly useful feedback. I thank my editor, Charles Grench, for lining up such knowledgeable and helpful reviewers for me, as well as for his faith in this project. Sara Jo Cohen and Jay Mazzocchi expertly shepherded me through the production process.

In acquiring Japanese and Japanese American source materials, I was ably assisted by Ashley Brennan, Akiko Kashima, and Yusuke Sekine. The good offices of Masaru Ikei, Akiko Ogawa, Jane Nakasako of the Japanese American National Museum, Naosuke Sekiguci of the Waseda University Archives, and Takeyuki Tokura and Mayumi Yamamoto of the Fukuzawa Memorial Center for Modern Japanese Studies were critical in obtaining some of the images used in this book. Jesse Draper provided valuable logistical support in preparing the final manuscript and the index. The bulk of research in Japan was conducted during my multiple stays at Keio and Waseda universities as a visiting scholar. Both are models of institutional commitment to international scholarly exchange and hospitality, and I am forever indebted to these global-minded universities and my faculty sponsors there, Kazuko Furuta, Aiko Kurasawa, Hatsue Shinohara, and Yoshihide Soeya. Being able to begin writing this book while staying in Keio University's guesthouse only a block from the Tsunamachi Grounds and to finish the manuscript in my office in Waseda University's main library—the site where Abe (Tozuka) Stadium once stood—was truly a treat.

A portion of chapter 1 appeared in my article "For Love of the Game," and materials used in chapter 7 were partially drawn from my contribution to Watanabe and McConnell, *Soft Power Superpowers*. I thank Yasushi Watanabe and David L. McConnell for permission to reprint the materials in this volume.

Saving the most emotional and heartfelt for last, I thank my extended families in Texas, California, and Tokyo for the love and support I have received from them at every step along the way. They have nourished me with their good cheer and spurred me with a well-timed question: "So, when are you going to finish that baseball book?" They know better than anyone that it has indeed taken a transpacific village to write this book. I thank my long-suffering immediate family for putting up with my eternal absent-mindedness and the mess created in our house over the years by the "Queen of All Available Spaces." Thank you, Danny and Reina, for not daring to disrupt the cosmic order structuring my piles of note cards, books, and photocopies. Finally, I dedicate this book to the people who lost their lives, possessions, and loved ones in the earthquakes and tsunami that devastated northeastern Japan on March 11, 2011. The disaster unfolded as I was undertaking the last round of manuscript revision, and the unspeakable physical destruction, loss, and human suffering transmitted through the global media affected me in most profound and life-altering ways. Although it can only amount to a tiny fraction of the pain and grief those directly affected by the catastrophe have endured and will no doubt carry into the future, the sense of loss and bereavement I share with them drives home to me that I, too, am a denizen of the transpacific world.

TRANSPACIFIC
FIELD OF DREAMS

INTRODUCTION

"Whoever wants to know the heart and mind of America had better learn baseball," Jacques Barzun famously wrote in 1954. Thus the French-born scholar of American culture identified baseball's unique place in American life. Barzun's paean to baseball has been so often quoted that it may almost sound like a cliché, yet its very staying power is an index of the evocative and even visceral qualities of the game's connections to some inner core of American civilization. But is it the heart and mind of America alone that baseball has made us privy to? How about the hearts and minds of others outside the territorial borders of the United States who also pledged emotional allegiance to this game of bats and balls? After all, parallel baseball universes existed elsewhere in the world at the very time the game was establishing itself as postbellum America's nationally played sport, as many baseball scholars, Peter Bjarkman foremost among them, have copiously documented. Cubans began taking enthusiastically to baseball in the 1860s after a cohort of youngsters returning from schooling in the United States brought their passion for the game to the Caribbean island under Spanish colonial rule. By the early 1870s, Cuba's first professional team, the Habana Baseball Club, had been organized, and by the decade's end, the first professional league was in place. That was contemporaneous with the formation of the National Association of Professional Base Ball Players (NAPBBP), the first professional league in the United States. Mexicans also began playing baseball at around the same time, and by the late 1870s they were challenging teams of North American sailors and railroad construction workers in places like Guaymas, Nuevo Laredo, and Tamaulipas. Halfway across the Pacific, the indigenous youths of the Hawaiian kingdom were facing off against children of white American settlers on the baseball diamond in the 1860s. That was decades before Albert G. Spalding, the paramount booster of American professional baseball, passed through the island during his ballyhooed tour to propagate "America's Game" worldwide. Farther afield, and more than a decade before Spalding's globe-girdling sporting expedition left the shores of California, a group of schoolboys were being won over to baseball on the other side of the Pacific Ocean, in the "Mikado's Empire." Given this surprising degree of contemporaneity and the amazing geographical span of the game's diffusion in its early history, is it not valid also to suggest that whoever wants to know the heart and mind of the late nineteenth-century world would do well to learn, or at least study, baseball?[1]

This book germinated in my belief that it indeed is valid—and rests on the premise I share with many baseball scholars and sports historians that, in truth, the United States could never claim a monopoly on a special connection with baseball, even from the game's early years.[2] Take, for example, Japan, a focal point of this book. As pioneers in the study of Japanese baseball Ronald Roden, Robert Whiting, and Ikei Masaru have variously demonstrated, the bat-and-ball game introduced by young American expatriates soon after Japan opened its doors to the Western world spread as a student sport through the country's new educational regime almost as quickly as the society modernized and industrialized. By the turn of the century, amateur baseball competitions had become a staple of the local cultural and social landscape. In the early twentieth century, Japanese collegiate squads began touring Hawaii and the U.S. mainland as well as Japan's newly acquired colonial possessions in Asia. Professional baseball, which first sprouted tenuously from the economic boom primed by World War I, reemerged as a still faltering but durable business enterprise in the 1930s. It was interrupted for a scant single season during World War II—in 1945.[3] Thus, I would like to expand the geographical and temporal purview of Barzun's time-honored adage and ask these recast questions: Why and how did baseball manage to become a transnational pastime in certain parts of the world (but not others) so soon after its emergence as a modern organized sport in urban bastions in the northeastern United States?[4] What do the adoption and adaptation overseas of a form of American sporting practice and its accompanying institutions reveal about the United States' engagement with the wider world?

Taking stock of this swift transmission and the enduring acceptance of baseball—the game that many Americans in the postbellum period came to believe was "their own"—in far-flung parts of the world such as the Caribbean, the mid-Pacific, and the Western-Pacific littoral, we see imbrications of the historical process through which that geographical dissemination occurred. For starters, baseball enables us to trace and analyze the interconnections, material and metaphorical, human and institutional, that began to sprout and thicken across national boundaries in many parts of the world after the mid-nineteenth century. Baseball also opens our eyes to the manifold ways in which technology transformed society and culture. It further illustrates how a cultural practice can powerfully mediate affective relationships between individuals, groups, and societies and sometimes even shape interstate relations in tangible ways. In the following pages, I will observe these historical constellations through the viewing lens of baseball and do so against the background of U.S.-Japanese relations. Bearing that purpose, this book is necessarily a study of globalization, "a process—or set of overlapping processes—in which the flows of peoples, ideas, and things accelerate and the networks of worldwide interconnectivity become even dense, facilitated in part by the increasing speed of communication and ease of transportation," in Charles Bright and Michael Geyer's useful definition.[5]

Many scholars have argued that globalization, though often referenced as a contemporary, post–Cold War phenomenon, provides an effective analytical scaffold for studying the world in earlier time periods as well. Some, like African historian Frederick Cooper, even take issue with the very concept of globalization partly because the term ("-ization") tends to underplay, at least implicitly, the historical depth of the world's interconnectivity, denoting the unwarranted degree of newness of that long-existing reality.[6] Not minimizing the conceptual problems arising from the capaciousness of the concept, I still find the idea of globalization analytically useful insomuch as it enlightens us about a force more intense and fundamentally different that was inaugurated in world history in the mid-nineteenth century. At that time, the transformative effects of new technology were crucial. The era's technological innovations, notably steam power, the telegraph, and, later, electricity, revolutionized transportation and communication, with manifold social and cultural implications. Practical applications of new technology, steamships, railways, intercontinental telegraph connections, and the mass proliferation of print media made it possible for many people, including North Americans, to become part of a larger world in ways previously unimaginable.[7]

It was during the 1870s that these technological innovations combined to connect the transpacific world, as well as the transatlantic world, as never before. Scholars of late nineteenth-century U.S. overseas expansion have ably elucidated the correlation between increased transpacific steamship operations, with continental railroad linkups, and the ubiquity and permanency of the American citizen's presence in the nation's new maritime frontiers in the last quarter of the nineteenth century.[8] Americans' semicolonial intrusions into foreign territories, such as Hawaii and treaty ports in East Asia, led to the emergence of vibrant overseas settler and expatriate communities in the latter half of the nineteenth century.

Yet this cohort of offshore Americans has only recently been given its rightful place in the literature on the United States' engagement with the world.[9] This book offers, through a tale crafted around baseball, a corrective to this relative historiographical inattention to Americans living and working overseas.[10]

This book also aspires to shine a spotlight on globalization's unlikely—sometimes almost accidental—participants. The same technologies that enabled Americans with wanderlust to be more mobile and travel-ready made communications and the acquisition of information and knowledge across distances less onerous and more reliable for those who stayed put. The late nineteenth century witnessed the advent of mass-circulating print media and a rapid increase in Americans' overseas mail and telegraph communications. Photography, lithography, and novel techniques in marketing such as magazine advertising and catalog merchandising came into wider use and stirred the imagination of their target audiences. It was thus only natural that Americans generally became more aware of the world "out there."[11] As Kristin Hoganson has shown, this enhanced global consciousness of the late nineteenth and early twentieth centuries was gendered but by no means the exclusive preserve of politicians and diplomats, merchants and businessmen, or even Christian missionaries—agents of American overseas activities most often highlighted in traditional narratives of diplomatic history. Women who led a homebound existence in Gilded Age and Progressive Era America partook of the incipient stage of globalization and claimed a piece of cosmopolitanism through their personal consumptive activities and aesthetic expressions. This gendered globality manifested in American women cut across class divides. The less fortunate of them were drawn to the low end of the international labor market, eking out a living in ill-reputed trades catering chiefly to their compatriots residing in expatriate communities in distant lands. Historical narration confined to the chambers of high politics thus cannot capture the full range and depth of diverse and often gendered social interconnectedness born of globalization. Neither can the nation-state as an analytical vessel fully reveal the costs and bounty of the expanding and more penetrating engagements with the world at large by builders and brokers of what Walter LaFeber elucidated half a century ago as the "New Empire."[12]

This line of transnational inquiry lends itself to another key goal of this book: to appraise the nature of American power in international relations in a less America-centric way. This objective resonates with several other ventures undertaken by scholars concerned with adding global textures to the writing of American history. The notion of overseas expansionism, perennially of paramount interest to historians of the United States, has been subjected to major conceptual overhaul in recent years. As Alfred Eckes and Thomas Zeiler have suggested, what diplomatic historians were once accustomed to portray as America's turn-of-the-century imperial ascent and its global ubiquity in the twentieth-century world should be reconceptualized in less self-possessed and self-referential terms. "American expansionism" can instead be reformulated as a local instantiation of global patterns and processes that may be encapsulated in the concept of globalization. This book, situating American history in globalization's multifarious ramifications, thus represents an effort to transcend, in Daniel T. Rodgers's apt phrase, the American "sense of world-historical centrality."[13]

One way to gain a more modulated understanding of American power is to consider the role of culture in American "imperial" ascendancy in the globalizing world. Pursuing this task, I have drawn inspiration from Jessica L. Harland-Jacobs's work on British imperialism, *Builders of Empire* (2007). Imperialism and its frequent fellow traveler, capitalism, were powerful agents of globalization and of connective, often violent and exploitative, forces in world history. World historians have thus long examined the role of imperial states and the trade and financial networks their citizens created in drawing together peoples and places across time and space. Using Freemasonry, Harland-Jacobs rigorously assessed the contribution of cultural institutions to the historical processes of globalization, in this case dating from the eighteenth century.[14] Examining the transoceanic circulation of baseball as a cultural formulation with accompanying institutions and ideologies, I argue, also offers an effective way to understand imperialism as complex relations of power, in both its formal and informal guises.[15]

Guided by these methodological and thematic concerns, this book brings to the foreground some lesser-known Americans—not those typically found in the corridors of power in Washington or behind the closed doors of diplomatic negotiations—who went global in the late nineteenth century and the first half of the twentieth century. These enterprising Americans with international aspirations played a part in the United States' transformation into a nation capable of, and certainly sanguine about, drawing the contours of transnational civil society. In this book, the careers and ventures of such American citizens with a global gaze will be juxtaposed with those of their kindred spirits in Japan, another society that was vigorously carving out gateways to the outside world in the second half of the nineteenth century. The United States and Japan began to engage and shape the transpacific world and ventured into overseas colonial enterprise at roughly the same juncture in world history, with energies, ambitions, and destabilizing proclivities emblematic of rapidly industrializing, urbanizing, and self-reinventing societies.[16] The mutual fascination, and even adoration, that characterized their initial contacts waned by the dawning of the twentieth century. A growing incongruity of visions and national interests defined by the respective states, differentiated positions in the global political economy, and a shared sense of racial irreconcilability put the two countries on a path toward estrangement. On the other hand, people from various social strata, along with capital, commodities, technology, and, less visibly, ideas, knowledge, ambitions, and dreams, flowed between the two centralizing nation-states through increasingly layered and intertwined material, human, and institutional networks.[17]

These transactions, taking place alongside, or despite, formal intergovernmental conduits, opened up and sustained a myriad of shifting and proliferating social spaces, or contact zones.[18] There, denizens of the nation-states *and* newly minted colonial empires consolidating themselves as the United States and Japan often embraced common practices and built shared, overlapping, or even mutually reliant institutions. While the strategic priorities of the two circum-Pacific empires often clashed, they nonetheless espoused comparable visions and formed individual and collective bonds neither totally amenable to state control nor summarily replaceable with local or national allegiances. Such alternative and overlapping human solidarities and communities of belonging flourished in peacetime and languished—but often persisted—in times of conflict and war. The story of baseball's diffusion and popularization across the Pacific highlights this enduring undertow of affinity and comparative historical parallels in multiple realms of U.S.-Japanese relations through the vicissitudes of the interstate contest and, ultimately, violent war in the mid-twentieth century. It thus opens a new vista on nationally unbounded communities, imagined or real, and allows us to explore how such alternative loyalties and bonds could often help sculpt the interstate relationship. Further, the tale of U.S.-Japanese encounters through baseball illuminates complex reciprocal exchanges brokered by a variety of local cultural intermediaries who helped disseminate what many Americans claimed to be an all-American cultural form by the dawn of the "American Century"—and beyond.

What unfolds in the following pages is this story of cultural cross-pollination, beginning with the game's first recorded play in early Meiji Japan and ending with the conclusion of the American-led Allied occupation of Japan after World War II. Throughout, my overarching objective is to highlight how intimately and often unexpectedly the two nations were intertwined through multitudes of networks, both apparent and hidden, directly related to baseball or not. In the process, I show how porous national boundaries were and how ubiquitous and variegated human webs were becoming in this period. This permeability and the mutual relevancy of historical developments across the Pacific require that what have traditionally been narrated as two relatively distinct national stories be retold as a braided historical narrative. Tracking the threads spun by border-breaching historical agents also compels us to integrate various nationally segmented historiographies and disciplinary subfields that have been developing largely separately from one another.[19] In this book, I aspire to combine vantage points and thematic concerns derived from U.S. and Japanese histories while weaving together U.S. ethnic history (Japanese American history) and Asian (Japanese) history.[20] Similarly, I hope to make sports a useful platform of international history. In his widely used textbook on American sports history, Steven A. Riess notes that sports and foreign relations (especially cultural diffusion and diplomacy) have not been adequately integrated into the study of American sports. Recent works by Barbara Keys and Thomas Zeiler have begun to fill this lacuna. My aim is to broaden the trail blazed by these pioneers with my own contribution to the literature on sports and international relations.[21]

Chapter 1 traces the diffusion of baseball in Japan during the Meiji period. In this incipient stage of U.S.-Japanese baseball exchange, American and Japanese apostles of the game played distinct but mutually reinforcing roles in diverse social settings, each side drawing from the sport different (but not discordant) meanings and varied notions of belonging and sociability. While baseball's ascendancy over the British game of cricket in Meiji Japan reflected a distant historical arc of American cultural influences eclipsing those of Britain in fin de siècle East Asia north of Shanghai, the chapter also foregrounds the contemporaneous process of the game's inexorable indigenization by the Japanese. Parallel to the spread of the sport to Meiji Japan was its circulation in multiple sites within the expanding colonial and semicolonial spheres that came under the control of the United States and Japan. Chapter 2 elucidates these regional eddies of baseball play that rippled from the two countries' imperial ascendancy in the Asia-Pacific world. In so doing, the chapter pays particular attention to the rise and evolution of American and Japanese settler communities in preannexation Hawaii and to Japan's newly acquired overseas colonial possessions in Taiwan and Korea.

A curious synchronicity existed between baseball's popularization in the nascent Japanese imperium and the baseball frenzy that swept across Hawaii and the U.S. Pacific Northwest[22] in the early decades of the twentieth century. Identifying the sources of this transoceanic pattern and unpacking the structure of multiple layers of organized baseball play encompassing the Pacific are the key themes of chapter 3. The explosion in baseball's popularity as a spectator sport and escalating competitiveness among its participants, both players and organizers, led to the sport's evolution into commercialized forms of recreation and entertainment in these two industrializing and urbanizing societies. The professionalization of baseball, occurring in the United States during the Gilded Age, was duplicated, albeit in a much different business model, in Taisho and Showa Japan. Chapter 4 explicates this staggered development of sports capitalism in the transpacific cultural zone and probes the actions and motivations of various historical agents who promoted or resisted that commercializing force. American semipro and professional baseball squads' barnstorming tours of Japan, its imperial outposts, and America's own colonial possession in the Philippines in the interwar period receive prominent treatment in this chapter, as does the tangled relationship between imperial nation-building and recreational activities.

Chapter 5 highlights an epoch-making postseason exhibition tour to Japan by Major League Baseball in the early 1930s. This and earlier "invasions" by American top-tier pro baseball led to the organization of Japan's first commercially viable professional baseball enterprise later in the decade. The chapter introduces the heretofore underrecognized fact that agents of Japan's nascent sports business enterprise initially envisioned it as the western fringe of American organized baseball until a critical mass of domestic competition was marshaled to ensure its sustainability as a new "industry." Two Japanese all-salaried baseball caravans through the U.S. mainland took place in the mid-1930s, at the same time that a semipro national baseball congress began to stake out its business niche in Depression-era America and laid the domestic groundwork for its unexpected overseas empire building after World War II.

How baseball endured in both countries through the war years is the central question upon which chapter 6 hinges. Requirements of military mobilization and social regimentation insinuated themselves into the transpacific world after a full-scale war between Japan and China began in 1937 and wholly dictated U.S.-Japanese relations after Japan's attack on Pearl Harbor in December 1941. Despite the creeping diplomatic crisis in the late 1930s, however, U.S.-Japanese baseball exchange tenuously continued in a variety of venues. Ultimately, Japan's baseball circuits, like the nation's diplomatic conducts, began to gravitate into distinctly "Asia for Asians" orbits by the eve of World War II. This chapter also locates baseball in a problem central to Japanese American historiography: World War II internment. What did playing baseball mean to those Issei (first-generation) Japanese nationals and Japanese American Nisei (second-generation) citizens who continued to patronize America's Game inside the barbed-wire fences erected by the state that condemned them as forever untrustworthy "enemy aliens"?

Chapter 7 examines the amazingly quick return of baseball at all levels—professional, semipro, and amateur—to Japan after its defeat by the Allied powers. Baseball was adroitly deployed by both the triumphal military occupier and the discredited occupied in the shared purpose of creating new postwar orthodoxies. Baseball, as a composite iconography, was expected to signal both change and continuity in the bilateral relationship, as well as a rebirth of the institution whose patronage of the sport was strategically publicized: Japan's imperial household. As the Cold War with the Soviet Union began to affect U.S.-Japanese relations, baseball as a shared American and Japanese pastime was painted with yet another coat of political symbolism that bespoke the future trajectory of the newly forged diplomatic and military partnership. Projecting continuities between the wartime and postwar years, aided by baseball as an interpretive fulcrum, this final chapter suggests a new temporal marker in U.S.-Japanese relations: that of a transwar period. Chapter 8 tracks the formation of post–World War II order in organized baseball in both countries and points to the dawning of a new era in transpacific baseball.

I close this introduction with a comment on the title of this book. *Transpacific Field of Dreams* is not just a sentimental and clichéd invocation of the 1989 Hollywood movie adaptation of the book *Shoeless Joe*. I fully intend to narrate in this book a tale of an expansive field of dreams— a contested terrain traversed by myriad visions, aspirations, and pursuits of greed and not-so-holy impulses in all shades of gray, espoused and enacted by both Americans and Japanese, and by those who played in between the two circum-Pacific empires.

A note about names and transliteration: Japanese, Korean, and Chinese names appear in this book in the conventional East Asian order, that is, with surname first, except for authors whose publications list their surname last, and names given in that form in a quoted source. The transliteration of Japanese names and words follows the Hepburn system. Most Chinese names and words are romanized in pinyin, except for those names that are better known to the Western reader in the old Wade-Giles system, such as Chiang Kai-shek.

1 PACIFIC CROSSINGS

On December 30, 1907, Abraham G. Mills, the fourth president of the National League of Base Ball Clubs (NL), issued the final report of a special seven-member panel appointed by Albert G. Spalding, a kingpin of American professional baseball's founding brothers, to determine "the true origins of America's national pastime." The commission, which included two U.S. senators, was charged to "weigh all available evidence" against the claim made by English-born baseball writer and statistician Henry Chadwick that the game had evolved from the British folk game of rounders. After three years of intermittent investigation, the Mills Commission definitively dismissed Chadwick's thesis, reporting that baseball was solely of American origins. The singular basis of this unequivocal conclusion was written testimony sent to Spalding by Abner Graves, a former resident of Cooperstown, New York. Sixty-eight years after the alleged event took place, the informant recalled that his childhood friend Abner Doubleday, a West Point graduate and a Civil War hero (who also happened to be Mills's commander in the Civil War), had single-handedly invented the game of baseball in 1839 on a playing field in the pastoral upstate New York village. Baseball scholars, such as Robert W. Henderson and Harold Seymour, have long since debunked this Doubleday-Cooperstown foundational myth. The current scholarly consensus holds that no single individual created baseball; rather, it evolved incrementally from various forms of bat-and-ball folk games, including British rounders. This cultural form of transatlantic hybrid pedigree grew into a modern team sport in Philadelphia, Boston, and New York in the early nineteenth century, with each of these burgeoning northeastern American cities developing its distinctive formats of the game. These regional archetypes competed for dominance in midcentury America, but by the eve of the

Civil War, New York's variant became ascendant. It spread far and wide across the reunited nation after the war, claiming the moniker "America's national pastime" along the way.[1]

Unlike the contested hagiology of baseball in the United States, the genesis of baseball in Japan has been free of the polemical debate and manipulation of historical evidence that surrounded the mythologizing of the game's "immaculate conception" in Cooperstown. Not surprisingly, Japanese baseball historiography has been unburdened by vested interests in either affirming or disputing the quintessentially "American"—as opposed to British—origin of the sport. Nor was there any compelling need or organized attempt, as there was in turn-of-the-century America, to make baseball serviceable to the narrative of post–Civil War intersectional reconciliation and link its "purely American origins" to overarching American nationalism.[2] Both scholars and popular chroniclers of Japanese baseball have long reached the consensus that rudimentary forms of baseball, introduced in the early 1870s, had multiple known roots. One pointed to a cohort of young American men who came to Japan as *oyatoi* (meaning "hired hands") employed by the Japanese government, provincial political leaders, and private patrons to participate in the nation's modernization project. Minor quibbles over particular "firsts" have existed among devoted aficionados and custodians of baseball trivia, but they never assumed divisive proportions, certainly not to the degree necessitating the creation of an investigative commission.[3] Scholars of Japanese baseball also widely acknowledge that disseminators of the American cultural form were not Americans alone. The game made its way to Meiji Japan, embraced by Japanese adolescents who, through various types of study-abroad opportunities, received education in Gilded Age America. By the end of the nineteenth century, baseball blossomed into a transoceanic pastime fostered in multiple networks built and sustained by aspiring Americans and Japanese who chose to cross the Pacific with a variety of aspirations in their hearts.

Baseball in Early Meiji Japan

As part of the state-driven modernization program, rulers in Tokyo recruited over three thousand experts, the *oyatoi*, from Europe and the United States after Japan's reluctant "opening" to the West, the historical process initiated by Commodore Matthew Perry of the U.S. Navy. These hired foreign nationals assisted, first, the decaying Tokugawa shogunate and the Meiji imperial government that replaced it in 1868 in adopting Western science and technology and building institutions of governance to handle the demands of a complex modern society. Four countries (Great Britain, France, Prussia, and the United States) supplied the bulk of these foreign consultants and technical assistants, and lines of specialization were clear from the inception of this top-down knowledge-importing program. British subjects figured prominently in engineering and finances. France and Britain rivaled each other in directing the organization of the Japanese military. Prussians became a key source of knowledge in economics, medicine, and theories of statecraft. Americans were valued chiefly for their expertise in public education, agriculture, and animal husbandry.[4]

Although the exact number of *oyatoi* is hard to ascertain, the United States sent the second-largest contingent (374), trailing only Great Britain. American *oyatoi*'s imprints in modern Japanese history are both deep and extensive. Two former diplomats, Henry Denison and Durham Stevens, helped the Japanese Foreign Ministry navigate the treacherous waters of modern diplomacy as the Asian nation sought to renegotiate its "unequal treaties" with the Western powers and, later, to fashion a negotiated settlement to the Russo-Japanese War.[5] Americans' expertise was also crucial to the development of the northern island of Hokkaido.[6] In the area of education, the contributions of two men, both alumni of Rutgers College, particularly stood out. William Elliot Griffith was instrumental in designing a college-level curriculum in the natural sciences. David Murray, a Delaware native, worked alongside Japan's education specialist, Tanaka Fujimaro, as the latter drafted and promulgated the Kyōiku Rei (Education Ordinance) of 1879, a government edict that steered Japan firmly in the direction of universal education and the virtual elimination of illiteracy.[7]

Baseball migrated from Gilded Age America to Meiji Japan with this cohort of offshore Americans. The earliest records of baseball played in Japan put the genesis of the game in the nation's capital in 1872. The American identified as the pioneer instructor of baseball was a twenty-eight-year-old *oyatoi* teacher at Daigaku Nankō (South Academy, renamed Kaiseikō a year later) by the name of Horace E. Wilson. A devotee of baseball and a Civil War veteran, Wilson sailed out of San Francisco in 1871 with his wife and a toddler son, carrying a bat and a ball in his suitcase. Holding a lucrative three-year contract with the Japanese government, Wilson joined the twenty-three-member foreign faculty at the just established all-boys academy to train Japan's "best and brightest" re-

Pacific Crossings | 13

cruited from across the country. After a series of reorganizations and a merger with other schools, the three-hundred-student academy where Wilson taught English and math would expand in 1887 into First High School, or Ichikō, the feeder program to the nation's first institution of higher learning, Tokyo Imperial University.[8]

Aside from his classroom instruction, the young American teacher from rural Maine taught Japan's future elite the military-style calisthenics and setting-up exercises he had learned as a soldier in the Union army. Wilson also showed his students how to play his favorite bat-and-ball game during recess and after hours. Spontaneous play blossomed into a major preoccupation of Kaiseikō students, to whom the notion of physical exertion for its own sake was thrillingly unfamiliar. By 1876, the Kaiseikō nine were ready to take on an American adult team assembled from residents of the foreign settlement in Yokohama and American *oyatoi* teachers in Tokyo. By the time Wilson completed his second three-year contract and returned to the United States, baseball had established a dedicated following among Kaiseikō students and curious spectators who thronged the school's newly opened playing ground every Saturday to watch this exotic public spectacle and the weekly ritual of male fellowship through athletic activity. Those Wilson awakened to the joy of playing ball included Aoki Motogorō, a preeminent scholar in engineering, and Komura Jutarō, who would go on to study at Harvard and pilot Japan's imperial expansion as an iron-willed foreign minister.[9]

This foundational tale of Japanese baseball not only highlights the imbrications of a world rapidly becoming interconnected in the late nineteenth century; it also illuminates the way in which the social fluidity of both early Meiji Japan and postbellum America, coupled with budding long-distance transportation infrastructures, broadened the horizons of a rural American of humble origins and actuated his transborder upward social mobility. Born in Gorham, Maine, in 1843, Wilson served in the Civil War and was discharged in Georgia in March 1866 at age twenty-three. Having spent his early adulthood in military service, Wilson never received a formal college education. Yet his life after the Civil War took an unexpected turn through the workings of a fraternal network built by veterans of the Union army. Voluntary mutual aid associations sprang up among Civil War veterans to ease their transition to civilian life. Among the services they provided were monetary assistance to the destitute among them and to war widows; they also brokered jobs for the unemployed.[10] Many veterans of the Union army in search of work moved west, aided by this fraternal network, riding on the newly completed Transcontinental Railroad. In 1870, Wilson moved from his hometown to San Francisco, where he found work as a clerk in the family business of a fellow Union army veteran. A year later, Wilson was hired by the just established Japanese Consular Office in San Francisco and set sail for Japan.[11] Historians of American baseball have shown that the Civil War, during which soldiers played the game as a fleeting recreation near battlefields and at encampments, helped to spread its appeal throughout the country. By exposing a cross section of the male population to the game, the war also contributed to the erasure of baseball's original mostly white, middle-class social moorings. The genesis of baseball in Meiji Japan points to yet another link between the Civil War and baseball's social and geographical dispersion: the human webs formed in the war's aftermath catapulted across the long expanse of the U.S. continent and the Pacific Ocean what by the 1870s many Americans were coming to identify as their nationally played pastime.[12]

Wilson was not the only young American schoolteacher who sailed across the Pacific in the early 1870s with a baseball bat and ball in hand. So did Edward Mudgett, who came to Japan as a language instructor in 1872 upon graduating from California's Oakland Military Academy. After a teaching stint in the provincial city of Fukui, twenty-year-old Mudgett moved to Tokyo and taught at Daigaku Yobimon, the foreign-language academy that would also become a feeder program to Tokyo Imperial University in the 1880s. Since only a fence separated Daigaku Yobimon and Kaiseikō, many of Mudgett's students, including Hisahara Kyūgen, the future president of Kyoto Imperial University, would drift into the adjacent playing field to try their hand at "Mr. Wilson's game." Wilson and Mudgett also became teammates on a "town team" formed among American expatriates in Tokyo.[13] Another young American who arrived in Japan with a cache of baseball equipment was Albert Bates, a nephew of American *oyatoi* Samuel Williams, who consulted for the Finance Ministry. In 1873, Bates, then age eighteen, landed a job teaching English at Kaitakushi Karigakkō, a technical school just opened in Tokyo as an adjunct to Kaitakushi (the Hokkaido Development Agency).[14]

Created in 1869, Kaitakushi was a bastion of American influence within the evolving Meiji officialdom. As the government agency charged with settling the northern island of Hokkaido, Kaitakushi mirrored and implemented the Meiji state's twin geostrategies relative to its northern periphery: limiting Imperial Russia's territorial expansion in the Far East littoral and its commercial encroachment on Hokkaido's west coast; and developing the island's rich natural resources for exploitation by the mainlanders.[15] In the spring of 1871, Kuroda Kiyotaka, Kaitakushi's youthful deputy commissioner, journeyed to the United States to recruit civil engineers and specialists in agricultural and animal sciences for Kaitakushi's Hokkaido development program. He considered the United States an ideal project partner for its putative tradition in settling and "civilizing" the nation's western frontiers. Further, the geopolitically astute Kuroda reasoned that, given America's preoccupation with the domestic imperatives of Reconstruction, it was unlikely to band together with European imperial powers, particularly Russia. Kuroda could not persuade the administration of President Ulysses S. Grant to formally contribute to the Japanese government's Hokkaido agricultural mission, but Horace Capron, U.S. commissioner of agriculture under Andrew Johnson and Grant, agreed to resign from his cabinet post to serve Kaitakushi as a private citizen. Until its dissolution in 1882, Kaitakushi employed forty-eight American agricultural experts, some recruited through Capron; others ventured to Japan guided by a vision of extending the missions of American land-grant colleges even overseas. This band of pioneering Americans introduced new techniques of dairy farming and cultivation of crops such as wheat, corn, and sugar beets in Japan's northern periphery. Some of them joined the faculty of the Sapporo Agricultural College (the institutional prototype of present-day Hokkaido University) when it was opened in 1876.[16]

Given this condensed American influence at its foundation, it was not surprising that Kaitakushi's technical school, in its initial temporary location in Tokyo, became another pocket of baseball fever. Bates was one of the instigators of this new rage on campus. His Japanese students quickly took to the sport, but language barriers and a lack of equipment beyond Bates's personal cache hindered both instruction and play. Fortunately, Bates soon received reinforcements: three Japanese students left in the United States by Kuroda in 1871 to study at the Massachusetts Agricultural College returned and enrolled in Kaitakushi Karigakkō. Thanks to their fluent English and souvenirs of bats and balls, Bates and his Japanese assistant coaches won new converts. When the school was relocated to Sapporo in 1875 and expanded into Sapporo Agricultural College, Karigakkō's students and teachers took their love of baseball and moved with it to Japan's northernmost island.

Hokkaido's harsh clime did not dampen their passion for the game, and they received a positive reinforcement from the school administration. The college's inaugural president, William Clark, a former president of Massachusetts Agricultural College, was an apostle of what would come to be called, both admiringly and pejoratively, "muscular Christianity" in the United States in the 1880s, a strain of religiosity that aimed to energize churches and to counteract the enervating effects of urban living. To achieve these goals, these stalwarts of Christian manliness promoted competitive sports and physical education.[17] Each day Clark exhorted his Japanese charges to give equal weight to studying indoors and playing outdoors, arguing that the healthy body was the keystone of moral and "manly" Christian life. As one of his first tasks as the college's headmaster, he supervised the building of a spacious outdoor playing ground. Students at Sapporo Agricultural College also had an avid baseball coach to spur them on: a botany and chemistry professor also recruited from Massachusetts Agricultural College by the name of David Penhallow.[18]

Circumstantial evidence suggests that at about the time America's national pastime migrated north with those young agricultural students and their American professors, seeds of the game were being planted in Japan's southern island of Kyushu as well. Another Civil War veteran, this one a graduate of West Point, is widely credited with this southern diffusion of the game. A former captain in the Union army, Leroy Lansing Janes was employed by the municipality of Kumamoto to direct a private school for "Western studies" chartered and funded by local benefactors who wished to expose the area's male youth to Western learning "in an environment suffused with manly martial spirit." Janes eminently fit the bill. This international teacher recruitment was a product of far-flung human networks connecting West Point, the U.S. War Department, the Dutch Reformed Church in New York, and Christian missionaries active in western Japan. At age thirty-five, Janes moved to the rural Japanese province with his wife and two young children to build a new career as a teacher of English, math, and chemistry. In August 1871, he sailed from San Francisco on the same ship with Horace Capron and other American *oyatoi* in Japanese government employ.[19]

According to Kumamoto's local lore, Janes's instructional activity was not confined to academic subjects. The American teacher also emphasized "practical learning," such as growing vegetables in the school garden. He also instilled in his Japanese students the notion of "healthful life," exposing them to a daily regimen of outside setting-up exercises styled after the military calisthenics practiced at West Point. Although Janes was not an ordained Christian minister, his pedagogy shared many elements with work of young American Protestant missionaries who were fanning out to various parts of the world at the time, such as a commitment to vigorous male physicality as a staple of Christian religiosity. Through such nonclassroom edification, Janes bonded intensely with his students. Many of them were sons of former samurai whose future became suddenly uncertain with the Meiji state's dissolution in 1871 of the old governing system based on the *han* (feudal domain). These socially disoriented youngsters came to identify with the stoicism of their American teacher's daily practices as a muscular Christian and found an alternative vision of future glory in his lay Protestant theology. In rural Kumamoto, as in Sapporo, baseball established itself as a vehicle of Christian male fellowship.[20]

Japanese physical education teachers who were beginning to staff primary and middle schools also contributed to the spread of baseball in the countryside in the early 1880s.[21] At the epicenter of these cultural ripples was yet another American whose expertise the Japanese government had enlisted: George Leland, a sports pedagogue and disciple of Amherst College's Edward Hitchcock, a pioneer in the development of physical education in the United States.[22] The School Ordinance of 1872 (Gakusei), which promulgated the notion of universal education for the first time in Japanese history, instituted physical education as an integral part of primary and middle school curricula. This represented a radical break from the past, for Japan had only just been initiated by enlightenment theorists such as Fukuzawa Yukichi into the Anglo-American notion that physical exertion was healthful and conducive to learning.[23]

In 1878, the Education Ministry opened Taisō Denshūsho (the National Institute of Gymnastics) in Tokyo to develop pedagogy of physical education in the public schools and to train gym teachers. Leland was recruited from Amherst to advise the institute's Japanese faculty on curricula and facilities. Under his guidance, Taisō Denshūsho became the incubator of the American model of physical education and a storehouse of sporting equipment donated by benefactors connected to Amherst. Taisō Denshūsho's graduates fanned out into primary and middle schools throughout Japan and propagated the knowledge of Western competitive sports with a decidedly American inflection. Tsuboi Gendō and Tanaka Seigyō, two key faculty members at the institute, took charge of spreading information on modern Western sports by compiling a widely disseminated instructional manual titled *Kogai Yūgibō* (How to Play Outdoor Sports). School records show that as early as 1892 the institute shipped eight sets of baseball equipment and copies of the manual in response to requests by provincial teachers' colleges.[24] Baseball, the representative of Western team sports, spread like a wildfire in the fertile ground of the nation's new national universal education regime.

In sustaining the Japanese interest in Western sports in general, Americans were assisted by an English *oyatoi* teacher, Frederick W. Strange, who joined the faculty of Kaiseikō in 1875. The twenty-one-year-old graduate of Eton and member of a British expatriates' amateur rowing team in Yokohama preferred playing outdoors to teaching English in the classroom. When weather permitted, the athletically inclined young Briton played sports with Kaiseikō students all day, teaching them a wide range of Western sports, including track and field, cricket, and baseball. His students at Kaiseikō would later credit him with inculcating with them an unfamiliar concept—that even a ball game must be governed by a set of codified rules.[25]

Returning from America with Bat and Ball

In considering the forces behind baseball's remarkably rapid acceptance in Meiji Japan, one cannot overemphasize the central role played by Japanese students educated in the United States who returned home to assume key posts in government and private industry. Many of these early study-abroad students came from aristocratic backgrounds. For instance, Kido Takamasa and Ōkubo Toshikazu, the youngest members of the Iwakura Embassy (which toured Europe and the United States in 1871–72 to survey Western institutions and lay the political groundwork for revision of "unequal treaties" with the West), became avid baseball players. Makino Nobuaki, a future foreign minister, also became enamored with baseball while studying in Philadelphia in the early 1870s. They were sons of key members of the Meiji oligarchy, and as such they helped solidify the game's patronage in Japan's patrician circles. By mid-decade, a steady stream of government-sponsored study-abroad students were also returning from the United States, ensuring that baseball would not fade away as an exotic fad doomed to oblivion once the imported American teachers finished their contracts and left.

Among the student returnees from the United States, none made a more lasting mark on the development of Japanese baseball than Hiraoka Hiroshi, a railroad engineer. The end of Japan's diplomatic seclusion created multifarious consequences, some intended and others unanticipated. One of the consequences of this systemic development in world history was the opening of a new option for those Japanese looking for a way to get rid of family black sheep and ne'er-do-wells. In 1871, Hiraoka, at age fifteen, was shipped off to school in the United States by his father, a minor samurai-turned-aristocrat exasperated by his son's behavioral problems. The elder Hiraoka successfully used his connections to place his unruly son in a United States–bound government mission headed by Mori Arinori, the Meiji government's first education minister. Upon arriving in San Francisco, the young and restless Hiraoka saw a moving train for the first time in his life and became captivated by this technological marvel. Determined to unlock the mysteries of the chugging iron, the prodigal son deviated from his father's plan, quit high school in Boston, and became a locomotive apprentice in Philadelphia.[26]

During the six years he spent in the United States, Hiraoka accumulated many intangible assets besides the technical knowledge he voraciously absorbed. First, he cultivated connections with members of Japanese political elites that would stand him in good stead. When the Iwakura Embassy visited Boston in 1872, this semiexiled youthful rebel was the only person in town capable of serving as an interpreter for the government delegation, which included Itō Hirobumi, later prime minister. While in Boston, Hiraoka also became an avid Red Stockings fan. It is easy to imagine why: between 1872 and 1875, Boston won four consecutive national championships in the newly established pro league National Association of Professional Base Ball Players. Obviously, it was during his Boston years that Hiraoka gained acquaintance with Albert G. Spalding, then a Red Stockings ace pitcher who would soon become a principal mover of American professional baseball as a club owner and equipment manufacturer.[27]

Hiraoka returned to Japan in 1877 as a seasoned railroad engineer but with his youthful playfulness intact. He repatriated with a set of baseball equipment and a pair of roller skates. Hiraoka's career in Japan began with a bang. The connection with Itō, then serving as the minister of engineering, landed him a job with the Shinbashi Railroad Bureau with a monthly salary of forty-five yen, an astoundingly high starting salary by the day's standards. It was perhaps one of the most glamorous jobs a young Japanese man could hope for at the time. The Shinbashi-Yokohama railroad line, Japan's very first, had just opened five years before, and this new and mechanized mode of overland transportation was rapidly changing life in the Tokyo-Yokohama metropolitan belt. Not one to be enslaved by his high-power career, Hiraoka began to teach "Base Ball" to the railroad bureau's managerial staff after hours. By 1878, he had assembled the nation's first private baseball club, the Shinbashi Athletic Club (SAC), naming it after the Philadelphia Athletics, his favorite "hometown" team.[28]

The SAC became a vehicle for introducing into Meiji Japan many of the organizational elements that had been taking shape in "America's Game" earlier in the decade. Besides legitimating the revolutionary concept of a dues-charging private club devoted solely to diversion and recreation, Hiraoka built Japan's first playing field set aside for baseball in the railroad bureau's compound and named it Hokenjo (Health Field). When the field opened in 1882, it was christened by a baseball match between the SAC and the Komaba agricultural institute, another program that would be consolidated into Tokyo Imperial University. In managing this playing ground, Hiraoka enforced the regimen of facility upkeep with which he had familiarized himself in Boston and Philadelphia—having his team roll and level the ground every Saturday—and tweaked the curiosity of city dwellers in Tokyo. The United States–trained railroad engineer made this public space a site for demonstrating the exotic ball game as a pleasurable, but structured, group enterprise that also entailed the discipline of work. The SAC's sporting of uniforms, a practice unheard of outside the military, police, and fire brigade, also fascinated people who gathered around Hokenjo to watch the team practice after work and play games every Sunday. Many Ichikō students asked to participate in the SAC practice and be coached by Hiraoka in state-of-the-art baseball techniques fresh from Philadelphia. These eager neophytes included some of the nation's top minds, such as Tanakadate Aikitsu, who would become the nation's premier geophysicist.[29]

Hiraoka's popularity in Japan's patrician circles was a boon to baseball. Many former feudal domain leaders, who had retained their social status after the Meiji Restoration in the new regime's peerage, sought out the returnee from America to learn English, the language of the future.[30] In no time Hiraoka initiated his language students into baseball as well. It was in this way that a scion of the Tokugawa family, Tokugawa Satotaka, became an avid patron of the sport. This cultural conversion was all the more interesting in that he once was a firebrand spearheading the shogunate family's antiforeigner faction. In 1884, Tokugawa organized a team rival to the SAC, named it the Hercules Club, and built the team's own playing field within his expansive private compound in downtown Tokyo. This second private baseball club led the way for other "sandlot clubs" that sprang into existence in the capital city in the 1880s. The vast majority of these early urban private baseball clubs were made up of sons of wealthy aristocratic families.[31] The dapper Western-style jersey uniform sported by these private baseball clubs, as well as the top-dog Shinbashi Athletic Club's affiliation with the railroad, metaphorically fused the American game and modernity in the imaginations of urban spectators. As historian Steven Ericson has shown, public transportation underwent rapid modernization in Meiji Japan. As in the West, the railroad became a potent symbol of civilization and progress. From the beginning, railway projects, railway openings, and railway travel received prominent coverage in newspapers and popular magazines in the early Meiji era. When the Shinbashi-Yokohama line opened, people marveled at the speed of the train and expressed that awe in songs and other arts. As spectators gathered around the athletic field inside the railway bureau compound to watch baseball played by a squad of railroad engineers and bureaucrats, the American-born sport became modernity incarnate, establishing its popular appeal and respectability as a civic enterprise to an urbanizing society eager for social experimentation and cultural innovation.[32]

The Rise of Collegiate Baseball in Meiji Japan

The private baseball clubs that first sprang up in Tokyo in the early Meiji period drew on a rather limited pool of a privileged few who could luxuriate in dues-paying nonproductive leisure activities. These pioneer clubs also relied heavily on the charisma and leadership of their founders, and for that reason, once the progenitors moved on to other preoccupations, sustaining the clubs became difficult. Even Hiraoka's Shinbashi Athletic Club disbanded in 1887 after the player in chief left the railroad bureau to devote himself to business ventures. Rather than these private clubs, what fundamentally drove and sustained baseball's popularization in Meiji Japan were school-sponsored clubs that began to emerge in large numbers in the late 1880s. At the top of this fledging structure of play were high school and college intramural teams. With the promulgation of the Daigakkōrei (University Ordinance) in 1886, Japan's inchoate government-funded higher education, which had undergone a series of reshufflings and false starts, finally stabilized into a two-tier system consisting of the three-year preparatory program (high school) and the four years of university. In Tokyo, those elite boys' academies that had undergone a series of name changes and mergers since 1869 were consolidated into First High School (Ichikō), which now functioned as the preparatory program for those seeking admission into Tokyo Imperial University.

Ichikō, from its early years, boasted several student athletic clubs thanks to its spacious outdoor athletic field and the presence of two faculty members in particular. One was Eton-educated Frederick Strange, who made a lateral move from Kaiseikō to Ichikō. Strange baptized the new student body with the ideology of British amateur sports and organized and coached in various athletic programs. This English language teacher also organized one of Japan's first school-sponsored Field Days modeled after Eton's in 1888.[33] In the following year, Strange purchased two boats from England with his own funds to start a rowing team at Tokyo Imperial University. There he found a partner equally committed to the British idea of gentleman amateur sports in Kikuchi Tairei, a professor of mathematics and physics. Kikuchi had been a government-sponsored student at Cambridge University. There Kikuchi imbibed the Victorian notion of gentleman sports and came to believe in character building of the male elite through sports. After his appointment as Tokyo Imperial University's chancellor in 1898, Kikuchi continued to exhort students at the nation's premier university to train both body and mind and encouraged sports as a way of male bonding.[34]

Besides the government-chartered elite high school and university, several private schools in Tokyo received accreditation as colleges in this period. They all began fielding a baseball team, as well as formal athletic programs, soon after their founding. Keio, a private academy founded by Fukuzawa Yukichi, was reorganized into a college in 1890, and within two years, seven student sports clubs, including baseball, were organized. Waseda, initially called Tokyo Senmon Gakkō, was upgraded into a college in 1901 and began fielding its baseball squad two years later. Several Christian mission schools that had originated in the foreign settlements in Yokohama and Tokyo's Tsukiji district similarly expanded into colleges. One of these early Japanese Christian colleges was founded by William Curtis Hepburn, a missionary-scholar dispatched to Japan in 1859 by the Dutch Reformed Church in New York. Hepburn, now known for the romanization system he developed for transliterating Japanese to the Latin alphabet, established a mission school in Yokohama that merged with similar academies supported by Protestant churches to become Meiji Gakuin in 1887.[35]

These early Christian colleges played institutional host to young American men serving in foreign missions in East Asia. Having been exposed to the muscular Christianity movement back home, many of them were committed to promoting physical activity among their (male) students as a way to attain the Christian moral rectitude that they believed could reside only in the healthy and athletic body. Theodore McNair, a Presbyterian missionary who joined the founding faculty of Meiji Gakuin, was one such American apostle of muscular Christianity in Meiji Japan. Besides his mission work and teaching psychology and economics at the newly launched college, baseball was McNair's passion in life. A former ace pitcher at Princeton, the twenty-seven-year-old missionary learned that he could overcome the language barrier and connect effortlessly with his Japanese students through baseball because most of them were already familiar with the game. McNair received support from Hepburn, who also encouraged students' involvement in athletic activities. When the school moved to its permanent location in Shirogane, then Tokyo's outlying area, Hepburn saw to it that an expansive outdoor field was built. Buoyed by this endorsement from above, McNair organized a baseball club and became its highly dedicated coach, frequently taking his squad to the Yokohama foreign settlement to practice with and play against a team of American expatriates.[36]

McNair's nine comprised youngsters of first-rate intellectual caliber. Meiji Gakuin's first captain and catcher, Shirasu Bunpei, would go on to study at Harvard. His younger brother Chōhei, a pitcher, later studied at Yale. One of their teammates, Matsumura Shōnen, would become Japan's preeminent entomologist. Then sixteen years old, Matsumura had an insatiable love of insects and plants, so he transferred to Sapporo Agricultural College. Matsumura soon became the college's ace pitcher.[37] The muscular Christian baseball fraternity McNair incubated in Tokyo extended west in 1891 when Shirasu Chōhei transferred to Dōshisha, a private Christian college in Kyoto founded in 1875, and took the initiative in organizing a baseball team at his new academic home. The squad's first known contender was Third High School (Sankō), the institutional forerunner to Kyoto Imperial University. Extant records indicate that the opposing teams played on the lawn adjacent to the Kyoto Imperial Compound. Most of the players were still wearing straw sandals, and not many of them were using gloves or mitts. The two squads had a rematch in 1893, this time at Sankō's newly opened home ground. The Dōshisha-Sankō matchup would become the centerpiece of intercollegiate baseball in western Japan in the early decades of the twentieth century.[38]

A biographical sketch of Dōshisha's founder, Christian educator Niijima Jō (Joseph Hardy Neesima), gives ample clues to why the newly created private college in Kyoto emphasized human fellowship through sports. In

1864, Niijima, a son of a minor samurai family, broke the shogunate ban on overseas travel and headed for America as a stowaway. His illicit transpacific journey originated in the port city of Hakodate in Hokkaido and culminated in Boston, assisted by sympathetic Russian and American seamen along the way. With the good offices of Horace Taylor, the captain of the freighter that secretly transported Niijima to the land of his dreams, he attended Phillips Academy in Andover, Massachusetts, and went on to Amherst College, where William Clark was one of his revered professors. In 1870, Niijima graduated from Amherst and became the first Japanese national to receive a degree from an American college. By then baptized, Niijima went on to the Andover Academy and became a member of the American Board of Christian Missions. Like Hiraoka Hiroshi, the young Niijima accompanied the Iwakura Embassy in 1872 as a locally recruited interpreter. The connection he made with the politically high and mighty accrued a pardon for his violation of the shogunate ban on overseas travel. In 1874, Niijima was able to return to Japan free and clear and founded Dōshisha the following year. Reflecting his Amherst roots, physical education and extracurricular club sports occupied a central place in Niijima's idea of a well-rounded liberal arts education modeled after Amherst. Physical education also became an integral part of curriculum in the all-girls school Niijima founded in 1876; education for girls, physical education no less, was a truly revolutionary concept in Japan at the time.[39]

Dōshisha's culture of athleticism was further reinforced when the college accepted transfer students from Janes's academy. By early 1876, Janes's position in Kumamoto had become precarious because his pedagogy had taken a more openly Christian evangelical turn, straining his relationship with the school's financial backers. A total break came when students at the academy converted to Christianity en masse. Janes incurred the wrath of the conservative local populace, and the benefactors cut off funding. The school was shut down, and many of Janes's devoted followers, future architects of one of Meiji Japan's influential Protestant groups called the "Kumamoto Band," moved to Kyoto to continue their studies at Dōshisha. Some of them became founding members of Dōshisha's baseball squad, including Miyakawa Tsuneteru, who would found a branch of the Young Men's Christian Association (YMCA) in the city of Osaka in 1882.[40] Through this organization, Janes's former student would become a key propagator of the recently invented American team sports, basketball and volleyball, in western Japan.[41]

The Ascendancy of "America's Game" in Meiji Japan

When private baseball clubs began to appear in Tokyo, baseball's ascendancy over cricket as Japan's bat-and-ball game of choice was not a foregone conclusion, for, as was the case in mid-eighteenth-century U.S. northeastern cities, both cricket and baseball were part of the cultural topography of Japan's foreign settlements in the 1870s, and American expatriates, like their British brethren, tended to play both.[42] By the turn of the century, however, even British observers, hardly impartial judges, grudgingly conceded that baseball had eclipsed cricket in the mikado's empire. Many factors contributed to this outcome, which mirrored what had happened to these bat-and-ball games in the United States. The length of a game and the need for playing grounds with a well-manicured surface worked against cricket. The fact that baseball squads of the U.S. Navy periodically visited Japanese ports for coaling tended to give an extra edge to the American game. In the 1870s, the U.S. Navy, angling to "open up" the hermit kingdom of Korea, was augmenting its presence in the adjacent waters.[43] In an unintended consequence of this emergent geopolitical interest in the Far East, American sailors began to take shore leave in Yokohama more often, creating opportunities to play baseball with local expatriates. But what decisively tipped the scale in baseball's favor was most likely the increasing ease of access to baseball equipment and technical know-how. This improvement in the infrastructure of play for baseball should be attributed in large part to the great entrepreneurial mind of A. G. Spalding.

In the early days of Japanese baseball, shortages of balls and other essentials were serious impediments, and playing without gloves and mitts caused frequent injuries. The shortages also forced ingenious improvisations and what in today's world would be considered industrial piracy. Kido, for instance, took apart a ball he had brought from the United States and ordered a neighborhood shoemaker to study the disassembled material and craft imitations. Hiraoka's SAC substituted *kendō* (Japanese bamboo sword fencing) masks for catcher's masks and upholstered railroad car material for protective gear. Cricket balls were often used by the private clubs in lieu of baseballs. Some Ichikō students even resorted to concocting homemade balls with a nucleus of lead pellets encased to maximize durability. They regarded the pain inflicted on catchers of this ultimate hard ball as "the price of being a real manly man."[44]

For Hiraoka, a long-term solution to the equipment shortage, as it turned out, lay in tapping an old Boston connection. He took a photograph of the SAC members in uniform and sent it to Spalding and mentioned the serious dearth of equipment in Japan and the rampant injuries endured by his suffering teammates. The letter was sent, not to Boston, but to Chicago because Spalding, now retired as a player, was running a baseball equipment manufacturing business in the Windy City and angling to assume the presidency of the Chicago White Stockings. In the 1880s, his company, Spalding & Brothers, began mass-producing baseballs and uniforms, capitalizing on the economic prosperity of the decade. The company's rapid growth was also fueled by a novel sales method enabled by the nation's increasingly reliable nationwide postal service: catalog merchandising. When the National League was established in 1876, Spalding's company acquired the exclusive right to publish its annual *Base Ball Guide* and standardized the size and weight of baseballs for the first time in the game's history. The expansion of Spalding's business and the greater use of standardized and factory-manufactured equipment by American ballplayers went hand in hand. An 1884 advertisement boasted that the company had sold 250,000 balls in the previous five years.[45]

As his biographer Peter Levine has shown, idealism and practical business calculations were always inseparable in Spalding's key decisions in life. When a letter from a long-forgotten Japanese acquaintance bemoaning the scarcity of equipment reached him, this Asian nation popped up on his radar screen as a potential market for his merchandise. In early 1884, the SAC received a free gift of balls, bats, gloves, and catcher's protective masks from Spalding & Brothers, a gift worth $500 to $600 at the time. In an accompanying letter, Spalding congratulated Hiraoka for starting Japan's first baseball club and expressed hope that Japanese baseball, along with the nation's civilization, would "rise like the sun." He was unabashedly candid in revealing the nature of this gift; it was a marketing tool "good for my business," and he offered to send additional supplies free of charge to help promote baseball in Japan. Enclosed catalogs and promotional literature for Spalding & Brothers' sporting goods vouched for the sincerity of the offer.[46]

As an ambitious entrepreneur who was aggressively absorbing rivals to establish a near monopoly in domestic sporting goods, Spalding had been ready to test the waters overseas for some time. His endeavor to spread the American gospel of baseball around the globe had gotten off to a disheartening start a decade earlier. In 1874, Harry Wright, the kingpin of the NAPBBP and manager of the Red Stockings, sent a mixed team of his Boston club, including Spalding, and the Philadelphia Athletics on a promotional tour in the British Isles. The expedition met with a lukewarm reception; Britons were not about to embrace the American game as an equal to cricket. In 1888, Spalding was ready to take up Wright's mantle—this time, with an extended exhibition tour during which he matched his Chicago squad against a team of National League all-stars. Storming through Hawaii, Australia, Ceylon, Egypt, Italy, France, the British Isles, and the Netherlands from October through April of the following year, the expedition was an unabashed business proposition. Spalding candidly told one reporter that he went to Australia to "extend his sporting goods business to that quarter of the globe and to create a market for goods there." At the same time, he was equally committed to spreading what he believed to be the American values of manliness and democratic virtue as embodied in the game. As far as he was concerned, it was both private business *and* an expression of American idealism, and the two were almost inseparable in his mind.[47] Spalding lost money on the world tour, yet his overseas baseball mission helped project a more expansive American presence in the late nineteenth-century world. Games played in the shadows of Egyptian pyramids, in the historical grandeur of Rome's Colosseum, and on England's leading cricket fields also adumbrated, as did Buffalo Bill's Wild West Show touring through Europe in the same year, the dawning of an era of American entertainment spectacles, of which sports would become an important part in the twentieth century.[48]

The marketing genius with which Spalding would spread patriotic baseball lore, including the Doubleday-Cooperstown founding myth, came into play as he touted baseball's global growth potential before launching his tour. Although the logistics of ocean passenger transport kept Japan out of the world tour itinerary, that did not deter Spalding from sending Hiraoka's old letter and the SAC's uniformed group picture to the *Chicago Tribune*, the National League's mouthpiece, to convince skeptics that the sport he was trying to sell as a respectable and stable business enterprise in Gilded Age America was achieving a following even in distant Asia.[49] It was indeed a well-grounded boast. His company's baseball equipment was by then quickly becoming an object of awe and envy among Japan's urban baseball-playing crowd, as members of the SAC and other patrician clubs flouted it as a trophy of social status and proof of privileged access to American consumer modernity.[50]

Included in the promotional package Spalding sent to Hiraoka in 1884 were several copies of *Spalding's Official Base Ball Guide*, just published in the United States on behalf of the National League. This self-congratulatory gift thus helped accelerate the standardization of play and rules in the land of eager neophytes. In the early years of Japanese baseball, rules of play were orally transmitted by *oyatoi* teachers and Japanese student returnees. As is the case with practices relying on oral tradition, they lacked uniformity and consistency, and various local rules coexisted. The first written illustration of baseball rules appeared in most rudimentary form in 1873 in a government-sanctioned primary school textbook. Translated from lesson 7 of *Wilson's First Reader*, brought back from the United States to Japan six years earlier by Fukuzawa, it explained in plain idioms the innocent fun of playing ball.[51] In 1883, a pamphlet written by Strange, then on the staff of Kaiseikō, marked the beginning in Japan of systematic efforts toward standardization and codification of baseball rules. Titled *Outdoor Games*, the fifty-five-page booklet devoted ten pages to baseball. Two years later, Tsuboi Gendō and Tanaka Seigyō included a Japanese translation of baseball rules in *Kogai Yūgihō*. Although it included slight deviations from prevailing American norms, *Kogai Yūgihō* clearly drew on *Spalding's Official Base Ball Guide*, made available to Japanese readership a year earlier. Circulated through the national networks of gym teachers emerging from the state-run physical education institute, this vernacular manual quickly spread across Japan and established itself as the holy scripture of the country's fledgling sporting culture.[52]

Beyond describing equipment use, rules of play, and methods of record keeping, the authors of *Kogai Yūgihō* also took pains to explain concepts associated with organized play, such as forming private "clubs" and the positive social value of doing outdoor bodily exercise as a group.[53] At a time when a limited number of informational outlets covering baseball existed in Japan, the system of play and organizational principles anointed by Spalding and his cohorts in the National League as *the* American national game achieved normative dominance in Japan with only slight delay. This swift cross-border transmission of information and ideology was possible largely because Spalding's official baseball guide penetrated the elite social networks revolving around the SAC and similar urban clubs, which were in monopoly control of private informational channels, and the central nervous system of the Meiji state's universal physical education regime. The growing conformity of rules and styles of play between the United States and Japan in turn created general compatibility, preparing the way for the international intercollegiate baseball exchange that would blossom in the twentieth century.[54]

The Rise of "City Games" in Japan

Historian of American sports Steven Riess has observed in his classic *City Games* (1991) that the process of urbanization, more than any other single factor, spurred the development of organized sports and recreational athletic pastimes in the United States.[55] Accelerating Japanese urbanization in the middle to late Meiji period similarly facilitated the rise and circulation of baseball at the structural level. One marker of the transforming force of urban development was visible in Yokohama's foreign settlement. Even before Japan unshackled itself from "unequal treaties" with the West and the nation's treaty port system formally ended in 1899, the boundaries between native and foreign expatriate populations, both spatial and social, were gradually breaking down. Initially, Japanese nationals were barred from the athletic field built in 1876 in the center of Yokohama's foreign settlement, but distant-range spectatorship of the game played on the settlement's outdoor field figured in early references to baseball in Japan. Inside that thinning boundary, other changes took place. When the playing field in the Yokohama foreign settlement was constructed "for the health and recreation of its inhabitants," British aristocratic athletic traditions, with an emphasis on "gentlemen's sports" and male-centered social activities built around them, predominated in that social space. By the 1890s, however, the Yokohama foreign settlement had evolved into an urban locale where American cultural influences eclipsed those of Great Britain. This contrasted with the other key treaty port, Kobe, in western Japan, where British influences predominated well into the twentieth century because of the port's closer integration with the British-controlled Chinese coastal trading network.[56]

The diverging cultural orientations of the two Japanese treaty ports reflected the reconfiguring regional maritime transport infrastructure, which itself was a spin-off of the changing geopolitics of East Asia. In 1889, the construction of steel-reinforced piers and modern port facilities in Yokohama Harbor began as a national public works project. The bulk of the funds disbursed by the Meiji state originated in a three-million-dollar indemnity the Western powers had extracted from the domain of Chōshū for its failed 1863–64 armed attempt to close the Straits of Shimonoseki. In 1883, the United States returned to Japan its cut in the multinational cash settlement. Itō Hirobumi and other erstwhile Chōshū domain leaders in the Meiji officialdom rewarded Americans for this act of goodwill by pledging most of the returned funds to the enhancement of port facilities in Yokohama. It was a move mutually understood as most beneficial to

Americans—silk importers, the Pacific Mail Company, and the U.S. Navy, in need of a better coaling station near trouble-filled China and Korea, which had recently opened its doors to American traders.[57] The modernized piers in Yokohama Harbor permitted moorings and dockings by large steamships, be they passenger liners, cargo vessels, or refueling American naval ships. The men-of-war's periodic port calls and their crew members' recreational activities during shore leave accelerated the Americanization of Yokohama's sporting culture by the century's end.

That visiting U.S. Navy ships provided opportunities for Japanese nationals and American expatriates to play baseball with American sailors is an aspect of the growing U.S. naval presence in the western Pacific in the late nineteenth century that has largely eluded diplomatic and naval historians' attention. There is no reason to assume, however, that the need for "fleets in being," a requirement of a far-flung maritime presence, did not affect the crews of these ships that were now steam-powered. As Harold Seymour has noted, the crews' permanent noncombatant status and the new technology left an ineluctable mark on their everyday lives. Short, daily drill and setting-up exercises and general athletics replaced the long, rigorous physical training that handling sailing ships had once necessitated. The typical regimen of young seamen during their first six to eight months at training stations came to include the use of spacious grounds for outdoor exercises, including baseball. The U.S. Navy's internal policies would reflect this change. A new government order issued in 1903 permitted naval vessels to requisition the Bureau of Equipment for baseball equipment and uniforms with the name of the ship on the breast so an esprit de corps might be fostered. It further directed each naval station's commanding officer to appoint a board for scheduling competition and awarding trophies. The U.S. Navy became an unlikely agent of the dissemination of American sporting culture overseas.[58]

In the late 1870s and early 1880s, the Yokohama foreign settlement's English-language weekly, *Japan Weekly Mail*, periodically reported baseball games between the Yokohama Baseball Club (YBC); the Yokohama Cricket Club (YCC), established in 1868 by Scottish merchant J. P. Morrison; and crew members of the U.S. Pacific fleet docked in Yokohama. The first call for assembling an ad hoc baseball team among residents of the Yokohama foreign settlement appeared in the paper on April 10, 1871. It was intended for an anticipated game against the USS *Colorado* in the fall.[59] On July 4, 1876, on the nation's centennial celebration, there was a major breakthrough surrounding America's Game in Japan. Residents of the Yokohama foreign settlement, and Americans who traveled from Tokyo, played against the team of the battleship *Tennessee* as part of the Independence Day festivities. The Yokohama-Tokyo "All Stars" beat the vaunted navy team. This unexpected feat boosted interest in baseball among the area's American expatriates and led to the formation of a club with more than forty members in Yokohama and a separate Tokyo-based squad of about thirty players.[60]

The two American expatriate "town teams" played at least five extramural matches that year. One of them took place on Kaiseikō's playing field against Wilson's students. The roster for that game offers an intriguing view into the makeup of the emergent American baseball fraternity in the urban belt linking Tokyo and Yokohama. It also reveals a texture of the American presence in Japan at the time. First, on the roster were three *oyatoi* teachers, including Wilson and Mudgett. The team was captained by U.S. vice consul in Yokohama Henry Denison, the same Denison who advised the Japanese Foreign Ministry through the renegotiations of the "unequal treaties" with the Western powers and the 1905 peace talks with Russia. Research by baseball scholar Philip Block has unearthed the fascinating background of this *oyatoi* diplomatic consultant: before coming to Japan, Denison had played baseball for pay for two years (1867–68) as a member of the Washington Olympics club, owned by none other than Abraham Mills, the latter-day chair of the Mills Commission. The 1876 American roster also included Samuel Hepburn, the son of Meiji Gakuin's James Curtis Hepburn, and Durham Stevens, another *oyatoi* diplomat who would serve Foreign Minister Inoue Kaoru. In 1904 Stevens would be appointed by the Japanese government to "advise" the Korean government on foreign policy matters after Korea became a Japanese protectorate.[61] The game's umpire was the U.S. consul general in Yokohama, Thomas Van Buren. The Americans walloped the Japanese students 35–11. The game was called after the seventh inning because many of the Americans had to catch a train back to Yokohama.[62]

Schedule constraints notwithstanding, because of Yokohama's direct railroad link to Tokyo, the games held there drew spectators from the Tsukiji foreign settlement in central Tokyo, U.S. diplomatic representatives, and Japanese nationals given privileged access to the foreigners' preserves, such as McNair's student nine at Meiji Gakuin. The same railroad connection in the urban belt enabled regular play between the American "town teams" in Yokohama and Tokyo. Baseball thus became America's Game in Japan also, providing a means for the socially isolated American expatriates, often hailing from radically divergent backgrounds but sharing the challenge of living in a foreign land thousands of miles away from home, to foster fraternal bonds among themselves.[63]

In 1883, the YBC and the YCC merged and became the Yokohama Cricket and Athletic Club (the YCAC). As Japanese private colleges organized extracurricular baseball clubs under school sponsorship between the 1880s and the early 1900s, the YCAC began to play against these Japanese collegiate squads as well, mostly at the latter's home grounds. Again, the Tokyo-Yokohama railroad link made such athletic outings a viable civic enterprise. The pattern of regular interaction and resulting sociability that developed between American expatriates and Japanese student elite athletes could not help but exert corrosive effects on the invisible boundaries separating the local and foreign populations at large. The gradual dissipation of social barriers between nationalities can be ascertained from other contemporary indicators, such as a greater number of government permits issued for foreigners' inland travels and the publication of tourist manuals for foreign travelers in the last two decades of the nineteenth century.[64] By the time Japan's foreign settlement system was formally abolished, baseball, the game that had been actively catalyzing the erosion of social boundaries between Japanese and Americans, had clearly eclipsed its British rival, cricket, the sport whose growth in Japan was stunted by the Englishmen's tendency to restrict play in both practice sessions and formal matches to themselves. Because of the greater class and nationality blindness with which it was played, America's Game carried the day in Japan. Sports sociologists Andrei Markovits and Steven Hellerman have argued that whichever sport fills a nation's "sport space" first and manages to do so in the key period between 1870 and 1930—the crucial decades of industrial proliferation and the establishment of modern mass societies—is likely to become the dominant one played in that particular country. Baseball's ascendancy in Meiji Japan eminently validates their thesis.[65]

Baseball and Nationalism in the Age of Imperialism
In terms of enhancing baseball's visibility among a wide spectrum of the Japanese people and linking the game directly to their sense of rising nationhood, perhaps nothing matched the historic four-game series between the YCAC and Ichikō in the summer of 1896.[66] In the early 1890s, Ichikō emerged as the unrivaled powerhouse of student athletics by dint of a head start over private colleges in developing athletic programs as

an extracurricular activity. To make Western competitive sports serviceable to Ichikō students' manly character building, the school authorities under the leadership of Headmaster Kikuchi Hirotsugu sponsored extracurricular clubs for eight sports, including crew, judo, and track and field. Needless to say, baseball was by far the most popular sport among Ichikō students. The school's newly approved self-governing dormitory system buttressed baseball's special place in Ichikō student life. The dormitory's spatial autonomy and freedom from adult supervision nurtured a self-contained peer culture steeped in distinct notions of the masculine young elite, and baseball's appeal broadened for both players and rooters in that gendered environment of institutionalized privilege. The Ichikō baseball club attained almost iconic status among its peers and baseball enthusiasts, who often waxed poetic about Ichikō players' ascetic devotion to the sport and self-punishing training regimen, analogizing them to samurai. Despite its foreign provenance, the adulators effused, baseball fostered "traditional Japanese virtues of loyalty, honor, and manly courage." This cultural construction, a product of the era's nationalistic backlash against the past two decades of Westernization and the contemporary rise of a student subculture, acquired a brand: "Ichikō Baseball" or "*Bushidō* (the way of samurai) Baseball."[67]

Unrivaled in domestic competition after 1890, Ichikō's baseball squad repeatedly challenged the YCAC, an embodiment of the foreign settlement's exclusivity and a reminder of Japan's inferior status vis-à-vis the West, in a manner modeled after rituals of Oxford-Cambridge or Harvard-Yale athletic exchange, but each time the YCAC spurned Ichikō's challenge. Twice, the reason cited for rejection was the Japanese student athletes' diminutive physique and implied lack of masculine vigor. This racialized and gendered insult deeply wounded the Japanese elite youths' pride, and it did so with a particular sting when their nation's recent victory in the Sino-Japanese War, tempered by the humiliation of the Triple Intervention (by Russia, France, and Germany), had sparked a nationwide outpouring of nationalist bravado and when conservative ideologues were churning out tropes of Japan as the new standard-bearer of Asia facing up to the White Men's West.[68]

In May 1896, William B. Mason, an American teacher at Ichikō and a longtime resident of the Yokohama foreign settlement, was able finally to broker a match, to the ecstatic joy of Ichikō students, supporters, and alumni. The depth of emotional investment the Japanese male elite had made in this sporting contest can be fathomed from the fact that a delegation of about four hundred faithful accompanied the Ichikō baseball squad to the Yokohama athletic field on May 23. American spectators, none too pleased with the idea of Japanese nationals unescorted by one of their own entering the privileged space of their playing field, received the Ichikō nine and their supporters with jeer and taunts. Ichikō's surprising 29–4 victory, however, left the same Americans in stunned disbelief. The victorious Ichikō squad was paraded on rickshaws to the Yokohama station with accompanying supporters shouting "Banzai!" The totally unexpected defeat prompted an immediate request for a rematch from the YCAC and stunned commentaries in both vernacular and foreign-language newspapers.[69] The Japanese newspaper coverage of the game and sensationalized reports of Ichikō's spectacular win over the white expatriates generated a rapturous reaction from primary and secondary schoolchildren across the country. Hundreds of congratulatory telegrams poured into the Ichikō dorm. In the second game, on June 5, the YCAC meant business, for it had recruited top players from the crews of American cruisers anchored in Yokohama, the *Charleston* and the *Detroit*. Yet even with these naval reinforcements, the YCAC suffered another defeat, 32–9. The English-language newspaper belittled the significance of this repeated rout, attributing the Ichikō's victory merely to the luxury of full-time training enjoyed by the Japanese students.[70]

The third match, played on June 23 between Ichikō and a team constituted from the crew of the USS *Detroit*, saw the Japanese student athletes again emerge victorious, 22–6, before a swelling crowd of ten thousand spectators, including American diplomatic representatives and Japanese government officials, thronging Ichikō's home grounds. The patriotic trappings of the event had been accentuated by the presence of a U.S. naval band playing "Columbia, the Gem of the Ocean" as the *Detroit* nine swaggered onto the field. The Ichikō ballplayers' repeated exploits generated banner headlines in the key metropolitan newspapers and drew attention from afar, including English-language newspapers in Kobe and Nagasaki.[71] The fourth and final game, played in the Yokohama athletic field symbolically on July 4 amid an ascending spiral of patriotic fervor, pitted Ichikō against the combined YCAC and top players from all the U.S. naval vessels moored in Yokohama at the time. The American naval ships in the nearby harbor were festooned with American flags, and the Japanese student athletes were received with a twenty-one-gun salute. Thanks to the recent arrival of the fleet's flagship and George Dewey's pride, *Olympia* from Shanghai, the American "all-stars" squeezed out a narrow 14–12 win.

To the chagrin of the Japanese players and supporters, the American nine included a former professional ballplayer on their roster. *Olympia* seaman and shortstop Hiram "Pop" Church had played outfield for the Baltimore club in the American Association in the 1890 season before joining the navy. An embittered editorial in the Ichikō student publication later complained that the American team had "an undue advantage" by using a professional and thus "breached sportsmanship." The American team, however, did demonstrate good sportsmanship after the game by giving its Japanese opponents a rousing "Hip, Hip, Hooray!"—a far cry from the catcalls with which they had greeted the Ichikō nine before the first game.[72]

The trope of linking Ichikō's 3–1 victory in the "international series" to Japan's national honor and America's "disgrace" typified the day's newspaper commentaries. Prominent examples were those that appeared in the newspaper *Nippon*. Starting on July 19, the newspaper known for its nationalistic editorial slant ran a three-part serial essay on baseball, explaining the game's rules and historical provenance in both Japan and the United States. The author of the lengthy exegesis, which did much to further familiarize the nation's general populace with the game, was Masaoka Shiki, who would immortalize himself on Japan's literary scene as the Meiji era's preeminent haiku poet. As an Ichikō student in the 1880s, Masaoka had been an avid baseball player himself. After dropping out of Tokyo Imperial University in 1892, he became a reporter for the newly launched *Nippon* and served as a war correspondent in the Liaotung Peninsula at the tail end of the Sino-Japanese War.[73] Before tuberculosis cut short his life in 1902, the dean of modern Japanese haiku would compose many poems themed around the game so dear to his heart.[74] In the wake of his alma mater's trouncing the physically imposing American baseballers, Masaoka participated in the press euphoria over Japanese manly honor avenged through baseball. Calling baseball "America's national game comparable to Spanish bullfighting and Japanese sumo," Masaoka the newspaperman triumphantly speculated about Americans' "wounded national pride" after "being beaten at their national game (*kokugi*)."[75]

Ichikō's four-game series against Americans in the summer of 1896, the passions it generated nationwide, and the blaring coverage it received in the popular press revealed not only baseball's growing significance as a cultural vessel of national identity but also its growing acceptance as a spectator sport and a vehicle of recreation and public entertainment in Japan. The rise of sport spectatorship in late Meiji Japan, as in Gilded Age America, was inseparably entwined with the rise of mass-circulating printing press and emerging social attitudes that legitimated sport as a consumptive, as well as participatory, act. Just as Gilded Age social critic Thorsten Veblen bemoaned the "addiction" to athletic sports by privileged Americans, such as college students and alumni groups, as another piece of evidence that the society was heading toward an operational paradigm defined by consumption, an imperceptible but equal sea change was under way in fin de siècle Japan.

One of the inducers of that tectonic shift was the emergence of a new social group. The institution in 1886 of the four-year middle school across the nation contributed to the conversion of young Japanese males into baseball devotees, as both players and rooters. Under this centrally directed decree, each prefecture was required to have at least one middle school. From the inception of this national system, all the schools sponsored extracurricular clubs that all students, at least initially, were required to join. According to the historian of Japanese sports Watanabe Tōru, about 80 percent of the middle schools sponsored sports clubs. By the late 1880s, twenty-one of them fielded a baseball team (followed by eleven schools that had a boat-racing club or track-and-field team or both). Many more baseball clubs came into existence by the start of the 1897 academic year. Clearly, Ichikō's baseball victories over Americans generated a boom in middle school baseball.[76] For growing ranks of children and youths engaged in compulsory full-time schooling in the new regime of universal education, life began to offer activities not exclusively tied to productive labor or contribution to the household economy. Increasingly, this new category of citizens, the full-time students, resembled the privileged socioeconomic class in their relative freedom from the imperative of constant work and personal sacrifice.[77] The nation's fledgling intercollegiate baseball and the popular following it was about to establish as a spectator sport were both a manifestation and a propellant of this incipient experiential consumerism that was beginning to seep through Japan as well as Veblen's homeland.

That Ichikō's victory over Americans was conjured as a symbol of national honor indicated that the game was coming to be invested with complex social meanings pertaining to self and nationhood and, transporting this cargo, was embraced as Japan's national game as well. Nothing attested to Japan's symbolic "nationalization" of baseball more eloquently than the coining of the vernacular word for baseball, *yakyū*, meaning "ball play in the field." Its progenitor was Chūma Kanoe, a former second baseman on the Ichikō team. A native of Kagoshima Prefecture on the southern island of Kyushu, Chūma was typical of Japanese males of the era in that he was initiated into the game of baseball in middle school gym class. After graduating from Ichikō in 1893 and becoming a literature major at Tokyo Imperial University, he remained involved as an alumni coach. It was Chūma who umpired in the third game of the 1896 U.S.-Japan series, played against the crew of the *Detroit*. In 1894, because of his literary gift, Chūma was given the task of writing the history of Ichikō baseball. In this process of chronicling, the former Ichikō second baseman came up with the Japanese translation for *baseball*. Ichikō's squad history bearing the word (*Ichikō Yakyūbushi*; History of the Ichikō Baseball Club) was published in February 1895—the first time the vernacular word *yakyū* had appeared in print.[78]

Later, Chūma published a pamphlet titled *Yakyū* (1896) as a consolidated response to the many queries about the intricacies of the game that the Ichikō baseball club had received from primary and middle school students across the country after the summer of 1896. The detailed explanations of the rules in Chūma's volume drew on the 1896 edition of *Spalding's Official Base Ball Guide* yet symbolized the nation's domestication of America's Game at a number of levels. Most obvious was the use in the title of the word *Yakyū* instead of the previously common *bēsubōru*, the direct phoneticization of the English word.[79] More important, Chūma made a few significant modifications of Spalding's guide to adapt the rules made for American professionals to Japan's local contexts. After consulting with his brothers in the Ichikō baseball fraternity, Chūma trimmed the guide's original seventy-two rule provisions to fifty-one. One of the eliminated provisions concerned the team captain's right to address the umpire to question his calls or interpretations of the rules, as the Ichikō baseball fraternity believed that questioning the presumed infallibility of authority was not appropriate for student baseball. Chūma's version also allowed an extra five minutes before the forfeiture of a game to make allowance for teams traveling by the still unreliable trains. Finally, Chūma deviated from Spalding by professing ambivalence about using baseball equipment, for the use of gloves might interfere with the attainment of "genuine techniques" in fielding, and the pain from catching a ball with bare hands might make for "manly fortitude."[80]

Chūma's baseball canon sold extremely well, going into seven printings in just four years. It also presaged Japan's rising imperial aspirations and the centrality of male physicality expressed in soldiering in that emergent national project. In the preamble to this volume, Chūma reflected in detail on "the dog-eat-dog world of international politics" and stressed the need for the healthy body and mental agility of its (male) populace in a nation that had to become "the fittest to survive." From this social Darwinist ideological perch, Chūma exhorted, as Theodore Roosevelt had done in the United States, the nation's youth to strive for a strenuous life and physical fitness in the service of their rising nation. Citing German *turnen* and British gentlemen's amateur sports such as rowing and cricket as an ideal, Chūma emphasized that Japan also needed a productive outlet for the excess energies of its young male population. The sport he recommended was, of course, *yakyū*, a game that, he argued, required one to be "agile in both body and mind, to be decisive, enterprising, and open to new ideas." Better yet, a game required only two *tan* (about two thousand square meters) of playing surface and could be completed in two hours.[81] Going into the new century, Japan, like the United States, had found its national pastime, carrying with it idealized visions of gendered citizenship, nation, and, increasingly, empire.

2 | COLONIAL BASEBALL

Baseball's spread across the United States in the postbellum period was notable for its contemporaneous diffusion outside America's national borders. As Adrian Burgos has instructed us, North American professionals' first documented travel to Cuba took place in 1879 when future major-league manager Frank Bancroft led the Rochester-based Hop Bitters on a tour of the Spanish colony. Other professional teams traveled to Cuba over the next two decades whenever the intermittent anticolonial insurgency on the island would permit such excursions. In the meantime, an embryonic structure of intra-Caribbean competition between Cuba, Puerto Rico, and the Dominican Republic emerged as sugarcane production on these islands expanded and refineries became key sites for local laborers to play *béisbol*. By the end of the century, an intrahemispheric circuit of baseball play was in place, linking New York, San Francisco, and Chicago with Havana, San Juan, and Santo Domingo. Through this transnational circuit, playing talents, management expertise, and technical and other information flowed both ways. The end of Spanish colonial rule in Cuba turned the Caribbean island into a regular winter stop for American professional squads and barnstorming players from the major, high-end minor, and Negro leagues in the early twentieth century. The growing presence of the U.S. Navy in the circum-Caribbean region also afforded more opportunities for local clubs, both professional and amateur, to challenge North Americans on the diamond.[1]

Almost concomitantly, a transoceanic loop of baseball play linking the United States with Hawaii, Japan, and the Philippines began to take shape. As was the case with the Caribbean, a wide variety of historical actors participated in the circulation of America's national pastime to places outside the Western Hemisphere. The lineup ranged from individuals, American or not, who loved the game passionately—so much so that they took baseball equipment along wherever they moved—to groups and organizations that patronized the game for a variety of objectives and institutional missions, and, ultimately, to larger and impersonal structural forces of global history. Some of these individuals and collectivities were guided by God, others driven by Mammon, and many inspired by varying combinations of both. Still others employed baseball as a tool of governance and social control. Baseball was also expected to "civilize" or pacify the alien populations encountered overseas. In the transpacific zone of cultural circulation, the deployment of the sport for these varied reasons resulted in diverse forms of "colonial baseball," a system of play predicated on decidedly asymmetrical relationships of power, some backed by raw military force and political subjugation and others enacted by subtly coercive or seductively co-optive power. This uneven and power-laden regime of athletic practices bore both American and Japanese emblems in the transpacific world and, in its unfurling, generated divergent social meanings and political symbolisms while fostering disparate and overlapping affinities and identities. Through it all, baseball grew into a cultural auxiliary of the two colonial orders.

Christian Missionaries and Early Baseball in Hawaii

One of the notable features of mythologies surrounding baseball is an apparently irrepressible impulse on the part of their progenitors and propagators to attribute "America's Game" to a sole inventor or to pinpoint a specific moment of creation. Besides the most glaring example of the Doubleday-Cooperstown foundational myth concocted by Spalding and his cronies on the Mills Commission, the legend built around Alexander Joy Cartwright and his historical role vis-à-vis baseball also fits into this pattern of baseball mythmaking. After Robert Henderson documented in *Ball, Bat and Bishop* (1947) Cartwright's contributions to the codification of the rules and regulations of a New York variety of the game, this former member of the New York Knickerbocker Base Ball Club acquired the title "Father of Modern Baseball." Further, this onetime Manhattan bank clerk and bookseller was credited with spreading baseball across the American West and all the way to Hawaii, as is claimed on his plaque at the Baseball Hall of Fame in Cooperstown. This anointment even received formal endorsement in June 1953 when Congress recognized Cartwright as the inventor of baseball as a modern organized sport.[2]

When gold was discovered in the Sierra Nevada foothills in 1848, "Alick"

Cartwright and his brother Alfred joined tens of thousands of gold rush prospectors who headed for California with the dream of instant riches. Alfred left first, in January 1849, setting sail on a clipper ship out of Newport. Alick went by land, taking 156 days to traverse the continent by rail and covered wagon and arriving in the Sierra Nevada in August. After a brief stop in the gold-crazed boom country, Cartwright realized that there was no money to be made there, at least not for him and his brother. So he embarked upon a westbound sea voyage, hoping to find better fortune in China before returning home to New York. On his way to the "flowery empire," Cartwright landed on the Sandwich Islands (Hawaii) and ended up spending the rest of his life on Oahu. According to popular accounts, including his biography by Harold Peterson, Cartwright brought bats and balls with him on his cross-continental journey, showing Indians and frontiersmen how to play the game along the way. The legend also has it that Cartwright planted the seeds of baseball in northern California and did much to promote the game in his new home, Hawaii; hence he was dubbed the "Johnny Appleseed of baseball."[3]

Alluring as such a folk hero might be, recent studies of Cartwright's life and the development of baseball in Hawaii have shown that the story does not stand the test of empirical scrutiny. Using a variety of contemporary records, historian Monica Nucciarone has argued persuasively that Cartwright's trek across the American West was simply too arduous and he was too sick for him to play a role as baseball missionary. True, Cartwright departed from New York with a catgut-covered ball and occasionally tossed it around with his fellow travelers in the early and relatively trouble-free legs of the cross-country trip. But his wagon almost collapsed later, and, as his brother Alfred put it in a letter to Cartwright's wife back in New York, Cartwright and his wagon party arrived in San Francisco with only "what they had upon their backs, a cup and a spoon apiece." Suffering from dysentery, Alick was too weak to concern himself with gold prospecting, let alone playing baseball. The Cartwright brothers summarily booked passage on a westbound Peruvian sailing ship and left California in less than a week. Given those circumstances, argues Nucciarone, Cartwright almost certainly did not plant any seeds of baseball in California. Rather, the game was borne to the territory by a myriad of outsiders who had poured in from all over before Cartwright's arrival and continued to do so after his hurried exit from the territory. Among such ball-playing California dreamers was another New York Knickerbocker, Frank Turk, who settled in San Francisco, where he served as an attorney.[4]

The claim that Cartwright promoted "the game he invented" in his adopted land, the Kingdom of Hawaii, rests on similarly shaky evidentiary grounds. Drawing on local newspapers and other indigenous records, Frank Ardolino has shown, quite convincingly, that Cartwright's role in the development and popularization of baseball in Hawaii was peripheral at best. First, the origins of baseball in the island kingdom preceded the New Yorker's arrival by decades, and here Ardolino points to multiple roots of baseball's entry and murky circumstances under which it spread. Baseball in its embryonic form was first introduced to Hawaii in the 1820s by New England Christian missionaries sent by the American Board of Foreign Missions, an interdenominational Protestant organization whose members were predominantly Presbyterians and Congregationalists.[5] Between 1820 and 1850, more than a hundred members of the organization were sent to Hawaii to "civilize" the native population into Christendom. In so doing, the proselytizing white Americans discouraged indigenous cultural practices they disapproved of, such as hula dancing.[6] Baseball was their game of choice with which to teach the native populace "civilized" physical exercise. One James H. Black, a Boston printer, has been credited with introducing the Massachusetts form of early baseball to the native people and providing the necessary equipment. Many native Hawaiians took to baseball because they had been playing their own indigenous bat-and-ball games for ages. British settlers also brought their favored bat-and-ball game, cricket, to the mid-Pacific islands, where the Anglo-American outsiders vied for dominance in multiple realms of local life through midcentury.[7]

The education and socialization of their own children provided added impetus for the American missionaries to patronize baseball in their white settler community in the mid-Pacific. Some of the missionaries sent their children back to the U.S. mainland for education, while many employed the game as a handier way to ensure that their children grew up properly "American" amid the native population. That was one of the reasons that America's Game was privileged at Punahou School, founded in 1841 to "create a class of learned men" out of children of white mainland settlers (haoles). It was built on a hundred-acre land grant that Hiram Bingham, a leading Congregational missionary, had received from Queen Kaahumanu. The Reverend Daniel Dole, the school's founder and first headmaster, happened to be an avid baseball player, and he demonstrated techniques himself and arranged matches between his students and children at other schools. A school record dating from 1866 reports a game played between teams of haole students and native Hawaiians as a Fourth of July function. After the 1876 centennial, Independence Day baseball games became a staple of the annual event calendar of the Honolulu haole community as well as the Punahou School's.[8]

According to the popular foundational tale about Hawaiian baseball, Cartwright and his son marked out, à la Abner Doubleday in 1839, a baseball diamond on the field at Honolulu's Makiki Park (renamed Cartwright Field in 1938) in 1852 and introduced the New York style of game. But was it really so?[9] Cartwright's two Hawaiian-born sons, Bruce and Allic, did attend Punahou School and played for the school team in the 1860s. They continued to play ball as alumni in the 1870s and for Honolulu's adult town teams in the 1880s.[10] But little, if any, evidence exists of the senior Cartwright actively involving himself as a baseball missionary in Hawaii. He did seem to retain his interest in the game per se, as intimated in his oft cited 1865 letter to an old Knickerbocker friend, Charles DeBost.[11] But once he decided to settle in Hawaii permanently and relocated his family from New York, his passion definitely shifted to business ventures, participation in local Freemasonry, and, later on, the annexation movement whose key members included his sons and their childhood friends. As a successful businessman, local civic leader, and, at one point, financial adviser to the Hawaiian royal family, Cartwright probably patronized the game in a general sense, but the nature of his actual engagement appears indirect. His obituaries in local newspapers in 1892 made no mention of his baseball-related activities in New York or Hawaii.[12]

The American Protestants missionaries' "civilizing" mission over time reconfigured into a semicolonial enterprise, or as Bruce Cumings would call it, "the purest American colony in the world."[13] The white missionaries wrote the island kingdom's first constitution in 1840, setting in motion the long-term historical process in which the haole establishment would increase its power at the expense of native monarchical authority. Ingratiating themselves with the royal family, the American "advisers" convinced King Kamehameha III to undertake the Great Mahele, a program in which Hawaii's historically communal lands were parceled out, commodified, and sold. Missionaries each obtained 560 acres of land at minimal cost. The Kingdom of Hawaii thus opened up to the "modern" capitalist land tenure system and, not so coincidentally, to large-scale landholding by white settlers. Native Hawaiians, whose indigenous subsistence economy had been based on barter and communal land use before the Westerners' arrival, found this new regime beyond the ken of their historical experiences. Hard put to pay newly instituted land taxes, many native Hawaiians were forced into selling their allotments, allowing the concentration of landownership in the hands of white settlers. By 1862, nonnative white settlers owned about 75 percent of Hawaii's acreage, paving the way for the development of large-scale plantations in the next phase in Hawaiian history. As it so happened, baseball became established as a cultural mainstay of this rising haole establishment during this period, with the Punahou School as its central organizational platform.[14]

As baseball went through various innovations on the U.S. mainland in the 1860s and 1870s, newer elements involving rules, playing techniques, equipment use, and record were brought back to Hawaii by Punahou School alumni who went on to attend mainland colleges. Among such cultural emissaries was William Castle, a son of Samuel Castle, a pioneer lay missionary and the founder of Castle and Cooke, one of the Big Five corporations that would come to control Hawaii's sugar industry. The young Castle returned to Honolulu in 1866 after two years of schooling at Oberlin College and introduced the New York version of baseball to local players. American northeasterners recruited as teachers at Punahou School also helped update the game to mainland standards. For example, William Chickering, a former shortstop for Amherst College, moved to Honolulu in 1871 as a teacher of the classics and began coaching the school squad and played on an adult town team. Punahou's students and alumni were present at the creation of Hawaii's first formal baseball league in 1866, officially adopting the California National Baseball Convention's rules and regulations. A game played by the league's founding teams, the Pacifics and the Pioneers, on August 24, 1867, was the first game to be recorded with box scores in a local newspaper, the *Hawaiian Gazette*. By all indications, it was a huge to-do for the local community. Businesses in town closed an hour before the game, and a hundred or so women traveled from outlying areas in carriages to join an overflowing crowd of men and boys to watch the game, won by the Pacifics 11–9 and followed by lavish social events. Within a few years, the league expanded into a five-team circuit, joined by the Whangdoodles, Pensacolas, and Athletics. In June 1871, King David Kalakaua attended a match between the Athletics and the Pensacolas, the first member of the Hawaiian royal family to do so.[15]

The players and officials active in early Hawaiian baseball constituted a virtual who's who of the haole power elite. Many of them descended from the original contingent of New England Protestant missionaries and successful mercantile families from the U.S. mainland. Most attended Punahou School and went on to achieve prominence in Hawaii's economic and political circles. Pacifics pitcher Charles Gulick, a nephew of missionary Peter Gulick, would serve Queen Liliuokalani, the last Hawaiian monarch, as minister of the interior. Pioneer catcher Allan W. Judd and his brother Charles were the sons of Gerrit Judd, a medical missionary and adviser to the Hawaiian monarchy. The father of Pioneers outfielder Harry Whitney Jr. founded the *Pacific Commercial Advertiser* in 1856 and acquired the *Hawaiian Gazette* in 1873 to form a newspaper monopoly on the island. This cohort of Honolulu male elite also counted among its ranks the Cartwright brothers and Lorrin Thurston, the drafter of the so-called Bayonet Constitution of 1887 and one of the instigators of the overthrow of the Hawaiian monarchy in 1894.[16]

League play in baseball grew in Honolulu in the 1870s, a cultural manifestation of the larger historical development in which white Americans and their sociocultural norms displaced rival British influences through settlement, trade, and investment, especially after the signing of the U.S.-Hawaiian Reciprocity Treaty of 1875. Under this bilateral trade agreement, Hawaiian sugar, now produced on large-scale plantations run by haoles, was given duty-free access to U.S. mainland markets. In exchange, the United States secured, among other things, the right for its navy to use the Pearl River Lagoon, the only natural deepwater harbor in the Hawaiian Islands besides Honolulu. When the reciprocity treaty was renewed in 1887, the U.S. Navy secured the exclusive use of Pearl Harbor and a right to build a coaling station and other improvements.[17] The island economy, now harnessed to white American commercial agricultural capital, began to gravitate decidedly toward a mainland U.S. economic orbit under the U.S. Navy's "protective" wings. It was during this period of the island kingdom's profound socioeconomic transformation that baseball, as the favored pastime of this white American governing class, displaced other forms of bat-and-ball games, including cricket, and solidified its dominance in the local recreational culture. One indication of baseball's growing spectatorship in urbanizing Honolulu was that, in 1884, Makiki Field was enlarged with the addition of a grandstand seating eight hundred.[18]

Spalding's 1888–89 world tour passed through Hawaii during these halcyon days of white settler colonial baseball. It was also a year after the haole Reform Party and its armed militia Honolulu Rifles forced King Kalakaua to sign the so-called Bayonet Constitution and stripped him of much of political authority.[19] Among members of the 408-member Hawaiian League who formed the core of the Reform Party were former Punahou baseball players such as Lorrin Thurston, Sanford Dole, and the Cartwright brothers. Cartwright Sr. was also a member of the Hawaiian League.[20] A group of local civic leaders who arranged the Spalding tour's stop in Honolulu, including Spalding's cousin George W. Smith, intended the occasion to showcase the white Americans' dominance in the island society. It was thus ironic that two games scheduled in Honolulu had to be canceled because of the local blue laws instituted by the original Protestant missionaries as an aspect of their "civilizing" program. Spalding and his traveling troupe docked in Honolulu early in the morning of Sunday, November 25, a day later than scheduled. Some one thousand local baseball enthusiasts signed a petition to have the ban on Sunday games waived. Many contributed money to pay for fines that would accrue from breaking the law. King Kalakaua, now a beleaguered and much weakened "constitutional monarch," came out publicly in favor of the game being played as scheduled. Spalding, however, opted to honor the local blue laws, contributing, intentionally or not, to the public diminishment of the king's political authority.[21]

The disappointment of game's cancellation notwithstanding, the visit by the professionals from the U.S. mainland ratcheted up the baseball craze that had been sweeping across Hawaii. The island's baseball fever culminated in the incorporation of the Hawaiian Baseball Association in 1890 as a commercial entity underwritten in large part by the local haole establishment. The association invited an all-star team from California in December of that year to play a seven-game series in Makiki Field against Honolulu's town teams. Drawing a cumulative twenty-eight thousand paying spectators, it was a rousing commercial success. King Kalakaua, in medical retreat in San Francisco twenty-five hundred miles away, died the next month. Within two years, the baseball-loving kingdom would morph into a baseball-loving "republic" when Kalakaua's sister, Queen Liliuokalani, was dethroned in a coup d'état choreographed by Thurston, Dole, and their haole coconspirators in the self-proclaimed Committee on Safety, emboldened by the reassuring presence of armed U.S. Marines from the USS *Boston*, anchored in Honolulu Harbor. The request for the marines' landing, ostensibly to "protect American lives and property," was made by U.S. minister John Stevens, a vocal Hawaii annexationist and appointee of fellow Maine expansionist James Blaine.[22]

The U.S. Military and the Origins of Baseball in the Philippines

While baseball leapfrogged across the continent and half an ocean to Hawaii, another organization equipped with transborder mobility, this one far more rigidly regimented than Protestant overseas missions, also contributed to the game's westward geographical dispersion in the late nineteenth century: the U.S. military. At first brush, the period after the Civil War might appear to be a sleepy interlude in the history of U.S. foreign relations, but it can be characterized as a gestational period during which the American state began incrementally to extend its military reach through the trans-Mississippi West and in the Pacific Ocean. During this era, the U.S. Army, fighting against Native American tribes in the high plains and mountain territories after the Civil War, set up a large number of forts and encampments for its military operations. Soldiers assigned to these new posts and garrisons were mostly volunteers, with an average age of twenty-three, and generally drawn from the bottom of the social ladder. Thirsty for camaraderie and reprieve from the gnawing tedium and desolation of fort life, these young American men typically found solace in playing baseball, among other improvised amusements. On holidays, they played prearranged ball games with the blessings of their commanders, often matched against local civilian town teams and "friendly" Native American inhabitants.[23]

At first, the army top brass gave little or no encouragement to organized recreation. They did not even provide the most basic of sporting equipment, leaving these young men in their charge to improvise their own. Signs of change first appeared in the 1880s as athletic enthusiasts within the army began to champion organized sports not just as the preserve of elite cadets at the military academies but also an adjunct to regular training for rank-and-file soldiers. In 1884, the *Army and Navy Journal* recommended that post commanders set aside an entire day each week for athletics based on a regular schedule of intercompany games of baseball and other team sports to maintain the physical vigor and combat readiness of troops. Baseball was second to none in popularity in this new internal regimen.[24] Efforts to incorporate athletics more systematically into military life followed. The most vigorous advocate of this new approach was Lieutenant Edmund Butts, who had been known as the best all-around athlete in West Point's class of 1888. Butts advocated sports of every kind, arguing that athletics would "see the men at once transferred into hardened veterans, upon whom the safety of the nation could depend." He particularly recommended baseball because it taught team play and "prompt and individual action" together with "subservience to the united action of the company needed by a skirmisher in the field." In 1893, he authored what came to be known as the army's "Butts Manual" for organized athletics. The army dispatched this sport advocate to various posts and encampments for demonstration. As far as baseball was concerned, the inchoate institutional support for intramural organized sports became manifest by the mid-1890s when a typical eight-company post housing about three thousand people was equipped with a baseball diamond marked out of the side of the quadrangle nearest the soldiers' barracks.[25]

The army's institutional commitment to organized athletics was proclaimed for the first time in 1896 by Commanding General Nelson Miles, a former commander in the Plains Indians war and a future military governor of Puerto Rico. He authorized the Quartermaster's Department to "transport gymnastic and athletic appliances, purchased with regimental or company funds, for the use of the troops, from the nearest market to the post or station of the troops." With this official mandate on the books, sports equipment now became available and could be shipped at the army's expense. Yet as historian Wanda Wakefield has chronicled, the real watershed in the military's approach to institutionally supported athletic programs came as a result of the Spanish-American War. The acquisition of an overseas empire and the advent of more expansive overseas missions compelled the military establishment to undertake a thoroughgoing reassessment of its future role and proper function. The notion of supporting organized athletics to maintain the health, morale, and discipline of troops stationed overseas for an extended period came to the fore during this process of institutional overhaul and resource allocation. Initially, the army's top echelons were slow to accept the paternalistic concept that its members' welfare needs must be met—let alone to do so through the provision of recreation and entertainment. Major General Leonard Wood, the first military governor of Cuba, was one of the first top army commanders to emphasize the value of organized athletics. A physician by training, Wood argued that athletic activities held the key to the physical vigor and general health of the troops engaged in occupational duties overseas. Civilian leaders provided an added impetus; none other than the commanding Rough Rider Theodore Roosevelt complained that his troops were lying idle with nothing to do in Cuba after the island had been secured. Reflecting this new awareness and organizational commitment, the army formally instituted organized sports in occupied Cuba as a recreational resource for its members.[26]

As has been shown by Louis A. Pérez Jr. and others, it took no time for baseball to become *the* game in U.S.-occupied Cuba because the sport had long been embedded in the culture of the local populace of all ages and been identified by Cuban nationalists during their recent decades of anticolonial resistance as a game in which Cubans could express their distinctiveness from and opposition to bullfight-patronizing Spanish colonial masters. There had also been a venerable tradition, going back two decades, of exchanging technical and other information on baseball between New York, Philadelphia, St. Louis, and Havana through the fledgling baseball journalism published out of these cities. The American baseball periodicals *Sporting News* and *Sporting Life* and Cuban baseball publications mutually contracted with local baseball writers as their "foreign correspondents." Even before the hostilities ceased on the island, North American baseball promoters, including equipment manufacturers, began spinning schemes to tour Cuba, a market expected soon to rid itself of unfriendly Spanish colonial rulers and open up to American products. It was no wonder, therefore, that as soon as U.S. military occupation began, American soldiers and Cuban civilians began to engage each other avidly on the baseball diamond, and an American military league was soon established on the island. Less than six months after the war ended, the first team of Cuban professional players toured the United States. Cuban barnstormers, landing in Key West, Tampa, or New Orleans after the end of their local seasons, would become a fixture in mainland American pro teams' spring training in the South in the second decade of the twentieth century.[27]

Similar cultural intermingling took place in the Philippines, another Spanish colonial possession over which the United States gained control. Filipinos generally responded to the game brought by Americans in the same way that their transoceanic colonial brethren in Cuba did—that is, they embraced it as a new recreational practice replacing cockfighting, a cultural bequest of their previous colonial ruler. Like other countries in Asia, the Philippines had been largely devoid of an indigenous tradition of organized team sports before the Americans' arrival. In the late nineteenth century, Filipinos generally perceived physical exertion in solely productive, not recreational and consumptive, terms. To them, bodily exertion was another form of manual labor, nothing more and nothing less. Such attitudes toward athletics began to change as Filipinos watched American soldiers and sailors play baseball and engage in other team sports in between their combat missions. The first known baseball game in the Philippines was played in May 1898 between sailors and marines under George Dewey's command, fresh from the rousing naval victory in the Battle of Manila Bay. The crew of the squadron's flagship *Olympia* was particularly renowned for athletic prowess, and its baseball squad, the Diamond Diggers, played five officially sanctioned games at Cavite Naval Base between May and October 1898, including one against a U.S. Army team. The star of the Diamond Diggers was pitcher Ernest "Pop" Church, the former pro who had been instrumental in beating the Ichikō nine in Yokohama two summers earlier.[28]

It was also in the Philippines that, once the insurrection by local guerrillas had been largely suppressed, the U.S. military sponsored for the first time in its institutional history an athletic program for soldiers and sailors, transitioning to a "peacetime" colonial administration in the early 1900s. The first baseball park with a covered grandstand, Paco Baseball Park, was built in Manila in 1902 for exclusive use by the Manila Baseball League. The circuit was initially made up entirely of U.S. service teams, but the loop expanded to encompass indigenous amateur and semipro teams in the second decade of the century.[29] The first contingent of locals to take a stab at playing the Americans' ball game was Filipinos employed on the U.S. Army encampments. They were followed by Filipino children in public schools established as part of America's new colonial regime. American Protestant missionaries and schoolteachers began to arrive in the archipelago in the first decade of the twentieth century to take part in the running of the new colony, and they too used baseball as a tool of educating and Americanizing their wards in an institutional framework of YMCA sports programs. The best known among such ball-playing Protestant missionaries in the Philippines was the Reverend George W. Dunlap, a former varsity catcher for Princeton, who helped turn the island of Cebu into a hotbed of youth baseball in the early twentieth century.[30]

Youth baseball in the Philippines first got off the ground in Manila, where the American presence was most secure and concentrated. By 1905, four local schools fielded baseball teams. Two others joined a team later to form the Philippines' first student baseball league in the colonial capital. Growing ranks of adult town and company teams also came into existence in urban locations and the "pacified" countryside in the first decade of the twentieth century and played organized and pickup matches against American expatriates and the U.S. service teams. Governor-General William Cameron Forbes (1909–13), a Republican investment banker and a William Howard Taft appointee, did much to spread baseball and organized athletic competition beyond urban areas to the countryside. The son of William Hathaway Forbes, president of Bell Telephone Company, Forbes was an athletic enthusiast, having fielded Harvard's varsity football team as an alumni coach in the mid-1890s. Also skilled in polo, Forbes founded the Manila Polo Club in 1909 soon after his appointment as governor-general. An unapologetic Anglo-Saxon racial supremacist, the patrician governor-general shared many of the tenets of racial and gender ideology professed by his contemporaries such as Theodore Roosevelt (who as president appointed him to the Philippines Commission for Police and Commerce). Anglo-Americans' excellence in competitive sports proved their innate racial superiority in this athlete-politician's worldview. Organized sports thus became Forbes's key proving ground for white American men's claim to world civilizational leadership in the Philippines.[31]

Forbes possessed a genuine, if racist, sense of mission to "uplift" his colonial wards in the Philippines through better public health and sports. Baseball, rather than his erstwhile favorites football or polo, became his chosen instrument of Western civilization because the local populace, particularly those at the lower rungs of the social hierarchy, readily took to this game, unencumbered, unlike upper-class Filipinos, by concerns about getting tanned. Most of the material and modern consumerist trappings of sports play, such as complete uniforms worn by the top divisional teams in baseball and basketball, trophies given out at track and field meets, and various prizes and commendatory paraphernalia for winners at baseball games at the provincial level, were a legacy of Forbes's gubernatorial initiatives. By the end of his tenure in 1913, more than fifteen hundred fully uniformed baseball teams competed in the Philippines, and 95 percent of the public schools' enrollment participated in organized sports. Forbes later boasted that "one of the most notable achievements of the Americans in the islands was the diversion of the attention of the young Filipinos from the cockpits, with their attendant vice of gambling, to the more healthful and vigorous competitive outdoor sports." The Philippines' shift from traditional folk games to modern organized athletics was no doubt facilitated by the fact that sports simulates equality, a fleeting illusion created by the application of uniform rules and regulations to all participants, both the colonizer and the colonized, in the circumscribed social arena.[32]

Voluntary civic groups subscribing to a similar sports creed assisted these athletic endeavors by the military and the civilian government in

Manila from the sidelines. Sport officials housed in the increasingly influential Amateur Athletic Union (AAU) became advocates for exporting to the Asian colony American-style team athletics and the manly "American" virtues they purportedly embodied, touting sports' "civilizing" effects on the "natives." James E. Sullivan, one of the AAU's founding members, emerged as a partisan particularly invested in this project. A sports journalist, a close business associate of Spalding & Brothers, and a member of the recently launched Mills Commission, Sullivan was heavily involved in the planning and execution of the 1904 St. Louis Olympics, held in conjunction with the Louisiana Purchase Centennial World Fair. In his capacities as head of the AAU and director of the St. Louis World Fair's physical department, Sullivan took every occasion to articulate his brand of American nationalism loaded with cultural ethnocentrism and racism during these twin events held in the Gateway City.[33] One of the most popular exhibits at the 1904 World Fair was the Philippines Reservation, in which the newly acquired colony was put on display as a land populated by "savages" and scantily clothed "tribal" people. Not surprisingly, the exhibits about the Filipinos and Native Americans were placed next to each other, mirroring their contiguous locations in the epistemological universe of the exhibit's organizers, the U.S. government. These symbolically loaded exhibits also received scholarly validation by W. J. McGee, the era's leading expert in anthropology. The Filipino and Native American villages together constituted the "Congress of Races," whose aim, McGee explicated as the exhibit's coordinator, was to "present human progress from the dark prime to the highest enlightenment."[34]

Historian S. W. Pope has argued convincingly that "Anthropology Days," held on August 12 and 13 as an ancillary event to the 1904 St. Louis Olympics, enacted on the athletic fields the arrival of the United States as a multiracial empire and the complex racial ideology undergirding that new body politic. About 3,000 indigenous people, including the Japanese Ainu, Native Americans, and Filipinos, competed in athletic contests designed purportedly to showcase their native cultures and innate physical attributes. A Filipino Igorot, for example, won the pole climb, and a Sioux Indian prevailed in the hundred-yard dash. The competitors in this "Special Olympics" (so called by Sullivan and his co-organizers) were made to wear their "native costumes" instead of athletic clothing to highlight their racialized and exotified differences. Sullivan was the chief impresario of these objectifying spectacles touted to provide "scientific" evidence that "uncivilized" natives and aborigines did not perform in modern sports as well as Caucasians. These ethnocentric athletic enterprises, Pope argues, enabled white European and American spectators as well as organizers to feel morally sanctioned to propagate the "civilization" encapsulated in modern Western sports to their imperial peripheries. The AAU's cooperation with the American state to transplant Western sports to the Philippines should be understood in this context of global racial politics.[35]

The Philippines' embrace of organized sports in the first decades of the twentieth century was also prompted by the YMCA in Manila. Ushering in this process of cultural shift was the physical director of the Manila YMCA, Elwood S. Brown. Born in Cherokee, Iowa, in 1883, Brown launched his career in the YMCA as a basketball coach for the organization's Chicago branch. Upon assuming the post in Manila in 1910, Brown exercised vigorous leadership that came to fruition in the formation of the Philippine Amateur Athletic Federation (PAAF) in January 1911. The American sport advocate also made a lasting footprint on Asia's regional athletic topography by masterminding the organization of the Far Eastern Games. Participated in by Japan (including Korea and Taiwan), the Philippines, north China (Shanghai), and south China (Hong Kong), the first of Asia's multi-event athletic meets took place in February 1913 as part of the Manila Carnival.[36] Brown had traveled to Japan and China in the previous two years to persuade the YMCA branches and government officials concerned with athletics in these countries to sign on to the American-proposed regional undertaking. Needless to say, the Far East Games received Governor-General Forbes's wholehearted support.[37] Until they went into abeyance in 1934 because of the controversy over participation by Manchukuo, the Far East Games were held biennially and contributed greatly to the dissemination in Asia of the new YMCA-invented team sports, basketball and volleyball, as well as Olympic events such as swimming and track and field. The Far East Games also provided a regular venue for fierce baseball rivalries played out every other year between Filipino and Japanese amateur champion squads during the interwar period.[38]

Early in that second decade of U.S. colonial rule, baseball established itself as the centerpiece of the Philippines' budding athletic culture. Major General James Franklin Bell, commander of the Philippines Department between 1911 and 1914, boasted that baseball had "done more to 'civilize' Filipinos than anything else" and to shield American servicemen stationed in the Philippines from tropical degeneracy. The *Sporting Life* gloated in 1912 about the American "National Pastime" displacing cockfighting, the residual Spanish colonial influence, thanks to dedicated efforts by American public school teachers. In a similar vein, Frank White, the director of the Bureau of Education in Manila, proudly proclaimed in 1914 that baseball had eclipsed cockfighting as the sport of choice among Filipinos. Given "the natural apathy of a tropical people," effused White, the "progress" had been "extraordinary." The conflation of America's "civilizing" mission in the Philippines, baseball, colonial modernity, and American manliness was trumpeted with flair when an expedition of American major leaguers headed by John McGraw of the New York Giants and Charles Comiskey of the Chicago White Sox played in Manila in early 1914 during their world tour. General Bell threw out the ceremonial first pitch and congratulated the touring American professionals for "stir[ring] patriotism . . . and impress[ing] foreign nations . . . with the cleanness and manhood of Americans." Baseball, the highest-ranking military man in America's Asian colony added, "foster[s] clean living, skill, and fair play, makes men, and is therefore a big factor in the upbuilding of a nation."[39]

Baseball among Americans of Japanese Ancestry in Hawaii

The rise of the white American oligarchy in Hawaii in the latter half of the nineteenth century joined with a crosscurrent of historical forces to create a realm of U.S.-Japanese baseball interaction mediated by the island U.S. territory in the twentieth century: Japanese American baseball in Hawaii. Private landownership enabled by the Great Mahele set the stage for the development of large-scale plantation economies based on tropical cash crops, notably sugar and pineapple, foodstuffs that had been long consumed by native Hawaiians but never commercially mass cultivated until the Westerners' arrival. Sugar, in particular, would chart the future trajectory of Hawaiian history in a most profound way. The first large-scale sugar plantation opened on the island of Kauai in 1835. The outbreak of the Civil War and disruption in sugar production and shipment by the South fueled the expansion of Hawaiian sugar production and the plantations that raised the capitalist commodity. The upward trend accelerated after Hawaii gained duty-free access to the U.S. mainland markets under the 1875 Reciprocity Treaty. There were twenty large-scale sugar plantations in 1875; five years later, there were sixty-three. Hawaii's fundamental economic role shifted from a midway point in America's China trade and whaling stations to an insular workshop of commercial agriculture. The massive wealth created by this new industrial sector, now firmly hitched to the global economy, was concentrated in the hands of haole plantation owners, who solidified themselves into the "Big Five" in 1882. This little oligarchy, interwoven through overlapping board memberships, intermarriage, and Punahou alumni connections, had two all-important agendas to pursue: safeguarding duty-free access to mainland sugar markets and "cheap servile labor" to till the fields.[40]

When sugar's commercial production began in Hawaii in the first half of the nineteenth century, native Hawaiians initially furnished the bulk of its workforce. Yet the plantation owners found it hard to sustain this indigenous source of agricultural labor. One reason was that the native Hawaiian population had dropped dramatically by the mid-nineteenth century because of diseases introduced by outside contacts. The Big Five responded to the labor shortage by turning to external labor sources, particularly from Asia. The first group of contract laborers arrived from China in 1852. By 1872, about 50 percent of Hawaii's sugar plantation laborers were Chinese, but they tended not to stay on the plantation after completing their three-year contracts. Some went back to China or migrated elsewhere in the world; others began business in Honolulu or became freeholders. Thus began systematic labor importation from other national sources, such as Portuguese from the Azores and Madeira (1878) and Germans and Scandinavians (1881).[41] To minimize the danger of collective action by laborers, the white plantation owners consciously diversified the ethnic mix of their workforce. The beginning of Japanese migration to the Kingdom of Hawaii in 1868 should be situated in this divide-and-conquer labor management strategy adopted by haole capital.

The first wave of Japanese immigration to Hawaii took place amid the political chaos attending the collapse of the shogunate government. One hundred and fifty-three so-called *gannenmono* (meaning "first-year persons") were recruited by the Kingdom of Hawaii's general consul, Eugene Van Reed, a Pennsylvania-born merchant in Yokohama appointed to that post by King Kamehameha V. Most *gannenmono* were urbanites not equipped with the requisite skills in agriculture. The newly inaugurated Meiji government had to dispatch a mission to Hawaii to investigate their complaints over wages and working conditions and arranged for forty of the laborers to return home in 1870. This negative experience made the Meiji government gun-shy about overseas emigration. That changed in 1885 when Hawaii's King Kalakaua visited Japan during his world tour. Concerned about the increasingly powerful haole oligarchy and the white American influence exercised through it, Kalakaua sought to use the rapidly modernizing Asian country as a counterweight in the island kingdom's racialized political economy. This strategic calculation prompted the Hawaiian monarch to request, among other things, that the Japanese government permit its nationals' labor migration to Hawaii. Afflicted by widespread unemployment and the deflation of its currency, the Japanese government responded positively. Japan's government-brokered labor migration to Hawaii thus began. Within ten years, about twenty-nine thousand Japanese nationals had signed a three-year labor contract and moved to the mid-Pacific kingdom. Most of them were young men from impoverished agricultural villages in southwest Japan, lured by the much touted prospect of "earning 400 yen in three years." After the overthrow of the Hawaiian kingdom in 1893, Japan's emigration brokerage was transferred to government-licensed private companies. About fifty-seven thousand Japanese moved to Hawaii under this new system before 1900, when contract labor was banned in postannexation Hawaii with the islands' incorporation into the U.S. mainland labor regime.[42]

When Japanese migration began in 1885, less than 1 percent of Hawaii's population was Japanese; within ten years, the figure exceeded 60 percent. By 1902, Japanese accounted for about 70 percent of the islands' increasingly multiethnic population.[43] The Japanese plantation workers in Hawaii endured conditions akin to slavery, working ten hours a day, six days a week, under the scorching sun, often whipped by Portuguese labor supervisors called *luna*. At sugar refineries, the workday stretched to twelve hours. The young Japanese men sought cheap amusements during a precious few hours of freedom from this punishing environment; many indulged in "vile amusements," that is, gambling, excessive drinking, and prostitution in an ethnic red-light district sprouting in Honolulu. Antivice campaigns by social reformers of various religious persuasions began soon after the arrival of Japanese contract laborers. In 1886, the Reverend Charles McEwen Hyde, an American member of the Hawaiian Board of Missions, launched a purity movement among the predominantly male Japanese sojourner community, later joined by Oberlin-educated Japanese congregational missionary Okabe Jirō. In 1892, Okabe returned to Japan to recruit more volunteers to minister in Hawaii. One of the young Japanese Christians who responded to the call for godly action Okabe made at Dōshisha, the hub of Protestant Christianity in Japan, was the Reverend Takie Okumura.[44]

Okumura, a native of Kōchi Prefecture, had been active in the Christian temperance society in western Japan and played a key role in the founding of the YMCA branch in Osaka. As soon as he arrived in Hawaii in 1894, the Japanese Congregational minister sought, against vast initial odds, to promote baseball among the young Japanese plantation workers as a recreational outlet. Since baseball had been a familiar part of rural children's play and public school curricula, Okumura reasoned, it would be readily accepted as a wholesome alternative to the "vice" rampant in the bachelor community. He also used baseball for "proper" socialization of Japanese children on the island. In 1896, Okumura opened a tuition-free Japanese-language boarding school, Okumura Home, for seven children of sugar plantation workers. From its inception, baseball was a staple of Okumura Home's Christian instruction. Three years later, Okumura orchestrated the organization of a first baseball team comprising entirely children of Japanese sugarcane workers. The team expanded into the Nisshin (meaning "daily progress") Club, a forty-five-member squad made up of varsity and junior varsity teams in 1904. It would later be renamed the Excelciors, a change signaling Okumura's commitment to the cultural assimilation of Nisei (second-generation Japanese) to Hawaii's white American cultural norms.[45]

By the 1900s, the Japanese population in Hawaii exceeded sixty thousand, constituting the territory's largest ethnic group. The expanding demographic base nurtured the rise and proliferation of various ethnic civic institutions, such as churches, both Buddhist and Christian, and associations of small business owners. Meanwhile, contract labor was banned in Hawaii, and Japanese, among other ethnic plantation laborers unbound from restrictive labor contracts, began to move to Honolulu for better wages and living conditions.[46] The Asahi (Rising Sun) baseball club, founded in Honolulu in 1905, was an offshoot of Honolulu's urbanization and the attendant formation of ethnic communities in the early twentieth century. The majority of the team's founding members were teenagers, both Japanese and Hawaii-born, who honed their skills in sandlot baseball in Honolulu in plantation settlements.[47] The name Asahi was picked by Steere Gikaku Noda, one of the team's founding members. Born in 1892 to a sugar plantation laborer in Ewa, Noda was only thirteen years old at the time of Asahi's founding, but the teenage standout led the team in pitching, hitting, and base stealing. Also among the Asahi's original members was Gotō Chimpei, born in 1887 in the northern Japanese prefecture of Iwate. He moved to Hawaii with his parents when he was eleven years old. Although raised a Buddhist, Gotō became an ordained Methodist minister and moved to Haneohe, the windward side of Oahu, in 1927. His rural ministry featured the three Bs (baseball, bicycling, and the Bible).[48]

While the Asahi and the Nisshin began to animate adolescent and youth baseball, layers of adult baseball play began to form in Hawaii's Japanese communities, the chief among them weaving themselves into Oahu's sprouting intraisland baseball league structure. As Hawaii's non-haole adult population took up baseball in the late nineteenth century, its sporting rivalries played out along the division of labor between ethnically segregated field gangs and mill workers. This structure of ethnically segregated play, informally abetted by the plantation management, tended to make America's Game the staging ground for interethnic competition encompassing work *and* recreation. It received official sanction and financial backing by plantation capital after the 1909 Oahu strike. During the labor stoppage that impeded sugar production on the island for three months, about seven thousand Japanese plantation laborers walked off the field, demanding elimination of the ethnically differentiated pay structure, higher pay, and better working and living conditions. The Hawaiian Sugar Plantation Association (HSPA) responded by bringing in Filipino and Puerto Rican substitute laborers from these new American colonies. As was the case with all previous labor revolts in Hawaii, workers failed to construct a cross-ethnic solidarity, allowing the plantation owners to prevail in the end. No major pay raises were conceded, but the prolonged large-scale strike made the plantation management recognize the need for a different approach to its disgruntled labor force.

Baseball—healthful, relatively inexpensive, and deemed "American" in symbolic association—became an integral part of the Big Five's new and more paternalistic labor management strategy. The HSPA committee that investigated the 1909 strike urged plantation managers to incorporate elements of welfare capitalism by providing workers and their families with more amenities and recreational resources, including "a baseball ground well paved out and grassed" to "encourage this sport, which every nationality of laborers is keen for." Baseball, in short, was expected to "cultivate a spirit of contentment among the laborers." This recommendation produced palpable results; baseball grounds were constructed in each company town built on the plantations, and playing baseball games for cash prizes and other giveaways provided by the plantation owners became a Sunday ritual in the decade following the strike. Each company town formed a camp league, in which Chinese, Japanese, Filipinos, Portuguese, Puerto Ricans, and haoles competed on their own ethnic teams. Champion teams of each camp league then competed in the overarching Plantation League.[49] America's Game thus provided a site for peaceful and orderly interethnic one-upmanship, but to the extent it fanned the flames of visceral interethnic rivalries, baseball perpetuated the ethnic division and animosities upon which haole capital built its dominance over labor. The practice of playing for prizes, including cash payments, introduced commercial elements into Hawaii's adult baseball scene, and many squads were operating as semipro by 1920.[50]

In this arena for interethnic contest, Issei, Japanese immigrants to America who were ineligible for citizenship in the United States, often expressed through baseball their undying allegiance to the country they had come from. When the Nisshin, coached and managed by Okumura, won the championship in the newly created interethnic youth baseball league in Honolulu in 1905, Issei community leaders rejoiced and trumpeted the athletic feat as evidence of the superiority of the Yamato (Japanese) nation. As the Asahi's founding members matured into adulthood, the club began to acquit itself well against other ethnic teams whose players often outsized the relatively diminutive Japanese athletes. Steere Noda, the Asahi's southpaw ace pitcher and leading slugger who led the team to multiple intraisland championships in the 1910s, earned the nickname "Banzai" Noda because of Issei spectators' synchronized banzai cheers each time the prized Nisei standout recorded a strikeout or hit a home run. For young Nisei boys in Hawaii, making the Asahi roster became the ultimate dream. As various adult semipro leagues in Honolulu stabilized into a six-team Hawaii League in 1924, the Asahi became one of its charter members and would win the league pennant seventeen times. The Asahi's league rivals were the Hawaiians, the Chinese, the Braves (Portuguese), the Wanderers (haole), and the Filipinos (replaced by the U.S. Navy team in 1933). These ethnic baseball subcultures, invested as they were with disparate social meanings and clashing ethnic pride, embodied the shoal of racial and cultural crosscurrents that was Hawaii.[51]

After Hawaii's incorporation into the United States as a territory, the secondary migration of persons of Japanese ancestry (Nikkei) to the North American continent increased. More than half of the two hundred thousand Japanese who migrated to Hawaii moved to the U.S. Pacific coastal states and Canada's British Columbia in the 1900s and began to form ethnic communities there. Most of the pioneering teams on the mainland were made up of Issei players, but as younger demographical groups reached adulthood in the late 1910s, Nisei teams took over the torch of athletic leadership. The expansion of the Japanese overseas diaspora thus dovetailed with the further geographical dispersion of baseball. Tellingly, America's national pastime came home to America on the backs and in the hearts of those who were labeled inassimilable by white mainstream society as well as by the American state.

Japanese Colonial Baseball: Taiwan

While Americans planted seeds of colonial baseball in the Caribbean, Hawaii, and the Philippines, Japanese duplicated that historical exercise in East Asia. If Hawaii was the easternmost perimeter of Japanese baseball at the end of the nineteenth century, its western frontier pushed to Taiwan with the island's 1895 cession to Japan as a spoil of war against the decaying Qing dynasty. When the Japanese arrived in this newly acquired colony, Taiwanese—neither Sinofied Han populations in the lowlands nor Austronesian aboriginals in the mountains—were familiar with modern organized sports. According to Andrew Morris, an expert on Chinese athletic traditions, the game of baseball found its way to Taiwan around 1897, just two years after the island's incorporation into the Japanese empire, brought by Japanese colonial bureaucrats, bankers, merchants, and their sons.[52] For several years baseball remained the colonizer's preserve, contained within the isolated bastions in the colonial capital in the north. The incremental military pacification of the island by the Japanese colonial authorities accounts for this rather gradual dissemination. Over the first decade following the territory's cession, Japanese faced an effective armed resistance by Taiwan's local populations. Armed with advanced weaponry, the Japanese army gradually subdued the regional revolts and expanded its colonial control southward. Between 1895 and 1902, thirty-two thousand Taiwanese were killed, over 1 percent of the island's population. By 1905, under the leadership of the fourth military governor-general, Kodama Gentarō, and his civilian administrator, Gotō Shinpei, Japan had finally stabilized its control in the lowlands. The systematic suppression of aboriginals in the highlands began under the fifth governor-general, Sakuma Samata, in 1907.[53]

As population centers in the lowlands became pacified, baseball began to spread in the northern parts of the island in tandem with the apparatuses of Japanese colonial administration. Mirroring the contemporary education regime in the metropolis, Western athletics were introduced as a part of the public school curriculum in Taiwan from the beginning of the Japanese colonial regime. In 1898, the governor-general's office established Taiwan Colonial Government High School (later to be renamed Taibei First Middle School) in Taibei for educating children of Japanese colonials and a select few Taiwanese. The school's second headmaster,

Tanaka Keiichi, who arrived in 1902, happened to be a baseball aficionado. He encouraged the game among students at the elite colonial school as a way to instill a "properly Japanese" identity among the expatriate youth. When a teacher's college was founded in the colonial capital in 1899, a former player for Nikō (Second High School in Osaka) recruited from the mainland as a faculty member coached his students as an extracurricular activity.

Baseball play at Taibei First Middle School languished between 1907 and 1912 because new headmaster Honjō Taichirō disapproved of the game, regarding it as a frivolous activity not germane to youth education. Yet by that time baseball's diffusion outside Taibei was well under way. As the Japanese colonial state extended its effective control early in the second decade of the century, Japanese settlement in the southern parts of Taiwan progressed. The fertile coastal plains in the south began attracting investment by Japanese sugar companies like Mitsui Sugar, and a large number of sugar plantations emerged in the south. Children of Japanese colonial settlers who returned during summer break from schooling in the north became the initial agent of baseball's southward diffusion. Company towns that developed around southern sugar plantations were typically equipped with the baseball fields along with company-provided humble dormitories for local laborers and Japanese-style modern homes for the plantation management class. As the Japanese public school system extended to all regions of Taiwan, baseball spread across the island with it. In 1915, the colonial government organized the Taiwan Baseball Federation, a national association of fifteen all-Japanese public schools fielding a baseball team. An interscholastic annual tournament at Butoku-kai Stadium, built near the governor-general's office in the city of Taibei, began in 1921.[54]

Education policies adopted by Governor-General Sakuma, who assumed the post in 1906, opened the way for baseball's acceptance by the young indigenous population. In the first decade of its colonial rule, the Japanese colonial state envisioned a distinctly two-track system of public school, reflecting Gotō Shinpei's thinking that "education is the sword with a multisided blade." Education for the colonial subjects was thus predicated on the idea that full and equal education for Taiwanese youth risked equipping them with knowledge and ideas that might prove detrimental to Japanese colonial control. The resulting segregated school system created a situation in which only Japanese colonial youth tended to play baseball. Most Taiwanese parents, on their part, tried to suppress their children's natural curiosity about the sport popular among their Japanese age cohort. That attitude reflected a larger trend in the local adults' response to the new education regime installed by the Japanese. Taiwanese parents fiercely objected, at least initially, to the introduction of athletic activities as unproductive and thus pointless exercises that would get in the way of their children's academic pursuits. Additionally, they generally viewed baseball as an injury-prone, dangerous pursuit that also carried a taint as the colonizer's favorite activity.[55]

A new regime of colonial public education that cohered during Sakuma's governorship lowered these social and ideological barriers to baseball's diffusion across the colonial boundary. An innovative aspect of Sakuma's policy included a new emphasis on Western athletics in the schools for Taiwanese children. The motive was hardly altruistic; Sakuma believed that modern Western sports would promote the physical fitness of Taiwan's young male population, which would then be ready to serve in the Japanese military. Similarly, he encouraged baseball among the Taiwanese youth, believing that cultural practices were a penetrating device that could facilitate comity between the colonizers and the colonized. A creeping second-generation problem for Japanese colonial settlers also highlighted the utility of baseball as a tool of cultural acculturation of children born and raised in Taiwan into the colonial metropolitan norms. In order to help Japanese expatriate children attain technical levels competitive with the those of the mainlanders, Sakuma recruited from Japan baseball specialists, mostly former collegiate players in Tokyo, to coach Japanese and Taiwanese youth at public schools.[56] Displaying an intergenerational variation in local response to Japanese colonial rule, Taiwanese children enthusiastically responded to this encouragement from above during the new phase in the Japanese colonial period.

Larger historical forces also came into play. A change of government in Tokyo in the early 1910s ushered in a new era of political liberalization in the colonial metropolis called the Taisho Democracy. This multifaceted opening in Japanese society and polity trickled down as liberal reform in Japan's imperial periphery. A far stronger and immediate impetus for greater political liberalism came from Korea, a new addition to the Japanese imperium after 1910. A massive popular rebellion that erupted in Japan's most recent colonial acquisition in March 1919, although brutally suppressed, forced the Japanese state to reappraise its colonial policies. In October 1919, the cabinet of Hara Takashi appointed Den Kenjirō as Taiwan's first civilian governor, signaling the adoption of a more paternalistic and assimilationist approach to the colony. Realizing that the older Taiwanese were irreconcilably hostile to the Japanese colonial presence, the new colonial administrators concentrated their mollifying efforts on younger demographic groups and, as a manifestation of that new approach, abolished the dual public school system. Under the new single-track system, educational opportunities available to the Taiwanese youth expanded dramatically. The locals were now permitted to attend middle schools alongside Japanese youth as well as vocational schools where baseball had been established as the most popular intramural and interscholastic sport. Despite Taiwanese parents' lingering resistance, baseball, now woven into the fabric of Taiwanese youths' daily life built around full-time schooling, spread unstoppably. Since the game required the equal treatment of all participants on the diamond, Taiwanese children naturally found this social space appealing.[57]

In the 1920s, playing baseball was thus crafted into an emblem of Japanese-Taiwanese cultural harmony. At the fifth Far Eastern Games held in Shanghai in 1921, the Japanese team included four "Taiwan athletes," of whom two were Han-ethnic Taiwanese and two were ethnic Japanese colonial settlers.[58] As Sakuma envisioned, baseball as a cultural practice proved highly infiltrating and subversive because the effects ran both ways. Baseball gave the colonized population a way to negotiate its relationship with the Japanese overlord on terms and in arenas acceptable to the latter. Taiwanese thus gained a circumscribed social space in which they could challenge Japanese with impunity as temporary equals and even showcase their superior abilities at the colonizer's game. Participation in what Japanese by then considered their national pastime and excelling in it allowed the Taiwanese at once to demonstrate their acculturation into the colonial order and to subtly undermine the ethnic hierarchy upholding that very order.[59] This innate subversiveness of baseball in a colonial context came into full display in early 1921, and American outsiders had much to do with that social allegory. After American Major League Baseball's 1920 season, an obscure utility player just traded out of the Boston Red Sox by the name of Herbert Hunter piloted a barnstorming tour of a mixed squad of major leaguers and Pacific Coast League players to Japan. After playing twenty exhibition games in Japan proper and a match with the U.S. Navy team in Shanghai, the American professional ballplayers visited Taiwan briefly in January 1921 on their way to their final destination, the Philippines.[60] The American travelers played seven games in Taibei against Japanese all-star teams with top players drawn from the local industrial teams. Despite high ticket prices, over five thousand spectators filled the ballpark, and many more climbed up on the outside fence trying to catch a glimpse of the game between the Japanese colonials and touring Americans. In the very first match the Americans mercilessly flattened the Japanese 26–0. On the next day a local newspaper carried the front-page headline "Sumo between Big Man and Little Child" to describe the game's brutally one-sided result. During the Americans' entire exhibition series in Taiwan, both Japanese colonials and the Taiwanese subjects witnessed in glaring light the superior baseball played by the American professionals. And it was more than games won or lost for sure; in the eyes of the Asian beholders operating in the racialized world imperial order, the whole scene was nothing less than Japanese colonials pummeled at their own game by the white Americans.[61]

Baseball in Southern Manchuria
In the first decade of the twentieth century, Japan gained an imperial foothold in the Asian mainland, and with it, baseball's sphere of influence extended to the tip of China's Liadong Peninsula and southern Manchuria. The Portsmouth Treaty of 1905, which settled the Russo-Japanese War, marked a milestone in modern Japanese history in a number of respects. Since the treaty, brokered by President Theodore Roosevelt, did not award a sorely needed cash indemnity to Japan, the perceived affront sparked angry antigovernment and anti-American popular outbursts in the country, displaying the first visible signs of souring U.S.-Japanese relations. Regardless, Russia's leasehold in the Liadong Peninsula changed hands, and the Japanese avenged the humiliation of the Triple Intervention engineered by Imperial Russia at the end of the Sino-Japanese War. The area of Japanese "rights" granted under the 1905 Russo-Japanese Treaty included the Kwantung Leasehold (3,462 square kilometers at the base of the Liadong Peninsula), the Southern Manchurian Railway, and a 5.296-square-kilometer strip of land called the Rail Zone that lay adjacent to the railway extending north from Pulandian (where the leasehold ended) to Changchun. This territorial cession opened up these areas to Japanese civilian settlement. Unlike in Taiwan, baseball fever kicked in immediately in these Japanese semicolonial "leased" territories. Middle schools for children of colonial settlers were established in Dalian and Ryojun (Lushun) in the late 1900s, and a structure of regular baseball play between two Dalian schools emerged as early as 1912. In 1916 the schools began competing in the leasehold-wide tournament that also en-

compassed industrial teams. From its very first year, the Southern Manchurian Baseball Tournament became a huge popular entertainment for recreation-starved Japanese settlers, drawing spectators from all over the leasehold and the Rail Zone south of Fengtian (Shenyang).[62]

The crown jewel of Japanese colonial baseball in southern Manchuria was industrial semipro clubs. Once the Kwantung Leasehold changed hands from Imperial Russia to Japan, Dalian became the target of massive Japanese commercial investment and a key destination of Japanese overseas settlers. Many former mainland collegiate baseball players, having achieved quasi-celebrity status, were offered plum jobs in Dalian, Japan's new overseas outpost brimming with commercial vigor and colonial ambitions. This recruitment pattern serendipitously concentrated Japan's top-flight baseball players seeking venues for playing ball after graduation in the colonial port city. Dalian's golden age as the baseball capital of the rising Japanese empire opened in 1912 with the organization of two industrial clubs, the Dalian Jitsugyōdan (Dalian Mercantile Club) and the Manshū Club, both boasting rosters loaded with former metropolitan collegiate standouts and their own ballparks complete with a grandstand. Once an economic boom sparked by World War I swelled the city's Japanese expatriate population, other local municipal clubs and smaller company teams burst into existence, and watching and playing baseball became the mainstay of the local social landscape. The two top industrial clubs' pickup matches with the U.S. Navy teams visiting nearby Port Arthur (Lushun) were considered the Kwangtung Leasehold's top-flight public entertainment. Billed "U.S.-Japan Face-off," these games were typically sponsored by two local Japanese-language newspapers, the *Liadong Shinpō* and the *Mansūu Nichinichi Shinpō*.[63]

Baseball was central to Japanese semicolonial life in Dalian in another way. As the Japanese expatriate community expanded in the booming 1920s, the settler colonials' demand for leisure activity also increased. As Yamazaki Yūkō has shown, commercial entertainments in southern Manchuria constituted a highly gendered social space. For Japanese expatriate women, movies were the only commercial diversion that did not compromise their female respectability. Men, on the other hand, heavily patronized horse racing. Interestingly, horse racing and associated gambling attained the kind of legitimacy, and even respectability, in southern Manchuria that was unimaginable in the imperial metropole because it was an integral part of the Kwangtung Army's horse-breeding program. The proceeds from horse races supported the program's research and development components. Free from the social stigma accruing from the antigambling ordinances on the Japanese mainland, horse racing grew into a well-regarded masculine form of commercialized leisure in the entertainment-scarce colonial outpost.[64] In this gender-segregated recreational life in southern Manchuria, baseball came to occupy a unique place. Because of the former celebrity status of many players for the industrial clubs in the Manchurian baseball circuit, games invariably drew a large number of young expatriate women to the ballparks. Baseball became the colonial settler community's only commercial entertainment equally patronized by men and women, friendly to family outings.

In the 1920s, improvements in the regional ocean transport network in the area surrounding the Bohei Sea added an extraterritorial element to southern Manchuria's student baseball circuit. Starting in 1926, Qingdao Middle School was integrated into the area's interscholastic tournament. When World War I erupted in Europe, the Japanese military attacked and seized Qingdao, and Japanese migration to the former German leasehold in the Shandung Peninsula began soon afterward. About two-thirds of the Japanese settlers in Qingdao had come from Japan's other colonial areas, mostly from southern Manchuria. Many of them were marginal merchants seeking new commercial opportunities. Geographical proximity accounts for this transmigration pattern as well as the fact that half of the ships entering the port of Qingdao originated in Dalian, the hub of regional commercial maritime transport.[65] Baseball, as well as the human and commercial webs spun by Japanese continental colonialism, cast invisible networks transgressing the existing national borders. In 1929, Qingdao Middle School even beat the local baseball powerhouse Dalian Commercial High School and became southern Manchuria's "regional representative" to the mainland national student baseball tournament.

Japanese Colonial Baseball: Korea

Tracking the diffusion of baseball affords an illuminating glimpse into the intersection of the American civic presence and Japanese colonial incursion in East Asia in the early twentieth century. That national juxtaposition was particularly salient in Korea, a kingdom that became a Japanese protectorate in 1905 and was formally annexed in 1910, a historical process facilitated in no small part by the American government's secret endorsement in the 1905 Root-Katsura agreement.[66] American private citizens in Korea, however, had different agendas for the beleaguered kingdom. Some sought to strengthen Korea from within and fortify it against imperialist predation by steeling its population and body politic with Western sports. Among these American anticolonialists was Philip L. Gillett, a Christian missionary and founder of the YMCA in Seoul. A native of LaSalle, Illinois, who later moved to Iowa City with his family, Gillett embodied the ethos of midwestern Christian athleticism, one of the driving forces of the muscular Christianity movement in the United States during the Progressive Era. After graduating from Colorado College in 1891, Gillett attended Yale Divinity School and went on to the International YMCA Training School at Springfield, Massachusetts. He received an appointment as general secretary of the YMCA's International Committee for Korea in 1901. Gillett and his colleague at the Seoul YMCA, Frank Brockman, used Western team sports as the fulcrum of their social engineering in Korea. In his report to the YMCA, Gillett proudly spoke of the contributions being made by his Seoul YMCA to "the young manhood of the city and country ... [whose] leadership should be held by 'energetic Christian men.'" Gillett is widely credited with introducing baseball as well as basketball, invented by his Springfield classmate James Naismith, to Korea in 1904.[67]

Various accounts of early Korean baseball identify the first formal baseball game played in Korea as a match between members of the Hansong YMCA coached and managed by Gillett and students of the German Language Institute, which took place in February 1906 on a military training ground near the current site of Seoul Stadium. Obviously, it was an under-resourced operation; some of the Korean players were wearing straw sandals, or wooden clogs, and traditional Korean clothing. Outfielders were not wearing gloves. Other oft cited annals of Korean baseball link "the official foundation of Korean baseball" to a game in February 1910 between Hansong Middle School (a school for Japanese expatriates) and a Hwangsong Christian School team fielded by an American Protestant missionary.[68] As if to display the dual American and Japanese presence in the city's baseball scene, the game was officiated by an American plate umpire and Japanese line umpires. Although members of the YMCA, as well as the Korean youth in general, took to soccer and basketball more readily than baseball, by 1912 Gillett's Seoul YMCA squads were playing over sixty baseball games a year. Its varsity team toured Tokyo and played against—and was walloped by—Japan's top collegiate teams in the previous fall.[69]

American muscular Christians' gospel of male physicality found fertile soil in Korea, where a series of sweeping social and education reforms had been under way since the mid-1890s. The indigenous reform initiatives entailed the adoption of a whole new approach to physical exercise, similar to the cultural self-reinvention that had taken place in Japan in the early Meiji period and China during the "self-strengthening movement." Korean reformers began to emphasize athletic exercises and Western organized sports to give the nation's rising generation the physical and intellectual capabilities to survive in the cutthroat world of Western *and* Japanese imperialism. In another parallel to Meiji-era Japan, study-abroad students were among baseball boosters. In July 1909, twenty-five Korean students who had recently returned from Japan, led by Yun Ikhyon, formed a private baseball club in Seoul and scored an easy victory over a team of American expatriates in the city. They are also said to have brought back uniforms and state-of-the art equipment, including spiked shoes, from Japan, turning American-born athletic paraphernalia into an alluring symbol of consumer modernity in the Japanese colony.[70]

Politics and diplomacy after Korea's absorption by Japan led to the gradual displacement of American influences in Korea's nascent baseball scene. In the tumultuous post-1905 era of Japanese intrusion, Gillett and his peers at the Seoul YMCA initially tried to stay out of politics as a strategy to ensure the organization's survival amid the colonial turmoil. Once Japan formally annexed Korea and intensified its colonial repression, political neutrality became progressively untenable. Since the Protestant Christian churches constituted a fulcrum of anti-Japanese nationalist activity by Koreans, American missionaries often found themselves providing refuge to Korean nationalists trying to elude the Japanese police by throwing themselves under American missionaries' protective wings. Meanwhile, the cresting Korean national independent movement wrought an internal division among Americans in Korea. One incident that took place in San Francisco in early 1908 dramatized America's divided heart on matters regarding Japan's political engulfment of Korea. Durham White Stevens—that same Stevens who was on the 1876 roster of American expatriate ball players in Japan—was assassinated in plain view of the Japanese consul general in San Francisco by a young Korean patriot belonging to the San Francisco Korean Methodist Church. Stevens, then a legal adviser to Japanese resident general Itō Hirobumi, was on his way to Washington, D.C., on a lobbying mission. His statement, "Japan is doing in Korea and for the Koreans what the United States is doing in the Philippines for the Filipinos," was prominently reported in the *San Francisco Call* and angered about a hundred Koreans residing in the city, including the assassin, In Whang Chang.[71]

After Japan's formal annexation of Japan, Americans in Korea were

Colonial Baseball | 69

further pressured to take sides. To co-opt Korean Christians, Governor-General Terauchi Masatake picked nineteen Korean church leaders to visit Japan on an all-expenses-paid trip in the fall of 1910. These "friendly" Korean Christians were treated royally and shown the marvels of "modern" Japan. Some American missionaries, such as the Reverend Arthur Brown of the Presbyterian Mission in Korea, contended that the "loyal recognition" of the Japanese rule was the right thing to do. He equated Japan's colonial rule with enlightened and efficient modern administration, a departure from the indigenous government's benighted and corrupt ways. The fact that the Japanese colonial state honored an arrangement between the Korean YMCA and the Korean government and continued to provide an annual subsidy of ten thousand yen to the Korean YMCA no doubt helped generate this favorable disposition on the part of some in the American missionary community in postannexation Korea.[72] In the winter of 1910–11, American Protestant missionaries grew increasingly polarized over the issue of how to keep peace with Korea's new political ruler.

In October 1911, the Japanese colonial state unleashed a crackdown on Korean Christian leaders in cities with a concentration of Christian populations such as Seoul, Pyongyang, and Sonchon. Japanese military police fabricated charges of an assassination attempt against Governor-General Terauchi. The plot supposedly had been hatched at the YMCA conference that summer. Some 600 Korean Christians were implicated in the alleged conspiracy, and 105 of them, including a leading member of the Seoul YMCA, Yun Ch'i-ho, were arrested, indicted for the assassination attempt, and jailed. In the course of the sham trial, Gillett decided to join other anti-Japanese Christian missionaries in Korea to petition for Yun's release and sent a detailed report on the roundup to seek assistance from the International Christian Missionary Association in Edinburgh. Not surprisingly, Gillett's action incurred the wrath of the Japanese colonial authorities. Under mounting harassment of the Seoul YMCA by the Japanese military police, Gillett was forced to resign from the Seoul organization and was transferred to Shanghai in 1913. The American missionary's virtual banishment bespoke the consolidation of the Japanese colonial regime in Korea under Terauchi's iron-fisted rule in the coming years.[73]

The Japanese presence in Korean baseball thickened in inverse relationship with the tapering American influence after Gillett's expulsion from the country. As elsewhere in its empire, Japan beginning in 1905 opened public schools to educate children of Japanese colonial settlers in Korea, and these colonial schools typically fielded all-Japanese baseball teams.⁷⁴ After formal annexation in 1910, Japanese commercial investment in Korea rose exponentially, and as in southern Manchuria, industrial teams, particularly those sponsored by the amply capitalized government-run railroad corporations and colonial administrative agencies, began to field high-powered rosters studded with former star collegiate players recruited from the mainland. Tournaments among top-tier industrial teams such as the Ryūzan Railway Club and the All-Kyōjō Club were sponsored by a local Japanese-language newspaper, *Kyōjō Nippō*. As Japanese colonial control solidified, layered structures of colonial baseball play emerged. In June 1913, the All-Korea Middle School Tournaments began with sponsorship by the city's other Japanese-language daily, *Kyōjō Shinbun*. In areas where Japanese settlements were particularly concentrated, such as Seoul and Pusan, regional tournaments emerged earlier than in other areas. Because of its proximity to Japan and the opening of a direct biweekly steamship line to Shimonoseki in 1905, Pusan emerged as a hub of settler colonial baseball. In 1928, Pusan Stadium was built to serve as the venue for regular regional baseball competition linking Korea, western Japan, and the islands of Kyushu and Shikoku.⁷⁵

By and large, early Japanese colonials sought to maintain a distinctly Japanese lifestyle to separate them from the colonized. As the Japanese settlement grew, a dual structure thus emerged in Seoul, Pusan, and other cities, separating Japanese residential and commercial districts from Korean ones.⁷⁶ Since Koreans played in mostly segregated all-Korean teams in the early years of Japanese colonial rule, beating the Japanese at their favorite sport became, as was the case in Taiwan, the ultimate expression of their anticolonial pride, and the competitive emotions at such interethnic matches often became overheated, beyond rowdiness to the point of blood-spilling violence. One example was a game in 1914 in which the all-Korean Osong Club trounced the Japanese championship industrial team Ryūzan Railway Club, 13–4. A postgame melee among spectators and players from both sides escalated into a pandemonium that required police intervention.⁷⁷ Since the Japanese colonial authorities initially associated baseball play by Koreans with an unfriendly American influence, they tried to suppress it. The May 1 Movement, the anti-Japanese nationwide revolt that lasted almost a year, induced a change in that official attitude toward Koreans playing baseball. During the 1919 uprising, an estimated seven thousand Koreans were killed by the Japanese police and military. Sixteen thousand people were wounded, and forty-six thousand Koreans were arrested before the revolt was finally subdued. Saitō Makoto, the new governor-general, arrived in Seoul in August 1919 and adopted Bunkaseiji, a set of more-conciliatory colonial policies, such as allowing the publication of Korean-language newspapers. Baseball play by Koreans was still not particularly encouraged but became tolerated to a greater degree by the Japanese colonial authorities under this general démarche.[78]

As baseball took root in the life of Japanese colonial settlers in Korea in the 1920s, the game furnished Japanese expatriates' children born and raised in Korea with an arena of performance in which to prove that they could compete on a par with mainlanders, and by extension, the Japanese colonial settler community in Korea was a legitimate part of the rising Japanese empire and not frontier riffraff. Talented players, coaching expertise, and technical and equipment information began to flow between Japan proper and the Korean peninsula through the exchange of coaches and recruitment of middle school standouts in Korea by top collegiate teams on the mainland. As Korea became a major outlet of Japanese general merchandise and low-end consumer product exports in the interwar period, Japanese sporting equipment, produced by manufacturers in western Japan, such as Mizuno in Osaka and Yamamoto Shōten in Kyoto, penetrated the Korean markets and contributed to the game's popularization. Despite the need for convoluted negotiations with absentee landlords in the colonial metropolis, several playing fields and ballparks were built across the peninsula during this period.[79] In many respects, the transoceanic baseball viaduct that linked Tokyo, Osaka, Pusan, Seoul, Dalian, Qingdao, and Taibei in the early twentieth century came to resemble the baseball network that had emerged between the United States and Caribbean islands in the late nineteenth century.

Whether one calls baseball America's or Japan's national pastime, there is no denying that the game traveled far and wide and in multiple directions across the Pacific around the turn of the century. Its developmental trajectories paralleled circuitous paths taken by the band of offshore Americans and Japanese who traversed the geographical expanse of the circum-Pacific hemisphere, carrying colonial aspirations and civilizational pretensions. The diffusion of baseball across the Pacific also affords another way to understand industrial growth, capital accumulation, and local regimes of labor in this era of high imperialism. Further, transpacific colonial baseball opens our eyes to heretofore underrecognized similarities and overlaps in the cultural practices of Americans and Japanese in ordering their newly acquired colonial spheres. Both countries employed baseball as a chief athletic means for molding the behaviors of their colonial subjects and acculturating their youth born or raised overseas into "mainland norms." Expatriate youth returning from schooling in the imperial metropole often served as cultural emissaries and agents of consumer modernity, introducing updated information and new artifacts of the game. Colonial service offered a flourishing job market to well-educated youth in the metropolis, and elite secondary schools and universities provided feeders for colonial employment.[80] Baseball traveled quite well in this corridor of colonial elite recruitment. Baseball also mediated American and Japanese relationships with the "native" populations they sought to govern, at turns serving as a "civilizing" tool and as an avenue of conciliation and insidious co-optation. Since these interactions are fundamentally two-way, if not equitable, baseball, as a cultural formulation and everyday practice, ineluctably became loaded with different social purposes and multivalent symbolisms and, not infrequently, was recrafted into a surrogate battleground where anticolonial resistance was enacted and ethnic/nationalistic pride was expressed.[81]

The shared pastime of baseball also provided a venue for warmly fraternal interaction between Americans and Japanese who came in contact with each other in a third country. One example was the U.S.-Japanese baseball exchange that became a social and culture fixture in the Chinese city of Tienjin, where a foreign settlement was set up in 1902 on the basis of the international agreement signed between the weakening Ch'ing dynasty and eight imperial powers to settle the Boxer Rebellion. Armed with extraterritoriality and the right to station troops to protect their citizens, Japan (1,149 troops) and the United States (1,367 troops stationed in the British settlement) were the two largest foreign contingents in this international contact zone. Not surprisingly, baseball became the basis for fellowship between Japanese and American expatriates against the backdrop of semicolonial privilege gained at the expense of Chinese. A baseball park with a wooden grandstand was built in the foreign settlement in 1911, and a variety of American teams—the Tienjin Marines, civilian expatriate teams, the Army Fifteenth Regiment team, and the Beijing Marines—engaged the Japanese Tienjin all-stars on the diamond in annual spring and fall tournaments. The biannual sporting events became an important seasonal ritual and top commercial entertainment for both American and Japanese expatriates. Many former Japanese residents in

Tienjin fondly reminisced years later that they had become tutored in "the American ways of baseball," such as Lady's Day, when women and girls were admitted free, learning baseball idioms in English (because all announcements and calls were made in English) and partaking in the "manly American" practice of drinking beer while watching the games.[82]

Similar cultural and social intermixing took place in Brazil, where Japanese immigration began in 1908 after Japanese labor migration to Hawaii and the U.S. mainland was practically banned under the U.S.-Japanese "Gentlemen's Agreement." After massive initial hardship, Japanese immigrant life in the South American country slowly stabilized by the late 1910s, and a variety of civic enterprises began to emerge. Japanese town baseball teams, including the Mikado Club established in Rio de Janeiro in 1920, regularly played against one another, but their premier games were always contests against American expatriate clubs in Brazil and U.S. Navy teams on shore leave.[83] The shared pastime enabled Americans and Japanese to find common ground and carve out a sphere of sociability and affinity in the countries where they were both strangers from different shores.

3

LEAGUES OF THEIR OWN

After Japan's narrow victory in the Russo-Japanese War, the national priorities and strategic objectives of the United States and Japan appeared increasingly at odds, especially in places like Manchuria, Japan's new sphere of influence taken over from Russia. U.S. Navy strategists and their allies in Washington had been sounding alarms over Japan's "stealth" control of Hawaii through settlement for some time. In American domestic debates regarding the annexation of Hawaii, they warned vociferously about the rising Asian nation's territorial ambitions vis-à-vis the mid-Pacific islands. The U.S. acquisition of the Philippines augmented America's sense of vulnerability in defending its distant colonial possession on the other side of the Pacific.[1] By 1907 American navy strategists were busy formulating possible war scenarios predicated on future conflict with Japan. The *Los Angeles Times* even lamented the lack of coastal defense for San Pedro (where there was a concentration of the Japanese labor migration population) against a possible Japanese amphibious attack. Ominous clouds were gathering in America's Pacific coastal states over the immigration issue, with the *San Francisco Examiner*, a Hearst paper, increasing its drumbeat against cheap Japanese labor stealing jobs from white American workers. The immigration issue reached crisis proportions in 1906 when the San Francisco School Board attempted to segregate Japanese children into schools for "Orientals." The deterioration of U.S.-Japanese relations was only temporarily allayed when President Roosevelt intervened and hammered out a series of agreements with the Japanese government commonly known as the U.S.-Japan Gentlemen's Agreement.[2]

The heightened tensions infiltrating the interstate relationship were dramatized by the Great White Fleet's Pacific Ocean practice cruise in

1907. Intended to awe, or at least impress, Japan with the United States' naval capabilities and battle readiness in the western Pacific, a fleet of sixteen battleships plus auxiliaries manned by a total of fourteen thousand sailors was sent by President Roosevelt from its Atlantic home on an unprecedented peacetime world cruise. Circumnavigating the southern tip of the South American continent, the U.S. Atlantic Fleet visited Hawaii, Oceania, and the Philippines before arriving in Japan in October 1908.[3] This historic visit occasioned direct U.S.-Japanese encounters in multiple realms. Confabulations between high-ranking Japanese government officials and the U.S. naval command were not the only highlight. Even schoolchildren lining the streets to cheer the visiting Americans, as if to give a lie to reports of U.S.-Japanese animosity, did not quite tell the whole story. While the U.S. Atlantic Fleet anchored in Yokohama, its crews challenged Japan's top collegiate teams in baseball games. On October 19, the fleet's all-star team lost to the combined Waseda-Keio team by a score of 5–4. The next day Keio faced the *Wisconsin*, and Waseda played the *Ohio*; on the following day, the matchups were reversed. The U.S.-Japanese "Pacific series" concluded on October 21 with the final game, again between the navy all-star team and the Waseda-Keio all-stars. It was a 1–1 tie. It was followed by a convivial gathering of players, politicians, and naval officers; libations flowed freely, and the happily inebriated participants from both sides congratulated each other on the shared ethos of manly sportsmanship.[4]

This little-known episode in U.S.-Japanese baseball fraternalism in the midst of interstate tension attests to the presence of a parallel social field the shared pastime was able to construct. The two circum-Pacific imperial nation-states grew connected through budding webs of sporting brotherhood in the early decades of the twentieth century when new local, regional, and national networks of baseball play sprouted in both countries. In the United States, the Pacific Coast League (PCL) was organized in 1903 as a premier minor league encompassing the three Pacific coastal states. The California Winter League became institutionalized in the second decade of the century as a seasonal but racially integrated professional circuit that operated in Southern California. Japanese American baseball embedded itself in semipro galaxies dotting the American West. Within the Japanese imperium, layers of student and industrial leagues rose and grew into a hugely popular spectator sport in the second and third decades of the century. Although a baseball enterprise openly run on the pay-for-play principle did not yet exist in Japan, some of the so-called amateur competitions were highly commercialized in their actual operation, foreshadowing the advent of inchoate sports capitalism in the Asian empire. All the while, U.S.-Japanese exchange grew among regional and national units of baseball play in the form of periodic barnstorming tours and structures of regular exchange. These institutional developments combined to ferment a baseball fever as a transpacific mass cultural phenomenon.

Organized Baseball's Wild Frontier: The U.S. West

Alexander Cartwright may have been too downtrodden and physically weakened to plant seeds of baseball in gold-rush California, but the Golden State had no shortage of baseball pioneers willing to do their part. One of them was John Fisher, a founding member of the San Francisco Eagles, the first known organized baseball club in California, which appeared in the early 1850s. Fisher was a prototypical California baseball man in that his evolving work life, in which the game transitioned from his avocation to vocation, dovetailed with the maturation of baseball as a business in the Pacific Northwest. In the 1870s, Fisher moved to Sacramento with his family and became a star outfielder for the semipro Atlas club while he worked as a mechanic for the Southern Pacific Railroad. He later became the club's highly popular owner-manager.[5] Meanwhile, San Francisco continued to grow as the hub of regional baseball. In 1866, representatives of seven of the city's clubs agreed to adopt standardized rules to be used to determine a champion. Two years later, California's first enclosed baseball field was constructed in the city. Called Recreational Grounds, the ballpark with a seating capacity of four thousand was the site of the year's Thanksgiving Day game, won 37–22 by the Eagles under Fisher's skippership against the cross-bay rival, the Wide Awakes of Oakland.[6]

Fisher was also present at the creation in 1885 of the California League, the state's first all-salaried professional circuit, comprising three clubs from the San Francisco Bay area and one from Sacramento. By then, one of Fisher's sons, Mike, played outfield for the Sacramento club. The junior Fisher would inherit the franchise and later move it to Tacoma, Washington, to tap a greater local spectator base expected to arise from the city's new railway linkup. Meanwhile, the California League extended south to become by 1890 an eight-city loop passing through the state's growing agricultural belt, linking San Francisco, Oakland, Sacramento, Santa Cruz, San Jose, Stockton, Fresno, and Watsonville. Then came a rival regional league. Once clubs from Portland and Seattle/Tacoma began to travel south regularly on the Great Northern Pacific Railroad to compete in the more populated and thus lucrative California, these northern West Coast clubs and two in Montana aligned themselves into the Pacific Northwest League in 1892.[7]

The Golden State's blossoming professional baseball immediately found itself in need of a defensive strategy against encroaching eastern capital. Taking advantage of the transcontinental transportation infrastructure, the National League teams headquartered in the East began barnstorming regularly after the conclusion of their regular seasons through Texas, Arizona, and California, where the climate permitted longer seasons. But this seasonal operation was a mixed blessing for baseball organizers in these sun-drenched regions of the United States. While visiting "majors" jazzed up the play and provided a boost at the gate, these easterners also had the nasty habit of snapping up the most promising local talent they played against—and they would often do so without paying due compensation to local club owners. Such predatory business practices by baseball's robber barons back east persisted even after the National Agreement of 1892, to which nearly all professional leagues in the United States were signatories. This nationwide industrial compact supposedly protected minor-league franchises' reserve rights over their players and codified rules for the recruitment of minor leaguers by National League clubs. Yet the majors' unmitigated player raiding was expected to grow even more ruthless after the infant American League (AL), which had been waging the so-called Great Baseball War against the NL under the command of president Ban Johnson, a former Cincinnati sports editor, declared itself a second major in 1901.[8]

In light of this dire prospect, minor-league executives nationwide banded together in self-defense, and a new national coalition, the National Association of Professional Baseball Leagues, was born. The umbrella organization, formed in the fall of 1901, systematized player transfers among minor-league clubs by dividing member circuits into A-to-D classifications on the basis of criteria such as the population of franchise cities, size of team rosters, and salary totals. The association also codified a system of player drafting within this hierarchical structure. Further, by signing on to the National Agreement of 1903 (which finally ended the Great Baseball War), the National Association incorporated itself into the nationwide regime of territorial monopolies governing all of what was becoming known as "organized baseball" in the United States. The 1903 truce agreement also instituted a new system by which the major leagues could draft players from the minors with agreed-upon rates of compensation to club owners. Any minor-league team not affiliated with the National Association was deemed an "outlaw" circuit outside the pale of organized baseball, now a vertically integrated industry.[9]

While this national industrial realignment unfolded, some of the franchise owners in the three Pacific coastal states, previously polarized into two competing regional leagues, reconfigured their alliances to produce a new and fortified minor league. The Pacific Coast League emerged at the end of the 1902 season as a result of this regional industrial realignment. At first, the newly minted minor league swore off membership in the National Association. Its constituent franchises remained locally controlled, and the owners were not obligated to make their players available for the draft by the majors. After seeing the PCL enjoy a highly successful inaugural 1903 season, National and American League executives began courting this "outlaw" let loose in organized baseball's wild western frontier. The baseball magnates back east feared that, instead of being their talent-hunting ground, the PCL might turn the West into a refuge for disgruntled major leaguers trapped within their organizational cage. Top officials of the majors thus made transcontinental train journeys to San Francisco to talk PCL president Eugene Bert, a business-savvy San Francisco attorney, and other league executives into joining the National Association and becoming a part of organized baseball as a Class A circuit, only one rung below the two major leagues. After a year's wheeling and dealing, the PCL top brass accepted that proposition. Some PCL owners, however, continued to grumble publicly about the subordinate position into which they had been placed in relation to the eastern major leagues over the draft issue and kept floating the idea of going outlaw again. The catastrophic earthquake in 1906, which destroyed a huge swath of the Bay Area, muted the talk of an immediate secession. Still, the majors continued to feel the need to mollify this fiercely independent maverick within organized baseball. Beginning in 1908, the PCL, along with the Eastern League, another premier minor league, was granted a new and enhanced classification of AA. That same year, AL president Johnson honored the PCL with a request to help field a team for the junior major circuit's first-ever overseas postseason tour. The job of heading that exhibition team went to the manager-owner of the PCL's 1904 champion Tacoma Tigers, Mike Fisher—the son of an original founding brother of California baseball, John Fisher.[10] As discussed in the next chapter, players who took part in this AL-sponsored

Leagues of Their Own | 79

off-season enterprise would become the first American professionals to set foot in Japan.

There was another notable development in West Coast professional baseball in the second decade of the twentieth century: the institutionalization of the California Winter League. Up and down the West Coast, centers of seasonal play developed in the 1910s with the bulk of the activity clustered around San Francisco in the north and Los Angeles in the south. Major leaguers on the prowl for additional income and a warm winter, including legendary Washington Senator pitcher Walter Johnson, and players from the PCL and other high-end minor leaguers played together during the majors' off-season months. The Southern California Winter League, later referred to as just the California Winter League, soon became the dominant circuit thanks to the area's balmy climate and the league's decision to bring high-performing Negro league teams into its fold. As early as 1909, talented black players made the trek west to play ball there, including one of the greatest Negro League pitchers of all times, Hall of Famer "Cyclone Joe" Williams, who played for the local Trilby Baseball Club. The Leland Giants, managed by the "Father of Negro League Baseball," Rube Foster, joined the California Winter League in 1910 and became a regular fixture thereafter. The technical level of the seasonal league rose by leaps and bounds from a semipro level in 1900, putatively reaching a Class A level in a decade, then a class AA and AAA level by the 1920s, fueled in no small part by the steady infusion of the Negro League's top talent. Southern California's growing black urban population, the westernmost spillover of the World War I–induced Great Migration, delivered a solid fan base for the country's first modern, integrated professional baseball circuit.[11]

The Instigators of Baseball Fever in Japan

The sanguine projection Spalding made in his 1882 letter to Hiraoka about Japan's future use of sports equipment proved prophetic. By the early twentieth century, baseball indeed "rose like the sun" in Japan, and the nation began to consume American-style sporting goods in increasing volume. But this commercial development did not yield the kind of business outcome Spalding had envisaged. Japan's growing demand for baseball and sporting goods in general was mostly filled by domestic suppliers that began to appear in large numbers at the turn of the century. In 1882, Japan's first sporting-goods retailers, Mimatsu and Junkōdō, opened in Tokyo within a few months of each other. These small, family-owned businesses initially sold gymnastic apparatuses, bicycles, and most important, baseballs imported from Spalding & Brothers, but they began manufacturing their own baseball equipment within a few years.[12] The typical modus operandi of these pioneer manufactures consisted of dissecting Spalding's originals to study the material and copying them. Predating international legal regimes regulating such industrial piracy, this reproduction of equipment was still considered a perfectly legitimate business practice in Japan at the time.

Imitating Spalding's business model also extended to an emphasis on publicity and advertising. In 1902 Mimatsu began to publish *Yakyū Nenpō*, its own annual baseball guide modeled after *Spalding's Official Base Ball Guide*. The company's 1905 price list carried in this advertising venue shows that a mitt cost as much as one yen at a time when a *shō* (1.8 liter) of rice cost only seventeen sen (1 yen was 100 sen). Undoubtedly, baseball equipment was still very much a luxury item beyond the reach of the general population.[13] Yet even a casual reading of Japan's popular baseball periodicals, which began circulating a few years into the new century, reveals increasing pictorial advertising by domestic sporting-goods producers. The dynamo of this budding light manufacturing industry was the Mizuno family partnership, located in Osaka. Started in 1892 by an Osaka merchant as an import-export business, Mizuno initially distributed general consumer merchandize imported from England and the United States. A year later, its founding owner died, and his oldest son, Rihachi, was forced to quit primary school at age nine to apprentice in a textile business in Kyoto. During his years in Kyoto, Mizuno Rihachi took up the hobby of watching baseball games between Dōshisha, Sankō, and American expatriates in the Kobe foreign settlement. In 1897 Mizuno finished his apprenticeship in the textile business and returned to Osaka as a devotee of baseball, starting his own business to import and distribute Spalding & Brothers' baseball equipment and other athletic equipment.[14]

Like Mimatsu and Junkōdō in Tokyo, Mizuno branched out into manufacturing in 1906. Its competition with chief regional rival Yamamoto Shōten in Kyoto spurred efficient production, quality improvements, and ferocious price-cutting. Within ten years, several Japanese firms were producing baseball equipment in numerous small family-run factories in the greater Osaka-Kyoto urban belt. Mizuno rose through all this industrial energy as a charismatic leader of national renown. In 1916, under his leadership, the size and weight of baseballs were nationally standardized. Spalding's free gifts and merchandise catalogs to prospective Japanese customers clearly achieved the intended goal of developing a new market. What Spalding did not quite anticipate was that, in the land of the Rising Sun, domestic equivalents—made with cheap local labor and natural rubber and cork that became procurable from plantations in Southeast Asia through expanding interregional maritime transport routes—held a distinct competitive advantage over the American company's expensive originals, burdened as they were with higher shipping costs in the less-developed transpacific routes and higher labor costs in the United States. In short, baseball was one of the early cases of Japan's successful import substitution.[15]

It is rather ironic that while the Osaka-based family-owned business progressively eroded the high-end market niche of Spalding & Brothers, Mizuno's patriarch, Rihachi, was a genuine apostle of Spalding's gospel of baseball. He grew up projecting onto baseball a mythical image of "America" as one open playing field where any young, honest, disciplined, and hardworking man, despite his humble social origins, could run free and find a way to excel—the kind of idealized vision of pastoral America marketed by Spalding and his fellow boosters of professional baseball. As a young business apprentice, Mizuno steeped himself in the cult of Gilded Age American entrepreneurship and idolized American self-made men such as Andrew Carnegie and John D. Rockefeller, whose legendary life stories of rags to riches were popularized among Japan's reading public through best-selling minibiographies like Mizuno's personal bible, *Seikō Taikan* (A Catalogue of Successors). At one point, it appeared Mizuno might even get to work in the land of his dream. At age twenty, he accepted an offer by a Kyoto silk-exporting company to dispatch him to its San Francisco branch as a sales agent. Then the Russo-Japanese War broke out. Mizuno was drafted into service, and his dream of moving to America was cruelly dashed.[16]

Mizuno displayed much of the business acumen and aggressive entrepreneurship that distinguished A. G. Spalding. Mizuno understood, as did Spalding, the importance of advertising and publicity in an age of widespread literacy and the cheap mass-circulating press. Mizuno would later claim that he had actually learned the importance of advertising from John Wannamaker, another American business baron featured in *Seikō Taikan*. Even from his business's modest beginning in 1906, Mizuno made a point of earmarking a separate budget for advertising and publicity, which was a revolutionary business practice in Japan at the time. Once Japan's sports journalism got off the ground in the early twentieth century, this new publishing genre gave Mizuno a handy platform for advertising his merchandise and the positive sport creed underpinning his business. By running pictorial illustrations of products in nationally circulated baseball publications such as *Yakyūkai* (Baseball World) and *Asahi Supōtsu* (Asahi Sports), Mizuno and his domestic rivals delivered to aspiring ballplayers even in the Japanese countryside concrete visual images of novel consumer products called baseball goods and sporting wear (as distinct from everyday wear and work clothes), planting acquisitive desires for them. Mizuno's wife, who daily scrutinized American merchandise catalogs for the latest fashion trends, was his unpaid in-house consultant.[17]

Mizuno also adroitly turned barnstorming tours by American baseballers into occasions for advertising his merchandise. The first opportunity to do so came when the baseball team of the University of Chicago toured through Osaka in 1910. Mizuno unabashedly made a public spectacle of himself in the wooden grandstand of a recently enclosed municipal playing field by cheering and dancing, dressed in an eye-catching crimson shirt (wearing red was very uncommon for Japanese adult men at the time). He repeated the same antics each time American baseball squads barnstormed through western Japan in the ensuing years and turned himself into an eccentric but endearing advertising mascot. Business sponsorship and ticketing of "amateur" sporting events also originated in 1911 with this sport entrepreneur. Once Japan's entry into the International Olympic movement and an economic boom brought on by World War I triggered a broad-based interest in sports and recreation, Mizuno seized business opportunities in the rapidly industrializing and urbanizing society by both fulfilling its growing leisure-time needs and creating and abetting those needs. In 1923, Mizuno Brothers became the first domestic sporting-goods company to be incorporated.[18]

The invention of a uniquely Japanese baseball artifact that effectively accommodated local needs, *nanshiki* (soft rubber) balls, also sparked the baseball craze in early twentieth-century Japan. As *yakyū* became popular among primary school children after Ichikō's 1896 feat, gloves and mitts still remained beyond the reach of the vast majority of Japan's juvenile players. Early in the 1910s, a Kobe rubber company developed a soft-cored but durable rubber-surfaced ball that made it possible for children to play baseball without mitts or gloves without the risk of injuries. This innovation further fueled a passion for baseball among young players. The advent of *nanshiki* balls also opened the floodgate for ball manufacturers to begin sponsoring youth and student baseball tournaments for marketing purposes.[19] Business sponsorship and ticketing of early twentieth-century Japanese versions of "Little Leagues" soon extended to the older age cohorts in middle school, and at one point in the 1920s twelve different "national championship tournaments" were held in Japan annually. More than three thousand adolescent squads from across the "empire"—including Taiwan, Korea, and southern Manchuria—participated in these commercially sponsored events during summer recess. Rival sponsoring firms and school alumni allied with them began to dictate the organization of these interscholastic ventures with the result that Japan's youth "amateur" baseball became heavily commercialized during the Taisho and early Showa periods.[20]

Meiji Japan's adolescent baseball craze also had a transpacific taproot. The advent of baseball publications made the transmission of information about U.S. major-league baseball and its stars more systematic and set off the cult of American baseball celebrities among Japanese youngsters. The infant stage of Japan's baseball journalism owed its existence to improbable agents: Japanese businessmen who reported on major-league baseball from the United States purely as a personal hobby. *Beikoku Yakyūjyutsu* (1909), the first book detailing the National League and the American League, the two leagues mutually recognized as "majors" in the United States six years earlier, was authored by Yamaguchi Ryūkichi, an employee of the Mitsui Trading Company's newly opened New York office. The second book, *Beikoku Yakyū Kenbutsu* (1910), was penned by Masaoka Geiyō, a member of Japan's first business mission to the United States headed by famed industrialist Shibusawa Eiichi. Written by baseball dilettantes with privileged access to actual major-league games, these self-published books included not only information about major leaguers' superb techniques but their biographical data and "human interest" stories as well. The theme of American professionals' huge salaries also received prominent play. Among other things, John McGraw's salary of more than $10,000 from the New York Giants, and the Pacific Coast Leaguers' average salary of $2,000 to $3,000, were admiringly touted as examples of the massive monetary reward that came with baseball celebrity in America.[21]

Parallel to such sporadic reporting by amateur aficionados was the advent of early sports journalism, inaugurated by Japan's oldest magazine specializing in sports, *Undōkai* (Sporting World) by advertising company Hakuhōdō in 1897. It was purportedly inspired by the launching of the modern Olympic movement by French aristocrat Pierre de Coubertin.[22] The magazine's motto, featured in its inaugural issue, was to "encourage physical education and produce physical fitness and sturdier and more robust bodies in Japanese men."[23] Within five years, the publication of *Yakyuū Nenkan* by Mimatsu began, annually updating rule changes reflected in *Spalding's Official Base Ball Guide*. An all-sport specialty magazine focusing primarily on baseball, *Undōsekai*, was launched in April 1908, followed by the nation's first monthly magazine devoted to baseball, *Gekkan Bēsubōru* (Baseball Monthly) in November 1908. The inaugural issue of the latter carried a detailed analysis of Christy Mathewson's pitching prowess and the previous year's World Series between the Detroit Tigers and the Chicago Cubs with box scores. Reporting on major-league baseball was the magazine's "foreign correspondent," an Issei named Furukawa Shigeo, a part owner of the all-Japanese semipro Seattle Athletic Club.[24]

The launching of rival baseball magazines at this juncture was a testament to the surge in popular interest in the game fueled in part by back-to-back bumper seasons in U.S.-Japanese baseball exchange, beginning with the University of Washington's Japan tour in April 1907 and culminating in the Great White Fleet's port call and the first visit by an American professional off-season exhibition team, the Reach All-Americans, in the fall of 1908.[25] Most of the Meiji-era commercial sports magazines, however, were short lived, a casualty of the still limited readership in Japan for sports. For instance, *Undōsekai* folded in April 1914. The World War I–induced economic boom and Japan's increasing exposure to international athletic competitions centered around the Olympic Games ushered in the next and more viable stage in the development of Japan's sports journalism. The first boost in public interest in sports came when Japan was invited to participate in the 1912 Stockholm Olympics as the first "non-white," "non-Western" country. In May 1917, the city of Osaka hosted the first international athletic competition ever held in Japan, the third Far Eastern Games. This competition, coupled with the winning of the first Olympic medals by two Japanese tennis players in the 1920 Antwerp Olympics, set off a major sports boom in the country. Against this backdrop the magazine *Undōkai* was relaunched in April 1920 with Tobita Suishū, a former Waseda star baseball player, as its editor in chief. A national daily with a robust capital base, the *Asahi Shinbun*, launched a full-service sports magazine, *Asahi Supōtsu*, in 1923. As soon as Mizuno learned of the launching of this bimonthly specialty magazine, he rushed to sign a contract for a full-page ad on the magazine's back cover. It was during this decade of sports fever that the word *supōtsu* (sport), as a translation of *undō* (athletic), entered Japan's popular lexicon.[26]

The rise of sports journalism spun off from the integration of Japan's mass-circulating print media and the resulting rise of nationwide information sharing. The late Meiji era marked a major watershed in modern Japan's media history. With the nationwide networks of railway and postal service now firmly in place, the national circulation of newspapers, magazines, and books began in earnest. Meanwhile, publishers and newspapers borrowed ideas from the United States about means of distributing their print products to the far-flung countryside, such as lending libraries and book clubs. The Japanese people in provincial cities and in rural areas thus began to read the same newspapers (such as the nationally circulating *Asahi* and *Nichinichi*), magazines, and books as their compatriots in metropolitan areas and, to use Benedict Anderson's celebrated term, shared in an imagined national community.[27] This nationally standardized reading public had access to common clusters of information organized around new and geographically unbounded social groupings, such as those focusing on hobbies and recreation. Baseball journalism, which achieved a stable commercial footing in Japan during the interwar period, also benefited from this structural development. At the deft hands of information purveyors ranging from amateur dilettantes to professionally devoted sports writers and journalists, exploits by baseball titans in the newly consolidated American major leagues and their outsized salaries became nationally shared and envied knowledge in Japan and provided fodder for the emergent cult of media celebrities.

The Birth of Intercollegiate Baseball in the United States and Japan

Another feeder of Japan's early twentieth-century baseball mania was the rise of periodic intercollegiate baseball exchange. In the United States, intercollegiate athletics, heralded by a crew meet between Harvard and Yale (1852) and a baseball game between Amherst and Williams (1859), became entrenched in higher education after the 1870s. Technological advances, particularly in transportation, became a critical ingredient of the emergent new subculture in student life built around athletic contests. Intercollegiate athletics depended on railroad service for transporting and assembling teams and supporters, just as the organization of the National League in professional baseball in 1876 became possible only with the development of intercity railway lines.[28] The rise of intercollegiate baseball in late Meiji Japan closely dovetailed with the organizational logic of its American counterpart. In the first decade of the twentieth century, with a critical mass of public and private colleges established and accredited, occasional challenge matches and pickup games among their officially sponsored athletic clubs were gradually subsumed into multi-team leagues and tournaments held on a fixed schedule. The first of such institutionalized intercollegiate contests emerged between the rowing teams of the two elite imperial universities in Tokyo and Kyoto after the latter was founded in 1898. The event was consciously modeled after the Cambridge-Oxford rowing match, down to the colors of the opposing teams' oars: light and dark blue.[29]

A similar two-way contest started in baseball between two private colleges in the Tokyo metropolitan area, Keio and Waseda, in 1904 after both schools beat Ichikō and Yokohama's American expatriate team and thus staked their claims as Japan's new baseball powerhouses. Believing that sports including baseball must not be the preserve of elite students attending the government-funded imperial universities, the faculty manager of the Waseda baseball team, Abe Isoo, proposed to Keio that the two schools conduct a regular home-and-away series so that baseball play and spectatorship would be made more accessible and stimulate esprit de corps among the student bodies of the recently founded schools. This intercollegiate sporting event became a huge draw, but the rivalry between the two private colleges got so intense on the diamond and student supporters' behavior at the games so rowdy and disorderly that the contest had to be canceled in 1906. The two Tokyo archrivals ended up not playing against each other for almost two decades thereafter.[30] In the intervening years, three other private colleges in the expanding Tokyo metropolitan area, Meiji, Hōsei, and Rikkyō, began to field formidable baseball teams. Waseda and Keio were finally persuaded in 1925 to bury the hatchet and join these three metropolitan private colleges to form a regular circuit. Tokyo Imperial University also joined, and the result was the establishment of the Tokyo Big 6 League. This athletic conference would become the key breeding ground of Japan's baseball celebrity culture and fandom and the reservoir of top-flight talent before World War II.[31]

As was the case with intercollegiate athletic leagues and regional conferences that began to develop in Gilded Age America, the operation of Japan's first multischool league depended on expanding intracity rail networks and decreasing fares in the Tokyo metropolitan area in the early decades of the twentieth century. In addition to the proliferation of private commuter lines, promotional techniques inspired by practices prevalent in England and the United States gave impetus to a rapid rise in rail ridership in urban population centers. Beginning with the government-operated Japanese Railway, railroad companies adjusted fare structures to emphasize commuter service, offering student discounts and group fares for featured attractions, including holiday festivals and sporting events.[32] These infrastructural enhancements in the urbanizing Tokyo metropolitan area were one of the factors that enabled Tokyo Big 6 baseball to evolve into a hugely popular spectator sport and public entertainment in the prewar period.

The Rise of U.S.-Japanese Collegiate Baseball Exchange

In a parallel historical pathway, intercollegiate baseball links between American universities and Japanese private colleges grew in the early 1900s, relying on networks of transoceanic transportation and on cheaper telegraph and mail rates that facilitated planning and organization of games.[33] The use of large steamships for transpacific passenger liners meant safer and more affordable oceanic travel. With British and Japanese shippers taking the lead, steamship companies increased regular routes connecting North American and Asian markets in the last decade of the nineteenth century. In a move toward "big government" boosted by the indemnity of 200 million taels (liang) in the spoils of the 1894–95 war with China, the Japanese state actively involved itself in these maritime infrastructure improvements. It furnished coordinated subsidies to the nation's merchant marine under the Sailing Promotion Law and Ship Construction Promotion Law of 1896. This government aid enabled Nippon Yūsen Company, Japan's leading shipper, to start regular routes between Seattle and Hong Kong with stopovers in Honolulu and several ports in Japan. After 1901, six Nippon Yūsen liners plied the Pacific every week. Not to be outdone, Tōyō Kisen opened Hong Kong–San Francisco routes in 1898, and Osaka Shōsen launched regular Tacoma–Hong Kong service in 1908. By the time of the Russo-Japanese War, the Japanese merchant marine had largely achieved the government goal of establishing parity with British and American shippers in East Asia's regional maritime transport.[34]

It is no accident that U.S.-Japan intercollegiate baseball began in the first decade of the twentieth century on the crest of this growing transpacific maritime traffic. Nor was it by chance that the early matches took place between Japanese teams and American colleges in Hawaii, San Francisco, and Seattle. Players participating in the first of these international contests, Waseda versus Stanford, were drawn together through the regular Yokohama–San Francisco maritime route. In April 1905, the Waseda team, headed by Abe Isoo, sailed off to an unprecedented forty-five-day overseas sport excursion amid a gripping national crisis—the impending naval showdown with Czar Nicholas II's mighty Baltic Fleet, the climax of the Russo-Japanese War. Undeterred by the exigency of the state or critics' indignation at the "unpatriotic frivolous excursion," the Waseda baseball team played twenty-six intercollegiate games in San Francisco, Los Angeles, Seattle, and Tacoma for a record of seven wins and nineteen losses, traveling overland on the Northern Pacific's railway linkups. By the time the team returned home in late June 1905, the war with Russia had been narrowly won as a result of the Japanese Combined Fleet's victory in the naval battle off the island of Tsushima. The Japanese government had just decided to send Komura Jutarō—a former baseball enthusiast and Wilson's student at Kaiseikō, incidentally—as plenipotentiary at peace talks in Portsmouth, New Hampshire.[35]

In many respects Waseda's 1905 West Coast expedition was a harbinger of future trends. First, the team's faculty manager, Abe Isoo, a Christian socialist educated at the Hartford Seminary and a known opponent of the war with Russia, engaged in fund-raising and accepted a share of the gate receipts generated in the United States to help pay for the tour. In defending these "venal" actions to the irate school administration, Abe cited statistics drawn from American professional and intercollegiate baseball records and emphasized the sport's ability to generate "clean" revenues and pay for itself.[36] Second, the sporting events Abe and his student squad put together in the United States opened a new venue for local Japanese American communities to sustain and affirm their connections, tangible or not, with the land still regarded by many Issei as their true home. Tellingly, Waseda's tour of the U.S. West Coast took place in the middle of anti-Japanese campaigns by white supremacists and labor groups in the U.S. West. Of two thousand spectators who came to the first Stanford-Waseda game, about five hundred were Japanese immigrants who had traveled from the Bay Area and outlying areas in California's Central Valley with gifts, Japanese food items, and cash donations for the traveling team. Waseda's games against other college teams in Los Angeles, Seattle, and Tacoma duplicated this pattern in spectator demographics and the critical role played by on-site contributions by the local Japanese communities to the tour's shoestring budget. Periodic expeditions by Japanese collegiate teams and their participation in the Hawaiian and West Coast amateur and semipro baseball would become an important social nexus between the Japanese homeland population and Japanese nationals on the labor migration frontier in the United States in the early twentieth century.[37]

Waseda's direct exposure to American collegiate baseball in 1905 also afforded an occasion for learning firsthand the "scientific baseball," or "inside baseball," then driving the sport in the United States. The Waseda squad brought back to Japan new concepts such as pitcher rotation and warm-ups. Other baseball techniques freshly introduced from America included the squeeze play, hit and run, and slide. Deeply committed to the idea of sports as a means of character building of democratic citizenry, Abe was not one to monopolize the acquired knowledge like a treasured secret. Working with the team's captain, Hashido Makoto, a gifted writer who would become one of Japan's most venerated sport journalists, Abe codified the fruits of their experiential learning in a manual titled *Saishin Yakyūjutsu* (Brand-New Baseball Techniques), which achieved a near canonical status among Japanese baseball players, replacing Ichikō's now antiquated manual. Hashido's new baseball manual distinguished itself in its obvious affirmation of "American-style baseball," which the author equated admiringly with scientific rationality, efficiency, and strategic coordination. The differing attitudes expressed in these two homegrown manuals toward the bunt are suggestive. While the 1897 manual compiled by Chūma considered bunts a "sneaky" tactic not befitting fair-playing and honorable men, Hashido's affirmed it as a legitimate component of "modern" coordinated offensive tactics. Similarly, Hashido, like Abe, portrayed the practice of collecting gate receipts as a rational cost-covering method about which there was nothing dishonorable or demeaning. In that spirit, *Saishin Yakyūjutsu* even came with an end-of-volume supplement devoted entirely to information about American professional baseball and explained the concept of playing baseball as a professional career.[38]

The precedent set by Waseda's pioneer West Coast tour was followed by other private colleges, and U.S.-Japanese intercollegiate baseball exchange became an increasingly common occurrence in the early twentieth century. For Japanese collegiate players, the opportunity to play against American collegians meant being anointed as national champion. For archrivals Waseda and Keio in particular, being a purveyor of modern, "scientific" American baseball became another domain of interscholastic competition, especially after they stopped engaging each other directly on the diamond. To match the feat of Waseda's West Coast tour, in October

1907 Keio invited Hawaii's semipro team, St. Louis, to Japan. Following the path cleared by Abe, Keio charged admission to help cover the costs of this expensive venture, which entailed payment of a guarantee to the semiprofessional athletes and covering their travel expenses. It was the first time gate fees were collected at a baseball game in Japan. As a spectator event the St. Louis tour of Japan turned out to be a huge success, drawing ten thousand people to Keio's Tsunamachi Grounds each time the Hawaiian semipro team played. In the following summer, St. Louis reciprocated by inviting Keio to Hawaii. Waseda's next U.S. expedition took it to the U.S. mainland, at the invitation of the University of Washington in Seattle. In the fall of 1908, it was Waseda's turn to bring the University of Washington to Japan. Again, gate receipts contributed to the tour's budget and helped bring the amateur sporting event to a successful conclusion. As binational intercollegiate baseball exchange became an annual event in the ensuing years, charging admission at the gate for cost-defraying purposes became routine in Japanese amateur collegiate baseball.[39]

The fierce rivalry between students of Tokyo's top private colleges combined with the boosterism of school administrations and alumni groups to push the horizon of Japanese collegiate baseball tours deeper into the U.S. continent. To one-up Waseda's sponsorship of the University of Washington's Japan tour, Keio invited the University of Wisconsin in 1909. Not to be undone, Waseda's next move was to underwrite the Japan leg of the University of Chicago's Far Eastern tour in the following year. Keio tried to outshine its rival by hiring two major leaguers, Arthur "Tillie" Shafer and Tommy Thompson of the New York Giants, as special coaches in the fine art of John McGraw's "inside baseball" during Major League Baseball's off-season in 1910.[40] In 1911, both Waseda and Keio toured the U.S. mainland, and in the following year, they both acquitted themselves well against the U.S. Army team in Manila touring Japan. After 1913, Tokyo's new powerhouse, Meiji University, joined the ranks of overseas Japanese collegiate barnstormers. In 1929, Meiji stunned its rivals in Tokyo Big 6 with an unprecedented three-month round-the-world tour, during which its baseball squad traveled eastbound from Hawaii through the United States, Europe, Egypt, Hong Kong, and Shanghai.[41]

American colleges were similarly on the move. During the Roaring Twenties, general prosperity in the United States created an economic environment in which an expanding phalanx of American college athletic teams would go on cross-country and overseas tours. For collegiate baseball, transpacific tours far outnumbered transatlantic journeys. In addition to upstart private schools like Stanford, the University of Southern California, and the University of Chicago, several midwestern state colleges, among them Illinois, Indiana, and Michigan, toured Japan during the interwar period. Similarly, it became an informal ritual for champions of the Tokyo Big 6 League to tour Hawaii, the U.S. mainland, and Japan's colonial outposts in Asia as the year's "national representative."

If one is to identify an American sports advocate who helped nourish the nascent channels of U.S.-Japanese collegiate baseball exchange more than any other American, it was perhaps Amos Alonzo Stagg, the inaugural director of the University of Chicago's Department of Physical Culture. Stagg is best known in U.S. sport history for his role in the growth of big-time American college football and as the nation's first full-time professional football coach with faculty status. Stagg's contribution to collegiate baseball, let alone U.S.-Japanese baseball exchange, has gone largely unrecognized by historians. Yet Stagg, during his forty-year tenure as Chicago's chief athletic officer, played a vital part in engineering four series of Chicago-Waseda dual meets (1910–11, 1915–16, 1920–21, 1925–27) and was instrumental in the brokerage of baseball matches between visiting Japanese collegiate squads and other schools in the U.S. Midwest. A brief look at Stagg's career and the entrepreneurial spirit that characterized his work in American collegiate athletics illuminates the intriguing mix of idealism, opportunism, and pragmatic managerial ideology that underlay Stagg's heretofore little-recognized contribution to the making of U.S.-Japanese baseball brotherhood.[42]

Born in 1862 to a shoemaker in West Orange, New Jersey, Stagg was a quintessential American muscular Christian in that throughout his life he firmly believed in physical vigor and bodily exertion as an essential aspect of manly character building. Stagg's life also embodied a Horatio Alger success story in which a young man's athletic talent, combined with the requisite drive, hard work, and serendipity, became a propellant for upward social mobility and an ingredient in a life of fame and fortune. From his humble origin, Stagg found a way into the elite Phillips Exeter Academy in New Hampshire at the mature age of twenty-one, excelling in various fields of athletics and finally beating down the jealously guarded door to Yale College in 1884. While playing football under Yale's legendary Walter Camp, often dubbed the "Father of Football," Stagg was selected in 1889 as a member of the inaugural all-American collegiate football team. At Yale, he was also a star baseball player and was offered a contract by multiple major-league clubs when he graduated. Stagg turned them all down to continue his studies at Yale Divinity School. As many of the era's Christian athletes did, Stagg went on to the International YMCA Training School in Springfield (currently Springfield College) after finishing his theological training. The YMCA school at the time was the epicenter of robust Christian athleticism, and Stagg's classmates there included a Canadian McGill University graduate by the name of James Naismith, who invented the game of basketball as a course project for the school.[43]

Among the valuable acquaintances Stagg made during his years at Yale was William Rainey Harper, an instructor of Semitic languages who left Yale in 1890 to become the first president of a university to be financed primarily by oil millionaire John D. Rockefeller. Harper's educational plans for the newly founded University of Chicago were considered revolutionary at the time, particularly for his explicit acknowledgment of the value of organized sport on campus as a "drawing card." Stagg was recruited by Harper in 1892 for the fine salary of $2,500 primarily to turn out a "team which we can send around the country and knock out all the colleges."[44] Stagg was in an enviable position of defining college athletic coaching as an embryonic profession at a new school with ample financial resources but unencumbered by institutional baggage. Under Harper, the "P. T. Barnum of higher education" (as a detractor quipped), and his immediate successor, Harry Pratt Judson, Stagg enjoyed almost unbounded institutional support to pursue accomplishments in intercollegiate sports as a way to generate publicity for the school and recruit students. He shrewdly discerned opportunities in the emergence of Harvard-Yale and Yale-Princeton athletic matches as an important social ritual in Gilded Age America. These eastern prototypes provided an inspiration for Stagg's own midwestern concoction, the Chicago-Michigan Thanksgiving football game. His field of vision, however, was not limited to the Midwest. In December 1894, Stagg boldly led his Chicago football players on a 6,200-mile cross-country tour to play against Stanford. This athletic extravaganza was planned and executed in cooperation with Walter Camp, Stagg's old Yale mentor and now Stanford's football coach, and the treasurer of the Stanford Athletic Association—a young engineering student by the name of Herbert Hoover.[45]

By pioneering long-distance tours by student athletes and breaking out of the local and regional confines of Gilded Age collegiate athletic events, Stagg revolutionized American intercollegiate sports and prepared the way for their future growth into a quasi-business enterprise predicated on interregional contests. It is therefore not hard to imagine why Stagg seemingly jumped at an invitation that came from Waseda's Abe in early 1910 for the University of Chicago baseball team to tour Japan that fall. To Stagg, it was first and foremost a business proposition. Having long fretted over the "small income which we derive from our baseball games, owing to the presence of the Sox and Cubs who dominate the whole city," Stagg saw in the novelty of Japanese collegians playing baseball an opportunity for generating publicity and not-too-shabby profits at the gate to boot. The possibility of extending the Maroons' "away" tour in Japan to elsewhere in Asia was another attraction for Stagg the sport entrepreneur, who intended to rely on his old YMCA contacts, Gillett in Korea and Brown in Shanghai. Stagg did not neglect to contact Frank White, U.S. commissioner of education in Manila, to arrange the Japan-Philippines leg of the tour; neither did he fail to contact Keio to arrange games with Waseda's rival to make sure that the tour of Japan would "get good financial returns."[46]

When Abe first approached Stagg, the University of Chicago's Board of Physical Culture and Athletics voted to decline the offer because financing the customary reciprocal invitation for Waseda to tour the United States was deemed too costly. Stagg, however, did not give up. He maneuvered to have Abe's invitation reconsidered at a sparsely attended board meeting held during college recess and generated a yes vote. Approval included partial funds for sponsoring a return visit by Waseda to Chicago in 1911. Having secured the board's approval, Stagg was quite clear eyed about how long the novelty value of Japanese collegians playing "America's Game" would last among local baseball viewers. His guess was "three games, and certainly not more than five," and it would be better "to send them around to the neighboring colleges, and thru [sic] this means seek to make up for the large expenditure which we will assume," as he confided to his alumni contact in Tokyo. Starting with the University of Wisconsin, Stagg aggressively enlisted his opposite numbers at Big Ten schools and other colleges in the Chicago area to help host an exotic athletic spectacle. It was every bit a business decision in the interest of cost-effectiveness as it was a reflection of Stagg's Big Ten fraternal spirit.[47]

That Stagg had no reservations about using his baseball team's Pacific trips as a recruitment tool targeting prospective high school student athletes is evident from the way those overseas baseball tours were hyped in his athletic department's promotional literature in the subsequent years. Stagg boasted that Chicago's baseball tours of Japan every five years were a "unique distinction. . . . What an experience for red-blooded young fellows to travel across the Pacific in a jolly group . . . all expenses paid . . . and touring the Orient, where games, sightseeing, banquets and hobnobbing with Nipponese dignitaries are part of the program."[48] Thanks to Stagg's entrepreneurship and hard-nosed bargaining regarding guarantees and expenses, the University of Chicago team, unique among American collegiate tours at the time, was able to tour not only Hawaii and Japan but also Taiwan, Korea, China (Shanghai), and the Philippines. From its first Japan tour, the University of Chicago baseball squad drew impressive crowds of 10,000–12,000 to its games against Japanese collegians and did much to demonstrate to the country's sports entrepreneurs, not the least of them Mizuno, the commercial promise of baseball. After their 1920 Japan tour, the Maroons even left their Japanese hosts with a net profit of about ten thousand yen, a nest egg that permitted the Waseda baseball club to move forward with its long-gestated plan to equip its campus playing field with the trappings of a "modern" ballpark, enclosing it with concrete walls complete with a grandstand.[49]

Student Baseball Madness in Japan

One of the distinctive features of Japanese baseball before World War II is a multilayered structure of "amateur" student tournaments that owed its existence to corporate involvement. Just as primary school and youth tournaments were organized and sponsored by *nanshiki* ball manufacturers, middle school competition also came to be subsidized by private businesses. The first initiative for organizing a large-scale middle school tournament came from Mizuno, who sponsored a tournament among twenty-five middle schools in western Japan in 1913.[50] Two years later, a major national daily, the *Osaka Asahi Shinbun*, took up Mizuno's mantle and expanded the tournament to a national scale with the purported objective of promoting "manliness and techniques uniquely suitable to the national character."[51] This announced lofty vision notwithstanding, the whole enterprise was driven from the very beginning by the newspaper's corporate interests.[52] The *Osaka Asahi Shinbun*, as a commercial entity, boasted solid distribution networks in Japan's two metropolitan areas (Osaka and Tokyo) but still lacked a broad nationwide readership. By bankrolling a national sporting spectacle highlighting students, the newspaper company hoped to gain nationwide exposure and brand recognition.

In the tournament's first year, seventy-one middle schools across the nation participated in regional preliminaries, from which ten regional champions advanced to the national finals held during the schools' August recess at Toyonaka Grounds in Osaka. The many local and regional tournaments that had previously coexisted randomly were now streamlined into a single system of national competition. The number of participating schools grew steadily in the subsequent years, reaching an astounding 410 by 1928. From its very first year, each game in the national finals drew over 10,000 spectators, forcing the venue to be shifted in 1917 to Naruo Stadium, a remodeled horse race track near Kobe with 20,000 seating capacity.[53] Even this multipurpose stadium with a wooden grandstand proved insufficient to accommodate the overflowing crowds. In 1924, the tournament was again moved, this time to Kōshien Stadium, its final home. The sixty-thousand-seat modern steel and concrete stadium had just been built by the Hanshin Railway Company at a cost of 15.6 million yen. Modeled after New York's Polo Grounds, Kōshien was billed by its proud management as "Asia's #1."[54]

Middle school baseball fever, which would become a national summer ritual similar to Thanksgiving football games in the United States, was ratcheted up to a higher pitch in 1925 when another national tournament, this one held during spring school recess, began at Kōshien Stadium. Again, corporate interests fueled this new athletic enterprise. By this time, the Osaka metropolitan area had turned into a media monopoly market where two national dailies, the *Osaka Asahi Shinbun* and the *Osaka Mainichi Shinbun*, engaged in a fierce commercial battle. The latter decided to sponsor a spring middle school national tournament as a marketing tool, but to differentiate itself from its crosstown rival, the *Osaka Mainichi* adopted a different format in which regional representatives selected by a committee of baseball experts were invited to compete in the national finals at Kōshien Stadium. It was about this time that these competing annual sporting events began to feature patriotic rituals, such as the pregame raising of the national flag and playing of the national anthem. Top government officials were invited to the opening ceremony as guests of honor, lending prestige to the events. In 1926 Wakatsuki Reijirō became the first prime minister to attend a game, a national championship contest, at Kōshien. Thereafter, either the prime minister or the education minister would honor the opening ceremony with his presence or a congratulatory telegram.[55]

The twin annual spectacles were also molded into a cultural framework of the Japanese empire. Beginning in 1921, the middle school tournaments in colonial Korea and southern Manchuria were designated as "regional preliminaries" by the organizers of these national tournaments. Taiwan was similarly integrated into the intraimperial structure two years later. The prospect of being able to compete in the hallowed Kōshien in the imperial metropole galvanized children of Japanese expatriates in the colonial domains thirsting for mainlanders' recognition. Becoming a "regional representative" to the national finals in Kōshien came to carry similar gravitas for colonial subjects as well, but with a different twist. During Japanese colonial rule, a total of twenty schools represented Korea in the national finals, but all except one fielded all-Japanese rosters. The exception was Fimun Middle School, which beat the all-Japanese elite Kyōjō Middle School 10–0 and won the regional championship in 1923. One can only imagine the intense nationalistic pride Koreans young and old must have felt in their hearts over this achievement. At the national championship tournament at Kōshien, Fimun beat another colonial representative but ethnically all-Japanese team, Dalian Middle School, 9–4 in the second round and advanced to the quarterfinals. In 1930, Daegu Commercial School, fielding a mixed Japanese and Korean roster, became Korea's regional champion and representative to Kōshien.[56]

Taiwanese student players similarly used the national limelight shone on the Kōshien diamond to showcase their caliber in the colonial master's favorite game, making an unspoken statement about their place within the colonial order. The governor-general's office set up several agricultural schools in Taiwan to promote agricultural (particularly sugar) production on the colonial island. One of them, the Jiayi Agriculture and Forestry Institute (abbreviated Kanō in Japanese), was founded in 1919. The colonial school achieved metropolitan fame through its baseball exploits at Kōshien. Under Japanese manager Kondō Hyōtarō, a former standout player on a mainland middle school championship team, the Jiayi team stormed Japanese student baseball's sacred ground from 1931 to 1936 as Taiwan's regional representative. In 1931, the team even advanced to the finals. The Jiayi nine's diamond exploits were all the more noteworthy in light of the equipment shortage they chronically endured and the short training hours they could afford; most Jiayi students came from laboring families and had to work part time while attending school.[57] The Jiayi squad was also unique within Japanese intraimperial baseball in that it was a "racially integrated," triethnic roster. Its 1931 starting roster was composed of two Han Taiwanese, four Taiwan aborigines, and three Japanese players. Historian Andrew Morris speculates that the Taiwanese members saw their victories over Japanese rivals as a statement of Taiwanese (Han or aborigine) excellence that could not be summarily dismissed by the Japanese.⁵⁸

Industrial Semipro Clubs Take the Field in Japan

Baseball fever was so intense across Japan's imperial domain in the interwar period because heat was also being generated by another dynamo: the industrial semipro league. World War I, fought mostly in Europe, was an economic boon to Japan, and many private enterprises were able to expand their operational scales, riding the crest of the robust business upturn fueled by the far-flung war.⁵⁹ The industrial sectors that did well in this boom cycle, particularly railroad and steel, became flush with internal resources with which companies and public railroad bureaus could sponsor baseball clubs. At a time when professional baseball did not yet exist, Japanese industrial league clubs typically became the destination of former student star players, who could continue to play baseball almost exclusively after graduation with the assurance of a spot on the full-time company or public sector payroll. Soon two men who were former collegiate star players, now established sports journalists, took the initiative to organize an intraimperial tournament for this expanding group of semipro players. Hashido, now a renowned sports writer, and Ono Michimaro, a former Keio ace pitcher, took up the banner together, touring Korea and southern Manchuria to drum up support for this proposed national enterprise. The two founding brothers, both great admirers of American professional baseball, structured it as an intercity tournament, a format inspired by the majors' franchise system. In August 1927, the first Intercity National Tournament began, with corporate sponsorship by the *Osaka Asahi Shinbun* and the *Tokyo Nichinichi*.⁶⁰

It proved to be a winning format. The idea of city-based identity and allegiance underpinning the tournament caught on in a country experiencing rapid industrialization, urbanization, and centrifugal social forces and demographic shifts resulting from that historical process. By fulfilling people's yearning for belonging amid social fluidity and geographical dispersion, this annual summer baseball ritual became massively popular in the late 1920s and 1930s, and this sporting institution, too, became a vehicle for shaping and nourishing Japan's grassroots imperial imagination. The twelve semipro industrial clubs assembled at its inaugural national tournament included two teams representing cities in the imperial outposts, Seoul and Dalian. The tournament's inaugural champion, Dalian's Mantetsu (Southern Manchurian Railway) Club, consisted mostly of former Tokyo Big 6 star players freshly recruited from the mainland. Its manager's remarks in the postgame interview made poignant reference to the colonial-metropolitan ties mediated through semipro baseball. After a shutout victory over the All-Osaka Club in the tournament finals, Dalian's field manager attributed the glory of the inaugural national championship to "the inspiration I and my players have drawn from the 200,000 *dōhō* [consanguineous compatriots] in the Liadong Peninsula." That Dalian's representative squad won the national semipro championship flag for three consecutive years until 1930 no doubt had the collateral effect, in the eyes of those who loved baseball, of naturalizing the city's place within Japan's imperium. These multiple seasonal civic rituals built around baseball, both amateur and semipro, gave flesh and bones to the grassroots imperial imagination in apolitical and deceptively benign ways, symbolically ennobling Japan's colonial project. Viewing these imperial outposts represented year after year as a part of "peaceful" national athletic competition naturalized their place within the empire and obscured from view the colonial violence that enabled their presence in the tournament to begin with. To that extent, colonial rule could be affirmed through seemingly innocent activities, such as going to the ballpark and cheering for one's favorite team and players. Even before the Japanese militarist state began to assert itself within its own territorial expanse and elsewhere in Asia in the 1930s, baseball had thus helped forge and reinforce an imperial identity for the fun-loving Japanese populace by lending its metaphorical power, and thus legitimacy, to the nation's colonial project.[61]

Grassroots imperial imagination could also be fostered by student baseball squads' barnstorming. In the interwar period, an increasing number of Japanese student and semipro teams began to tour overseas, not only eastward to Hawaii and the U.S. mainland but also westward to Japan's colonial possessions in East Asia. Starting with Waseda's 1916 tours to southern Manchuria, Korea, and Taiwan, Tokyo Big 6 squads and several colleges and middle schools in western Japan barnstormed in these northern colonial outposts in the summer and the Philippines in the winter. Like Stagg, many school administrators and team managers thought of these overseas tours as a publicity generator and a recruitment tool. Because of its proximity and the ease of travel, Taiwan emerged as a favored destination for schools in western Japan. The cost of these student tours was usually covered by gate receipts, alumni donations, and other school resources, but in Taiwan's case, expatriate trading firms, a local daily (the *Taiwan Nichinichi Shinbun*), and a consortium of smaller local Japanese-language newspapers often worked in cooperation with the governor-general's office to bankroll the athletic junkets.⁶²

The student baseball tours traveled in the other direction, too. In 1925, a nineteen-member squad, nicknamed Nōkōdan after the nearby mountain, from the Taiwanese eastern coast prefecture of Karen, toured Japan. The squad was made up exclusively of aboriginal children of the Ami tribe. Behind this much publicized travel to the Japanese mainland was Karen's colonial administrator, Eguchi Ryōzō, who sought to use the aboriginal players' baseball prowess to draw attention to "progress" toward civilization purportedly made by inhabitants in his outlying prefecture. While Eguchi no doubt loved baseball, his ultimate goal in showcasing "native" sporting accomplishment was to attract investment by mainland capital to build a port that would make this eastern coast area more accessible to the regional maritime network. The team played a series of games in Kyoto, Osaka, and Yokohama. The box scores, which listed the athletes' Japanese names, belied the players' true identity as aboriginals. Three aboriginals on the team were later recruited as players by a middle school in Kyoto.⁶³

Nikkei Baseball in Hawaii and North America

In the first few decades of the twentieth century, overseas Japanese and Japanese American (and Canadian) communities in Hawaii, the U.S. mainland, and Canada's western provinces also became home to multitiered baseball leagues. While these circuits were institutionalized first and foremost as part of the local networks of play, they often spun transnational links to Japan's "national" and "imperial" baseball networks through circulation of players, barnstorming tours, and diasporic imaginations embraced by players, spectators, and organizers. Given Issei's familiarity with the game, it is not surprising that they began to form baseball teams wherever they moved in substantial numbers. For Issei, the game gave them more than a social and recreational outlet. It also afforded them a means to connect with their American-born sons, to take pride in a Nisei son's Americanness. Such intergenerational mutual identification was particularly meaningful for the entire Nikkei community, where a legal divide in citizenship status existed between the generations and within households.⁶⁴ Baseball also helped Nikkei communities dispel suspicion of white Americans, make friendly contact, and create arenas of sociability with members of the surrounding society. For Nisei in particular, baseball constituted a cultural passport to acceptance by the white mainstream society, allowing them to enact their assimilability or cultural citizenship and, of course, to simply have a good time on the diamond.[65] The game also provided a way for Nikkei communities to mitigate or obscure the often divisive impulses spawned by religious divides, rivalry among different *ken* (i.e., the Japanese prefecture from which an Issei came), and other fault lines of intraethnic struggles.

One of the earliest of Issei Japanese baseball teams known to have appeared in mainland North American was the Fuji Athletic Club, formed in San Francisco. Among the team's founding brothers was Chiura Obata, who later became an art professor at the University of California at Berkeley. Born in the northern Japanese city of Sendai, Obata arrived in San Francisco in 1903 by way of Tokyo; he served an apprenticeship to a painter in the Bay Area and tried to carve out gainful employment as a commercial artist. The Fuji Club soon found a playing partner in another Issei team, the KDC. Organized by Shohei "Frank" Tsuyuki, it was made up of young men hailing from Kanagawa Prefecture who began to play in the city's parks and sandlots. Other early Issei teams in the Bay Area included the Oakland Asahi and the Harbor View nine of San Francisco.[66]

The 1906 San Francisco earthquake caused a wide range of dislocation in the area, and it forced some Issei to leave the city to look for work elsewhere, among them KDC founder Tsuyuki, who headed south to California's Central Valley. Between 1903 and 1915, many Nikkei baseball teams began to appear in new agricultural communities in Florin, Stockton, Sacramento, Lodi, and San Jose. Setsuo Aratani, Obata's Hiroshima-born teammate in the Fuji Athletic Club, also moved south after the earthquake. He ultimately settled in Guadalupe, near San Luis Obispo. He later acquired thousands of acres of agricultural land and established a successful vegetable-growing business. The wealth accumulated from commercial agriculture in central California enabled him to sponsor a Nisei semipro baseball team, the Guadalupe Packers. Other Issei who achieved success in the growing ethnic economy would also become financial backers and owners of Japanese American semipro teams in the economically flush times of the 1920s.[67]

California's Central Valley, in which many Japanese agricultural laborers settled, emerged as an epicenter of Japanese American baseball in the 1920s. In 1904, a young Issei named Abiko Kyūtarō, a San Francisco newspaper publisher, started a utopian settlement known as the Yamato Colony in California. It, too, had its own ball club, which regularly played against other Central Valley Nikkei teams, such as the Lodi nine. In Sacramento, a team called the Nippon Cubs played in the city's Municipal Baseball League in the 1920s.[68] Many Japanese agriculture laborers gravitated toward California's fertile Santa Clara Valley, where they established a Japantown adjacent to the existing Chinatown at the northern city limits of San Jose. The Asahi Club was one of the first Issei teams to be formed in San Jose in 1913. Nikkei baseball spread farther south to Fresno, Florin, and Stockton. The L.A. Nippons, the "pride of Little Tokyo," became part of the Los Angeles County League, playing other semipro and merchant clubs.

Up north, the formation of Japanese communities in the state of Washington lagged about ten years behind California. Settlement by Issei in and around Seattle was stimulated by the opening of Nippon Yusen's Seattle route in 1896, closely followed by the Canadian Pacific Company's Asia routes. Nippon Yūsen's ocean transport route was linked up with the Great Northern Railroad, the fifth transcontinental railroad, which reached Seattle in 1893. By the second decade of the twentieth century, the state of Washington had nearly 13,000 Japanese residents, with 7,000 to 8,000 in the city of Seattle alone.[69] The city's pioneer Issei teams, the Seattle Nippon and the Seattle Mikados, were formed around 1904. By 1910, an all-Issei league had developed in Seattle, and its teams sometimes played not only among themselves but against the area's all-white squads as well. The Seattle Mikados were one of the local squads that challenged the University of Chicago's Maroon baseballers before the latter's first Japan trip. By 1920, Seattle boasted its own Asahi club, organized by Frank Fukada, an Issei banker and teacher. In 1928, the *Japanese-American Courier*, a Seattle-based weekly newspaper, began promoting baseball and other recreational activities as a means of "strengthening cohesion and reinforcing 'American' ideals within the Japanese community." In its heyday, the *Japanese-American Courier* baseball league would administer thirty-five teams under its organizational umbrella. It also acted as a local sponsor and booking agent for barnstorming squads from Japan proper and Japanese Americans traveling from elsewhere through the Pacific Northwest.[70] The Wapato Nippons, active after the early 1900s, were another early Issei team in the state. Baseball was also a popular recreation among Japanese agricultural laborers and their Nisei children in the Yakima Valley in the state of Washington.[71]

Japanese American baseball clubs in British Columbia should also be situated within the network of Japanese diasporic baseball in North America. The earliest Japanese settlers in British Columbia were stowaways and drifters. One of them, Nagano Manzō, a fisherman from Nagasaki, arrived in New West Minster near the mouth of the Fraser River in 1877 as a boiler man working on a British ship. Early Japanese settlers to British Columbia were mostly lumbermen, fishermen, and miners. The Japanese population in British Columbia numbered 4,515 in 1900, but between 1907 and 1908, 7,600 more Japanese entered Canada. Many of them were transfer migrants from Hawaii seeking to thwart the U.S.-Japanese Gentlemen's Agreement and enter the United States via Canada. The sharp rise in the city's Japanese population led to an anti-Japanese riot in Vancouver in 1907.[72] As it so happened, the first newspaper article about Japanese baseball appeared in the same year. It was about a contest between a Japanese baseball team and a black baseball squad. The Japanese team lost 13–7. Another Japanese team, the Fuyō Club, was formed in Vancouver in July 1907.[73]

Vancouver, too, had its own Asahi Baseball Club, formed in 1914 by five young Japanese men who hailed from the same village in Shiga.[74] The team, comprising both Japanese-born and Canadian-born players, was organized around the community's Japanese-language school and was a means by which Japanese community leaders tried to dispel local white Canadians' suspicion about Japanese-language instruction for second-generation Canadian citizens. Like its namesake in Hawaii, the Vancouver Asahi became the pride of the local Japanese community because the squad, as one of the eight teams that constituted the Vancouver City League, often beat its white Canadian rivals. After 1918, the Vancouver Asahi played regularly against Japanese American teams in Seattle and Tacoma across the international border, including the Seattle Asahi. Crossing the international boundary was a matter of daily business in the U.S.-Canadian borderland, and seven hours on night trains on the Great Northern Railway brought the most distant teams together for a game. After 1928, these eleven Nikkei teams competed in the North American Pacific Northwest Japanese Baseball Championship. The area's Japanese-language newspapers, Vancouver's *Tairiku Nippoō* and Seattle's *Hokubei Jiji*, donated a trophy to the event. The rise of stable regional circuits was enabled by the gradual maturation of local ethnic economies and greater security in the lives of Japanese nationals and their offspring on the labor migration frontiers.[75]

In the late 1910s, Nisei players, as a new demographic bloc, started to rise through the ranks of Nikkei baseball in the Pacific Northwest. Many of them were recruited from Hawaii because as native-born American citizens they could move to the U.S. mainland even after the Gentlemen's Agreement virtually choked off Japanese labor migration to the United States. Many of them worked as farm laborers in California's expanding agriculture during the week and played baseball only on the weekends. The large influx of Hawaiian Nisei ballplayers, many of them veterans of the Honolulu Asahi and well seasoned in the competitive cauldron of the Hawaii League, pushed baseball on the U.S. mainland to a more competitive level. As the player base expanded, Japanese American community leagues sprang up across the U.S. West, and some had a big enough base of local supporters to go semipro, another marker of the ethnic capital accumulation and a cultural manifestation of the economic growth of Japanese America. In the 1920s, the Northern California Japanese Baseball League included high-powered semipro teams like the Alameda Taiiku-kai, the Lodi Templers, the Mt. Eden Cardinals, the San Jose Asahi, the Sebastopol Sakura, the Stockton Yamato, and the Walnut Grove Deltans. In the Central Valley, the Independent League included the Clovis Commodores, the Fresno Athletic Club (FAC), and George Aratani's Guadalupe Packers. Still largely excluded from white society, these Nikkei teams initially played games against one another in the 1920s, yet they could not help being a microcosm of mainstream white America. At the same time that a more organized "farm system" in organized baseball was developed by the St. Louis Cardinals' innovative manager Branch Rickey, Japanese American baseball built a multitiered system of talent development of its own. It consisted of the A-league, which represented semipro ability; the B-league, which was high school level; and the C-league, the junior-high level. The talent pipelines in white-only organized baseball and those in Japanese American baseball bore an uncanny resemblance to each other, even across the walls of racial exclusion.[76]

Just as Japanese American baseball grew into a multilayered league structure within a given area, it also expanded geographically, spreading outside the Pacific Coast to the Rocky Mountain states of Utah, Colorado, Wyoming, and Idaho. By 1920 eight Nisei teams played in a league that spanned the Rocky Mountain region. Nisei baseball ranged from as far south as the Tijuana Nippon to the Vancouver Asahi in the north, and from the Hawaiian Asahi in the west to the Nebraska Nisei in the east.[77] As early as 1914, Nisei semipro teams began to travel transregionally, as did white collegiate athletes. The more ambitious and better funded among them even sailed across the Pacific to barnstorm in the Japanese main islands. Arguably, such mainland Nisei barnstorming tours were an athletic variation of the *kengakudan*, Nisei study tours of the ancestral land that increased in numbers after the mid-1920s.[78] The first Nisei team to venture to Japan was Frank Fukuda's Seattle Asahi. Their 1914 trip was sponsored by two newspaper companies, the *Tokyo Nichinichi* and its affiliate in western Japan, *Osaka Nichinichi*. The Seattle Asahi engaged college and semipro industrial squads in the Japanese mainland again in August 1921. Along with a Native American squad, the Sherman Indians, the team was hosted by the Nippon Undō Kyōkai, a professional club newly organized in Tokyo. The Seattle Asahi left Victoria on the same steamship as the University of Washington squad, whose Japan tour was sponsored by Waseda. The roster for the Seattle Asahi's second Japan tour was bolstered by four Caucasian American "stringers" recruited from the semipro city league and the local industrial league. The reason for the interracial reinforcement was to make sure that the team's offensive power would be up to par with that of the Japanese professionals.[79]

The Seattle Asahi's trip, successful both commercially and in terms of bonding with the Japanese homelanders, paved the way for other Nisei semipro clubs to cross the Pacific to visit their parents' homeland for challenge, profit, and recognition. The next one up was the Honolulu Asahi, captained by "Banzai" Noda. It was a victory march of sorts for the Nisei team, which had just won the 1915 all-Hawaii interethnic championship to the rapturous delight of Hawaii's Nikkei community. In 1924, the *Osaka Mainichi* newspaper partially funded a Japan tour by the Fresno Athletic Club, composed of top-of-the-line Nisei players drawn from the entire San Joaquin Valley. Spearheading the powerful semipro squad was Kenichi Zenimura, often referred to as the dean of Japanese American baseball. Born in Hiroshima in 1900, Zenimura moved to Hawaii as a boy, cut his teeth in baseball in Oahu's sandlots, and won a place on the roster of the Honolulu Asahi. In 1920 Zenimura left Hawaii for the U.S. mainland in search of further challenge. While working in a restaurant and as a mechanic, Zenimura organized the area's Nisei standouts into the FAC. During their 1924 Japan trip, Zenimura's Nisei all-stars compiled an undefeated record against Japanese college and industrial teams, putting the overseas Nisei talent pool on the radar screen of homeland baseballers. The FAC returned to Japan in 1927 with a squad that included three Caucasian American players recruited from Fresno State College. In 1937, the FAC toured Japan for the third and, as it turned out, last time. Again, the tour fielded a racially mixed roster. This time, the Californians extended their journey to Korea and Manchuria. The San Jose Asahi also crossed the

Pacific in 1924, and this team, too, barnstormed in Japan's colonial outposts. The extended itineraries of these Nisei tours show that the Japanese imperium was becoming integrated as a network for semiprofessional baseball. Further, the growing presence of white "stringers" on their roasters adumbrated the erosion, if not yet elimination, of informal racial barriers in California's amateur and semipro baseball.[80]

In 1928, another all-Nisei baseball team from Stockton, the Yamato Athletic Club, stopped and played in Hawaii on its way to Japan. There the California squad recruited a local high school standout named Henry Tadashi Wakabayashi as an extra pitcher. Born in 1908 on the island of Oahu to a family of freeholding pineapple growers from Hiroshima, Wakabayashi was a typical Hawaii Nisei standout in that he commenced his baseball career as a member of the Honolulu Asahi. Barnstorming through Japan, Korea, and Dalian, the Stockton Yamato prevailed over the mainlanders, compiling an 18–6 record against the Tokyo Big 6 and industrial clubs. Wakabayashi's decision to join his *dōhō* from California for a summer of fun and adventure changed his life forever. The young Nisei took to the country his parents had come from — so much so that he decided to go to college there. Wakabayashi became an ace pitcher for Hosei University and one of the early stars of Tokyo Big 6.[81]

Going to Japan as a member of the 1931 L.A. Nippon tour similarly affected George Matsuura's life. Through the contacts he made in Japan, Matsuura would be recruited six years later by a newly organized Japanese professional team, the Nagoya club. That same year the Alameda Kono All-Stars, comprising central and northern California's top Nisei players, traveled to Japan, Korea, and Manchuria. Four of the Alameda players stayed in Japan to play in the infant professional baseball league. Serving as the Alameda Kono All-Stars' assistant coach was Kenso Nushida. Born in Hilo on the "big" island, Nushida launched his semipro career as a pitcher for the Honolulu Asahi. In 1923, the "Boy Wonder," the moniker that stuck with him into adulthood because of his diminutive five-foot frame, toured the U.S. West Coast on a Hawaiian all-star team. In 1932, Nushida would become the first Japanese American to become a Class AA Pacific Coast Leaguer when he had a brief stint with the Sacramento Solons.[82] The peripatetic careers of these Nisei semipros show how the baseball networks in the American West, Hawaii, and Japan became intertwined, until World War II disrupted them. These transpacific baseball circuits and talent pipelines fed the Janus-faced Japanese empire, a political formulation encompassing both labor migration frontiers in the east and colonial frontiers in the west.

World War I left Japan, a nominal British ally, physically unscathed yet rewarded with new semicolonial territories in China and the South Pacific taken over from defeated Germany. The military conflict fought mostly in Europe also helped prime a robust war boom for geographically removed Japan. Amid the economic expansion, many of the preconditions for the evolution of baseball into a commercial enterprise began to appear. Foremost, leisure-time pursuits, embraced by larger segments of the populace with rising standards of living, became increasingly commercialized. This process, reinforced by industrial development and capital accumulation, gave rise to new types of entrepreneurs eager to fill those emergent social needs and commercial niches. The advent and rapid proliferation of a new mass-communications technology, the radio, provided an added catalyst for baseball's metamorphosis into a business after the mid-1920s.

As baseball achieved nationwide popularity in early twentieth-century Japan, contradictory tendencies tenuously coexisted in Japanese attitudes toward the game as a civic enterprise. By the late Meiji and early Taisho periods, star players in student and industrial semipro baseball were idolized at the ballparks and in the nationally integrated media, much like major-league standouts turned national celebrities in the United States during baseball's "Golden Age." So-called amateur tournaments came to involve large-scale monetary transactions far beyond the collection of minimum gate fees to defray costs, and games among principal contenders featuring star players frequently entailed the payment of substantial guarantees and other forms of compensation. The talent search often resulted in sub-rosa payments of cash or gifts to student athletes and their adult guardians. Quests for technical excellence, spurred by rising competitiveness among clubs and teams, generated inexorable pressures for the sport's professionalization from organizers, players, and spectators alike.

Creeping commercialism in turn elicited a range of ideological responses from old guards and amateur sport purists, including discomfort over, if not downright aversion to, the play-for-pay movement. Such initial ambivalence about baseball's commercialization was in no way unique to Japan, where the discourse of ascetic Bushido baseball first emerged with Ichikō baseball and the dogma of idealized student amateur baseball embedded itself in the nation's modern sport ideology. As David Voigt has documented, commercialized baseball's origins in the United States—much murkier than the Cincinnati Red Stockings' 1869 "immaculate conception" myth postulates—were similarly fraught with uncertainties and ambivalence about how, or whether, to legitimize the game as a business, while the lure of good money and fans' increasing willingness to pay to see skilled play was making professional ball playing a coveted vocation, especially among working-class youths.[83] Even after the birth of professional leagues in the 1870s, some of baseball's stakeholders in America, particularly custodians of student athletics, wrestled continually with the question of where to draw the line between amateur and remunerated play. Commercial play was a force that organized athletic enterprises with a popular appeal would inevitably confront, albeit to varying degrees, in a capitalist, industrializing society. In Japan's case, however, the ambivalence about commercialized baseball was laden with an added layer of colloquy because recreation and entertainment—or "fun and games"—as forms of experiential consumerism were often associated with the distinct but closely related historical arcs of the nation's modern history: Westernization and American-style consumer modernity.[84] As baseball frenzy in Japan grew, so did this unresolved tension in Japan's sport ideology.

4. THE BUSINESS OF BASEBALL

Just as "winter ball" in Mexico and Cuba evolved into a commercially viable seasonal institution of American organized baseball in the early decades of the twentieth century thanks to improved trans-Caribbean transport, communications infrastructures, and a growing fan base, American baseballers began traveling across the Pacific in search of money, fame, challenge, and, of course, fun and adventure. The expansion of regular passenger-liner services in the first decade of the twentieth century accelerated with the opening in 1905 of the Canadian Pacific Railroad's new bimonthly ocean-liner routes originating from Vancouver. Now with three major ports of embarkation along the North American continent, transpacific oceanic travels became more affordable and reliable, furthering the integration of the circum-Pacific regions as a social field, a site of cultural cross-pollination, and a market for commercial entertainment. Baseball was but one of many cultural and business forms that flowed through this widening transnational circuit.[1] By sports sociologist Kiku Kōichi's count, in a ten-year period between 1905 and 1915 alone, twenty American, Japanese, and Filipino amateur baseball teams, the bulk of them collegiate, toured across the Pacific and engaged one another on baseball diamonds.[2]

Paralleling this growing traffic in amateur baseball, various formats of commercialized squads began venturing out of the U.S. West Coast to offer their athletic virtuosity and visual spectacles for pay in Hawaii, Japan, and the Philippines. Some traveled with sophisticated business prearrangements. Others took off with only preliminary or tentative plans—or no plans at all. Every American professional expedition introduced new business and crowd-pleasing elements to Japanese baseball and left a taste of what playing ball commercially was like. By the beginning of the 1930s, swaggering big leaguers were ready to travel west to Asia on this well-trodden route of American athletic entertainers. They found a fitting partner in the ambition and promotional genius of a Japanese media magnate. The result was the major leagues' first formal postseason tour to Japan in 1931.

The Reach All-Americans' 1908 Far Eastern Tour

The first American baseball professionals to hit the shores of Japan were the Reach All-Americans, a traveling team of four major leaguers recruited from the upstart American League, including Pat Flaherty of the Boston Nationals, and fourteen minor leaguers based in California. The amalgamated troupe, which landed in Japan in late November 1908, was assembled by the A. J. Reach Company, a sporting-goods company founded in 1874 and headquartered in Philadelphia. The team's manager was Mike Fisher, a key mover of the Pacific Coast League. The life of the A. J. Reach Company's founder, Albert Reach, an English-born former second baseman for the Brooklyn Eckford club and the Philadelphia Athletics, epitomized the growth of baseball as a business and the monopolistic enterprise it had become in Gilded Age America. Reach's contemporaries, including A. G. Spalding, considered him America's very first baseball professional when Brooklyn's star infielder was recruited away by the Philadelphia Athletics club, or A's, in 1865 for a full-time salary of twenty-five dollars. Upon retiring from his position as the team's playing manager in 1875, Reach bought into the incorporation of the Philadelphia Phillies, a franchise in the newly organized National League, and served as the club's president between 1883 and 1899. In the interim, Reach the entrepreneur ran a variety of retail businesses in Philadelphia. In 1881, he partnered with a Philadelphia sporting-goods manufacturer and small shareholder in the A's franchise, Benjamin Franklin Shibe. The result was the A. J. Reach Company. Having invented and popularized a novel two-piece cover for baseballs, Shibe supplied manufacturing knowledge and Reach the sales skills and business connections. It was a winning combination.[3]

As the sporting-goods markets grew in the 1880s, Reach's company at one point threatened to cut seriously into Spalding & Brothers' market shares and even began publishing its own "official" annual baseball guide in 1882 to compete with *Spalding's Official Base Ball Guide*, the NL's annually published baseball authority. Spalding responded to this challenge the same way he had been dealing with other lesser competitors, that is, by buying them. Ever a shrewd businessman, Spalding allowed the A. J. Reach Company to keep its name after the 1889 buyout so his company's monopolistic presence might not be flagrantly apparent. Reach himself was given an executive position within Spalding & Brothers. While Big Al's company continued to exclusively supply balls, equipment, and uniforms to the National League, the American League, acknowledged grudgingly by the NL as another "major" in 1903, designated the A. J. Reach Company as its official ball and equipment supplier and publisher of annual baseball guides. Thus, the advent of the era of two big leagues did not in the slightest affect Spalding & Brothers' monopolistic reign in the industry. Not coincidentally, Reach was handpicked by Spalding to serve on the Mills Commission, which shamelessly ratified the Doubleday-Cooperstown mythology.[4]

The Reach All-Americans' 1908 "Oriental Tour" was officially endorsed by American League president Ban Johnson. It reflected American pro baseball's "imperial turn" in the new century at a number of levels. For one, as boasted in the company's (and the AL's) post-tour report, it was the first "round-the-world" tour since the 1888–89 Spalding World Tour, a grand venture that supposedly "made more converts to the great National Game in every location it played." By making a foray into countries not reached by Spalding's preceding mission, the Reach All-Americans purported to extend the gospel of American baseball farther and wider on behalf of organized baseball. The tour's officially stated goal expressed bluntly the imperial vision propelling the "Oriental" venture. The touring athletes were going to "Americanize" through baseball the inhabitants of the newly acquired colonial possession, the Philippines. In *The Reach Official Base Ball Guide*, American schoolteachers were lauded effusively for their "commendable work" the past several years in guiding Filipino boys in acquiring "the physique and the wholesome spirit that go with that most excellent of games," and baseball "promise[d] to become universal . . . long before the English language accomplishes that feat." The Reach All-Americans' other key objective was to serve U.S. Army troops stationed in the far-flung colonial outpost by giving them holiday entertainment. True to this goal, the Reach All-Americans arrived in Manila on Christmas Day and played a total of ten games in the colonial capital, six against U.S. Army teams and four pickup matches with American expatriates in Manila and Filipino boys enrolled in secondary schools run by American Protestant missionaries. The tour departed for its next and last stop, Honolulu, on January 8, 1809. En route to Hawaii, the touring squad played one quick game against a U.S. Navy team in Shanghai to make the most of the ocean liner's coaling and resupplying stop in the treaty port.[5]

Although the Reach All-Americans' main destination was the Philippines, Japan was as much a point of interest to the tour's organizers. Baseball's popularity in the rising Asian nation had long been known to the A. J. Reach Company and its parent company headquartered in Chicago. This very first visit by American professionals was expected to raise baseball mania in Japan to a higher pitch. Besides, since the *Pacific Mail* ocean liner on which they journeyed made scheduled stops in Yokohama and Kobe along the route, it made good business sense to schedule exhibition games during layovers. The touring ballplayers left San Francisco on November 3, 1908, reaching Yokohama on November 22, and played—and won all of—seventeen games against Japan's top collegiate teams, Waseda and Keio, their combined all-stars, club teams made up of former collegiate standouts, and American expatriates in Tokyo, Yokohama, and Kobe. Because of considerable prearrival publicity in the Tokyo and Osaka metropolitan newspapers and baseball magazines, an average of six thousand spectators attended these games, an impressive number considering that Japan's playing fields, only recently enclosed, did not yet have so much as wooden grandstands.[6]

The Reach All-Americans' clean sweep was an ego-crushing experience for Tokyo's top collegiate players, who were growing accustomed to public adoration as vigorous masculine heroes in Japan's nascent metropolitan sport culture. The humiliation was particularly bruising for the Waseda nine, which on November 28 lost their second game to the Reach All-Stars, 3–0, with the Reach hurler pitching a perfect game.[7] Commentators humbly acknowledged the gaping technical gap between themselves and the American professionals, conceding that their Japanese athletic heroes had been "girly fish in a tiny Japanese pond."[8] Three years after Abe Isoo and his Waseda squad brought back state-of-the-art American baseball techniques and strategies, the Japanese, both players and spectators, were treated to the American professionals' play in live action and were simply awed by their speed and superior skills. The direct exposure to American pros' technical mastery thus germinated the idea among Japan's baseball devotees that achieving higher levels of play, and someday catching up with Americans, would require full-time devotion to the "craft" by dedicated—and paid—experts.

The Japanese made other discoveries in the Reach All-Americans' performance that would warm them to the concept of trained specialists playing baseball for pay. They were deeply struck by the serious "craftsmanship" with which the visiting American and Pacific Coast Leaguers played all seventeen of their games. Many contrasted it favorably with the previous year's barnstormer, Hawaii's semipro team St. Louis, which appeared to deliberately let Keio win a game as a misguided courtesy to the host. At the same time, Japanese baseball lovers were able to sample a taste of the crowd-pleasing flair and gaiety of commercialized baseball showmanship. At the beginning of the Reach All-Americans' first game in Japan, versus Waseda, team manager Fisher led the college's founder and chancellor, Count Ōkuma Shigenobu, clad in frock coat, from the bleachers to the pitcher's mound. Pitcher Jack Granney switched Ōkuma's top hat with his white baseball cap. Before the puzzled crowd of eight thousand, a flustered yet amused Ōkuma was then prompted by Granney to throw a ball into the catcher's mitt. The seventy-year-old former opposition parliamentarian with an artificial leg—the casualty of a bombing attack by an ultrarightist—smilingly obliged. The ritual of an attending dignitary throwing the ceremonial first pitch was thus introduced to Japan. That was almost two years before William Howard Taft established the precedent for the ritual of the president opening each season by throwing out the ceremonial first ball—a tradition that has survived until the present day.[9]

The Major-League World Tour of 1913–14

Five years after the Reach All-Americans' tour of Asia, international tensions were mounting perilously in the Old World. But organized baseball launched another overseas venture, and this time it was an around-the-world expedition undertaken by a combined force of National and American Leaguers. Billed at the time as one of the grandest events in the history of American sports, the 1913–14 major leagues' world tour was designed to parade America's commanding stature among the world's powers through the game its people had come to call their national institution. It was the brainchild of two towering figures in organized baseball in the early twentieth century: John McGraw, president and part owner of the New York Giants and the legendary National League manager whose detractors called him the "Little Napoleon," and Charles Comiskey, owner of the Chicago White Sox. Conceived on a cold December night in an alcohol-stoked conversation at a bar on Chicago's East Side, the 1913–14 tour was indeed one of the most ambitious sporting enterprises ever undertaken.[10]

The motive behind this bold venture was both professional and personal. For McGraw, it was a second attempt to put his team on display abroad; in 1896, he had explored the idea of touring Europe with his Baltimore Orioles, but the plan never materialized. Both McGraw and Comiskey despised Spalding on a number of accounts. For one, they considered the carnival-like atmosphere that flavored Spalding's 1888–89 world tour unbecoming to the serious athletic and freestanding professional enterprise that baseball had become in the intervening quarter century. Both men disapproved of the way the tour was used ostentatiously as a Spalding & Brothers' marketing tool. The duo naturally took delight in the idea of upstaging Spalding's self-congratulatory exploit on its twenty-fifth anniversary. In its geographical coverage, theirs would certainly be a step above Spalding's antecedent by including three countries he had bypassed: Japan, China, and the Philippines. In truth, the 1913–14 tour's more northern path of circumnavigating the Pacific was fundamentally dictated by the Canadian Pacific Railroad's passenger-liner route. Yet major-league executives, Ban Johnson foremost among them, emphasized the significance of including Japan and China in the itinerary so that the "Asiatic" corner of the globe would be firmly harnessed to "our great national game" and baseball's "civilizing influence on the Philippines" would be replenished.[11]

Their dislike of Spalding notwithstanding, McGraw and Comiskey modeled their world tour after Big Al's 1888 prototype in one important way: they divided the tour into two parts, the first phase a barnstorming jaunt across the western half of the North American continent. The second phase was a maritime expedition to Japan, China, and points east (Australia, India, Ceylon, Egypt, Italy, France, and the British Isles). The idea was to make profits from the domestic leg of the tour to help cover the losses to be anticipated from the leg outside the U.S. continent. Still, Comiskey, putatively one of the richest men in baseball at the time, had to pick up most of the $90,000 tab for steamship travel. He also carried with him a letter of credit for 25,000 pounds sterling (about $121,000) to meet contingent expenses to be incurred overseas.

The baseball caravan, consisting of twenty-five players, two umpires each representing the NL and the AL, and families and officers, departed from the tour's point of origin, Cincinnati, on October 18. It was a rushed departure for sure; only five days earlier, the Giants had suffered a crushing 4–1 defeat to the Philadelphia Athletics in the 1913 World Series at their home grounds in New York. The star-studded amalgamated squad, fortified by several "borrowed" players such as the Detroit Tigers' slugging outfielder Sam Crawford and the Boston Red Sox's centerfielder Tris Speaker, made a whirlwind expedition across the lower Midwest,

Oklahoma, Texas, and Arizona and up through the three Pacific Coast states, playing thirty-one games in twenty-seven cities in thirty-four days. Roughly one hundred thousand local baseball enthusiasts were drawn to these first-ever matchups of the NL and AL clubs held west of the Mississippi. On November 19, the touring squad left the port of Victoria, British Columbia, on board RMS *Empress of Japan*, one of the crown jewels of the Canadian Pacific Railroad's biweekly shipping routes.[12]

After seventeen days of an energy-draining, nonstop ocean voyage, the players and their entourage reached the first overseas stop, Japan, on December 6, three days behind schedule because of tough sailing. Unfortunately, this delay, caused by a late-season typhoon in the Pacific, would force the cancellation of two games scheduled in western Japan (Osaka and Kobe), to the great disappointment of ticket holders there. The reception of the touring big leaguers in the port of disembarkation, Yokohama, carried a hint of official pomp and a sign of things to come during their brief three-day stay in the country. U.S. consul general Thomas Sammons and representatives from the Tokyo Mayor's Office were on hand to receive the visitors. The docks were jam-packed with flag-waving Japanese baseball enthusiasts and newspapermen. The tourists' mode of transportation to and from the Grand Hotel, the premier Western-style luxury hotel in Yokohama, was a convoy of rickshaws. The typhoon-truncated schedule forced the Americans to defy their fatigue from the sometimes hazardous seventeen-day sea voyage and immediately board a specially arranged train to the nation's capital. There they became the first major leaguers to play against each other before Japanese spectators, bursting with anticipation. A crowd of seven thousand filled Keio University's Tsunamachi baseball grounds, the venue for the game. Overflowing spectators occupied every available space, with many sitting on straw mats spread on the ground. The White Sox bested their National League opponent 9–4. On the following day, McGraw's nine took the victory, 12–9. Prior to this second match, the Giants–White Sox All-Stars played a courtesy exhibition game against Keio's student squad to thank the school for the use of the ground. Following the recently imported "tradition," Keio's president, Kamata Eikichi, threw the ceremonial first pitch to Consul General Sammons, crouching at home plate. From the newly built grandstand, Waseda's manager, Abe, looked on as a guest of honor. The score was a walloping 16–3 in favor of the American professionals.[13]

Like the Reach All-Americans' tour five years earlier, the direct engagement with the American pros presented an opportunity for Japanese players, organizers, and spectators to acquaint themselves with the finer points of "authentic" American baseball. They discovered and delighted in the novel concept of a doubleheader and were engrossed by the precision and intricacies of "inside baseball" masterfully orchestrated by its pioneer, McGraw. Two umpires accompanying the tour, Bill Klem and Jack Sheridan, demonstrated the latest styles and rigors of their craft. The Japanese were at once stunned and entertained by home plate umpire Klem's booming bass voice and elaborate gestures. Postgame commentary by observers expressed an unalloyed admiration for these professional umpires' rigorous execution of their "craft." At the same time, the American pros also amused the Japanese spectators with a game of shadow ball. Yet more than anything else, the big leaguers' supreme athletic talent and physical stamina left the Japanese awestruck. Even after two weeks of debilitating seasickness and travel fatigue, they subdued the Keio varsity squad hands down.

The Keio team, which included four future Japanese Hall of Fame inductees, was summarily humbled. Context is useful here to fully appreciate the sense of humility planted among the Japanese collegians. Baseball followers in Japan had been elated by the way the Keio team had acquitted itself against American collegians during its first barnstorming through the U.S. mainland in 1911. The Japanese collegiate ballplayers had also held their ground four games to three in a seven-game series against the vaunted U.S. Army all-star team visiting from the Philippines. Thus, Japanese baseball fans had reason to wonder whether their top collegians were getting close to parity with Americans. Now completely flattened, they were forced to acknowledge anew the gigantic technical gap that separated them from American major leaguers. Again, yearnings to enhance their play as full-time professionals stirred among this generation of top-notch Japanese baseballers, including Keio's ace pitcher, Sugase Kazuma, whose valiant efforts against the physically imposing American pros generated warm praise from spectators and commentators.[14]

The absence of the famed Christy Mathewson from the Giants' roster — he had bowed out of the overseas part of the tour for fear of seasickness — disappointed assembled Japanese fans, but for some, the tour's other attraction was Jim Thorpe, the hero of the 1912 Olympic Games in Stockholm, who had joined McGraw's National League dynasty at the beginning of the 1913 season. When this "rookie" Giant disembarked from the *Empress of Japan* in Yokohama, he and his honeymooning wife, Iva, were feted more loudly than anyone else in the delegation. A Native American born in 1888 in Oklahoma, Thorpe blossomed into a superb football player and all-round athlete while he was enrolled at the Carlisle Indian School in Pennsylvania. He gained worldwide renown and became America's national hero when he achieved the unprecedented feat of winning gold medals in both the pentathlon and decathlon at the Stockholm Olympics. But his Olympic glory was short lived. The United States Olympic Committee (USOC) shortly discovered that Thorpe had played minor-league baseball during the summers of 1909 and 1910 and, on that ground, disqualified him as an amateur. Thorpe was stripped of his medals, and his Olympic records were expunged. In a perverse irony, though, one of Thorpe's contributions as a member of the U.S. national team at the 1912 Olympiad was to play baseball, a demonstration sport in the games.[15]

Thorpe's fall from grace with the USOC, and its parent organization, the International Olympic Committee (IOC), revealed the contorted relationship between sports, class, amateurism, and the politics of labor and leisure—a tangled question that the modern international sporting community had only just begun to acknowledge, let alone address. Many Americans had trouble coming to terms with the Olympics' underpinning principle of amateurism, a concept originally developed by nineteenth-century aristocratic elites in Britain. In the 1910s, no firm consensus yet existed in the United States regarding how to define and systematically enforce amateur eligibility. A national sport governing body such as the National Collegiate Athletic Association (NCAA, established in 1905) had yet to get a handle on this knotty problem. In the early decades of the twentieth century, playing baseball for remuneration was a fairly common summer job among American collegiate ballplayers. The high-caliber players among them would earn extra money playing in minor leagues during summer recess. The less skilled but socially gifted often played ball to entertain well-heeled clientele in mountain vacation destinations and summer seaside resorts in the East.[16]

In the summers of 1910 and 1911, Thorpe played in the minor Eastern Carolina League for a meager wage of two dollars (no more than fifty dollars in current dollar terms) per game; hailing from an impoverished household, he needed to earn extra money during summer months. But unlike the savvier and better informed among his cohort—including latter-day major-league greats Lou Gehrig and Mickey Cochrane and future U.S. president Dwight D. Eisenhower—he did not play under an assumed name to protect his amateur eligibility. Once Thorpe lost his amateur status, all that remained of his career options was to become a bona fide professional athlete. Since there was no professional football in America yet, his logical choice was to play baseball. The major-league clubs, too, found the former Olympic champion's fame and box-office draw eminently attractive, and eight out of sixteen teams courted him. The best deal came from the New York Giants, which offered a three-year contract of $6,000 a year. When the planning for the off-season world tour began, Thorpe was one of the first Giants that McGraw recruited into this off-season project.[17]

The rise and fall of Thorpe's fortunes as an Olympian had been reported and known among Japan's sport enthusiasts partially because the 1912 Stockholm Games were the very first Olympics to which this rising Asian nation proudly sent its athletes. Sports-attuned Japanese sympathized with this fallen American hero, and the heightened national sensitivity of the day to the racial dimensions of U.S.-Japanese relations even led some to detect and decry racism at the roots of the American domestic controversies surrounding this Native American athlete. Some editorials even juxtaposed the USOC's harsh treatment of Thorpe with white Californians' anti-Japanese nativism, which had crystallized a few months previously in California's Alien Land Law. The 1913 legislation denied Issei, "aliens ineligible for citizenship," rights to own land and property in the state. During the Giants–White Sox tour, some of the Japanese attuned to this brewing problem in U.S.-Japanese relations expressed their racialized sense of camaraderie with Thorpe, whom they viewed as a fellow victim of white American racism, through warm cheers and synchronized chanting of his name with the title "Champion." Tellingly, similar public idolization of Thorpe by the locals resentful of Western-imposed racial hierarchy showed itself during the Shanghai and Hong Kong legs of the tour.[18] This metaphorical link drawn by some Asians between race, class, honor, and amateurism pointed to the emergence of a transpacific symbolic world in which sport came to play an important mediating role. In this cultural arena, athletes, both amateur and professional, functioned as carriers of social meanings, national identities, and ethnic pride.[19]

After the ensuing three months of globe-circling travel through the British imperium encompassing Asia's southeast and southern flanks, McGraw, Comiskey, and their ballplayers journeyed through the Middle East and western European capitals. On February 28, 1914, they sailed out of Liverpool and arrived in New York on March 4, just in time for spring training. They crossed the Atlantic on board the Cunard Line's luxury passenger ship *Lusitania*. Little did they know that, in two years' time, the sinking of this British luxury ocean liner by a German U-boat would push their country a notch closer to entering the Great War, soon to be triggered by a Serbian assassin's bullet.

Herb Hunter and the Making of an American Baseball Ambassador to Japan

World War I put a temporary halt to organized baseball's interest in overseas promotional efforts, but when peace returned and major-league baseball was on the cusp of its golden age, McGraw and Comiskey attempted to reprise their successful 1913–14 world venture by sending another combined exhibition squad overseas. This time, they only targeted Europe, where they hoped that "America's Game" would serve the cause of peace and postwar reconciliation. The expedition left directly from New York, now the undisputed global capital of wealth, information, and cultural influence. The duo's 1922 itinerary purported to take the American ballplayers to the British Isles, France, Belgium, Germany, and Italy, but the ill-conceived and poorly funded sport entertainment mission to a continent still reeling from the recent war got only as far as France before collapsing on the road.[20] On the Pacific side of organized baseball's field of vision, a much less ambitious but far more successful enterprise had been under way. In November 1920, a band of Pacific Coast Leaguers, spiced up with a handful of major leaguers from the East, toured through Japan to play exhibition games among themselves and against the four top-flight private-college teams now dominating the Tokyo metropolitan area's baseball landscape (Waseda, Keio, Meiji, and Hosei). On the roster of this hybrid troupe, somewhat deceptively billed the "All-American National Team," was Herbert Harrison Hunter, an obscure utility infielder who had just been traded from the Boston Red Sox to the St. Louis Cardinals.

By all standard measures of excellence, Hunter's career in major-league baseball up to that point had been less than illustrious. Joining McGraw's New York Giants in 1916, Hunter was traded at midseason to the Chicago Cubs, for which he played a grand total of five games in two seasons. Hunter played unceremoniously for the PCL's San Francisco Seals in the 1918 season and missed much of the 1919 season, serving in the U.S. Navy during Woodrow Wilson's war to make the world safe for democracy. In 1920, Hunter, now back in civilian life, attempted to resuscitate his baseball career on the roster of his hometown team, the Red Sox, but he again spent far more time warming the bench than playing. His contract was then sold to the Cardinals, but his performance there proved just as unimpressive. The year 1922 marked the end of his brief and unfulfilling major-league career. His "lifetime" record in the majors consisted of ninety-nine games played for four teams in four years with a batting average of .163.[21]

It was during this disheartening transition from Boston to St. Louis that Hunter landed the postseason gig—part playing and part umpiring—in the barnstorming tour headed for Japan. Despite its grandiloquent billing, the 1920 "All-American National" squad actually fielded only two players on an active major-league roster—Detroit Tigers catcher Edward Ainsmith and Brooklyn Robins (Dodgers) outfielder Wallace Hood. The rest comprised Pacific Coast Leaguers and Hunter, a token major leaguer. Regardless, this off-season job became a life-changing experience for this Bostonian who, at age twenty-five, was already in the twilight years of his career as a player. While in Japan, the visiting American professionals successfully replicated the splendor of the McGraw-Comiskey team's pre–World War I tour, dazzling baseball lovers in Tokyo and several other cities with twenty exhibition games. Again, they routed Japan's top-flight ballplayers, most of whom were collegians. Resignedly, Waseda's new manager, Tobita Tadayori (pen name: Suishū), compared his nine's 19–2 and 11–2 losses to the American visitors to "children brawling with adult men" and speculated that "even with a 100-run handicap, those Americans would still come [out] on top." Keio suffered back-to-back shutouts. Meiji and Hosei together could score only one run in two games.[22]

Early on in the Japan tour, Hunter took a liking to the country and its people so afflicted with baseball fever. He was enormously flattered by the adoring fans following him everywhere, but the real highlight of his stay came during the additional six weeks he spent in Japan. Although the tour was partially funded by the *Daimai* (*Osaka Mainichi*) newspaper company, the operation failed to break even. In order to cover the shortfall, Hunter took an offer to coach Japan's top-three collegiate squads—Waseda, Keio, and Meiji—after the tour ended. He coached the eager Japanese disciples in a dedicated fashion (even breaking his leg as he tried to demonstrate a slide) and thereby earned the trust of the grateful Japanese baseball fraternity. Abe even invited him to join Waseda's winter training camp in Nara, a picturesque ancient capital city that Hunter came to love. During these weeks of intensive interaction and male camaraderie, Hunter and his Japanese apprentices genuinely bonded and developed mutual respect for their shared devotion to the game.[23]

The connections and goodwill that Hunter cultivated during this visit—the first of seventeen that he would make over the next fifteen years—became a bonanza of social capital at the end of the following season, when he became a young ex–major leaguer in search of a new career. In the fall of 1921, Hunter returned to Japan, this time mainly to coach the Keio squad, but he was again courted by other Tokyo Big 6 players and managers and became something of a jointly owned treasure trove of "American baseball" expertise. This junket was followed in the fall of 1922 by a visit with an off-season exhibition tour of American pros headed by American League umpire George Moriarty. Reflecting Japan's growing allure as a market for baseball entertainment, its roster included major-league star players and future Hall of Famers such as pitchers Waite Hoyt and Joe "Bullet" Bush of the New York Yankees and George Kelly and Charles "Casey" Stengel of the New York Giants. The visiting Americans bested the Japanese challengers in all but one game.[24]

Touting his knowledge about and extensive connections in Japan, Hunter garnered a job serving this star-studded delegation as its "official guide." The 1922 troupe was billed as the "Hunter All-Stars" in the Japanese press—a fact that Moriarty, the tour's general manager, did not appreciate. The high profiles of its members sealed Hunter's reputation in Japan as an international baseball promoter. The timing could not have been better. Baseball was creating various opportunities for profit making in post–World War I Japan. Domestic sporting-goods manufacturers and retailers were competing fiercely for a piece of this growing market. Sports (particularly baseball) journalism was an emergent genre, and many newspapers were expanding their sports sections. These new industries had a vested interest in hyping baseball and its heroes. Hunter, after being released by the last of his four major-league affiliations, the St. Louis Cardinals, threw himself into this social matrix and groomed himself as Japan's conduit to organized baseball.

As he began to build a new career as a baseball impresario, Hunter had his Japanese admirers to rely on. In late 1921, an Osaka baseball-equipment company, seeking to outdo Mizuno's publicity genius, sent a letter to the *Sporting News* that lionized Hunter as American baseball's goodwill ambassador to Japan. This flattering write-up was accompanied by a photograph of Hunter in a Cardinals uniform alongside Takasu Kazuo, the captain of the Keio University team, with the caption: "Arm in Arm for Baseball." The material received big play on the front page of the magazine's "New Year" issue. The bible of American baseball boasted that "all the so-called 'peace conferences'" would have less real effect on U.S.-Japanese understanding than "the common ground of the diamond." The allusion was to the Washington Conference, held in the winter of 1921–22 to codify the international relations of post–World War I Asia. This self-congratulatory rhetoric of diamond diplomacy as being the real crafter of U.S.-Japanese *entent cordiale* held a kernel of truth that was no doubt unintended by the article's author. During the Japan tour in the fall, Hunter and his traveling major leaguers would deliver their visual display of U.S.-Japanese brotherhood forged through baseball to ballparks in Korea, southern Manchuria, and Taiwan. The tour's final destination was Manila.[25]

The 1922 tour that Hunter shepherded was also significant in that it was the first off-season exhibition tour sanctioned by Kenesaw Mountain Landis, organized baseball's inaugural one-man commissioner. A former federal judge with close ties to Chicago's Republican Party, Landis was put in the office by major-league club owners in 1921, replacing the previous three-person National Commission. The challenge that organized baseball then faced was to restore public confidence in the sport whose reputation and image had been badly tarnished by the 1919 Black Sox Scandal. Landis was picked by the club owners over other serious contenders for the position, including U.S. Army generals John Pershing and Leonard Wood, in part because he had been a compliant judge in the antitrust court challenge to organized baseball posed by the Federal League.[26] From the inception of this newly created one-man executive perch, Landis assumed almost unlimited authority as the final arbiter of organized baseball, becoming a power unto himself within the enterprise until his death in 1944.[27] One of the very first actions Landis took as commissioner was to enforce the ban on postseason barnstorming by players who participated in that year's World Series. Although on the books since 1911 in the form of a series of edicts designed to rein in players' postseason activities, the ban had been routinely ignored by top players, who knew their infraction would only cost them token fines, especially if their club owners were coconspirators. The New York Giants who had responded to McGraw's summons to the 1913–14 world tour were in fact among such purposeful transgressors. As inaugural baseball commissioner, Landis put an end to this state of benign neglect by enforcing the existing edicts.

Pointing to the openly racist views for which the former judge was well known, some critics claimed that Landis reinstated the ban because he wanted to prohibit World Series teams from barnstorming as a whole unit during the off-season; that is, as racist, he could not abide the "disgrace" of white major-league champions being beaten by Negro League clubs, even in postseason play. Given his role as federal judge in the permanent ban of African American boxer Jack Johnson from the sport and his dogged resistance to the major leagues' racial integration for the next quarter century, the charge was probably not too far off the mark. Others protested Landis's action as unwarranted interference by the new office and an abridgement of the players' right to off-season income and "additional experience" through postseason play. In August 1922, the commissioner amended this rule slightly: World Series participants could petition for permission to join a postseason exhibition tour, but only a maximum of three players from the most recent championship club could be included in a given squad. Landis made this rule modification in part to accommodate his friends in the Republican administration, including fellow former jurist Secretary of State Charles Evans Hughes, to utilize postseason baseball tours as a platform for reinforcing U.S.-Japanese amity in the post–World War I Far East.[28]

In November 1922, the majors' traveling troupe—headed by Moriarty, Landis's friend in Chicago baseball circles, and "guided" by Hunter, the "baseball ambassador" to Japan—played seventeen games against Japanese amateur and semipro clubs around the country. The American visitors' overall record of shattering wins was certainly to be expected, but it came with one surprise that had significant long-term ramifications: the major leaguers at the top of their game ceded one loss to the Mita Club, a squad composed of Keio varsity players and alumni, by a 9–3 score.[29] When news of this unexpected loss reached Landis by way of Moriarty, who charged Hunter with throwing the game, the iron-fisted commissioner exploded in anger—and not simply because the American pros had let foreign amateurs prevail in that particular game. For Landis, the loss represented a desecration of the supremacy—and perhaps the integrity, if it was indeed a thrown game—of white American manhood for which the game of baseball stood. The irate commissioner clamped down on major leaguers' postseason play all over again. Starting in 1923, the World Series teams' exhibition plans had to be approved first by the unanimous consent of the club owners of both leagues before they could even be submitted for the commissioner's consideration. In light of the big egos and disparate corporate interests clashing within organized baseball's highest echelon, this edict amounted to a virtual ban, which may well have been Landis's intention. Japanese baseball lore posits that as a result of this 1922 "game of infamy" in Tokyo, Landis became fearful of losing again to nonwhite, physically diminutive Asian ballplayers; this dread lay behind his reluctance, until 1930, to give his blessings to major leaguers' tours

The Business of Baseball | 123

to Japan.[30] More likely determents for Landis, however, were the massive earthquake that hit the greater Tokyo metropolitan area in September 1923 and the lack of large stadiums capable of making a cross-oceanic off-season venture profitable. These problems, more than Landis's racism, kept the major leagues' top echelon from contemplating a tour to Japan, at least for several years.

The Philadelphia Bobbies, 1925–26

The major leaguers and club owners were not the only American baseballers who saw new opportunities and pursued higher ambitions in the expanding transoceanic field of play in the Roaring Twenties. It was a time of overseas expansion of American commercial activities in general. The general economic prosperity at mid-decade democratized the idea of travel and gave inspiration and wherewithal to myriad categories of Americans, including hurlers, hitters, fielders, and runners who wished to explore the possibility of becoming a professional athlete within or outside the American nation's territorial boundaries. One such venturesome band of athletes was the Philadelphia Bobbies, an all-female baseball squad consisting of teenage girls and young women ranging in age from thirteen to twenty. This youthful outfit barnstormed through Japan from October 1925 through early January 1926. Its breakaway contingent even extended its journey to Korea.

As a social and cultural force in American history, the Philadelphia Bobbies, founded in 1922, were an offspring of the so-called Bloomer Girls, pioneer female baseball players who dated back to the 1860s. From the Gilded Age through the early decades of the twentieth century, a dozen or so baseball sororities appeared across the United States, mostly in the northeastern region. Some played for the simple pleasure of an afternoon on the diamond; others sought personal fulfillment in travel and adventure. In greater numbers they played for prizes, money, or other forms of compensation. They sometimes played against men as well as other women's teams. Until organized baseball developed the farm system and began training players on the climb to the big leagues systematically in this gender-segregated setting, many of these Bloomer Girl squads, whose rosters often mixed in a few men, provided playing partners and competition to male semipro players and minor leaguers. The Philadelphia Bobbies, who took their name from the "bob" hairstyle popular at the time, were a more self-consciously "professional" offspring of these free-spirited sporting women who had first taken the field in late nineteenth-century America.[31]

The Bobbies were the entrepreneurial dream incarnate of a twenty-six-year-old ballplayer and businesswoman named Mary O'Gara. A "New Woman" aspiring to become a "club owner," O'Gara performed multiple duties, playing center field for her own team, working with local and regional booking agents to schedule games as far afield as New York and Virginia, and chaperoning her adolescent charges when they traveled. The team she organized through tryouts was an uneven lot. Shortstop Edith Houghton, the team's youngest player, was only thirteen years old. Nettie Gans, an eighteen-year-old outfielder, had grown up in an orphanage in Philadelphia. Later, Leona Kearns, a seventeen-year-old pitcher from Illinois, came on board. Standing more than six feet tall, she was a superb athlete capable of playing solid competitive ball against men. Their diverse backgrounds and skill levels notwithstanding, they all aspired to visit different parts of the country, see the world outside America, and to make good money from their play. Ace pitcher Kearns's goal was to earn $300 from the tour of Japan and buy a Ford coupe. That did not appear to be an impossible dream for the bubbling Bobbies. According to Paul Barth, a local Philadelphia promoter who arranged the tour, booking agents in Japan had guaranteed $800 per game and paid for the outbound oceanic passage from Vancouver in first-class cabins. The team was assured that the handsome gate receipts that could be expected in a country bursting with the love of baseball would cover all expenses with plenty left over to net a profit. To make that prospect into a reality, O'Gara decided to fortify her roster by recruiting Earl Hamilton, a pitcher who had just retired from the Philadelphia Phillies the previous year. The former major leaguer brought his new wife along to make a honeymoon out of the tour.[32]

O'Gara's outfit operated on the pay-as-you-go financial model typical of shoestring tours by marginally professional squads. So before leaving for the "promised land" in Asia from the West Coast, the Bobbies went on a cross-country barnstorming trip to raise money. After leaving Philadelphia on September 23, they journeyed through North Dakota, Montana, and Washington, playing local men's town teams. On October 2 they reached Seattle, where O'Gara met up with another former major leaguer through her booking agent in Philadelphia who had arranged the Japan tour. The player was Eddie Ainsmith, the former Detroit Tigers catcher who had toured Japan with Herbert Hunter as a member of the 1920 postseason tour. Ainsmith claimed to have established a fan club during his trip to Japan, and one of his fans supposedly handled the business side of things there. Reinforced with the addition of two former big leaguers, O'Gara's traveling company left Vancouver in high spirits on board the Dollar Shipping Company's ocean liner *President Jefferson*. During a stopover in Honolulu, the team played three games against local semipros and replenished its coffer. On October 18, the seasick travelers arrived in Yokohama. To their surprise, their booking agents, some newspaper reporters, the collegians they were scheduled to play, and many curious locals were on hand to welcome them. From the Tokyo station, they were whisked to a recently renovated Western-style hotel in rickshaws.[33]

Because of the novelty of young American women playing Japanese men with two former American major leaguers thrown into the mix, the Bobbies initially attracted considerable attention. Interviewed by baseball writers, the Bobbies effused that they "came to Japan to promote baseball among Japanese women" and to "encourage them to come to America." The blond haired among them, such as Houghton, were showered with gifts and flowers; the players' biographical sketches that appeared in local publicity pieces invariably referred to their "beautiful blond hair." Some fans said they came to the three games in Tokyo simply to watch Ainsmith and Hamilton play. Clearly, the former Detroit Tiger still commanded a following among Japanese fans, and it was his chance to reprise his glorious 1922 visit. Beginning with Nippon University on October 23—a contest that was opened by Tokyo mayor Nakamura Yoshikoto's ceremonial first pitch—the travelers played a total of eleven games against mostly second-tier collegiate and industrial teams in Tokyo and several cities in western Japan. Among their opponents were movie-studio teams in Kyoto, so they got to party with Japanese actors and actresses after the games. Ticketing in Osaka and Kobe was handled by the Mizuno Company, which advertised the games in several print media and admitted female students free of charge as a promotional tool.[34]

In contrast to the gaiety of the travel and the off-field festivities, the Bobbies languished on the diamond, even with the added power provided by the two former major leaguers. Spectators jeered the skill levels of many of the Bobbies and complained that Ainsmith and Hamilton were "not playing seriously enough." Out of eleven games, the Bobbies won only two—not a performance strong enough to retain fans' interest. The curiosity quickly wore off, and crowds dwindled as the tour proceeded west. Then two of the local promoters skipped town, leaving behind a stack of unpaid bills. The third promoter, who stuck with the Bobbies, ran out of cash. Such money troubles were a fact of life for barnstormers operating on narrow cash margins and often working with unreliable, small-time booking agents. Still, the crisis aggravated the conflict that had been brewing between O'Gara and the two accompanying ex–major leaguers. Claiming knowledge of the local baseball market, Ainsmith insisted that they go on to Korea and Dalian to turn their box-office fortunes around. When O'Gara refused, Ainsmith and Hamilton persuaded three Bobbies, including ace pitcher Kearns, to join them and four locally recruited semipro players in trying their luck in the Japanese colony just across the straits of Tsushima. They left Kobe on November 13. In Seoul, the contingent played and won two games against Japanese expatriate clubs and lost one to an all-Korean squad. Without local connections, however, no more games could be arranged, so Ainsmith's financial revamping plan did not pan out.[35]

Meanwhile, what happened to O'Gara and the nine Bobbies left penniless in Kobe gives a glimpse into the curiously cosmopolitan yet communal aspect of expatriate life in the former treaty port. Most overseas expatriate communities have a way of providing cushions and lending a helping hand to wayward sojourners, particularly those from their homeland. In this case, an American hotelier and a Canadian Christian missionary came to the rescue of the stranded young American barnstormers by providing free food and lodging. Taking pity on the adolescent American travelers' plight, a charitable British Indian banker wrote a personal check for twelve thousand yen to pay for their return travel. Thanks to the kindness of the strangers in the Japanese port city's multiethnic expat community, O'Gara and her players were able to sail for Vancouver in late November. From there, they took the train through the Canadian Rockies and down through upstate New York, returning safely to the City of Brotherly Love on December 6. By then, Ainsmith's breakaway group was back in Kobe, still without enough money for return fares. At that point, Ainsmith had money wired from the United States — enough for him and his wife to get back home. The three Bobbies were left stranded in Kobe to find their own way back. Again, the network of local Anglo-American expatriates bailed out the American teenagers. They raised money for the remaining Bobbies' return travel with a charity holiday ball.[36]

The story of the Philadelphia Bobbies' relentlessly eventful Japan tour had a tragic ending. A few days into their voyage back to Vancouver, the ship carrying the three remaining Bobbies, the *Empress of Asia*, encountered a violent winter storm. Kearns was swept up from the deck by a giant wave and thrown overboard. The seventeen-year-old knuckleballing southpaw, along with her unfulfilled dream of a gainful career in professional baseball, perished in the Pacific Ocean in January 1926.[37] Ultimately, the Bobbies' tribulations in Japan illustrate in a magnified form the perilous contingencies that could arise in a traveling enterprise with a minimal capital base. In a world connected with networks of trains, steamships, telegraphs, and increasingly sophisticated systems of money transfers, even marginal commercial entities could sometimes be tempted to try their luck in a far-flung location, but often with disappointing, and even harrowing, results.[38]

The Philadelphia Royal Giants, 1927
Shoestring tours and uncertain booking prospects were a way of life for Biz Mackey and his teammates in the Philadelphia Royal Giants, a band of fourteen African American ballplayers who also crossed the Pacific to barnstorm in Japan in the 1920s. In the fall of 1926, Lonnie Goodwin, a black baseball promoter based in Philadelphia, a hotbed of Negro League baseball, assembled a winter-ball squad with four accomplished Negro Leaguers and nine players of mixed and lesser talent. Mackey, who played for the powerful Philadelphia Hilldale club during the regular season, captained this off-season outfit. Born in 1897 in Eagle Pass, Texas, Mackey began his career in the Negro League in 1920 as a catcher for the Indianapolis ABCs. Three years later, he moved to the Hilldale club, where he contributed to its three consecutive Eastern Colored League (ECL) championships between 1923 and 1925. Joining Mackey on the jumbled roster were three other Negro Leaguers, slugger Frank Duncan and pitcher Andy Cooper of the Kansas City Monarchs and Rap Dixon of the Harrisburg Giants. Formerly organized in 1920 as a national governing body, the Negro League was a fount of baseball excellence whose level of play rivaled, if not surpassed, that of the major leagues—a determinedly racist American institution that refused to allow blacks to join its ranks until 1947.[39]

After winning the California Winter League championship for the 1926–27 season,[40] Goodwin and his off-season squad went on to do something that they had not planned: they embarked on a barnstorming tour in Asia to earn some more money before returning to regular season play back east. The impetus behind this change of plan was George Irie, an Issei booking agent they met in California. The Seattle-based baseball promoter offered to arrange all of the games to be played in Japan, as well as some in Honolulu on their journey back to the United States. The fourteen-member Philadelphia Royal Giants thus left San Pedro (Los Angeles) on March 9 in the steerage of the Nippon Yusen's ocean liner *La Plata* and arrived in Japan, the first stop of their Asian barnstorming tour, on March 29. There was virtually no prior publicity about their impending visit. Some of the early media reports after their arrival even called them an "American Indian pickup team," probably imagined to be like the Sherman Indians, who had toured Japan a few years before.[41] While Japan's baseball insiders, such as members of the collegiate teams that had traveled in the United States, knew about the Negro League and the major leagues' policy about racial segregation, most Japanese spectators only became aware of the fact that American baseball was not just a "white men's game" after their direct encounter with the visitors from Philadelphia in the ballpark.[42]

During the Japanese leg of the tour, which included Korea and Dalian, the African American travelers compiled a shattering 23–0 record against top-class local collegiate and club teams, with only one tie with the Daimai Club, a powerhouse in the nation's semipro industrial league. Contemporary write-ups about the black ballplayers' on-field performance as well as off-field deportment indicated that they very favorably impressed the Japanese who came into contact with them. Japanese baseball officials and players praised the Royal Giants' impeccable sportsmanship and fair play. Some noted with amazement that the Giants even graciously went along with a patently wrong call made by an inexperienced Japanese umpire. The Japanese contenders were also awed by the Royal Giants' masterful enactment of "inside baseball," aggressive base running, and astounding throwing and offensive power. Mackey in particular immortalized his play in Japan by blasting the first three home runs in the annals of Jingū Stadium, the first modern steel-and-concrete ballpark in the nation's capital, which had just been completed the previous year. Similarly, Rap Dixon slugged the first home run driven directly over Kōshien Stadium's outfield fence. After completing the twenty-four-game series on the Japanese mainland, Mackey and his teammates headed for Seoul, Dalian, and a few games in Shanghai. On their way back to the United States on board the Nippon Yusen's *Siberia*, the African American ballplayers stopped in Honolulu to play ten more games; local newspaper reports similarly noted approvingly their exemplary sportsmanship, including their respect for a local umpire's questionable calls.[43]

The Philadelphia Royal Giants' 1927 transpacific barnstorming tour provides one more example of how active African Americans were in playing other racial groups during organized baseball's Jim Crow era. Since the late nineteenth century, blacks' opponents on the diamond frequently included Cubans, Mexicans, and, later, Asian Americans in Southern California. Such interracial engagements were indeed a common practice of American baseball outside the big-league and high-end minor circuits that had self-segregated with the "Gentlemen's Agreement" among club owners. Like many African Americans who began playing in Mexico and Cuba in the early twentieth century, the Philadelphia Royal Giants took the "American practice" of racially mixed baseball outside the borders of their country. One of the teams they played while in Japan was Zenimura's Fresno Athletic Club (FAC), also touring the country at the time. The FAC's traveling squad featured three white American players and a Mexican American, including a former Pacific Coast Leaguer. An estimated 12,000 spectators came to watch the game held on April 20 at Jingū Stadium. The Royal Giants and the multiethnic FAC had a rematch in Seoul and Dalian, and thus African and Japanese Americans found an unlikely venue to showcase their prowess in America's Game overseas. Similar enactments of racial politics took place in the American territory of Hawaii. The Royal Giants beat the all-Nisei Asahi, but they lost to the all-Chinese team 3–1 a few days later. The proud Chinese who were packed into Honolulu Stadium roared in joy, just as the Japanese groaned in despair. Outside of major leagues' color line, vigilantly policed by Commissioner Landis and his kindred spirits, there existed myriad multiethnic fields of play that together enriched America's Game. From this decentered vantage point, the major leagues and their racial practices were arguably an aberration in the world of American baseball, not the norm.[44]

The Major Leagues' "Western Expedition" of 1927

Besides insisting on "splendid isolation" from the world of multiracial baseball, the major leagues in the first half of the twentieth century remained a decidedly self-contained entity in geographical terms as well. Even during the "golden age" of the 1920s, the majors still had no franchises west of St. Louis. Thus, fans in the western states could only read about the splendor of big-league play in printed forms or see it in newsreels. The stirrings of the majors' attempt to alter that state of affairs came after the end of the 1927 season—a season in which Babe Ruth hit sixty home runs and the Yankee dynasty was at its peak. To cap off that glorious season, the major leagues dispatched their first-ever official postseason cross-country exhibition tour by a World Series champion team, with the club owners' unanimous consent and Landis's approval, of course. Any doubts that baseball's big capital meant business in this first serious attempt to penetrate the nation's western half were dispelled by one look at the tour's banner bearers: Babe Ruth and Lou Gehrig. After routing the Pittsburgh Pirates in the 1927 World Series, the twin Yankee kingpins and their select teammates embarked on this western expedition. Ruth played on an exhibition squad called the Bustin' Babes; Gehrig spearheaded its opponent, the Larrupin' Lous. At each stop along the way, they invited local players to round out their rosters, a clever marketing scheme designed to tickle the pride of local fans and fulfill the fantasy of playing big-time baseball for local minor leaguers and semipros. The 1927 offseason tour of the West was a spectacular commercial success. It drew an estimated 250,000 spectators in eighteen states. Throngs of fans showed up to welcome them at the train station, and the Yankee travelers paraded through the city in motorcades and enjoyed royal treatment by local political and civic leaders. Evenings were filled with gala events and elaborate banquets at the area's premier hotels.[45]

The same scene was reenacted for the tour's last leg in California. The major-league troupes invited local players, mostly Pacific Coast Leaguers, to join their rosters as they proceeded through a north-south crisscrossing itinerary beginning in San Francisco and ending in San Diego. Journeying through the Central Valley, the Yankee caravan stopped and played in Fresno, where four of the locally recruited ringers bore Japanese surnames, all members of Zenimura's Fresno Athletic Club. The FAC's successful tour of Japan and its colonial appendages earlier that year had reinforced the Japanese immigrant nationalism of older Issei in the area. And now, the pride of the Japanese American community's Nisei members was boosted by the enlistment of the FAC's finest in the teams of white major leaguers—Ruth and Gehrig, no less. Nothing validated their pride and sense of identity as an American citizen more viscerally than seeing their own play ball alongside the majors' reining superstars.

The majors' cross-country postseason tour in 1927 was a harbinger of the next chapter in the chronicle of transpacific baseball in another important way. One of the Pacific Coast Leaguers who played for the Bustin' Babes was a young power-hitting outfielder named Lefty O'Doul, then of the San Francisco Seals. This native San Franciscan would fashion himself into a key middleman between organized baseball and the Japanese baseball fraternity in the next three decades.[46]

It was not long after this hugely successful and profitable western tour that major-league executives finally decided to extend their off-season territorial reach beyond the shores of California. At the forefront of this renewed promotional outreach to Asia was none other than Herbert Hunter, self-styled American baseball's ambassador to Japan. Landis's new edicts in 1923 frustrated Hunter's designs to become a conduit between the baseball worlds of the two countries. Nor did the big earthquake and the reciprocal ill will over the U.S. Immigration Act of 1924 help his cause. But Hunter patiently bided his time, playing in the Pacific Coast League during the regular season and coaching Japanese collegians during off-season months. Hunter also exhibited political savvy and organizational skill by arranging a series of working vacations—or larks—in Japan for just-retired major leaguers and their wives, beginning with Larry Doyle, a former Giant, who had field managed the 1922 "Hunter All-Stars." Hunter scored a great coup at the end of the 1928 season when he arranged for Ty Cobb, fresh from his retirement from the Athletics, to visit Japan and give a baseball clinic for players in the Tokyo Big 6 League. Accompanying Cobb on this junket were two other former major leaguers, Freddy Hoffman, a member of the 1922 Hunter All-Stars, and Bob Shawkey, a former Yankee pitcher; the National League's chief umpire, Ernie Quigley, also went along. In the first two years of its existence as a formal league, Tokyo Big 6 was rocked by frequent disputes over umpiring and threats of game forfeiture. Hunter helped the infant Japanese collegiate league to institute a system of full-time and certified umpires instead of relying on untrained alumni volunteers. Hunter arranged for Quigley to take charge of their training.[47]

Hunter's careful constituency building on both sides of the Pacific finally paid off in late 1930, when Landis, after years of refusal, finally gave his permission to send an off-season exhibition tour featuring players from the next year's World Series champion to Japan. In every sense of the term, it was a product of "old boys" networking. Hunter approached Fred Lieb, a prominent New York sportswriter, a frequent contributor to the *Sporting News*, and, most crucially, a close friend of National League president John Heydler and Commissioner Landis. Hunter offered to split any profits from the Japanese trip fifty-fifty if Lieb could broker the necessary official sanction by organized baseball's bigwigs. Meanwhile, Hunter appealed to the club owners with a vision of overseas empire building. He defined Japan as a logical extension of the Yankees' successful western tour in 1927 and of the barnstorming visits to the American territory of Hawaii. The owners readily bought this geographical argument. Besides, Japan had built two modern steel-and-concrete stadiums with a combined seating capacity of more than 100,000 in the two metropolitan areas—Kōshien Stadium in 1924 and Jingū Stadium in 1926.[48] This enhanced playing infrastructure, made possible by Japan's urban industrial growth and capital accumulation after World War I, seemed to ensure that it was well worth it for major leagues to dispatch their players across the Pacific to play off-season games in that country. Faced with the owners' unanimous endorsement, Landis grudgingly approved Hunter's proposition, but with certain stipulations. First, his crony Lieb must be the tour's official head and, in that capacity, sign the players to individual contracts; second, Hunter was not to play in a single game during the tour; and finally, this Japan trip was "not to be used as an entering wedge to let down the bars on the present barnstorming rules." In its 1931 "New Year" issue, the *Sporting News* trumpeted the major-league executives' long-awaited approval of "the first Oriental Diamond Missionary Tour in nine years," during which Lieb and Hunter would "carry the Gospel of Major League Baseball to Japan in 1931." Clearly, a naked profit motive and personal greed were key elements of that "gospel."[49]

In the winter of 1930–31, a magnetic force was emanating from the other shore of the Pacific as well, as hard-nosed corporate interest began to be attracted by the moneymaking potential of American media celebrities. At the epicenter of this commercial vortex was Shōriki Matsutarō, a highly ambitious and ruthlessly calculating helmsman of an upstart daily, the *Yomiuri Shinbun*. A former national police commissioner, Shōriki assumed the *Yomiuri*'s mantle in 1924 and threw himself boldly into the rapidly shifting world of the Japanese news media. The mission he defined for himself was to boost this Tokyo-based, late-starting daily's nationwide circulation against the more established and nationally networked *Asahi* and *Mainichi*. He sought to achieve this goal through coordinated and massive publicity campaigns built around gala events, exhibitions, shows, and other forms of public spectacle inciting and in turn catering to the middle- and low-brow consumerist thirsts of the urban masses. Naturally, baseball was at the front and center of his P. T. Barnum–like publicity campaigns. By late 1930, Shōriki was determined to garner a promotional appearance by the ultimate American hero: the home-run king, Babe Ruth.

Using his political connections as a former national police commissioner, he first tried to persuade the Railroad Ministry to sponsor his machinations. Failing this, Shōriki then prevailed upon the Foreign Ministry to throw its weight behind his company's corporate agenda to bring Babe Ruth to Japan to "further U.S.-Japanese friendship." The Japanese government bought this argument. "The main prize was Mr. Ruth," Foreign Minister Shidehara Kijuro's telegram to the consul general in New York read; "the rest could be junior varsities or even lesser ones." The entrepreneurial Japanese newspaperman thus presented himself as an ideal business partner for Hunter.[50]

In late January 1931, Hunter, armed with Landis's seal of approval, arrived in Japan to negotiate the terms of the *Yomiuri*'s corporate sponsorship of a Babe Ruth tour. The discussions were driven by the unabashed determination of the two baseball boosters, one Japanese and one American, to profit commercially from the game. Hunter held out for a guarantee of 250,000 yen. Shōriki managed to have the figure lowered to 100,000 yen but offered to let Hunter keep all profits beyond the guarantees and expenses; if any losses should accrue, the *Yomiuri* would bear them. Still burdened by an unsettled debt from Ty Cobb's 1928 junket, Hunter jumped at the offer. Meanwhile, Shōriki mobilized all of the resources and connections at his disposal for this enterprise. Shōriki hired Suzuki Sōtarō, a Japanese businessman based in New York, to be his point man in the United States. Born in 1890, Suzuki moved to New York in the early 1920s as an agent for a Japanese silk-exporting company. Through his business connections, Suzuki gained the acquaintance of President Charles Stoneham and manager McGraw of the New York Giants. Besides his "day job," Suzuki began writing about American major-league baseball as a self-appointed foreign correspondent for a Yokohama foreign trade newspaper. In 1930, Suzuki was recruited as the *Yomiuri*'s consultant in charge of arranging the baseball tour.[51] In the meantime, Shōriki launched a massive advertising campaign to the tune of 49,000 yen. The Tokyo Big 6 League, now presided over by Abe, also contributed 30,000 yen to publicity.[52]

Despite the *Yomiuri*'s persistent courting, Ruth's visit to Japan did not come to pass in 1931. Money proved the insurmountable obstacle. The minimum guarantee of $50,000 each required to obtain Ruth and Lou Gehrig was too much for the company, so Shōriki had to settle for only one superstar on the roster. Ruth was also busy making a series of one-reel film "photoplays" known as the *Babe Ruth Baseball Series* in Hollywood. Yet the delegation of the fourteen major leaguers that the Lieb-Hunter duo put together carried an unprecedented clout on the diamond and at the box office. They featured seven future Hall of Famers, including Gehrig, Lefty Grove, Mickey Cochrane, and Al Simmons. The majors' four-star diamond army arrived in Yokohama on November 15 on board Nippon Yūsen's luxury liner *Tatsutamaru*. Their fellow passengers included the Japanese government delegation returning from the largely fruitless London Naval Limitation Conference. This coincidence, or sign of the times, indicated that U.S.-Japanese baseball exchange was reaching another plateau just as the interstate cooperative structure built after World War I was showing early signs of unraveling.[53]

Even more relevant to the intersection of baseball exchange and the shifting landscape of U.S.-Japanese diplomacy was the fact that the 1931 majors' tour took place only a few weeks after the Manchurian Incident. In the aftermath of what some historians regard as the opening shot of World War II in the Asia-Pacific world, the major-league executives chose to go forward with, rather than cancel, the ballyhooed transpacific tour. Lieb, Hunter, and their fourteen players received red-carpet treatment nearly comparable to that granted to official state visitors. The Japanese Railroad Ministry ran a special train arranged by the Railway Bureau to transport the American baseball travelers from Yokohama to Tokyo, which was an unprecedented government courtesy extended to a private-sector undertaking. Once in Tokyo, they met with U.S. ambassador William Cameron Forbes—the man who promoted baseball in the Philippines as governor-general—at the embassy and were honored with a tea at the official residence of the prime minister, Wakatsuki Reijirō, who was then busy deflecting worldwide opprobrium over the nation's military aggression in Manchuria. Foreign Minister Shidehara, who had weighed in to help engineer the tour, also hobnobbed with the American guests alongside Ambassador Forbes. Press photos of the festivity were produced and circulated to the foreign press corps to showcase U.S.-Japanese friendship seemingly unperturbed by the military aggression perpetrated by the loose-cannon Kwangtung Army in Manchuria. The facade of normalcy and cordiality in U.S.-Japanese relations continued to be generated through the majors' monthlong tour. Japanese fans of both sexes and all ages flocked to the games, showering their American idols with gushing adoration. Japanese Boy Scouts presented them with a gold medal of honor in a ritual of international and intergenerational brotherhood. Lieb's *Sporting News* blared reports of the riotous reception of the visiting Americans in Japan, paying gushing tribute to "the success which our neighbors of the Pacific have made in America's national sports."[54]

Nor did Ruth's conspicuous absence affect the American visitors' collective firepower on the playing field. They won all seventeen games against Tokyo Big 6 teams, a collegiate all-star squad, and top industrial league clubs, even though a stray pitch broke two small bones in Gehrig's right hand and the Iron Horse was forced to sit out the rest of the tour. The 1931 Japan tour produced huge commercial dividends for all parties concerned. On their way to Japan, Gehrig and his teammates played in San Francisco and Honolulu and reaped handsome profits from these early legs of the tour.[55] Once in Japan, the major leaguers played before sellout crowds everywhere in the country. Fans began queuing up around the stadiums long before dawn. Some of them traveled as far as a hundred miles to get tickets. Available statistics vary, but both *Spalding's Base Ball Guide* and *The Reach Baseball Guide* placed average per-game attendance at 30,000, a figure far exceeding the average attendance for stateside big-league games. Lieb later boasted in the *Sporting News* that 450,000 Japanese came out to watch the American pros play. The American visitors pulled in more spectators in seventeen games in Japan than the Pittsburgh Pirates and St. Louis Browns drew to their combined 155 home games that year. The *Yomiuri* reaped a huge boost to its national subscription. True to his agreement with Hunter, Shōriki handed over to his American business partners all of the 200,000 yen in net profits. By then, there was no doubt in the minds of major-league kingpins: big money could be made in postseason tours to Japan.[56]

Another historic aspect of the majors' 1931 tour was Lefty O'Doul's presence on its roster. The Dodgers outfielder initially led all hitters in this exhibition series with a .600 batting average until he broke his ribs in a collision at first base the day after Gehrig's injury. Like Gehrig, O'Doul had to be sidelined for the rest of the tour. Yet with his early exploits and jovial persona, O'Doul made his mark among Japanese fans and became one of the most adored American players on the tour. O'Doul's life and his participation in the major leagues' Japanese (or "Far Western") expedition at this point in his career trajectory brought into relief the growing nexus between organized baseball, California, and Japan. Born in San Francisco in 1897, Francis Joseph "Lefty" O'Doul grew up playing sandlot ball in "Butchertown," San Francisco's tough, predominantly Irish meatpacking district. He quit school after ninth grade to join his father and uncle in their butchering trade. He worked six days a week at the slaughterhouse and played as a southpaw pitcher in San Francisco's city leagues on Sundays.

In 1918, at age twenty, O'Doul was recruited by the San Francisco Seals, a PCL club on the lookout for young Irish prospects to appeal to the city's large working-class Irish population. (Incidentally, one of his teammates in the 1918 Seals roster was Herb Hunter.) "Lefty" O'Doul pitched splendidly for the Seals, which led to a big-time contract with the New York Yankees at the season's end. O'Doul had only lackluster years at the Yankees, however. He pitched in just eight innings in two seasons, while playing occasionally as an outfielder or pinch hitter. O'Doul was sent back to the PCL for the 1922 and 1924 seasons, and during his second retreat to the minor circuit, he became a full-time outfielder, a conversion that sparked his late-blooming success in the big leagues. In 1927 he led the PCL in hits and RBIS and was named MVP. It was in the postseason of that glorious year 1927 that O'Doul was chosen to play for the Bustin' Babes touring through California.[57] In the 1928 season, at the mature age of thirty-one, O'Doul went back to the big time, and he spent the next seven seasons playing for the New York Giants, the Philadelphia Phillies, and the Brooklyn Robins/Dodgers.[58]

The 1931 tour was O'Doul's first visit to Japan, and it affected his life profoundly because he fell in love with the country, its culture, and its people. The following fall, O'Doul asked if he could join two other major leaguers, Washington Senators catcher Moe Berg and Chicago White Sox pitcher Ted Lyons, in the postseason baseball clinic for Tokyo Big 6 players organized by Hunter. It was an odd mix; Hunter chose Berg and Lyons for this coaching trip specifically because he believed that their college education—Princeton for Berg and Baylor for Lyons—would allow them to fit in well with their Japanese apprentices, who were highly conscious of their elite status. Berg and Lyons were also reputed to be the most linguistically gifted among major leaguers. O'Doul lacked a university education or proficiency in foreign language, but he made a real effort to learn Japanese and won over Japanese baseball officials and players with his earnest admiration of Japanese culture. As a player anticipating retirement in the not-so-distant future, O'Doul probably realized that his future place in the sun belonged in a niche afforded by his Japan connections. Having spent most of his life in San Francisco and playing before San Francisco's cheering crowds as a member of the majors' 1931 Japan tour, he understood the city's strategic location connecting the baseball metropolis in the American Northeast/Midwest and this burgeoning baseball market in

Asia. From his career in the Seals, O'Doul was also aware of the growing importance of Nikkei spectatorships for PCL clubs. From the inception of this long-standing relationship, O'Doul's interest in Japanese baseball was both genuine and calculated, and the two did not need to be mutually exclusive.[59] The cachet O'Doul built during these two Japan trips would position him to play liaison between organized baseball and Japan's baseball entrepreneurs in the decade leading up to the outbreak of the Pacific War—and well beyond.

Preceding Hunter and O'Doul's 1932 coaching junket by a few weeks was a Japanese tour by another group of highly accomplished American ballplayers: the Philadelphia Royal Giants barnstorming Japan for the second time. Arriving in Yokohama on September 7, the reconstituted Royal Giants included three returning members of the successful 1927 squad, including Mackey, and nine new members, including Jose Peréz, who had debuted with the Cuban Stars and was playing for the Philadelphia Hilldale that season.[60] As on the previous tour, the Philadelphia Royal Giants played twenty-four games, losing only one to the local challengers. But their experience in Japan was vastly different from their previous visit. This time, the Royal Giants played in sparsely attended ballparks against mostly second-tier industrial and private-club teams because a Japanese government decree issued earlier in the year had banned collegiate teams—the cream of the crop of Japanese baseball—from playing against professionals, either Japanese or foreign. Further, after the spectacularly successful 1931 majors tour, the focal point of Japanese fan interest had shifted to the "real thing." This grim reality awaiting the Royal Giants was evident in the stark contrast in the Japanese reception for these two groups of American professionals. In 1932 there was no motorcade for the Royal Giants; there was no special train arranged for their travel from Yokohama to Tokyo; there were no receptions at the Japanese prime minister's official residence or a meeting with Ambassador Forbes.[61]

The timing of the Royal Giants' second visit also conspired against them. They docked in Yokohama on board the same ocean liner that transported the Japanese National Olympic team from Los Angeles, a triumphant delegation that included the two-time gold medalist Tsuruta Yoshiyuki, a swimmer.[62] Also disembarking from the same ship was Miura Tamaki, a Japanese opera singer who had made a name for herself in America for her self-Orientalizing performance as Madam Butterfly. She was visiting her home country en route to a performance in Italy. In the shadows of these homegrown sport and entertainment heroes and heroines, hardly anyone in the press corps noticed the African American ballplayers' arrival.[63] After playing twenty-four games in Japan, the Royal Giants barnstormed in the Philippines and returned to the United States in late October, but a cruel reality awaited them at home. While they were away in Asia, many of the Negro League teams, including Mackey's Philadelphia Hilldale club, had collapsed under the weight of the Depression. This unprecedented crisis gripping the U.S. economy spared no one, and it hit commercially vulnerable entities like African American baseball outfits with brutal force.[64] In this punishing economic environment, many minor-league clubs also folded, while a different kind of baseball entrepreneurship rose to capitalize on employment opportunities created by the New Deal state and quasi-wartime mobilization, the two key macroeconomic stimulants that would animate America's economic life after the mid-1930s. The next chapter will discuss this Depression-era baseball venture.

5

EMPIRES OF FUN AND GAMES

In the early and middle 1930s, the governments of the United States and Japan cast about for ways to iron out their growing differences in the realm of diplomacy and military strategy. The Japanese military aggression that erupted in Manchuria in September 1931 severely strained the nation's relationship with the United States. Yet as historian Inoue Toshikazu has shown, throughout an era bookended by Japan's withdrawal from the League of Nations in March 1933 and the start of its full-scale military aggression in north China in 1937, Japanese officialdom still defined its geopolitical interests largely within the time-tested formula of keeping peace and cordiality with the Anglo-American informal entente in Asia. Since most of such diplomatic efforts and maneuvers took place outside the formal collective security framework of the League of Nations, and because Japanese government officials periodically blurted out bombastic anti-Western rhetoric that was often miscontextualized or unduly magnified by the international media, the underlying continuity from earlier times could all too easily be obscured from view, missed both by contemporaries and by historians in later decades.[1] In this period of uneasy transition, baseball, too, was an element of the continuity in U.S.-Japanese relations. The game beloved by both Americans and Japanese was one of the cultural forces that helped to keep, albeit peripherally, the bilateral relationship from drifting irreversibly apart. Since Waseda University's pioneer West Coast tour, the tradition of regular U.S.-Japanese baseball exchanges taking place in the U.S. mainland, Hawaii, Japan (including Korea and Taiwan), and the Philippines had already spanned three decades and, as such, entrenched itself as a fixture of U.S.-Japanese cultural trade and social interaction.

This transoceanic institution had a renewed flowering in the middle part of the 1930s, the decade described by some historians as a "dark valley" in international affairs, including U.S.-Japanese relations. In the fall of 1934, yet another major-league world tour squad, this one consisting solely of American Leaguers and featuring Babe Ruth, stormed through Japan. From there, the traveling extravaganza took the American League all-stars to the Philippines, through the Suez Canal to Egypt, and finally to Western Europe. This sporting and media spectacle again left in its wake visible, and at times ostentatious, affirmations of U.S.-Japanese harmony and cultural affinity that belied the increasingly unconcealed discord at the level of high politics. As it turned out, the majors' 1934 world tour was the last hurrah of their pre–World War II overseas empire-building efforts. Like Gehrig and O'Doul, injured in play during the 1931 tour, Clint Brown of the Cleveland Indians was seriously injured by a pitch in the 1934 tour. The club owners feared that future foreign outings might pose similar hazards to their high-value investments, and Commissioner Landis decided once again to ban off-season overseas tours by major leaguers, sealing off this avenue of U.S.-Japanese fraternal encounter and the tempering cushion it had provided to bilateral relations. This chapter shines light on this mid-decade interlude in U.S.-Japanese relations by examining what kind of role baseball played in that period of relative stability—or perhaps the deceptive calm before the stormy years of wartime mobilization that would begin in earnest later in the decade.[2]

The Making of *Yakyū Tōseirei* (1932)

As the lines separating amateur, semipro, and professional baseball became progressively blurred in Japan amid the baseball boom of the 1910s and 1920s, incipient sports capitalism gave rise to the nation's first joint-stock baseball club whose members openly declared themselves to be "professionals" playing ball to make a living from it. The Nippon Undōkai (later renamed the Shibaura Kyōkai), organized with fourteen players chosen through rigorous tryouts in late 1920, was in that sense Japan's first frontal attempt at fully salaried professional baseball. The founding officers of this pioneer enterprise were Kōno Atsushi and Hashido Makoto, both members of Waseda's 1905 West Coast tour. From their formative experience in the United States, these senior members of the Japanese baseball fraternity had imbibed the "American" way of professionalism as a positive sports creed; that is, the attainment of higher technical levels required full-time commitment by dedicated experts, and, more to the point, there was nothing morally corrupting or demeaning about playing for monetary compensation in and of itself. They also believed, as did their longtime mentor Abe, that creating a separate enterprise for play-for-pay baseball might actually help rescue "amateur" student baseball from the banes of commercialism and crass materialism.³

The time, however, was not yet ripe for baseball as a self-standing business enterprise in Japan. The Shibaura club suffered chronically from financial instability. Its uncertain status of being neither amateur nor semipro proved an impediment in scheduling games with existing squads. Further, the earthquake that hit Tokyo and its outlying areas in September 1923 dealt a crushing blow to the club. As disaster-relief materials donated by U.S. charitable organizations poured in, the Tokyo municipal government impounded as an emergency measure the club's waterfront stadium and office building for storage space and operational headquarters for relief work. Unable to absorb the loss of these assets, the club disbanded as a joint-stock company within a few months of the natural disaster. An Osaka industrialist and owner of railroads, Kobayashi Ichizō, tried to resuscitate the club under the new name Takarazuka Undō Kyōkai (the Takarazuka Athletic Association), but the parent company's halfhearted commitment, compounded by the financial panic of 1927, doomed the revived club. The aspiring Japanese pros, first captained by pitcher Yamamoto Eiichirō, toured as far as Korea and Dalian in search of competitors and playing venues, but this organization also folded in the summer of 1929. For a brief period in the mid-1920s, another squad, the Amakatsu Baseball Troupe, fielded by a professional magician, took a stab at professional play, but the 1923 earthquake also dashed this experiment.⁴

While these early attempts at professionalization failed to take off, commercialism in student "amateur" baseball continued to rage uncontrollably. During the interwar period, a combination of historical circumstances—the invention of the *nanshiki* softball version of the game; widespread business sponsorships of amateur contests; a spike in domestic and overseas tours by student squads, most of them cosponsored by newspapers; and the beginning of radio broadcasting of games—turned student baseball, both collegiate and high school, into a mass entertainment in a society where sumo was still the only professionalized sport in town. The emergence of multiple playing venues bred a neglect of academic work in youth baseball; adult involvement increased and developed into parental zealotry and meddling by, and feuding among, alumni and school administrators tied up with their own outside sponsor influences. Gate receipts became a critical revenue stream for some schools, not just for their sports teams and athletic programs but for general operation as well. Payment of guarantees to top teams became a common practice. Overzealous rooting by supporters often turned into rowdiness and violence that spilled onto the playing field. This mania for student baseball created practices and athletic creeds that sports purists like Tobita Suishū (Tadayoshi), conservative social ideologues, and traditionalist government officials considered antithetical to the ideals of "wholesome" and ascetic student athletic practices, whose paramount, if not sole, purpose must be moral development and character building.[5]

The problem of commercialism infiltrating student, particularly collegiate, athletics was intrinsic to the popularization of sports as a civic enterprise in an industrializing and increasingly networked modern mass-consumer society. American intercollegiate sports, too, had been tackling this unruly question since their inception in the mid-nineteenth century. As a signpost on this long-running historical process, sports stakeholders in the United States devised various regional and national governing bodies in the late nineteenth and early twentieth centuries to formulate and enforce uniform rules of amateurism governing such questions as player eligibility, scheduling, and hiring of professional coaches. The National Collegiate Athletic Association (NCAA) was established in 1905 out of this movement for self-reform, reflecting the ethos of the Progressive Era. Despite such regulatory efforts, intercollegiate athletics, particularly football and baseball, continued to take on the attributes of a business enterprise in the early twentieth century. Misconduct and financial scandals involving student athletes and school administrators grew in tandem.

Against this backdrop, the Carnegie Foundation commissioned a study of commercialism in American college sports. The report, *American College Athletics* (1929), exposed damning evidence of corruption and abuses. Three-quarters of the 112 colleges and universities studied were found to be in violation of NCAA codes and the conventionals of amateurism. While the report contended that the "heart of the problem facing college sports [was] commercialization," it also pointed out that the sociology of American college sports was part of that problem; for many college athletes coming from relatively humble social origins, playing sports was a way to achieve upward social mobility. The commercialization of college sports, the report concluded, was thus a tangled problem stemming from multiple factors, such as expanded press coverage, public enthusiasm, excessive alumni and administrative involvement, aggressive player recruitment, and professional coaches abetting neglect of academics.[6]

Although not to the same extent as football, American collegiate baseball was engulfed in scandals and controversies in the period preceding the Carnegie Commission report. One particularly high-profile dispute involved Ray Fisher, a pitcher with the Cincinnati Reds who had a coaching stint at the University of Michigan in 1921. Having suffered a pay cut, Fisher left the Reds to coach the Wolverines for additional income. When he attempted to return to the Reds after the end of the college baseball season, he got into a predictable conflict with the Reds front office, which placed him on the permanent ineligibility list. Fisher took the case to the newly created Commissioner's Office for adjudication, but Landis allowed the Reds' harshly punitive measure to stand. Despite his reputation as a "trust-busting" federal judge appointed by Teddy Roosevelt, Landis, a long-term fan of the Chicago Cubs and a friend of many major club owners, had been chosen in part because he was in fact an apologist for the fundamentally monopolistic nature of organized baseball as an industry. Not contradicting this expectation, Landis ruled that actions such as Fisher's—jumping a major-league contract to coach at the college level and then trying to return to pro ball—threatened to undermine the reserve system, one of the bedrock rules upon which the enterprise of pro baseball rested. As far as Landis was concerned, college coaching jobs were as much a part of the market for professional ballplayers as rival teams or leagues.[7]

Thus, since the early years of Landis's reign as commissioner, the coaching of amateurs by professional baseball players became strictly regulated in the United States, but the awarding of gifts, prizes, and even straight cash payments to high-end collegiate players remained unabated, especially during overseas tours. Far removed from the supervisory gaze of the NCAA, Hawaii emerged as a protected sanctuary for "amateur" collegiate baseballers to partake in remunerated play. Between 1905 and 1930, a number of American collegiate teams from the Pacific coastal states and the Midwest toured Japan, the Philippines, and Australia, with Hawaii as a semirequisite stopover. Reports in local Hawaiian newspapers reveal that the payment of guarantees beyond travel expenses and hefty prize money for winners were common practices in the American territory in the mid-Pacific. In Japan, the costs of underwriting American collegians' tours and the need to pay a guarantee necessitated the charging of fees at the gate. This expediency, initially limited only to "international" matches, expanded into a normal revenue-generating instrument for Tokyo Big 6 and other forms of student play, as baseball grew into a popular spectator sport and leagues became complex bureaucratic organizations with large overheads. The commercializing tendencies in collegiate baseball thus became an interconnected, transpacific pattern in the development of sports capitalism, although the symptoms and the remedies applied varied significantly across national boundaries.[8]

A series of money scandals involving star players, as well as open squabbles among school administrators over the sharing of gate revenues, rocked Tokyo Big 6 in the late 1920s and early 1930s. By then, the collegiate league's estimated annual net profit was 500,000 yen—a hefty sum at a time when a public schoolteacher's starting annual salary was 500 yen. Each time irregularities surfaced, the Education Ministry ordered Tokyo Big 6 to reform itself through a self-governing body like the NCAA, but the member colleges and league executives persisted in wrangling over revenue sharing and other issues of self-interest. The ministry finally decided to step in directly to "purify" student athletics. The result was the issuing in March 1932 of *Yakyū Tōseirei* in the name of Education Minister Hatoyama Ichirō. The new administrative edict stipulated wide-ranging restrictions and proscriptions for each and every level of student baseball. First, it made national tournaments for elementary-school players contingent on government approval and banned corporate sponsorship of their games and tournaments; only local, nonprofit sports governing bodies or school boards were authorized to sponsor youth baseball tournaments. At the middle-school level, restrictions were even harsher, limiting the authority to organize tournaments and collect gate receipts only to the prefectural governments. Games could only be played on Saturday afternoons or Sundays. Amateur eligibility was also tightened, and grade repeaters or transfer students were made ineligible to play extramurally for one year. School headmasters had to approve all games, and no tours outside of the area were permitted without approval by the prefectural governments. All gate receipts from middle-school and collegiate games had to be reported to the Ministry of Education, and the money could only be used for covering actual expenses. No rewards or gifts from sponsoring organizations and no financial backing by alumni groups were allowed. The prohibition bearing the greatest significance for collegiate baseball— and by extension for pre–World War II Japanese baseball in general—was *Yakyū Tōseirei*'s immediate ban on amateurs playing against professionals, whether Japanese or foreign, under any circumstances.[9]

In considering this unprecedented interventionist action by the Japanese state, it is important to note that, at least at the time of the policy's proclamation, two distinct strands of thought and administrative agendas uneasily coexisted among government officials. There was one group who genuinely wished to rid student baseball of the bane of excessive commercialism. Others in officialdom harbored a more ambitious political agenda: to harness sports and physical education into a state-directed centralized regime of national mobilization. This latter impulse was not newly activated by the militarization of Japanese foreign policy after the Manchurian Incident, as some historians have suggested; rather, it dated back to the previous decade of relative peace and calm in Japan's domestic politics and foreign-policy conduct. It was during the 1920s, for example, that the Ministry of Education took the lead in legislating Athletics Day for all schools and the Ministry of Home Affairs began to sponsor the Meiji Jingū Meet, which was an annual, national, multievent sporting competition emulating the Olympics. Even pro-Western, "liberal" politicians like Wakatsuki lent their prestige to the top-down nationalistic sporting event—held adjacent to the "sacred" Meiji Shrine, dedicated to the late Emperor Meiji—by appearing at opening ceremonies and exalting the supposed link between individual physical improvements and the bolstering of the national body politic.[10]

Quite aside from these incremental steps taken toward the state control of the national body and the appropriation of sports for mobilization purposes, some athletic specialists, housed in the Education Ministry, began a plan to rein in student baseball, which, in their view, was degenerating into a moral-compromising "revenue sport." In this administrative initiative, the ministry's young bureaucrats trained in the new academic discipline of sports pedagogy consciously referred to the United States—the nation that pioneered this field of study as an academic discipline—for inspiration. In the early 1930s, they carefully studied the Carnegie Commission's report on American college athletics and identified a number of disturbing common elements in the situation they faced in Japan. Newspapers' abetting the sports mania and fanning the cult of sport celebrities was foremost among them. In the case of Japanese baseball, the two leading newspapers sponsored national high school baseball tournaments, and local newspapers and railway companies with ballparks situated along their train routes sponsored lesser (regional) tournaments. The sports critics also noted that a vicious circle identified in the Carnegie Commission report—excessive numbers of interscholastic games and tours driving up the costs of maintaining a team and, in turn, necessitating aggressive revenue generation through gate receipts and securing, via guarantees, the "services" of players and teams with box-office appeal—also applied to Japan. Similarly, cutthroat player recruitment by rival schools bred morally questionable if not illegal practices, and the imperative to win at all costs often bred the neglect of academics by players and coaches.[11]

The recognition of these striking parallels between the problems afflicting American and Japanese amateur sports pushed reform-minded ministry officials to take steps to arrest the morally corrosive tendencies in student athletics, particularly baseball. They determined that what may be called the "baseball-industrial complex" lay at the heart of the problem, and that liberating the game from the grips of corporate profit motives and crass materialism was the way to "clean up" the sport and bring it back to its original healthy status. The ministry's sport reformers were also concerned about the effects of the economic depression on student athletics. In light of diminishing public funding for sports and, conversely, greater reliance on private resources, including corporate sponsorship, the task of bridling commercialism appeared all the more urgent.[12] The Education Ministry then appointed Taiiku Undō Shingikai (Physical Education and Athletics Council),[13] the Japanese version of the Carnegie Commission, to explore possible remedies. This government initiative received broad support at the time because of the widely shared public (mis)perception that Shōriki and his media company had made huge profits from the 1931 majors' tour by prostituting collegiate players to play against the money-grubbing, morally bankrupt American professionals. The council was similarly well regarded by baseball stakeholders because its membership included such venerated senior members of the baseball fraternity as Abe (now a socialist-populist parliamentarian), Hashido, and Tobita. In January 1932, this policy-advisory council recommended that the ministry enforce top-down controls of student baseball "until such time as officials of student baseball would set up a system of self-policing to safeguard amateurism." What followed from this recommendation was the decreeing of *Yakyū Tōseirei* in March 1932. With this administrative edict, Japan's "amateur" student baseball formally came under state control, a move that would have profound ramifications during World War II.[14]

In its immediate aftermath, this extraordinary state intrusion into the Japanese national pastime elicited surprisingly muted reaction from baseball promoters and boosters. Student baseball's two corporate sponsors, *Asahi* and *Mainichi*, both refrained from openly criticizing the decree in their editorial pages and seemingly acquiesced in the top-down government regulation, although the *Yomiuri* harshly denounced it. Many colleges consented, albeit reluctantly, to open the books of their baseball program to the ministry's auditors to document amounts of gate receipts and use of funds. Still, officers and leaders of collegiate baseball were unable to organize themselves into an NCAA-like, intermediary self-governing organization because of an internal conflict of opinions and parochial institutional interests. In the absence of such a civic mechanism for self-regulation, the Ministry of Education continued, almost by default, its administrative controls (until they were finally rescinded after World War II).

Perhaps the most consequential outcome of the 1932 *Yakyū Tōseirei* was the birth of the first commercially viable professional baseball clubs in Japan. When Shōriki managed to orchestrate another postseason tour of major leaguers in 1934—this time with his ultimate prize, Babe Ruth, atop its roster—Japan's top players, most of them Tokyo Big 6 players, were no longer available to play against the visiting American professionals. Shōriki's response to this predicament was to organize his own squad of newly minted "professionals." The Dai Nippon Tokyo Yakyū Kurabu (All-Nippon Tokyo Baseball Club) was thus hastily assembled in June 1934 to play against the Sultan of Swat and company. The first contest between American and Japanese professionals took place that fall. Judging through the lens of high politics, it is rather remarkable that it was during the first half of the 1930s—a time of reemerging intergovernmental tensions—that U.S.-Japanese baseball exchange entered another growth spurt, as it had during the earlier period of diplomatic estrangement after the Portsmouth Treaty. Clearly, the heart of the transnational sporting culture was pulsating on a rhythm distinct from that of interstate geopolitics.

The 1934 All-Americans Tour

In early 1933, Shōriki embarked on another bold business venture that linked baseball and media-driven celebrity culture, deploying the familiar idiom of U.S.-Japanese compatibility and harmony. By then, he had an unshakable faith in sports as an item of mass entertainment. In June, his media company sponsored an eight-round bantamweight boxing match between French world champion Emile Pladner and Japanese challenger Horiguchi "Piston" Tsuneo, a member of Waseda University's boxing team at the time. The sporting event drew an astounding 30,000 spectators to its open-air venue, Waseda's Tozuka Stadium (turned into a venue with a seating capacity of 25,000 in 1926 with funds partially generated from the highly profitable Waseda–University of Chicago series).[15] After this highly rewarding experience, the kingpin of the *Yomiuri Shinbun* became even more determined to deliver Babe Ruth, the ultimate American sports icon, to Japanese "consumers." Meanwhile, back from another coaching junket for Tokyo Big 6, Hunter began lobbying major-league executives and the Japanese Foreign Ministry about the next postseason Japanese tour.[16]

By that time, however, Hunter was no longer Shōriki's business partner on the American side. After the 1931 tour, the two men found themselves mired in a dispute over the tour's publicity costs. The contract had the *Yomiuri Shinbun* responsible for all expenses, but Shōriki argued that Hunter should contribute part of the huge profits he had handed over intact to his American business partners. Hunter resisted this proposition, sticking to the "Western" notion of the sanctity of contractual terms. In the end, Abe had to intervene and broker a face-saving compromise that involved, among other things, Hunter donating part of his cut in the profits to the city of Tokyo as a contribution to the proposed construction of a modern steel-and-concrete stadium in the metropolitan area. Shōriki, however, used this dispute over money as an excuse to part with Hunter because he had found another, more pliable, and better-connected liaison to organized baseball: Lefty O'Doul. Not only had O'Doul endeared himself to Shōriki during the coaching junket arranged by Hunter in the previous fall; Shōriki also calculated that his new pet Japanophile's connection to Ruth as a former Yankee teammate might prove useful in enticing his object of affection to Japan.[17]

As soon as the 1933 season ended, O'Doul began to maneuver assiduously among the majors' executives on behalf of his Japanese patron. By year's end, he had successfully engineered club owners' unanimous endorsement of a postseason overseas tour and cleared the biggest hurdle: getting Czar Landis's permission. O'Doul did so by capitalizing on the old-boy networking that typically shaped organized baseball's key decisions at its highest echelons. He piggybacked on a blessing the commissioner had already given to Connie Mack's plan to organize a world tour in partnership with the Canadian Pacific Railroad. It was understood among baseball insiders to be a gift by Landis and club owners to this longtime manager-owner of the Philadelphia Athletics, who was experiencing financial difficulties during the Depression. O'Doul brokered a deal whereby the *Yomiuri Shinbun* would pay Mack 150,000 yen as a guarantee for the Japanese leg of his world tour.[18] On July 18, the *Yomiuri* made a bombastic sponsorship announcement of a postseason tour by American League all-stars, including Babe Ruth. There was one problem with that notice, however: Shōriki had not yet secured Ruth's agreement to come to Japan.[19]

In early October, with the tour's departure from the United States only a few weeks off, the *Yomiuri* was at long last able to persuade Ruth to come on board. This last-minute breakthrough was a product of a combination of circumstances, including where Ruth stood in terms of his career after his disappointing 1934 season. He was clearly no longer at the top of his game, with Gehrig and Jimmie Foxx far outslugging him in home runs. Ruth announced his intent to retire as a player at the end of the next season but also let it be known that he wished to round out his career by becoming a manager—of his beloved Yankees, he hoped. Various considerations of Ruth as a manager came and went. Perhaps his best opportunity for receiving an offer of a major-league managerial position had been undermined by his decision to go to Hawaii when the 1933 season ended. Detroit Tigers president Frank Navin was seriously considering signing Ruth as manager to replace Bucky Harris, who had just led the Tigers to a disappointing sixth-place finish. But Ruth, contractually committed to playing a series of exhibition games in Honolulu, left without meeting with Navin. He did call Navin from Honolulu, but the Tigers' president was not pleased about the time of the call (reportedly 2:00 A.M. Detroit time). Whether or not that factored into his hiring decision, Navin opted two months later to hire Mickey Cochrane to be his player-manager.[20]

After this disappointment, Ruth probably knew as well as anyone that his managerial prospects were not bright. It was at that juncture that the Japanese sponsor strategically stroked the battered ego of the former home-run king. Paying personal homage to Ruth in New York, Shōriki's agent Suzuki showed Ruth the *Yomiuri*'s promotional poster for the upcoming major-league tour. Ruth's king-size face was the only player portrait featured on it. A flattered and amused Ruth finally agreed to join Mack's world tour, or so goes Japanese baseball lore.[21] Shōriki made Ruth's commitment airtight by arranging for him to be the team's player-manager in the Japanese leg of the tour, even though Mack did most of the actual managing. The first Japanese book-length biography of Ruth, complete with an ad for a Babe Ruth trivia contest with an autographed ball as a prize, was published before his arrival to raise the hype.[22] On October 20, the fourteen-member American League all-stars left Vancouver for Japan on board the *Empress of Japan*. The dazzling squad included five future Hall of Famers besides Ruth: Gehrig, Jimmie Foxx, Lefty Gomez, Earl Averill, and Charlie Gehringer. Gehrig, accompanied by his newlywed wife, Eleanor, was the only returning member from the 1931 tour. O'Doul, now a New York Giant, was only able to join the tour as a nonplaying assistant manager because in late 1933 the National League had prohibited off-season overseas competitions by its players for fear of injuries.[23]

Their monthlong, twelve-city tour of Japan was a replay of the spectacularly successful 1931 tour and much more. The Americans were again treated like royalty, and the Japanese government made sure that its embrace of the American travelers and their games was widely publicized, both at home and abroad. When Ruth and company landed in Yokohama on November 2, an estimated 100,000 Japanese fans gathered on the docks and along the road to the train station, waving national flags of the two countries. The Railroad Ministry again arranged a special Tokyo-bound train for the American professional athletes and their travel companions. The *Yomiuri* issued an extra to report the arrival of Ruth and company. When they arrived at Tokyo Station, the travelers were feted by an estimated one million people crowding into the capital city to catch a glimpse of the home-run king and other shining stars of U.S. major-league baseball. The American guests were then transported in a motorcade from the Tokyo station to the Imperial Hotel, the architectural feat of Frank Lloyd Wright that had withstood the crushing power of the 1923 earthquake.

The highlight of the grand parade came when the delegation was engulfed in a deafening chorus of "Babe Ruth, Banzai!" cheers as it proceeded through the Ginza district, commonly referred to in U.S. newspapers as the "Broadway of Tokyo." All other traffic was stopped to make way for this lordly procession. Riding atop a Ford convertible, Ruth paraded down the thoroughfare like a triumphant war general returning home victoriously; some observers even analogized the scene to Charles Lindbergh's ticker-tape parade in New York City in 1927. At the welcome ceremony in downtown Hibiya Park, the American delegation was formally greeted by top Japanese government officials and U.S. ambassador Joseph Grew. Among the Japanese dignitaries in attendance was the Foreign Ministry's information director, Amou Eiji, who relayed well wishes from Foreign Minister Hirota Kōki (who later would be condemned and hanged as one of Japan's thirteen Class-A war criminals after World War II). The original articulator of the so-called Amau Doctrine[24] waxed poetic about "manly sportsmanship," which "transcends national boundaries and contributes to international good neighborliness." There was not even a hint in these carefully choreographed enactments of U.S.-Japanese friendship that the two governments had been dueling fiercely over geopolitical issues that included, but was certainly not limited to, the puppet state of Manchukuo, created two years earlier.[25]

Ruth's tour of Japan in 1934 outstripped the preceding tour by major leaguers not just in pomp and festivities but in a commercial sense as well. A sellout crowd of more than 55,000 watched the series opener at Jingū Stadium on November 4. On the tour's western swing, 60,000 spectators reportedly packed into Kōshien Stadium, yielding a profit of 20,000 yen for the ticketing agent in the region, the Hanshin Railroad Company. A grand total of 700,000 spectators attended the sixteen games, in which the Americans invariably walloped the Japanese all-stars. Regardless of the one-sided results, the *Yomiuri* still netted upward of 300,000 yen, which the company split 30 percent to 70 percent with its American business partners.[26] Ruth, who played right field and appeared in every inning of every game, was by far the brightest shining star of all. He also emerged as the triple crown of the series, hitting thirteen home runs, with twenty-seven RBIs and a .408 batting average. Everywhere he went, the Japanese let him know with their thundering banzai cheers and chanting of his name that he was still the king of baseball in Japan, even though his playing career might be soon ending in America.

The rhetoric of baseball as evidence of U.S.-Japanese compatibility was employed not only by the Japanese press and government; the tour's members, the American press, and the game's boosters back in the United States similarly harped on that theme for all it was worth. According to Lieb's *Sporting News*, Babe's visit was almost "a religious experience" for "these little almond-eyed fans." In the same magazine, Mack went so far as to suggest that there would never be a war with Japan as long as the Japanese loved and played baseball, because through "our national game" Japan could be made to understand "the true Yankee spirit." All major American journalistic outlets—newspapers, magazines, newsreels, and radio programs—participated in this self-congratulatory lovefest. The effusive remarks by Ruth and Mack about brotherly friendship between the two countries forged through "our game" were spread far and wide, transmitted through Japan's national radio network and in an NBC radio broadcast from Tokyo. Years later, Grew would reminisce about these high points of the major leaguers' 1934 tour and praise Ruth as the goodwill ambassador who "accomplished more in U.S.-Japanese comity than he could ever hope for." Perhaps all these effusions were meant to be innocent boasts, well-meaning mutual cheerleading, a promotional pitch, or diplomatic pleasantries. As an amalgamated symbolic message spread through diverse informational channels, however, they assumed propagandistic properties, some unintended and some probably fully intended.[27]

The effusive media reports of baseball diplomacy notwithstanding, U.S.-Japanese relations were imperceptibly yet inexorably shifting toward a wider rift in the fall of 1934. That much was clear from the mysterious off-field activities of the Americans' backup catcher, Moe Berg, a former Washington Senator who had just moved to the Cleveland Indians in a midseason trade. The literature abounds on Berg's unconventional life, his possible activity as an undercover agent for the U.S. government during the 1934 Japan tour, and his subsequent work as an intelligence officer during World War II.[28] A graduate of Princeton University and Columbia Law School, Berg was one of the most erudite major leaguers of all times. Gifted with innate linguistic abilities, Berg mastered multiple languages, including Japanese. His proficiency in the language had made Berg immensely popular with the Japanese baseball fraternity and press during his coaching junket in 1932. His performance during the 1934 season had been mediocre at best, but Berg was added to the 1934 tour at the last minute, supposedly for his familiarity with the country and his language skills.

He arrived in Japan with a letter of reference from Secretary of State Cordell Hull and a 16mm Bell and Howell movie camera tucked away in his personal effects. On November 29, Berg was a no-show at a game near Tokyo. That day, he went to St. Luke's Hospital in downtown Tokyo, presumably to visit Ambassador Grew's daughter, who had just given birth. Rather than visit her, however, Berg ascended to the rooftop of the hospital building (one of the highest in Tokyo at the time), panned the surrounding skyline with his camera, and recorded images of the city's industrial areas and harbor facilities. The images Berg filmed that day were later used in mapping the flight path of the famous 1942 bombing raid on Tokyo by Lieutenant Colonel Jimmy Doolittle. During the war, Berg would work in Nelson Rockefeller's Office of the Coordinator of Inter-American Affairs and later contract with the Office of Strategic Services, the institutional forerunner to the Central Intelligence Agency. Whatever the real reason behind Berg's last-minute inclusion in the 1934 tour or the motive behind his pseudo-detective work, this oft-quoted anecdote about his mysterious AWOL conduct in Tokyo serves as a reminder of the precarious balance upon which the bilateral relationship was teetering during that turbulent mid-decade. Underneath the media-enhanced symbolic images of U.S.-Japanese camaraderie via baseball was a dark sea of mutual suspicion that was definitely deepening.[29]

Blissfully unaware of the American intelligence gathering in their midst, Japanese fans soaked in the major leaguers' overpowering athletic and technical prowess during the sixteen-game series. To them, the tour's finest hour came during the tenth game, held in Shizuoka on November 20. Sawamura Eiji, a fresh-faced seventeen-year-old rookie from Kyoto, pitched seven shutout innings and struck out nine batters, including four consecutive strikeouts of Gehringer, Ruth, Gehrig, and Foxx in the first and second innings. Sawamura lost the game 1–0 after surrendering a home run to Gehrig in the eighth inning, but this magnificent performance against the major-league greats instantly earned him a permanent place in the pantheon of Japanese baseball. He also acquired the moniker "School Boy Sawamura"—an obvious reference to Lynwood "Schoolboy" Rowe, who pitched the Detroit Tigers to the AL championship that season—and a reputation among the tour members and baseball commentators in the United States as a fireball hurler to be watched for. Connie Mack, in particular, considered the Japanese teenager potential big-league material and tried to recruit him.[30] On December 2, the "Tall Tactician" and his fourteen-member crew left Tokyo for their next stop, Seoul, by way of Kobe. From that Japanese colonial outpost, the tour preceded to Shanghai and Manila, delighting the colonial capital's foreign expatriates, both American and Japanese. Wherever there was a concentration of Japanese expatriates in Asia, the major leaguers could count on robust business for their games.

The Rise of Japanese Professional Baseball
The majors' 1934 tour helped usher in the era of full-blown professional baseball in Japan. The 1932 *Yakyū Tōseirei* made players of Tokyo Big 6, the fount of top-notch baseball talent, unavailable to play against professionals. As a result, while Shōriki and his agents negotiated to be integrated into Connie Mack's world tour, they concurrently faced the challenge of organizing a crash team of "professionals" to challenge the visiting major leaguers. The hurriedly assembled squad consisted mainly of semipros drawn from the industrial league and high school players who were willing, for one reason or another, to have their amateur status forfeited. The latter category of newly christened "professionals" consisted of Sawamura and Victor Starffin, a six-foot-four pitcher from the city of Asahikawa in Hokkaido.[31] For Sawamura, the oldest son of a petty merchant with a large family to support, turning pro before graduating from high school was an economic necessity; for Starffin, it was an existential im-

perative stemming from his less-than-secure residency status in the country. Starffin's White Russian parents had fled their homeland after the Bolshevik Revolution and ended up in the Manchurian city of Harbin. In 1925, when Starffin was nine years old, the family defected to Japan using the Nansen Passport, the identification document the League of Nations began issuing for refugees. As they assembled the all-Japan squad, Shōriki and his agents browbeat this stateless teenager into leaving high school and turning pro with a veiled threat of having him and his parents deported to the Soviet Union under Stalin. Also rounding out Japan's original thirty-member, multiethnic roster were players recruited under various circumstances from Korea, southern Manchuria, and the Japanese American communities in Hawaii and California. In that sense, the newly launched professional team was a microcosm of the multiethnic Japanese empire.[32]

Only three weeks after the major leaguers left Japan, Shōriki and baseball boosters coalescing around him took steps to incorporate the 1934 all-Japan team into a permanent commercial entity, with start-up capital of 500,000 yen. The pool of originally contracted players formed the nucleus of the resulting nineteen-member squad, Dai Nippon Tokyo Yakyū Kurabu (Greater Japan Tokyo Baseball Club). As a show of appreciation for his successful lobbying of major-league club owners enabling the 1934 tour, Shōriki gifted 200 shares of the company's stock to O'Doul and named him "adviser."[33] The club's other founding brothers, including Suzuki and Ichioka Tadao, a former manager of the Waseda University baseball team, envisioned a two-stage plan for building this new enterprise. In the first phase, the team would raise its level of play to one comparable to America's AA minor leagues. To achieve that goal, the squad would barnstorm in the U.S. West Coast and play at least sixty games against Pacific Coast League clubs and other lesser teams. In the second phase, they hoped, the club would begin challenging big-league clubs, with the ultimate goal of being a party to a "true World Series." With this exceedingly ambitious blueprint, the Dai Nippon Tokyo Yakyū Kurabu left for the United States in February 1935.[34]

Within a year of the club's departure for the United States, six other "professional" clubs fielding all-salaried rosters emerged in Japan. The instigator of this industrial development was none other than Shōriki. Ever an astute businessman, he understood exactly why the pioneer Japanese pro clubs of the previous decade had failed: they did not fill the most fundamental requirement for building a viable, freestanding sports enterprise, which is to have a critical mass of rival teams to play against and to constitute a stable regime of regular competition to sustain fan interest. Guided by this self-administered caveat, Shōriki aggressively lobbied other entrepreneurial-minded industrialists and businessmen to join him in this new "industry."[35] Shōriki first approached the Hanshin Railroad Company as the most obvious potential partner in this brave new world of business. There were several reasons why this railway corporation in western Japan would be interested in starting a pro baseball club. First, the company owned Kōshien Stadium, located along one of its suburban commuter-train routes. Hanshin had also served as the ticketing agent in western Japan for the highly profitable 1931 and 1934 tours by major leaguers, so its top executives understood that baseball could be a real moneymaker. As Shōriki expected, Hanshin proved receptive to the idea. In December 1935, a year after the launching of the Dai Nippon Tokyo Yakyū Kurabu, the Osaka Tigers, bankrolled by the Hanshin Railroad Company, became incorporated as Japan's second professional baseball club.[36]

The birth of the Osaka Tigers had a ripple effect. First, Hanshin's rival rail line in the greater Osaka area, the Hankyū Railroad Company, announced that it would launch its own pro baseball club. Having tried his hand at the baseball business sponsoring the doomed Takarazuka Association, the company's imaginative owner-president, Kobayashi Ichizō, had been waiting for an opportune moment to reprise his effort.[37] A spate of other corporations attuned to baseball's commercial potential followed suit. One was *Osaka Mainichi Shinbun*, the national daily that had been sponsoring various "amateur" student tournaments and major leaguers' off-season jaunts arranged by Hunter. The newspaper company had also been sponsoring the semipro Daimai club since the late 1920s. *Shin Aichi*, a regional newspaper in Nagoya, also signed on, prompting its rival regional newspaper, *Nagoya Shinbun*, to get into the action. By early 1936, a total of seven professional clubs had lined up to form an all-professional league, Nippon Shokugyō Yakyū Renmei, or the Nippon Professional Baseball Association (NPBA). The league opened for its inaugural season in April 1936.[38]

This second generation of Japanese professional baseball clubs[39] offers an illuminating view into patterns of Japanese industrial development in the interwar period. The parent companies of the NPBA's original seven clubs were private railway companies (Hanshin, Seibu, Hankyū) and newspapers (*Yomiuri, Shin Aichi, Kokumin Shinbun, Nagoya*), two of the industrial sectors that had undergone rapid expansion and capital accumulation over the previous three decades. They were the drivers and, in turn, chief beneficiaries of urbanization and the arrival of an incipient mass-consumer society in Japan, creating and serving train riderships or newspaper readerships.[40] The media companies did not look at ownership of a baseball club as an independent revenue stream; rather, they expected it to serve as the parent company's advertising division. The same applied to the private railways, to which the operation of a pro baseball club was only one part of an overall corporate strategy built around fulfilling the nation's growing recreation-related demands. Hankyū was the most salient example of this business model, which was unique to Japanese professional baseball clubs. During the company's expansive interwar years, its charismatic helmsman, Kobayashi, fashioned and pursued an integrated strategy often referred to as the "Takarazuka Strategy" (*takarazuka senryaku*), which tailored his commuter-train services to an emerging middle-class lifestyle that featured increasing leisure-time activities. To lure greater ridership and to cater to customers' needs as residents and consumers, Hankyū built a variety of attractions and recreational facilities—such as department stores, amusement parks, and sports facilities— along its suburban train routes. The Hankyū club's home ground, Nishinomiya Stadium, was completed in May 1937. The construction of the stadium and the operation of a baseball club to maximize its use were integrated into that multifaceted corporate strategy. To that extent, netting a profit from the baseball club, in and of itself, was not considered critical. Four months later, Kōrakuen Stadium, which would become home to two Tokyo-based clubs, opened in downtown Tokyo with a future plan to expand into multiplex sport facilities.[41]

The diffusion of a new communications technology, radio, also brought the still-born Japanese professional baseball of the 1920s back to sustainable life in the mid-1930s. After acquiring a technology license from General Electric, radio broadcasts by government-run JOAK (NHK) began in Japan in March 1925. More than any other technology or household appliance up to that point, the radio spread quickly in Japan[42] and reshaped the nation's cultural landscape. Its rapid diffusion owed much to government industrial policy. The Ministry of Communications made concerted efforts to install a nationwide radio network in time for the coronation of Emperor Showa in Kyoto in November 1928. Many eateries and businesses tried to draw customers by playing a radio at their storefronts. The national radio broadcasting of the middle-school national tournaments began in 1927. Tokyo Big 6 games also went on the national airwaves two years later, and listening to the much-hyped Waseda-Keio matchups became a national craze. The new medium made baseball more popular and accessible to those lacking time and resources to go to the games. Stylized game reporting by a handful of pioneer radio broadcasters groomed some collegiate and middle-school standouts into national celebrities, or "stars." The outbreak of the media-abetted baseball fever in interwar Japan and the rise of sports celebrity culture thus owed some of their impetus to this new electric channel of informational flow. The radio as an informational medium also became a key advertising venue for many of the professional baseball clubs' parent companies. Shōriki's *Yomiuri*, in particular, self-consciously aligned the content of its newspaper reporting with that of radio broadcasts.[43]

These early pro baseball clubs also mirrored the fact that the Japanese imperial metropole and the overseas diasporic communities constituted an integrated labor market for those with specialized skills. As a new enterprise, Japan's professional baseball drew extensively on Nisei talents imported from Hawaii and the U.S. mainland, and many of the prewar pro teams included Asian colonial subjects on their rosters. The most prominent among them was Wakabayashi Tadashi, an Oahu-born *kibei*[44] who pitched for the Osaka (Hanshin) Tigers between 1936 and 1949 (except for a brief wartime interlude).[45] Another leading Nisei player in prewar Japanese professional baseball was Fumito "Jimmy" Horio, born in 1907 on the island of Maui. When his Issei parents gave up on unrewarding plantation work and returned to Hiroshima in 1928, Horio, a dual citizen, elected to move to the U.S. mainland instead to pursue his dream of becoming a major leaguer. He played for the semipro L.A. Nippon while working as a truck driver. He then moved up to minor-league baseball, playing a couple of stints in South Dakota and Nebraska. In 1934, Horio turned west and moved to Japan in search of new playing opportunities. With a heavy load of American-style self-promotion, he landed a contract to play for the all-Japan team during Babe Ruth's Japan tour and later made a lateral move into the Dai Nippon Tokyo club. Premier Taiwanese players, such as Go Ha (who later Japanized his name to Go Shōsei) joined the Dai Nippon Tokyo Yakyū Kurabu in 1937, similarly attesting to prewar Japanese pro baseball's circum-imperial player recruitment.[46]

There was also a surprisingly color-blind quality to pre–World War II Japan's professional baseball in its infancy. One of the founding members and the inaugural captain of the Nagoya club was a former minor leaguer from Los Angeles named Andrew Harris McGalliard. After attending the University of Southern California for two years, McGalliard joined the

AA Pacific Coast Sacramento Club in 1928, but he was unable to achieve his dream of moving up to the big leagues. In 1930, McGalliard joined the semipro L.A. Nippon as a ringer and toured Japan for the first time in his life. He struggled through the Depression years, working for an oil refinery and playing for the L.A. Nippon. In early 1935, McGalliard was "discovered" by Suzuki Sōtarō, then barnstorming in the United States with the Dai Nippon Tokyo Yakyū Club. Impressed by McGalliard's earnest commitment to baseball and eagerness to learn Japanese, Suzuki later recommended this white American catcher to Kōno Atsushi, the Nagoya Club's inaugural field manager, who was seeking to recruit talent from the United States. McGalliard arrived in Japan in early 1936, along with three teammates from the L.A. Nippon. As a member of the Nagoya Club, Andrew Harris McGalliard went by the field name "Bucky Harris" to evoke association with the famed former major-league second baseman Stanley "Bucky" Harris. The Japanese "Bucky" Harris's hustling play and round-the-clock dedication to his craft garnered widespread admiration from Japanese pro baseball's founding brothers. Kōno even called him an "American with the [martial] Yamato spirit (*yamato damashii*)."[47] Harris was elected the Most Valuable Player (MVP) in the 1937 fall season (Japanese pro baseball played split spring and fall seasons at that time) as a member of the Kōrakuen Eagles and became the home-run king in the 1938 spring season.

The Tokyo Giants' 1935 North American Barnstorming Tour
When it was launched in December 1935, the Dai Nippon Tokyo Yakyū Kurabu was the lone professional club in the country, and it was in need of competitors. That reason—as well as the club's founding brothers' vision of attaining a AA minor-league level of play and "tapping into the baseball fever of the 120,000 *dōhō* [consanguineous partners] on the Pacific Coast"—lay behind the club's spending a good portion of its inaugural year in business barnstorming across the United States. It bears reiterating that, at its inception, the club's gaze was decidedly cast eastward across the Pacific for training and a fan base. When the nineteen-member squad sailed from Yokohama for San Francisco on February 14, 1935, its business manager, Suzuki, expected to schedule sixty to eighty games against PCL clubs in spring training and against California semipros. At that point, he still envisioned a tour geographically restricted to the Pacific coastal states. However, it ended up evolving into a four-month, 104-game, 59-city grueling expedition crisscrossing the western half of the North American con-

tinent. Along the way, the Japanese baseballers traversed thirteen American states and Canada's four western provinces, crossed the U.S.-Canadian border twice, and even ventured south of the U.S.-Mexican border.[48]

Initial robust attendance, solid gate receipts from games against PCL teams, and substantial press coverage in the West Coast cities created an illusion of commercial success and provided the motivation for the tour's managers, Ichioka and Suzuki, to continue it beyond the initially arranged schedule. The itinerary grew unexpectedly dispersed also because Japanese American community leaders in isolated locations implored the club to come and play for the area's *dōbō*, who were enduring punishing life circumstances and recurrent waves of anti-Japanese campaigns—especially over landownership (even by American-born Nisei)—by white nativists. Venturing outside the Pacific coastal areas, the Japanese pro ballplayers trekked through Idaho, Utah, Colorado, Nebraska, midwestern states, and Canada until finally returning to the West Coast again in late June. Their fortunes at the gate dropped precipitously in areas without a substantial Japanese American population, and they had to play a wide gamut of American contenders—minor-league, semipro, student, town, company, and sandlot teams. The tour almost ran out of money while traversing Saskatchewan and Alberta, at one time finding itself in real danger of being stranded in the middle of the Canadian Rockies. Overall, it turned out to be a money-losing operation.[49]

Regardless, the 1935 North American barnstorming trip mapped the future of the newly launched Japanese professional club in profound ways. It was during the first leg of this U.S. tour that the Dai Nippon Tokyo Yakyū Kurabu began to call itself the Tokyo Giants to make the team easily recognizable to American audiences. The advice for the name change came from O'Doul, the club's American founding brother and official adviser who was a ubiquitous presence in the early phase of the tour in California.[50] O'Doul was invested, both professionally and emotionally, in the success of this Japanese experiment. While touring the world with the American League players the previous fall, O'Doul was informed that his longtime friend and the owner of the San Francisco Seals, Charlie Graham, had bought his contract from the New York Giants. Graham sought to bolster his club's box-office appeal during the Depression-era doldrums by bringing this popular native son back from the east to manage the financially faltering AA team.[51] This meant that the thirty-seven-year-old O'Doul's career as a major leaguer was over, but he took solace in returning to his beloved hometown. It was through O'Doul's good offices that Suzuki was able to schedule games against PCL teams on short notice. Thanks to O'Doul's extensive connections in the Bay Area, the traveling Japanese ballplayers also received a substantial welcome from local politicians and civic leaders, despite the anti-Japanese feelings swirling in the region. One of the local dignitaries who welcomed the Japanese baseball tourists at a public reception was San Francisco's Italian American mayor, Angelo Rossi. In a historic encounter at a game in Fresno in late March, the Giants' nine engaged for the first time a Seals standout clearly on his way to the big time. No one imagined that, nineteen years later, this Italian American slugger by the name of Joe DiMaggio would choose Japan as the destination for his honeymoon with Marilyn Monroe.[52]

The presence of large Japanese American communities was instrumental to the team's relatively solid commercial performance on the West Coast leg of the tour. The aging Issei, in particular, rushed to watch "their own" play against, and sometimes beat, all-white Pacific Coast Leaguers.[53] The tour's opening game against the San Francisco Missions, held in Marysville, was attended by 1,500 mostly Japanese and Japanese American spectators. A match against the Sacramento Senators drew nearly 5,000 spectators from the Japanese American communities in and around the state capital. The two teenage hurlers, "School Boy" Sawamura and Starffin, piqued the interest of PCL scouts and became the darlings of the local Japanese American communities. Issei were delighted, or perhaps bemused, that Starffin, often referred to in the local press as the "Russian pitcher," spoke better Japanese than their Nisei children.[54] As the team traveled through the Central Valley and into Southern California, the Tokyo Giants played against local Japanese American semipro clubs such as the San Jose Asahi, the Fresno Athletic Club, and the Stockton Yamato. They fared less well at the gate playing those ethnic semipro squads, although a three-game series against the L.A. Nippon was a definite moneymaker. Billed as the "Japanese World Series," it received extensive advance publicity by the city's Japanese-language newspaper, *Rafu Shinpō*. It was also a "homecoming" for Horio, who still commanded a local fan following. The series opener on April 13 was honored by the presence of the Japanese consul general in Los Angeles, Hori Kōichi, who threw the ceremonial first pitch in front of 3,000 spectators. The Tokyo Giants won two of the three games in the series at White Sox Park.[55]

As they traveled farther south, the Japanese ballplayers stepped into the world of multiracial baseball in America and learned a general pattern that came with it: as the racial and ethnic makeup of the contenders got more diverse, the conditions on the road became more austere and the playing fields more Spartan. In the Imperial Valley near the U.S.-Mexican border, the baseballers from Tokyo played against a local all-black semipro squad. The morale of the area's several thousand Japanese agricultural settlers received a huge, if ephemeral, boost from the Tokyo Giants' 4–0 win. The interracial match temporarily brought together on the playing field the town's Japanese and black populations, who hardly ever interacted, living in separate residential sections across the Southern Pacific Railroad tracks. Passing across the national border into the town of Mexicali, the Tokyo Giants routed the Mexican all-stars, 20–6, on a makeshift playing field set up on an airstrip.[56]

The team then headed up to the Pacific Northwest to play in Oregon and Washington before traveling across the Rockies. The tour became quite grueling and shoestring during the trek across the mountainous states of Utah and Colorado. The highlight of the ensuing midwestern leg of the journey took place in Michigan, which turned out to be the tour's easternmost stop. In Detroit, the traveling Japanese ballplayers received an unexpectedly warm reception by the Ford Motor Company, whose corporate semipro team was handily subdued 6–0. They were paraded through the auto city in shiny red V-8 Fords, escorted by police motorcycles. In the other bastion of automobile production in the state, Flint, the Japanese travelers were treated to a guided tour of General Motors's Buick plant and a lavish banquet given by company and city leaders. The rival American auto companies had set up assembly plants in Japan in the mid-1920s and were competing fiercely to gain an edge over each other in this overseas market. The royal treatment that the Giants' nine received was part of the American automakers' promotional campaigns targeting this promising Asian market.[57]

Throughout the tour, the baseball games played by the Tokyo Giants' nine became a site where ideas about race, manliness, and American-style consumer modernity were articulated and practiced in complex and interwoven ways. This amalgam had a long genealogy in Japanese attitudes toward the game, but it had also been reflected in American commentaries about Japanese baseball as well. Noting the Japanese enthusiasm for baseball in *America's National Game* (1911), A. G. Spalding opined that it was in keeping with "what we know of the little brown men of the Orient." Baseball being a "combative game" embraced by "aggressive, competitive, and progressive people," the Japanese loved the game because they shared those attributes that made (white) Americans the heir apparent to mastery of the world order that was emerging in the early twentieth century.[58] "The little brown men" had been a consistent refrain in American press remarks about Japanese collegiate barnstormers ever since Waseda's 1905 tour. As for the Giants' North American barnstorming tour in 1935, baseball historian Nagata Yoichi has offered a meticulous tabulation and analysis of racialized references that appeared in local and metropolitan newspapers. The phrases "yellow-skinned all-star team," "visitors with almond-shaped eyes," "slanted-eyed professionals," and "short-legged, black-haired base runner" give a sample of the racially loaded descriptors Nagata unearthed in these venues for expressing Depression-era American racial ideology. The tour's sole Caucasian member, Starffin, was often touted as a scion of the Russian nobility who escaped persecution by the Bolsheviks. Interestingly, the word "Jap" hardly appeared in the West Coast newspapers during the Giants' 1935 tour but did quite often and nonchalantly in the press comments in America's heartland, where there was no history of organized anti-Japanese campaigns. Nagata suggests that avoidance of the term "Jap" might stem from the fact that the newspapers most likely to use that epithet, the Hearst papers, had just entered into an international syndicate agreement with Shōriki's *Yomirui Shinbun*.[59]

The traveling Japanese ballplayers also elicited positive press reactions, specifically about their politeness, civility to the umpire, manly sportsmanship, and apparent dedication to teamwork. These attributes were often cited as evidence to support broader social commentaries, such as U.S.-Japanese brotherhood and the reconcilability of their cultural differences and the diplomatic agendas of the two countries. The most often cited example of such Japanese "politeness" involved players taking off their cap and bowing to the plate umpire before going to bat.[60] Actually, such "positive" qualities ascribed to the Japanese ballplayers were self-consciously enacted. The strategy of playacting "Japanese politeness" and "fair playing samurai" was adopted at the very beginning of the tour at the suggestion of O'Doul, who was convinced that the technically deficient Japanese players would not be able to sustain fans' interest with their skill alone. He also suggested that the Giants' nine form a circular huddle—like football players—between innings, a show of cultural exotica mixed with elements familiar to American sports viewers. The players' numbers on the Giants uniform were written in Chinese characters (*kanji*) to make them look more Asian to the untutored American eye.[61] Such contrived civility and acts of self-exotification were further highlighted by staged photos and press releases distributed by the tour's publicist and booking agent, Webster Nolan. The San Francisco sports promoter was a friend of O'Doul and had cut his teeth as a journalist working for media outlets syndicated with the Hearst papers. As Adria Imada has shown in her study of Hawaiian hula-dancing tours in the continental United States in the 1930s, white American consumer tastes and their idealized notions of "what Asia [Hawaii] is like" profoundly shaped the actual practices of a commodified entertainment. In this sense, the Japanese baseball players and the Hawaiian hula girls traveled in the same boat in the metropolitan market of the American consumer empire. The only difference was that the Japanese ballplayers' cultural merchandise was served with a masculine flavor.[62]

The self-orientalizing enactments by the Giants' nine offended some local Issei and angered baseball purists back in Japan. Tobita, now a baseball writer for the *Asahi Shinbun*, jumped to the forefront of the criticism that erupted in early 1936. In a series of editorial commentaries, Tobita reacted scathingly to the reported showboating by the Tokyo Giants traveling in America. He took the occasion to denigrate the very notion of commercialized baseball, or at least its Japanese variety, as a "vulgar burlesque," and he reiterated his position that only purely amateur student baseball reflected the true essence of the sport in Japan. Tobita's public fulminations against baseball as a commercial spectacle resonated with the larger and more ideologically charged contemporary debate arising from Japanese ambivalence about Western (American) consumerist modernity, of which "fun and games" were a central element. For many traditionalists, professional baseball encapsulated these tangled questions. That ideological amalgamation was most dramatically and violently demonstrated when an outraged ultranationalist attempted to assassinate Shōriki in Tokyo in February 1935 for allowing "American baseball mercenaries" to desecrate Jingū Stadium, the "sacred grounds of student amateur baseball" located within the hallowed compound of the Meiji Shrine.[63] In a public rebuttal to Tobita's criticism on behalf of the traveling Tokyo Giants, Ichioka contended in a *Yomiuri* editorial that the club embodied "the genuine Japanese way of baseball steeled with the spirit of the Yamato nation" (*yamato damashī*) and that his barnstorming ballplayers were thus a vanguard of the "expanding [Japanese] empire." This public catechism betrayed the fact that even advocates of professional baseball legitimated the enterprise by emphasizing its value to national mobilization and overseas expansionism.[64]

The metaphoric power of baseball as intertwined with Japan's imperial greatness also became manifest at the final stop of the 1935 Giants tour: Hawaii. After playing their last game on the U.S. mainland against a semi-pro pickup squad fielded by the retired Ty Cobb, the Tokyo Giants departed San Francisco for Honolulu on June 24. The travelers played five games at Honolulu Stadium, all arranged by Steere Noda (now the territory's first ever Japanese American lawyer) and heavily publicized by the local Japanese-language newspaper, *Nippu Jiji*. The Giants beat the U.S. Navy team 6–2 in a game played as a companion event to the July 4 festivities at nearby Pearl Harbor. Three days later, however, the Giants surrendered their last game in Hawaii to the All-Chinese squad by a score of 2–1. Angry Nikkei spectators in the ballpark jeered and heckled, throwing food and *zabuton* (sitting cushions) at the prostrate Giants' nine. In contrast, jubilant Chinese fans celebrated the subduing of Japan's finest ballplayers with firecrackers. Exactly two years before the Marco Polo Bridge Incident opened an eight-year war between Japan and China, Sino-Japanese tensions were already flaring up in the playing field on the Pacific island.[65]

In February 1936, as Shōriki and the other industrialists enlisted by him launched Japan's first multiteam professional baseball league, the Tokyo Giants went on another barnstorming trip in the United States. This second tour drew a geographical loop stretching from California to Texas, Utah, Idaho, and the state of Washington. They played against PCL clubs, Japanese American and other semipros in California, and Class-A and Class-B minor leagues in Texas and elsewhere, compiling an overall record of 43 wins, 33 losses, and 1 tie. The Giants returned to Japan in June to join the newly launched, seven-team pro league, which had just opened in April for its inaugural season. With the domestic circuit of regular play in place, coupled with the beginning of war mobilization in the summer of 1937, the Tokyo Giants would not undertake another tour of the faraway United States before World War II.[66]

A New Baseball Entrepreneurship: The National Baseball Congress

Many of the American semipro squads that the Tokyo Giants played against in rural areas during their two U.S. tours were town and industrial teams of relatively recent vintage. By 1935, the U.S. federal government's multiplying efforts under the rubric of the New Deal, especially its relief and work programs administered by the so-called alphabet-soup agencies such as the Works Progress Administration (WPA) and the Civilian Conservation Corps (CCC), had ameliorated the economic hard times for several million Americans. As for the CCC, the federal government pushed this macroeconomic lever to assemble unemployed young American men in rural work camps, paying them $22 per month to put out forest fires and implement small-scale nature-conservation projects. These young men, now with some money in their pocket, also played baseball after work and on weekends, and many of their sandlot outfits evolved into town teams. By the late 1930s, a significant number of low-end minor leaguers had once worked for the CCC.[67] Semipro baseball clubs were a ubiquitous presence in Depression-era America's cultural landscape. Most were sponsored by local small and medium-sized businesses and consisted of employees who played ball only as an avocation. But in a number of well-organized and more competitive leagues with teams playing three or four times a week from May to September, a high-performing player could expect to supplement what he made at his day job by as much as $400 to $500 earned in this half-time vocational venue. By 1940 the National Baseball Congress (NBC), established as the governing body of American semipro baseball in 1934, claimed 25,000 affiliated teams and 500,000 players nationwide.[68]

Headquartered in Wichita, Kansas, the NBC was a curious outgrowth of Depression-era, county-seat business boosterism. In early 1933, Raymond "Hap" Dumont, a Wichita sporting-goods salesman, began organizing semipro baseball games among town teams and barnstorming semipro clubs in the state after receiving inspiration from a well-attended Sunday baseball game between circus clowns and local firemen. That summer, Wichita, Dumont's hometown, played host to sixteen Kansas semipro teams in a statewide tournament charging a team entry fee of $10 and offering a first prize of $400. To the local civic leaders' surprise and delight, 5,000 people paid 40 cents each to attend. The following year, the tournament attracted sixty-three teams and 35,000 spectators, with the state champion earning $2,074.00. Then a misfortune struck: a fire destroyed Island Park, Wichita's municipal stadium, leaving Dumont's state semipro tournament without a home. Trying to convince Wichita's city council to fund the construction of a new municipal ballpark with federal funds channeled through the New Deal, Dumont pledged to city manager Bert Wells that he would put on a national semipro tournament in the Depression-wracked community. The city of Wichita, with the help of the WPA, constructed the 20,000-seat Lawrence Stadium (now Lawrence-Dumont Stadium) by the Arkansas River. Dumont delivered the promised national tournament in August 1935, billing it as a "world championship" to boot. The event's 1935 ad touted that thirty-two invited teams would share $16,000 in prize money and $4,000 in expense money, with major-league scouts in attendance.[69]

Dumont's plan for establishing a successful tournament hinged on luring a big-name star to participate in the inaugural championship finals. With major leaguers still in the middle of their season, Dumont hatched the idea of enlisting the services of the biggest name competing neither in the American nor the National League: Negro League star pitcher Leroy "Satchel" Paige, then playing for the racially integrated Bismarck (North Dakota) Churchills, run by a local auto dealer. To entice Paige and his team to Wichita, Dumont offered Paige a whopping $1,000 appearance fee and promised a $7,000 winner's purse to be split among Paige's teammates if his outfit won the championship. Paige struck out sixty batters and won four games, beginning with one against a team made up entirely of nine brothers from Waukegan, Illinois (the Stanzal Brothers). Among the squads Paige bested at the tournament were Kenso Nushida's Japanese American All-Stars from Stockton, California, and a Native American squad from Wewoka, Oklahoma. In Dumont's mind, the participation of these teams validated his preposterous claim that his was a "world championship."

The inaugural 1935 NBC tournament, featuring a motley assortment of thirty-two teams "representing" twenty-four states, was a solid commercial success, with well over 50,000 spectators attending over a two-week period.[70] It also received extensive coverage in the *Sporting News*, whose editor, J. G. Taylor Spink, was thirsty for newsworthy events amid the doldrums of the Great Depression. An aura of respectability lent by the endorsement by baseball's premier publication was augmented when, in 1938, Dumont hired George Sisler—the legendary two-time .400 hitter then several years into retirement—to become NBC's new "commissioner." Somewhat tired of his sporting-goods retail business, Sisler gladly accepted this position. Dumont's humble midwestern semipro circuit achieved transcontinental reach in the ensuing years by bringing myriad obscure sandlot teams made up of the New Deal's key beneficiaries—CCC and WPA workers—into the NBC's organizational umbrella as affiliates.[71] With this sprawling domestic network under his belt, Dumont would next set his sight on opportunities overseas.

The mid-1930s produced a curious contingent of American baseball entrepreneurs aspiring to not only "national" but also "international" relevancy. They mostly operated outside the pale of organized baseball, but despite that marginality—or perhaps because of it—they sanguinely advocated making baseball an international sport with a multinational constituency. Along with Dumont, Leslie Mann, a former outfielder for the Boston Braves, the St. Louis Cardinals, and three other major-league clubs, falls into this category of unlikely American cultural internationalists. Mann, a graduate of Springfield YMCA College and a former college coach, retired from his fifteen-year major-league playing career in 1928. He then found a new mission in campaigning for baseball to be made into an Olympic sport, like soccer had been. Although the sport had been played in three previous Olympics (1904, 1912, and 1928) as an exhibition event, it was played mostly by track-and-field athletes on the U.S. national team. Mann wanted the great American game played by real ballplayers in front of a worldwide audience. Mann's efforts were largely spurned by organized baseball's insiders, but he was able to ally himself with amateur sports organizations like the NCAA and the AAU. Despite his fierce maneuvering through these groups, Mann failed to have baseball placed on the program of the 1932 Los Angeles Olympics, even though the games in North America did not include soccer.

Undeterred by this setback and armed with financial support from Louisville Slugger baseball-bat manufacturer Frank Bradsby, Mann shifted his attention to the 1936 Olympics to be held in Berlin. In 1935, Mann and his fellow Olympic baseball hopefuls created a national governing body of "amateur" baseball, the USA Baseball Congress, and gained an endorsement by the American Olympic Committee (AOC). Through the AOC's intercession—particularly helpful was assistance rendered by the organization's politically ambitious president, Avery Brundage—Mann engineered an invitation in November 1934 from the German Olympic Organizing Committee (by then firmly under the control of the Nazis) to send a team of American amateur baseballers to play a demonstration contest as part of the Olympics in the capital of the Third Reich. The Americans' opponent was going to be Japan, also invited by the German Olympic Organizing Committee. Whether by design or not, the announcement in Japan of this dual invitation was made at the same time as the arrival of the Babe Ruth tour.[72] In July 1936, the USA Baseball Congress held a national tryout in Baltimore with the endorsement of Babe Ruth, urging young American men to represent their country to "Bear the Name of Our Country and Carry Your Flag" as the "United States Demonstrates Its Greatest Game to the World." A squad of twenty-six collegiate players was assembled, including players from Stanford, the University of Southern California, the University of Oregon, and the University of Texas.[73]

Mann's campaigns on behalf of baseball becoming an Olympic sport brought together Americans and Japanese into a strangely collaborative setting at a time when their governments were rapidly becoming estranged over Japan's military adventurism in Asia. In November 1935, Mann sent a troupe of amateur baseball players—the Wheaties All-Stars, with General Mills underwriting the expenses—on an eight-game series in Japan to drum up the baseball-loving Asian nation's interest in his Olympic endeavors. The Japanese sponsor of this marketing enterprise was Meiji University's baseball club. Matsumoto "Frank" Takizō, the Meiji team's former Nisei student field manager and then a faculty member of the university, played host to the American visitors. The idea of sending a squad composed mainly of Tokyo Big 6 star players to the Berlin Olympics was batted about among Japanese amateur-sports officials through the fall and the winter. The Dainippon Taiiku Kyōkai (Japan Amateur Sports Association, or JASA), the national governing body with jurisdiction over the nation's Olympic teams, in the end declined the German Olympic Committee's invitation to a "U.S.-Japanese Berlin Series," forcing Americans to play an intrasquad contest instead. The reasons for Japan's last-minute withdrawal are not entirely clear, but the game's status as a non-medal-yielding demonstration event likely played a part. The JASA was far more intent on impressing Europeans with Japan's growing prowess in soccer in an effort to garner their endorsement of Tokyo's 1940 Olympic bid.[74] Discomfort caused by an increasingly vociferous international call for boycotting the "Nazi Olympics" may also have been a factor, at least among some Tokyo Big 6 officials. Senior statesmen of the Japanese baseball fraternity were also unimpressed by the level of baseball played by the amateur Wheaties All-Stars, who won only three games against Tokyo Big 6 teams. The fact that the American visitors wore a jersey bearing a corporate logo ("Wheaties") did not endear them to amateur purists in the Education Ministry; this marketing and publicity flop probably did not help advance Mann's cause, either.[75]

The exhibition game between two American squads, the "U.S.A. Olympics" and "World's Champions," was held on August 12 after the conclusion of all official events. Although Japan bowed out of the contest, Matsumoto, participating in the Berlin Games as a JASA officer and later receiving a swastika-bearing medal of honor from Hitler, served as one of the umpires. The game, held at night in a poorly lighted stadium, drew a crowd of 125,000, though a much smaller estimate of 90,000 spectators has also been mentioned in some historical sources. The turnout was substantial enough to convince the IOC to approve baseball as a formal event, not just an exhibition game, for the next Olympics, to be hosted by the city of Tokyo. American and Japanese baseball brothers who were invested in this project immediately began making plans for a "World Baseball Tournament" to be held as part of the 1940 Olympics. They approached amateur baseballers of twenty-one countries and organized the International Amateur Baseball Federation (IABF). The new organization, fancying itself an equivalent of FIFA, the International Federation of Association Football, was headquartered in Miami, Florida, where Mann's baseball school, the first of its kind, was located. Officials elected for the IABF included Mann (secretary-treasurer); Matsumoto (vice president); and Dinty Dennis, sports editor of the *Miami Herald*, serving as assistant secretary. Mann was also given "full authority" by IABF's constituent members to choose a prominent American as the organization's president. Eight countries and one "territory" (the United States, Japan, Mexico, Cuba, Germany, England, the Philippines, China, and Hawaii) signed up to compete in the 1940 World Baseball Tournament. It was to be preceded by a United States–Japan amateur "World Series" in Tokyo in 1937, a United States–Panama dual contest in 1938, and a third series between the United States and Japan in Honolulu in 1939.[76]

This little-known episode in America's overseas baseball mission and the pas de deux between American and Japanese amateur baseball officials was emblematic of both America's role in international sport in the 1930s and U.S.-Japanese relations at mid-decade. While Americans remained averse to foreign political and certainly military entanglements in the 1930s, as the legislation of the series of Neutrality Acts attested, many of them were quite active internationalists in the realm of sport. Indeed, as Barbara Key has aptly observed, "For these Americans, political isolationism went hand in hand with an aggressive, idealistic internationalism in the cultural sphere."[77] When it came to "fun and games," it might be argued, Americans in the 1930s could even be considered aggressive empire builders. The tale of Mann's international marketing of baseball and Japan's supporting role in it also demonstrates that the game of baseball gave American and Japanese nationals a space in which to work together against the grain of the era's interstate relationships, which were caught in a descending spiral.

A portrait of Horace Wilson. (Courtesy of the Japanese Baseball Hall of Fame Museum and Library)

A group picture of the Shinbashi Athletic Club, ca. 1878. Hiraoka Hiroshi is in the center of the middle row. The same picture was printed in the *Chicago Tribune* on July 15, 1888. (Courtesy of the Japanese Baseball Hall of Fame Museum and Library)

The 1896 Ichikō team that trounced the American teams. Chūma Kanoe is in the center of the back row. (Courtesy of the Japanese Baseball Hall of Fame Museum and Library)

The Waseda University 1905 West Coast tour. Abe Isoo is in the middle of the second row; Hashido Makoto is third from the right in the front row. (Courtesy of Waseda University Archives)

St. Louis of Hawaii, the first American semipro team to tour Japan in 1907. (Courtesy of the Keio University Fukuzawa Memorial Center for Modern Japanese Studies)

(opposite) Players of Keio and Waseda Universities with spectators, 1907. Abe Isoo is in the center of the middle row. (Courtesy of the Keio University Fukuzawa Memorial Center for Modern Japanese Studies)

Keio University vs. St. Louis at the Tsunamachi Grounds, 1907. Fees were collected at the gate for this game for the first time in Japan. (Courtesy of the Keio University Fukuzawa Memorial Center for Modern Japanese Studies)

The U.S. Major League tour of Japan with Herb Hunter, 1931. (Courtesy of the Keio University Fukuzawa Memorial Center for Modern Japanese Studies)

(opposite) Front-page picture of *Yakyūkai*, featuring Neal Pullen of the Philadelphia Royal Giants and Shinji Hamazaki of the Mita Club, 1927. (Courtesy of the Japanese Baseball Hall of Fame Museum and Library)

A group picture of the 1931 Major League All-Stars tour of Japan. (Courtesy of the Japanese Baseball Hall of Fame Museum and Library)

(opposite) The 1931 Major League All-Stars, accompanied by players' wives, U.S. ambassador William Cameron Forbes (center), and Japanese prime minister Wakatsuki Reijirō (next to Forbes). (Courtesy of the Japanese Baseball Hall of Fame Museum and Library)

A poster for the 1934 Major League tour of Japan, featuring Babe Ruth. (Courtesy of the Japanese Baseball Hall of Fame Museum and Library)

(opposite) Pictures of the 1934 Major League tour of Japan featured in *Yakyūkai*; Ruth was besieged by fans in Tokyo. (Courtesy of the Japanese Baseball Hall of Fame Museum and Library)

入場式、前から鈴木氏、マツケ、ルー、ブラウン、ゲーリッグ、ミラー、ゲーレンジャーの一団

マツケ監督と鈴木惣太郎氏

大陸候の始球式、後ろは讀賣新聞社運動部長岡本キトイ氏

操手すべる東林倶主将とルー

日米交驩右からルー、大陸候、ダール米國大使、正力讀賣社長

A Japanese American baseball team at Manzanar Internment Camp, California, 1942. (Gift of Jack and Peggy Iwata; courtesy of the Japanese American National Museum)

(opposite) Scenes from the 1934 Major League tour, including Connie Mack with Suzuki Sōtarō (top left) and Shōriki Matsutarō, U.S. ambassador Joseph Grew, Count Okuma, and Babe Ruth (bottom right). (Courtesy of the Japanese Baseball Hall of Fame Museum and Library)

Ken Zenimura at bat, Heart Mountain, Wyoming, 1944. The inscription reads: "Ken Zenimura." (Gift of Mori Shimada; courtesy of the Japanese American National Museum)

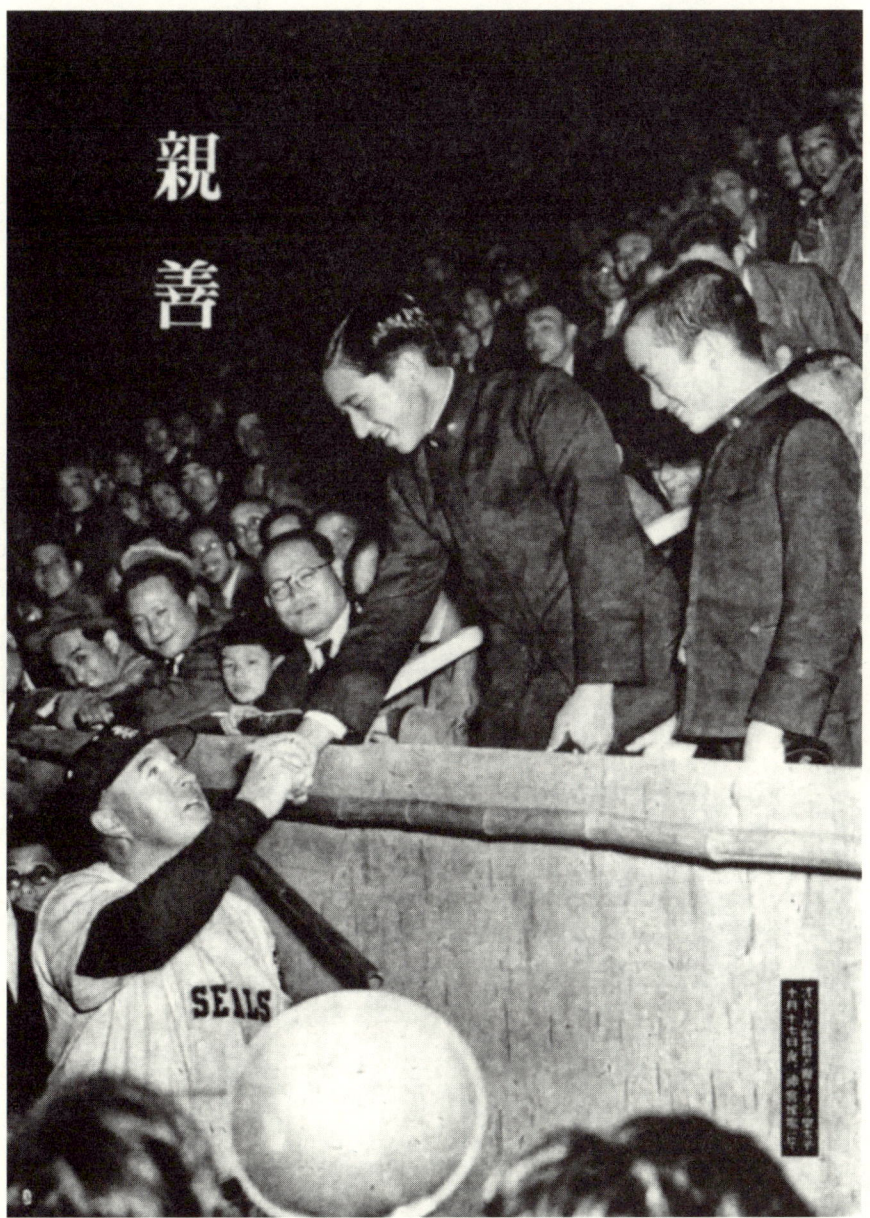

Lefty O'Doul shaking hands with Crown Prince Akihito (the current Japanese emperor) at Jingū Stadium, October 1949. The caption reads: "Amity." (Courtesy of *Asahi Gurafu*)

Tokyo Giants manager Shigeru Mizuhara shaking hands with Joe DiMaggio, with Lefty O'Doul looking on, before an exhibition match at Kōrakuen Stadium, October 20, 1951. (Courtesy of the *Yomiuri Shinbun*)

6 SPARTAN LEAGUES

When Japanese troops in north China became implicated in the Marco Paulo Bridge Incident in July 1937, a full-scale war began between Japan and Chiang Kai-shek's Nationalist China. As Japan mobilized for war, a Japanese tour by Pacific Coast League all-stars scheduled for the fall, O'Doul's brainchild, had to be canceled. Activities in amateur baseball similarly suffered. A year after the outbreak of the Second Sino-Japanese War, Tokyo was forced to forgo its right to host the 1940 Olympic Games, and consequently IABF's planning for a "World Baseball Tournament" in 1940 had to be aborted. Plans for a U.S.-Japanese amateur "World Series" in Tokyo (1937) and Honolulu (1939) similarly became the casualty of the Second Sino-Japanese War. Leslie Mann and his fellow amateur baseball boosters in Miami had to content themselves with a geographically contained "World Series," which took place in London in 1938. Mann's All-Americans played five games against the British team composed mainly of Canadian college players. The Americans won only one game. The IABF would host three more "world championships" in the Caribbean region, the first one in Cuba (1939) among the United States, Cuba, and Nicaragua and the second one in Puerto Rico (1940), with the United States, Nicaragua, Cuba, Mexico, Venezuela, Hawaii, and Puerto Rico as participants. Cuba emerged victorious on both occasions. The last prewar "world amateur championship" took place in Puerto Rico in 1942, with nine teams participating. This time, Venezuela won and Team USA finished a humiliating sixth. It had become embarrassingly clear that American amateurs could no longer hold a candle to their Caribbean brethren and that the reservoir of the best amateur talent now existed south of the Gulf of Mexico shorelines.[1]

Curiously, during the four years leading up to that fateful seventh day of December 1941, U.S.-Japanese baseball interaction continued. In late 1938, Foreign Minister Arita Hachirō and the Japanese ambassador to the United States, Saitō Hiroshi, explored the possibility of sending a team of collegiate baseball players to participate in the "centennial celebration of baseball's founding in Cooperstown, New York."[2] Although this goodwill gesture did not bear fruit, baseball exchange between the United States and Japan persisted in 1939 and 1940, albeit in a geographical alignment definitely not pleasing to custodians of American geopolitical interests. The Tokyo Giants toured the Philippines twice in 1939 and played against local semipro and amateur squads. While two other baseball-playing territories under U.S. control, the Philippines and Hawaii, failed to send their delegations to the IABF-sponsored "World Championships," they both sent their all-star teams to a multination baseball tournament held in Japan in conjunction with the Far Eastern Championships in 1940. Once the governments of the United States and Japan broke off diplomatic relations and the Pacific War began, baseball, like many aspects of civil society, morphed into an instrument of wartime morale boosting and national mobilization on both sides of the Pacific. Being young, able-bodied, and extremely fit, many professional baseball players, both American and Japanese, were drafted into military service and displayed to the wartime public as an embodiment of idealized masculine soldiering and heroic patriotism.[3] The wartime service of major-league greats was touted, and even commodified, by organized baseball and the U.S. military as a shining example of the citizen-soldier valiantly defending the American Way of Life. The vast majority of major leaguers ended up on the rosters of service teams a safe distance away from the battlefront. Exhibition games played by major leaguers became a big drawing card for the American war effort. In Japan, exemption of college students from the draft lasted until 1943, but many professional ballplayers began being drafted into the Imperial Army as soon as their country entered a full-scale military conflict with China. One of Japanese professional baseball's early standouts, the Tokyo Giants pitcher Sawamura Eiji, was drafted three times between 1937 and 1944. His offensive rival, former Tokyo Big 6 star and Osaka Tiger Kageura Masaru, was called up twice. Their multiple inductions and battlefield deaths were another telltale sign of the pathetically narrow human and material margins upon which the Japanese war machine operated during the Asia-Pacific War.

Perhaps the most painful and immediate impact of the war was felt by the Japanese American community. Three months after the Pearl Harbor attack, President Franklin D. Roosevelt signed Executive Order 9066, and with it, virtually the entire Japanese American populations of California, Oregon, and Washington were forcibly relocated to internment camps set up in the West Coast and mountain states. Within this miserably circumscribed life, Issei Japanese nationals and Nisei Japanese Americans cleared land for baseball diamonds and built wooden grandstands amid the sagebrush dotting barren deserts. There, baseball became a way to sustain a sense of community, a semblance of normal life, and ethnic pride and human dignity under terribly humiliating circumstances. Playing baseball games made their embittering experiences slightly more tolerable and brought a little joy into the lives of those in the camps while defusing (or sometimes inflaming) the tensions dividing the camp populations. These bush leaguers also played their games on a field of dreams—dreams of someday getting out of the incarceration camp and being accepted back into American society—but for the moment, the field was fenced in with barbed wire, and among the spectators were white soldiers watching from armed guard towers.

War and Baseball: Playing for the "True Japanese Spirit"
In the late 1930s, interlocking historical forces, both domestic and international, began to coalesce to move Japanese baseball into a more self-contained, intraimperial orbit. A powerful centripetal force emanated mainly from the Japanese state, which was beginning to intrude more invasively onto the national body and athletic culture in general for purposes of domestic mobilization and external recognition. This trend accelerated after the Japanese athletic feats at the 1936 Berlin Olympics and the IOC's decision to award the next Olympics to Tokyo.[4] Student baseball, which had been placed under the Ministry of Education's direct administrative control in 1932, was immediately affected by this new state policy of deploying sports for war mobilization. Beginning in 1937, all participants at the annual national middle-school tournament were required at the opening ceremony to pledge their allegiance to "the spirit of Bushido" and to "make all of their bodily faculties available to serve in national exigencies." Everyone at the stadium—players, umpires, and spectators—was made to bow in the direction of the Imperial Palace in Tokyo in a synchronized move and to offer silent prayers for fallen soldiers.[5]

When the city of Tokyo and its industrial boosters sought to host the 1940 Olympics, the Games were purported to be part of *Kigen 2,600-nen Hōshuku*, the mythical 2,600th anniversary of the ascension of the first emperor of Japan, Emperor Jinmu, to the imperial throne. The combining of the Olympics and this mythology-laden national event commemorating the imperial enthronement in 460 B.C. would have signaled the ultimate fusion of sports and the symbolism of ultranationalism. The Japanese government was initially slow to grasp the synergic power of the dual festivities. When it witnessed the glitz of the Berlin Olympics and the kudos that Hitler's regime apparently reaped from it, Japan's national government rather belatedly became persuaded that a successful execution of this international athletic spectacle would indeed add to its prestige. The dual spectacle of the Olympics and the *Kigen 2,600-nen Hōshuku*, however, did not materialize after all. Once it became clear that the conflict with China was going to be a drawn-out affair, the Japanese government adopted a military-first resource-allocation policy, enacted in the National Mobilization Act in April 1938. Faced with the scarcity of resources available for civilian projects, especially construction materials such as steel, the city of Tokyo decided to relinquish its right to host the 1940 Olympics and announced the forfeiture in July 1938.[6]

With a heavy dose of wishful thinking, however, the Tokyo city government and industrial boosters clung to the idea of hosting the Games in 1944 (with the assumption that the war with China would be over within a year or two), receiving strong encouragement from IOC president Henri de Baillet-Latour and his European aristocratic colleagues. In their effort to reclaim the games in 1944, Japan's Olympic lobby relied heavily on Avery Brundage, an American member of the IOC. They chose Brundage as their advocate for multiple reasons. Known as an avid Asian art collector and frequent visitor to that part of the world, Brundage was expected to be sympathetic to Japan's bid to take the Olympics outside of Europe or North America for the first time. Further, Brundage had famously blocked the movement in the United States to boycott the 1936 "Nazi Olympics" and staunchly supported Japan when calls to boycott the Tokyo Olympics erupted after the Japanese atrocities in Nanking in late 1937. Finally, Japan's sports officials knew that Brundage's intercession as a member of the AOC was instrumental in Mann's garnering an invitation from the German Olympic Organizing Committee to play exhibition baseball with Japan at the Berlin Games. In April 1939, the city of Tokyo, the Foreign Ministry, and the Railways Ministry's tourist board invited Brundage and his wife to Tokyo. Among other festivities, the couple was escorted through cherry blossom viewings and treated to the 1939 season opener of the Tokyo Big 6 at Jingū Stadium. At the end of the all-expenses-paid junket, Brundage lavishly praised Japan and its contribution to world amateur sports, pledging his support for Japan's bid to reenter its candidacy as an Olympic host city at the upcoming July IOC session in London. Although the 1944 Games were awarded to Helsinki, the outbreak of war in Europe within a few months made all of this a moot point.[7]

Brundage was not the only high-profile American sports official who remained favorably disposed toward Japan even after Japan's aggression in China proper began in 1937. A surprising level of cordiality and camaraderie characterized the American baseball establishment's contemporary relationship with its Japanese counterpart, the NPBA. Although the PCL's Japan tour and Mann's amateur "World Series" were canceled because of Japan's rush into war mobilization, the NPBA's top officials continued to work toward its grandiose goal of challenging the American majors in a "true World Series." Throughout 1938, Connie Mack and other major-league club owners continued to express support for Japan's endeavors along those lines, if only as public pleasantries. As late as January 1939, Commissioner Kenesaw Landis sent cordial New Year's greetings to NPBA chair Ōkuma Tsunenobu, expressing hope for a future U.S.-Japanese "World Series."[8] Some went farther and proffered a specific plan. J. A. Adelman, the chairman of the San Francisco World's Fair organizing committee, was one of them. In late 1938 he proposed on behalf of the Golden Gate International Exposition that the first U.S.-Japanese "World Series" be held in conjunction with his city's 1939 expo; the second round was to take place in Tokyo in 1940 as part of Tokyo's own planned world's fair. Given the San Francisco Expo's central theme of a "Pacific Rim Future," such a baseball contest would have snugly fit into the enterprise.[9]

Even that revised game plan was not meant to be. When the Japanese army blockaded the British and French leaseholds in Shanghai in the spring of 1939, disrupting American expatriate life there and incensing American public opinion, the relationship between Washington and Tokyo took a nosedive. In July the administration of Franklin Roosevelt informed the Japanese government that the United States would not renew the 1911 United States–Japan Commerce and Navigation Treaty. Any forms of baseball exchange as a commercial venture became practically impossible with the expiration of the treaty in January 1940. The Japanese professional baseball league, four years into its existence, revised its charter for the first time and eliminated any reference to a world series from the text.[10] Japan's war mobilization intensified exponentially after the Pearl Harbor attack, and all aspects of baseball began to feel the brunt of the regimentation of national life. The end of the 1941 season ended up marking the cessation of radio broadcasting of baseball games. Among other civilian resources, the rationing of rubber, leather, and yarn began, and the quality of baseballs plummeted; in addition, only six balls could be used per game, even by professional teams.[11] The national middle-school baseball championship at Kōshien was canceled in July 1941, accompanied by no official explanation. The fact was that the government banned all "nonessential" movements of people and resources during the large-scale military operations the Kwantung Army was engaged in along the Manchurian-Soviet border. For reasons of military security, the newspapers were not permitted to report these activities. In March 1942, the spring middle-school tournament was also suspended, again with no public explanation.[12] Baseball magazines became the target of hostility from anti-American radicals. In January 1943, in order to deflect criticism, *Yakyūkai* (Baseball World) voluntarily changed its name to *Sumō to Yakyū* (Sumo and Baseball), only to drop the name *Yakyū* entirely from its title a few months later.[13]

Officials of collegiate baseball initially tried to prevent outright persecution by the militarist state by voluntarily cooperating with its agenda. After 1937, Tokyo Big 6 began donating a substantial part of its gate revenues to the Imperial Army and Navy while voluntarily adopting nationalistic pre-game and after-game rituals similar to those imposed on middle-school baseball by the Ministry of Education. Tokyo Big 6 also demonstrated its loyalty to state orthodoxy by sending its all-star team to the Far Eastern Athletic Championships, the athletic event held in Tokyo and Osaka in June 1940 as part of the yearlong commemoration of the 2,600th anniversary of imperial rule and as a substitute for the forfeited 1940 Tokyo Olympics. The list of participants in this nominally multi-nation athletic meet signaled the increasingly untenable position into which Japan had driven itself in the international arena. Aside from Japan, only Manchukuo (fielding an all-ethnic Japanese team), Wang Zhaoming's Nationalist China (the Japanese collaborationist regime—it did not compete in baseball), the Philippines, and Hawaii sent their athletes to this bizarre athletic meet. Baseball was its main attraction, and the Tokyo Big 6 all-stars won the "Far Eastern championship" by beating in the finals the Asahi squad representing Hawaii. The Filipino team mostly comprised semipros in the employ of the Calamba Sugar Refinery, owned by Japanese capital. The bulk of the Asahi's travel expenses came from funds raised in charity events sponsored by Honolulu's Issei leaders, to whom the Asahi's participation in the metropole's commemorative celebration appeared to validate their own place in Japan's imperial glory.[14] Baseball's strategy of preemptive cooperation with the government, however, did not pay off. In March 1943, the Ministry of Education designated baseball as one of many "low priority" athletic categories, for which interscholastic scrimmages were allowed but multiteam tournaments were not. Claiming that it had lost its raison d'être, the Tokyo Big 6 League voluntarily disbanded a month later. After the government rescinded exemption from military service for college students in the fall, collegiate ballplayers, including many of the Tokyo Big 6 stars, also began to be drafted and sent to the battlefields. Industrial semipro baseball's annual intercity tournament was also suspended in 1943.[15]

Professional baseball survived the longest, continuing its play, albeit on a much-reduced scale, until the fall of 1944. Initially, it felt the immediate impact of the war mobilization more acutely than did student baseball because of the demographic makeup of its player pool. At the end of the 1937 season, nineteen professional ballplayers, including the year's spring-season MVP, Sawamura, were drafted and shipped off to fight in China. Once he was put at the forefront of Japanese military expansionism, Sawamura's service—especially his spectacular eighty-seven-meter hand-grenade throw—was featured in the wartime press as a rousing symbol of the nation's military advance in the Chinese theater and a model of masculine soldiering that would "guard our great empire at the [Asia's] continental front line." The tales of military exploits of other former baseball star players were similarly featured in the wartime press.[16] After two years of military service, Sawamura was discharged and returned to play early in the 1940 season, but he was drafted again at the end of the following season soon after the outbreak of war with the United States. This time, he was shipped off to Mindanao in the Philippines.[17] Between 1941 and 1942 alone, thirty-six other professional ballplayers were conscripted and sent to Japan's overexpanded war theater on the Asian mainland. Halfway through the 1941 season, four Nisei players, including Horio and his former L.A. Nippon teammate George Matsuura, returned to the United States to comply with the U.S. government's repatriation order to American citizens residing in Japan. Others, like Wakabayashi, who was married to a Japanese woman, chose to give up their U.S. citizenship and stay in Japan.[18]

Like collegiate baseball, Nippon Yakyū Renmei, or the National Baseball Association (NBA, formerly the NPBA but dropping "Professional" in

1939 to accommodate the rising social dogma vilifying commercialism), sought to elude outright state persecution by preemptively adopting militaristic rituals and tailoring its practices to emerging ultranationalist orthodoxy. Starting in October 1939, the NBA began donating 10 percent of its net profit on the first day of each month to the military.[19] In order to "domesticate" the game being attacked by rabidly anti-American militarists for its origin in the enemy's country, clubs dropped their English nicknames (such as the Giants and the Tigers) at the beginning of the 1940 season. A "hand grenade derby" by players began as a pregame attraction in 1942. The targets for this supposedly morale-boosting yet entertaining event bore the motto "Attack and Destroy Anglo-Americans!" Beginning in the 1943 season, all English words, including count calls, were replaced with Japanese words. The uniform designs were militarized, and khaki became the only permitted color. The Roman alphabet was banned in the team logos on the uniforms, and numbers had to be represented in *kanji*—as on the Tokyo Giants' 1935 American tour jersey. The rules of the game were also "Japanized" to demonstrate "the true fighting spirit of the imperial subjects." No longer were tie games allowed, and teams were required to "fight to the bitter end"; six and a half innings (instead of four) had to be played before a game could be rained out. Starffin, who had escaped conscription only because of his "stateless" legal status and had established himself as the Giants' ace pitcher during Sawamura's absence, was forced to Japanize his name to Suta Hiroshi in 1941. When the NBA banned registration by foreign-born players, he was taken off of the roster at midseason, ostensibly for illness. Finally, in 1944, numbers were purged from uniforms altogether to rid the game of any hint of "individualism," supposedly the signature—and contemptible—attribute of the enemy Americans and its "self-centered" culture. It bears underlining here that all of these changes were introduced as the NBA's "self-reform" to make itself relevant in the "new domestic order" proclaimed by Prime Minister Fumimaro Konoe's cabinet. To that extent, they were first and foremost the results of self-co-optation, not of the peremptory edicts foisted by the militarist government.[20]

The NBA also rode the bandwagon of the national celebration of the 2,600th anniversary of imperial rule by holding a monthlong series in Manchukuo in the summer of 1940. All nine professional clubs sent their entire squads to play sixty-seven games in a circuit set up by the *Manshū Nippō* daily, a loop linking four Manchurian cities (Xinjiang, Mukden, Anshan, and Dalian). While this undertaking was touted as a contribution to the yearlong national commemoration, holding a month of its regular-season play in Manchuria made eminently good business sense for the NBA and its local business partners. Baseball was hugely popular on that Japanese semicolonial frontier to begin with. After the termination of the U.S.-Japanese Commercial and Navigation Treaty, the Japanese mainland economy grew more systematically regimented into a "yen bloc" that also included Manchuria as its constituent part. NBA officials began to look at Manchukuo as its "rich untapped market," which they thought might well rival the Tokyo and Osaka metropolitan areas in the future. The NBA thus considered the 1940 Manchurian Summer League the inaugural year of a continual annual practice and reprised this summer enterprise in 1941.[21] Sawamura, who had been honorably discharged from the army in April, was rushed back on the Giants' active roster in July to ensure that this huge drawing card would be among those participating in the expedition to the inaugural Manchurian League. In all of these Manchurian cities, tickets were sold out on the day they went on sale, giving a needed financial boost to the clubs struggling to survive in the shrinking civilian economy of the war years. Part of the gate proceeds from the Manchurian series was dutifully donated to the war effort. Zheng Xiaoxu, the prime minister of Manchukuo, and President Kimura Takuichi of the Southern Manchurian Railway awarded championship trophies to the winner of the 1941 Manchurian series, the Tokyo Kyojingun (the Giants).[22]

Before the NBA embarked on this industrywide "northern expedition," the Tokyo Giants had gone on a single-team "southern swing," undertaking two rounds of monthlong off-season play in the Philippines (January–February and December 1939) against all-Filipino squads in the semipro Manila Bay League and local collegiate teams. After the first tour, the Giants even brought back with them a local recruit, Adelano Rivera, the captain of the semipro Manila Customs Office team.[23] The Giants' 1939 Manila tours were cosponsored by a large group of local benefactors and ethnic Japanese civic leaders. They mostly came from the capital's Japanese expatriate community (formed around the general consul's office) and nonprofit organizations that planned and implemented various people-to-people exchanges between the two countries, such as the Philippines Society and the Philippine-Japan Society. With the prospect of independence from the United States looming on the horizon after the attainment of commonwealth status in 1935, the Filipino political and economic elite searched for ways to safeguard the nation's postindependence future against twin external threats: infiltration by ethnic Chinese and economic and possibly even military control by Japan. This defensive Filipino experimentation generated a variety of cultural-exchange programs with Japan in the period leading up to World War II. Many Japanese expatriates in Manila served as intermediaries in this process. The Tokyo Giants' testing waters in the Filipino baseball market and the presence of the Filipino baseball delegation in the 1940 Far Eastern Championships should also be situated in this larger context of a brief efflorescence in Japan-Philippines grassroots interaction—a phenomenon no doubt annoying, if not disconcerting, to American geostrategists.[24] By the time World War II broke out in the Asia-Pacific world, Japanese professional baseball's gaze was definitely cast inward to Japan's Asian imperium, whether actual, imagined, or coveted.

Despite desperate attempts to survive the rigors of the wartime economy, Japan's professional baseball shriveled into a shell of its previous self between the 1942 and 1944 seasons, not so much because of state persecution—though there definitely was that—but because the nation's hemorrhaging wartime economy could no longer support anything beyond the tapering war effort and the rationing of bare-minimum necessities to its deprived population. Two years into the war, the resource insecurity that had dogged the Japanese military machine from the start of the war began to affect directly baseball's infrastructure of play. In August 1943, Kōshien Stadium's steel canopy was dismantled, appropriated by a military desperate for steel and other strategic metals.[25] Similarly, 18,000 metal seats were removed from the stands of Kōrakuen Stadium in October for recycling use by the military.[26] The number of the NBA member clubs shrank from the prewar nine (as of 1939) to six. In January 1944, the NBA renamed itself the Nippon Yakyū Hōkokukai (the Japan Baseball Society to Serve the Country) and formally offered up its players' labor to munitions factories on weekdays, only playing ball on the weekends. The 1944 season thus consisted of only thirty-five games. Even this trickle of an operation came to a complete halt with the season-ending, nine-day series named "The Empire's Final Charge," which was held in Tokyo, Osaka, and Kobe in September. Nippon Yakyū Hōtokukai closed its doors as of November 13, citing the deteriorating circumstances of the war.[27] With this, Japanese baseball at all levels became dormant—though not for long, as it turned out.

War and Baseball: The American Way

As baseball historian Steven Bullock has shown, World War II constituted a unique interlude in the latter stages of American baseball's "golden age." When the United States itself entered the war in December 1941, diamond legends such as Babe Ruth, Ty Cobb, and Walter Johnson had not yet receded into distant memories, while a new generation of shining stars such as Joe DiMaggio, Hank Greenberg, and Ted Williams were already gliding around the playing field and capturing American imaginations. The eruption of war in Europe in September 1939 and the ensuing war boom was a boon to the American economy, and baseball attendance was up for a while. The Pearl Harbor attack took place at that juncture in the halcyon days of American professional baseball. Once the United States became a belligerent, the game would go through nearly four years of profound changes.[28]

There is no denying that during the war years, major-league baseball suffered a severe decline both in fans' interest and in quality of play. With so many of the game's best talents serving in the military, so-called hole-pluggers had to fill the majors' depleted rosters. A one-armed player unexpectedly found a place on the major-league diamonds. In 1944, a publicity-hungry Cincinnati Reds even hired fifteen-year-old Joe Nuxhall for one game. Aging veterans long past their primes, such as Jimmie Foxx and Al Simmons, had a new lease on life as far as their playing careers were concerned. According to an estimate by baseball scholar Bill James, only 40 percent of the major leaguers who played during World War II actually possessed the deserving talent. He cites as evidence the fact that out of sixty-four regulars (eight players from each team, with pitchers left out of the count) that played in the National League in 1945, only twenty-two played 100 or more games the following year. The wartime conscription of players dealt a crippling blow to some major-league clubs. The prime example was the Detroit Tigers. The team went from an AL championship in the 1940 season to the second division in 1942 and 1943, only to recapture the pennant in 1945 when its key players, such as Greenberg and Virgil Trucks, finally returned from military service and rejoined their teammates. In contrast, the AL's perennial doormats, the St. Louis Browns, fortuitously found themselves at the top of the heap during the war, winning their only pennant in 1944.[29]

World War II also played midwife for women's professional baseball in the United States. The instigator of the wartime business of women's baseball was a corporate magnate who knew a thing or two about pro baseball. In 1942, Philip K. Wrigley, the chewing-gum titan who had inherited the Chicago Cubs franchise from his father, came up with the idea of using female ballplayers as a way to cope with the wartime depletion of major-league talent and to maximize the use of stadiums. Wrigley sent his scouts out all around the United States and Canada to find technically qualified players. After tryouts in various cities in the Midwest, about 280 finalists were invited to Wrigley Field in Chicago for the final selection process. Sixty-four women were chosen to play on the first four all-salaried teams, located in South Bend, Indiana; Rockford, Illinois; Kenosha, Wisconsin; and Racine, Wisconsin. The All-American Girls Professional Baseball League (AAGPBL) thus began regular-season play with Wrigley's financial backing in the spring of 1943.[30]

As soon as he realized that major-league baseball would survive the war even with second-tier talent and be able to sustain fans' devotion in a nation hungry for fleeting diversions, Wrigley quickly lost interest in his new wartime business venture. He sold his share of the AAGPBL after only one year to Arthur Meyerhoff, his publicist and advertising agent. Meyerhoff's Chicago-based Management Corporation would administer the AAGPBL until 1950. The all-women's pro league drew some 450,000 fans in its second season (1944). The AAGPBL's early success sparked the formation of a rival league, the National Girls Baseball League (NGBL), in 1944. It initially consisted of four semipro softball teams in the Chicago area and later expanded to a six-team baseball league. In its peak years in the late 1940s, the NGBL attracted nearly 500,000 annual paying spectators, as did the AAGPBL in 1948.[31]

World War II gave Ray Dumont, the Kansas baseball entrepreneur once called "Baseball's Barnum," an unexpected opportunity to extend his bailiwick beyond North America. Once a wheat and oil center in America's heartland, Wichita, Dumont's hometown, underwent profound transformation with the advent of the global conflict in 1939. By the end of World War I, Clyde Cessna, a farmer who had been building aircraft and learning to fly as a hobby in western Kansas and Oklahoma, had constructed the "contraption" that would come to bear his surname at an automobile plant in the city. A man named William Burke built an airstrip on a wheat field. A successful wildcatter and bold investor from Oklahoma by the name of J. M. Moellendick got an aircraft-manufacturing plant called the Swallow Manufacturing Company off the ground. By 1929, three men who had worked for the Swallow Company—Cessna; Lloyd Stearman, an engineer; and Walter Beech, who had been recently discharged from the Army Air Corps—started their own plane-building ventures in Wichita. Later, Stearman's company became Boeing. Although their factories were forced to lie idle during much of the Depression-wracked 1930s, the impending international crises resuscitated Wichita's nascent aviation industry. In 1937, the U.S. government relaxed neutrality laws and allowed foreign belligerents to purchase American-made war material on a cash-and-carry basis. In 1939, anticipating war, the U.S. military began placing large orders for munitions and aircraft. The outbreak of military conflict in Europe in 1939 and then in the Asia-Pacific in 1941 turned Wichita into a war-borne boom town. Dumont's National Baseball Congress was one of the in-town beneficiaries of this economic bonanza.[32]

The coming of World War II also gave rise to a bevy of new "semipro" baseball teams in military camp towns and in the form of a greater number of service teams. At the beginning of the 1942 season, Army Special Services captain Leroy Mounday of Fort Riley, Kansas, the manager of one of the better military squads in the Midwest, suggested to NBC commissioner Sisler and other executives that the organization amend its bylaws to better accommodate service teams; for example, he proposed that they be exempt from district qualifying and allowed greater flexibility in the scheduling of games. When NBC gladly obliged, a huge contingent of service teams became the NBC's constitutive members.[33] As will be discussed in the next chapter, World War II and its legacies would fuel the engine of the NBC's empire building to reach a new frontier beckoning across the Pacific.

In the immediate aftermath of the Pearl Harbor attack, baseball boosters—who had been pointing to Japan's love of baseball as "gospel truth evidence" of the game's universal appeal and usefulness as a tool for converting the world to the American creed of democracy—had a lot of reinterpretation, if not recantation, to do. Editors at the *Sporting News* fumed that "the spirit of the game [never] penetrated their yellow hides" because "no nation which had as intimate contact with baseball as the Japanese could have committed the vicious, infamous deed of the early morning of December 7, 1941." A few weeks later, they concluded, in chameleon-like fashion, that the Japanese had learned a few skills of the game but "the soul of our national game never touched them." After the news of the Pearl Harbor attack reached Ruth, he wished that "every Jap that mentions my name gets shot." Even Herb Hunter, long outside the limelight and running a business in St. Louis, was quoted by *Sporting News* as sprouting his righteous indignation about Japan's "war-mongers." The forty-six-year-old Hunter tried to enlist in the navy but was rejected because of "a dental deficiency."[34]

For weeks following the United States' entrance into World War II, speculation swirled within the baseball establishment that professional leagues would not be permitted to play in the new season. Given the possibility of Japanese attacks on the West Coast, the PCL's 1942 season in particular was called into doubt. To put an end to this state of uncertainty, Landis made a formal inquiry to President Roosevelt on January 14, 1942. In the now-famous "green light" letter to the baseball commissioner dated January 15, Roosevelt stated that the game should be allowed to continue during the war. FDR, a baseball fan since boyhood, believed that professional baseball would become a precious diversion for the war-weary working population and a source of morale for the fighting nation: "There will be fewer people unemployed and everybody will work longer hours and harder than ever before.... [I]f 300 teams use 5,000 or 6,000 players, these players are a definite recreational asset to at least 20,000,000 of their fellow citizens." There was to be no preferential treatment for players, however, and everyone at eligible draft age should serve in the military. That was Roosevelt's only proviso.[35]

The president had plenty of company in championing baseball's uninterrupted play during the war. A phalanx of public officials, including New York mayor Fiorella LaGuardia, enthusiastically endorsed the idea. In Washington, Senator Albert "Happy" Chandler of Kentucky could not have agreed more. The future Major League Baseball commissioner professed his faith in the nation's ability to both "win the war and keep baseball." Spearheaded by the *Sporting News* and *Baseball Magazine*, baseball journalism waged propaganda campaigns of sorts from the sidelines, claiming that the game had been woven into the very fabric of American society and was synonymous with the "American Way of Life." Throughout the war years, these publications circulated laudatory comments about the game made by high-ranking military officers and important civilian leaders and highlighted in editorials and news articles major leaguers' service to the country in the war.[36]

When the war broke out, American military leaders quickly recognized the importance of baseball to the majority of soldiers and sailors, and they made a systematic effort, unlike their Japanese foe, to build the game into military life. Shortly after Pearl Harbor, the War Department conducted a survey on sports and identified baseball as American fighting men's number-one favorite, so it became military policy to ensure that the nation's troops had abundant supplies of baseball equipment and received daily updates on major-league standings and statistics (along with information on other sports) in the military publication *Stars and Stripes*. This policy reflected the top brass's recognition, arising from its experience during the previous world war, that new challenges would arise from the influx of a large civilian population into its fighting force. The institution frontally acknowledged the need to ease citizen-soldiers' transition into military life, build a sense of cohesion out of this socially and ethnically diverse population drawn from disparate parts of the country, and assure the home-front population that their sons, grandsons, brothers, and husbands were given "a wholesome environment" to the extent that wartime circumstances would permit. Maintaining good civilian-military relations in locales hosting military bases and newly built encampments also required concerted efforts. For these reasons, various aspects of peacetime civilian culture, including sports and other forms of popular entertainments, were actively incorporated into military-sanctioned events.[37] The U.S. military also utilized athletic programs as a way to boost soldiers' morale and maintain their physical fitness and combat readiness. By the end of 1942, virtually every significant American military installation around the world had formalized athletic teams and leagues. In one estimate, as many as 75 percent of the American fighting forces either played in or watched baseball or softball games during the war years, far outdistancing the second-place sport, football. This surfeit of newly spawned service teams also became a huge reservoir of affiliates in Dumont's NBC organization.[38]

For these new programs officially sanctioned by the military to function smoothly, material contributions by the baseball establishment were crucial. Major-league owners and baseball executives willingly donated their resources to the war effort to showcase the game's loyalty to the nation at war. They contributed millions of dollars in cash subsidies to the intramural athletic programs of both branches of the military. They also donated baseball equipment to the service teams through the Ball and Bat Fund directed by Clark Griffith, owner of the Washington Senators, and Ford Frick, president of the National League. This program was an outgrowth of a similar entity created during World War I.[39] Starting in the 1942 season, the major leagues donated most or all of the proceeds from their annual all-star games and World Series contests to various war-related charities, such as the United Service Organization (USO) and the

American Red Cross. The 1942 World Series raised nearly $365,000 for these nonprofit organizations.[40] The baseball establishment and the military also cosponsored exhibition baseball games that were opened to the area's civilian population as well as to members of the military. Between 1942 and 1944, every major-league club set aside at least one game during the season as a charity event, with its gate receipts donated to the military. The major leagues also actively campaigned for the sale of war bonds. Players spent their off days lobbying businesses and wealthy patrons to replenish the government's war coffer through their bond purchases, and booths were set up in stadiums to promote bond sales to spectators. This "business partnership" between the military and organized baseball grew stronger as the war went on, representing another instance of wartime military-industry cooperation.[41]

In addition to organizing participatory baseball programs for the rank and file, the armed forces also assembled their own elite baseball squads to boost servicemen's morale, cultivate unit pride, and, most importantly, generate money and positive publicity for the institution gifted with this pool of fortuitously acquired talent. The massive influx of professional players made such projects relatively easy. Within a few months after the nation declared war on Japan, the U.S. military boasted among its ranks major-league stars at the top of their game, such as Hank Greenberg and Cecil Travis of the Detroit Tigers and Bob Feller of the Cleveland Indians. By the second year of the war, names such as Joe DiMaggio, Ted Williams, and Phil Rizzuto were added to the list. The 1942 season was a time of trial for some big leaguers who initially eluded the draft. DiMaggio, whose marital status had pushed him well down the draft list, was harangued mercilessly throughout the season by spectators booing him for his alleged "draft dodging." In February 1943, an exasperated Yankee Clipper enlisted, but he requested and was summarily granted assignment to the Army Air Force. Soon, DiMaggio was playing center field for the Santa Ana Air Base team in Riverside, California. San Francisco's two other homegrown major leaguers played on the same squad: St. Louis Browns outfielder Wally Judnich and Chicago Cubs backup infielder Dario Lodigiani.[42] These elite service teams became a kind of protective sanctuary for the growing ranks of major leaguers who joined the armed forces, either by draft or by enlisting. A spillover of their highly profiled military service during World War II was that it helped previously ethnically labeled players such as Greenberg (Jewish American) and DiMaggio (Italian American) to shed their ethnic associations in the press commentary and public discourse; they were now referred to as generic "American" major leaguers.⁴³ As the war progressed, the number of elite players in the service increased proportionately to over 90 percent of the major-league players who had been active in the 1942 season. The caliber of several of those elite military squads was such that they often bested the talent-depleted major-league teams in exhibition games and all-star contests. In the waning months of the war, some of the military's fund-raisers were played almost exclusively by major leaguers. In short, the U.S. military temporarily became organized baseball's senior circuit.⁴⁴

The top-flight major leaguers' service on the playing field was highly valued by the military's top brass, and not only because it provided first-rate entertainment to servicemen and civilians around the military installations. It also generated positive publicity and helped to create the public perception that the United States, as the shining citadel of democracy, was willing to send its best and finest to the war against enemies abroad—just as the president said it must in his "green light" letter. The notion that American soldiers, preeminently citizen-soldiers, were civilians first and part of the military second was crucial to the official rhetoric of the war.⁴⁵ In reality, military leaders were reluctant to place America's most prominent sports heroes in harm's way, and unwritten rules seemingly governed the military's treatment of high-profile athletes during the war. Thanks to their status as national celebrities, the vast majority of major leaguers were shielded from front-line duty and given assignments in stateside or secure overseas locations where their commanding officers usually allowed, and often encouraged, them to render their service on the playing field instead of on the battlefield. Some of the major leaguers became instructors at the military's physical training institutes. It was almost as if the U.S. armed forces entered into a "gentleman's agreement" with major-league executives to protect the high-value commodities entrusted to them by their key benefactors.

The contrast with the Japanese military could not be starker in this regard. The Japanese Imperial forces, particularly the army, were brutal and inhumane institutions, not only to enemy combatants and civilians but also to their own servicemen. Despite its obsessive drive to "modernize" itself, the Japanese military woefully lagged behind the modern militaries of the Anglo-American world after World War I in one important aspect: the Japanese military failed to adopt a system of furloughs and R & R as human-resource management policy in the era of total war, which entailed a massive mobilization of a nonprofessional, "national" fighting force. Similarly, organized recreational sport for servicemen was an alien concept to the World War II–era Japanese military establishment, except for random instances of pickup games played with the consent of local commanders in outlying areas where there were few hostile actions. Given the severely limited resources earmarked for enemy captives, as well as the ideologically rooted institutional disregard for the most fundamental requirements of their welfare, letting the Allied POWs indulge in recreational diversion, such as playing baseball, was simply out of the question for the Japanese military.[46] In such a labor-extractive and dehumanizing institutional culture, even those Japanese professional ballplayers who managed to survive their tours of duty typically came back with their health severely compromised. Because of the abuse that his shoulder took from excessive hand-grenade throwing and the carrying of heavy machine guns, Sawamura, when he returned to the pitching mound in 1943 after his second tour of duty, could no longer throw overhand and had to switch to a sidearm delivery.[47] Such divergence in the way they treated their professional ballplayers provides another illustration of the diametrically opposed organizational philosophies guiding these dueling militaries, as well as the vastly superior resources the United States was able to marshal for its war against Japan.

As the war in the Asia-Pacific progressed and the front of the U.S. island-hopping campaigns shifted westward, Hawaii became home to some of the best service teams outside the continental United States. Once the Japanese military threat in the Pacific had largely dissipated, as it had by late 1943, the army began transferring a number of its top players from West Coast military installations to the mid-Pacific island base, and many, including Joe DiMaggio, took up residence at Hickham Air Field in Honolulu. After Saipan fell in the summer of 1944, the navy also began to relocate its stockpile of major-league talent to its operational base in Hawaii. The resulting high-powered army-navy games became an enormously popular entertainment for American servicemen, who sometimes turned out in Honolulu Stadium in record numbers (for example, there were 26,000 in attendance for the Hawaii League playoffs in July).[48] The culmination of this interservice rivalry on the diamond came in September. An eleven-game series called the Servicemen's World Series was staged between an army select team and a squad of navy all-stars to entertain soldiers, sailors, and marines who had been enduring some of the war's most gruesome battles in the Pacific theater. The chief impresarios of this military baseball gala event were Lieutenant General Robert Richardson Jr. of the army and Admiral Chester Nimitz of the navy's Pacific Fleet. The event signaled the symbolic fusion of the U.S. military and the game of baseball, together constructing an arm of the emerging American transpacific empire of fun and games in close cooperation with the USO. Prior to the army-navy series, both service branches shipped in emergency reinforcements of top in-house ballplayers by formal orders. The navy, for example, transferred to Honolulu two blue jackets named Dom DiMaggio and Phil Rizzuto a few days before the series opener. The navy all-stars emerged victorious, winning eight games and losing two, with one tie.[49]

Once the U.S. forces retook control of the Pacific, American fighting men were dispatched to newly secured areas. Nearly all of the army-affiliated major leaguers stationed in Hawaii were transferred to new advance posts in Tinian, Guam, and Saipan to compete in leagues and individual games to entertain the troops stationed there and to establish, through "America's Game," a rapport with the local populace just liberated from Japanese military rule. In more-isolated areas where playing fields were not readily available, American fighting men improvised their own baseball infrastructures, often in a most resourceful fashion. In New Guinea, Army troops, while still encountering isolated Japanese resistance, built a lighted diamond on an artillery field by installing floodlights tied to coconut trees. The playing field, surrounded by twelve 800-million-candlepower lights, permitted them to play night games in the jungle.[50] The navy mobilized bulldozers to chisel playing fields from the tropical surroundings in Saipan. On the island of Leyte (in the Philippines), army commanders ordered coconut trees knocked down and tons of dirt removed to transform jungles around a camp into a baseball diamond. Elsewhere in the Pacific, American servicemen took over playing surfaces and arenas that appeared to have been constructed and abandoned by the Japanese troops, as they did in the Marianas.[51] After the Americans recaptured Manila in the spring of 1945, baseball returned to the colonial capital with the triumphant general who had famously sworn three years before that he would return. Navy teams began competing against an Army Air Force squad at Manila's Rizal Stadium, where Connie Mac's American League all-stars featuring Babe Ruth had played three exhibition games in 1934 and the Tokyo Giants had played against Filipino semipros in 1939. In the summer of 1945, Rizal Stadium also became the venue for the "Philippines World Series" played by American service teams. Through baseball, America symbolically reclaimed its old colonial outpost from the Japanese military interlopers.[52]

Baseball behind Barbed Wire: This, Too, Was the American Way

In addition to heralded military intramural baseball and glitzy exhibition games featuring major leaguers temporarily on the GI payroll, World War II created a different kind of baseball in wartime America. The game flourished between 1942 and 1945 behind the barbed wire surrounding ten "relocation camps" in the West Coast and mountain states. Approximately 120,000 persons of Japanese descent, about 77,000 of them U.S. citizens, were forced to live in confinement during the war. In his chronicle of baseball in California, historian Kevin Nelson narrates an illuminating story of what happened to the L.A. Nippon on the afternoon of December 7, 1941. The team, the "Pride of Little Tokyo," was playing against an all-white semipro team sponsored by the Paramount movie studio when FBI agents arrived. The government agents did not interrupt the game—they just watched it from the sidelines. After the Paramount team won, 6–3, the FBI agents summarily rounded up the Nisei players and took them in for questioning. The players were later released without being charged.

What happened that day to the L.A. Nippon nine was illustrative of Issei and Nisei experiences all around California, the state with the largest population of Japanese Americans. Law-enforcement authorities sought to ferret out possible "saboteurs against the United States," and their nationwide sweep focused particularly on people of Japanese descent. Over the next weeks, they faced a series of restrictive measures that culminated in Executive Order 9066, signed by President Roosevelt on February 19, 1942. The law, providing for the detention of all persons who posed a potential threat to the American war effort, led to the forced relocation and incarceration of virtually the entire Nikkei populations of California, Oregon, and Washington.[53] Once the order was signed, most families were given little more than a week to prepare for relocation. They were forced to sell their assets and belongings for a fraction of their worth, only taking money and whatever possessions they could carry in two suitcases. In San Jose, a ten-year-old Nisei boy by the name of Norman Mineta and his family reported to a designated "temporary assembly center." The youngster, dressed in his Cub Scout uniform, was carrying his most prized possession: his baseball bat and glove. A guard took the bat away from him because it could be used as a weapon.[54]

A similar fate befell the Nikkei community north of the United States–

Canada border. Following the Pearl Harbor attack, pressure mounted in British Columbia to remove persons of Japanese ancestry into the interior. In early 1942, the Canadian government bowed to the exclusionist demands and adopted a policy of relocating about 23,000 Nikkei—about three-quarters of them naturalized or native-born Canadian citizens—from coastal regions. Although the underlying ideas were the same, the Canadian version of the internment program had distinct characteristics. The Japanese were given a choice of either moving east or being repatriated. Unlike in the United States, where families were generally kept intact, Canadian Nikkei men being removed were forced to choose among road-construction camps in the British Columbia interior, sugar-beet projects on the prairies, or incarceration in a POW camp in Ontario. Women and children were sent to six inland towns newly created or revived for this purpose. Historians consider this to be the greatest mass migration in Canada's history.[55]

In Hawaii, where more than 150,000 Nikkei comprised nearly one-third of the territory's population, a wholesale relocation and internment did not take place, although, as Gary Okihiro has demonstrated, a scenario built around a declaration of martial law and the internment of Japanese American leaders had been floated and seriously considered by the local military authorities for decades.[56] The internment of Nikkei during World War II turned out to be a much more selective program in the island territory. About 1,200 to 1,800 individuals suspected of sabotage, the vast majority of them Buddhist monks and Japanese-language schoolteachers, were rounded up and sent to internment camps in Oahu and on the mainland. Japanese-language schools and newspapers were closed by military order. Shintoism was banned. Meanwhile, some local Japanese American community leaders, spearheaded by Takie Okumura, became the standard-bearers of the "Speak American Campaign," earning much fanfare in the press.[57] In this atmosphere of suspicion and fear following the Pearl Harbor attack, the Asahi baseball team voluntarily changed its name to the Athletics. Nisei team owner Doc Kometani enlisted in the U.S. Army, as did many players, such as centerfielder Joe Takada, who would become the first Nikkei soldier to be killed in combat in Italy as a member of the 442nd Regimental Combat Team.[58] Asahi's executives found a backup business partner in some white Americans who were active in the local baseball circles. John (Jack) Burns, a police captain and future governor of Hawaii, became the interim owner of the club, which had up to that point famously taken pride in its all-Japanese management and roster. Neal Blaisdell, future mayor of Honolulu, took over as manager. The club recruited white players while trading some Japanese American players away to other, less "ethnically suspect" clubs in the league. For example, the Asahi's second baseman, Jimmy Wasa, was "traded" to the all-Portuguese Braves, the 1942 champion of the Hawaii Baseball League. He was paid $900 a month while suiting up in a Braves jersey. Horio, who had repatriated from Japan in June 1941, became a member of the Athletics while working as a painter at the U.S. military installations, posing as a Chinese laborer.[59]

Executive Order 9066 did not specifically target Nikkei; it broadly applied to Americans of German and Italian descent as well as to foreign nationals from those countries. The task of interpreting and implementing the law fell to the Army Western Defense Command. In February 1942, Congress held hearings in Seattle, Portland, San Francisco, and Los Angeles to consider General John DeWitt's proposals on "National Defense Migration." His recommendation was to evacuate all three of the national groups of the Axis Powers from the West Coast and detain them in isolated camps during the war. German Americans, who had fallen victim to prejudicial treatments and persecution during the previous world war, successfully had their national group exempted from that order. Angelo Rossi, who had welcomed the Tokyo Giants as mayor of San Francisco in 1935, made a similar case for treating German and Italians differently from the Japanese. A San Francisco lawyer, Chauncey Tramutolo, also argued for the exemption of Italian Americans. In doing so, he highlighted to good effect the potential plight of two immigrants from Sicily, Giuseppe and Rosalie DiMaggio, neither of whom was a U.S. citizen at the time. Tramutolo argued (successfully as it turned out) to the congressmen in attendance that to force the parents of the DiMaggio brothers into a camp would badly damage the nation's morale. There were no Japanese major leaguers who could be conjured at these congressional hearings as silent advocates on behalf of the Japanese Issei, or Nisei Americans for that matter.[60]

The major figures in Japanese American baseball responded to this tyranny by the wartime American state in a variety of ways. Kenso Nushida, the former Sacramento Solon pitcher and the first Japanese American Pacific Coast Leaguer, managed to leave California and return to his native Hawaii before the incarceration actually began. Chiura Obata, the Issei founder of the first mainland Japanese baseball club, Fuji Athletic Club, felt, as many Issei did at the time, that he had no choice but to comply with the order issued by the government, no matter how unjust he felt it was. At the time, Chiura was an artist and a professor at the University of California, Berkeley. The youngest of his three Nisei sons, Gyo Obata, disagreed with his decision. Contending that the U.S. government was violating the Constitution and transgressing on his rights as an American citizen, Gyo refused to report to the detention center. With assistance from a white American friend of the family, an attorney who worked in General DeWitt's office, he managed to finagle a travel permit and arranged a transfer to Washington University in St. Louis, where he hoped to continue with his studies in architecture. With the evacuation scheduled to begin the next morning, Gyo narrowly escaped, making it onto an eastbound train.

Kenichi Zenimura also surrendered to the government order to vacate his home. In February, Zenimura and his family reported to the Fresno Assembly Center, one of the temporary detention centers set up to house the internees before they were moved to permanent "relocation camps." There, some converted horse stalls became the Zenimuras' new abode. One of the first challenges he and his fellow detainees faced was to establish a semblance of normalcy and continuity amid an uprooted life filled with indignities. For Zenimura and his two Nisei teenage sons, the way to do that was to create a place for playing the game that was a central part of their life. In May 1942, Zenimura gathered his fellow detainees to build a baseball field. Once they built it, they organized a league of their own, consisting of a six-team "A" semipro-level division, a high school–level "B" circuit, and a junior-high "C" league. With most of the draft-age Nisei players already in the armed forces, the camp's baseball fraternity had to do what the major-league owners were doing at the time; that is, they patched together ragtag teams with the available talent, consisting mainly of aging veterans and inexperienced young players. Zenimura's two sons, fifteen-year-old Howard and his thirteen-year old brother, Harvey, played on the Fresno "B" team.[61]

In October 1942, the Nikkei inhabitants of the assembly centers were uprooted again and moved to one of the ten permanent camps scattered through seven western states (California, Arizona, Utah, South Dakota, Wyoming, Colorado, and Arkansas). Despite this wide geographical dispersion, all of the camps had one thing in common: they were built in a remote location on inhospitable terrain. Regardless, one of the first tasks undertaken by the internees after "resettlement" was again to build baseball diamonds. Just like those GIs who would build makeshift playing fields in the jungles of the Pacific islands, the detainees exercised amazing Yankee ingenuity in building theirs in the deserts. At Tule Lake, a dry lake bottom in northeastern California, volunteers cleared one area of rocks and seashells and used food-delivery trucks to haul in dirt from the camp farm. At Manzanar in the Mojave Desert, the internees went up to the hills in a dump truck to load decomposed granite. It was unloaded and packed in with shovels to create a building surface for dugouts and wooden bleachers. At Gila River, where the Zenimuras were transferred to, the camp inhabitants built a formidable structure in the middle of the Arizona desert. Volunteers cleared sagebrush with shovels and leveled the ground with a bulldozer. They took out every other four-by-four of the fence surrounding the camp and built a backstop, a grandstand, and bleachers. The completed ballpark was named Zenimura Stadium. Apparently, camp officials and guards were fully aware of what the internees were up to, but they approached the not-so-clandestine construction project with benign neglect.[62]

In each camp, the internees organized a wide range of activities, including other sports such as football and basketball, but baseball was by far the most popular of the athletic diversions. Given the game's prominence in the prewar Japanese American community, that was hardly surprising. By early 1943, every camp had baseball leagues and teams. At Gila, where the climate permitted year-round play and there was a ballpark complete with grandstands and bleachers, as many as thirty-two teams competed at one point, and intense rivalries developed among them. Close to 6,000 people, half of the camp's population, would attend some of the premier games. At every game, a hat was passed around to collect donations, which were used to purchase baseball equipment from Zenimura's white American friend and sporting-goods dealer back home in Fresno. At Tule Lake, one camp team ordered its jerseys through a Sears catalog. They made pants out of heavy cotton potato sacks from the camp farm. The fabric was bleached white and then fitted and sewn by women in the camp. Another resourceful Tule Lake club made uniforms with canvas taken from mattress coverings. Headed by Yoshio Nakamura, the Tule Lake Baseball Association even compiled and circulated a mimeographed "annual baseball guide" complete with detailed game records and player statistics.[63] Occasionally, teams were even permitted to travel to other camps for "away" games. Ironically, such intercamp "tours" gave some internees the opportunity to meet Nikkei residents in the other parts of the United States for the first time in their lives.[64]

In mid-1943, thousands of camp residents were once again transferred, this time based on their response to a loyalty questionnaire administered by the U.S. government. Two key questions in the survey proved most problematic; they asked about the respondent's willingness to pledge allegiance to the United States and forswear allegiance to Japan and to serve in the U.S. armed forces. All who answered no to these questions were moved to Tule Lake as disloyal elements and security risks. The loyalty test caused enormous anguish among the incarcerated, particularly for Issei who were "ineligible for citizenship." Aside from their undying emotional attachment to the country they had grown up in, renouncing their allegiance to the Japanese government was not really an option for them unless they were willing to become completely stateless. As a result, many Issei were sent to Tule Lake, and their families, wishing to remain together, often ended up there as well.

After this major reshuffling of the Nikkei population, Tule Lake became a camp bursting with internal tensions and anger. There were preexisting divisions along lines drawn by the socioeconomic and regional backgrounds of the camp population, which was polarized between dark-complexioned farmers from the Sacramento Valley and others from Oregon and Washington. These social tensions were aggravated by the new fault line running between the pro-Japan faction and those who considered themselves "loyal Americans." The mutual animosities that poisoned the camp's living environment sometimes spilled over onto the baseball diamond, as in the 1944 season opener on May 2.[65] More than half of the 17,000 camp residents showed up for the heralded game. Even before the games began, the air was charged with nationalistic electricity, for preceding the games were festivities celebrating the birthday of Emperor Hirohito (*tenchōsetsu*). Later, in a finals game between Poston (Arizona) and Manzanar "major-league" teams, overheated rooting and an argument over a fly ball and the ensuing melee on the diamond turned into pandemonium, causing injuries and spilled blood among players and spectators and requiring intervention by the camp guards.

Whether to sustain individual hope, ethnic pride, or community cohesion or, as in the above cases, to become a vehicle for playing out group tensions and pent-up frustrations, America's Game continued to be the keystone of Nikkei's life, in war or in peace. The unaltered centrality of the game to the displaced Nikkei communities was the same in Canada. Regardless of which town or labor camp they settled in, Nikkei men of all ages, including former members of the elite Vancouver Asahi club, continued to organize baseball teams to ease the anguish and desperation of their disrupted lives during that uncertain period. Playing baseball also did much to generate a more cordial atmosphere among the local white residents, helping to remove the fear and animosity they felt toward the unwanted outsiders.[66]

On January 2, 1945, the exclusion order for persons of Japanese descent was rescinded, and the legal procedures for closing the internment camps began. The previous fall, as the U.S. Army and Navy were constructing baseball fields in the newly secured locations in the South Pacific, Sawamura, by then married and with an infant daughter, had been drafted for the third time. He died on December 2, 1944, when the transport ship carrying him to the Philippines was torpedoed by an American submarine and sank. The twenty-seven-year-old former pitching sensation, whom Connie Mack considered major-league material, perished in the East China Sea off the coast of Taiwan. Sawamura's proverbial rival, Kageura, drafted twice, died from starvation on one of the islands in the Philippines in May 1945. All told, sixty-nine Japanese pro baseball players were killed during World War II. One of them was Ishimaru Shinichi, a former infielder for the Nagoya club and the only kamikaze pilot among former pro baseballers. An eyewitness account had Ishimaru playing catch with Honda Kōichi, a former Tokyo Big 6 player, right before he took off on his first—and last—mission to Okinawa in a Zero plane on May 12. Honda also died in a kamikaze mission. In April, the Japanese government rounded up about 20,000 foreign residents in Japan as possible enemy spies and put them in an internment camp in Karuizawa, a town about 100 miles north of Tokyo. Among the incarcerated foreign nationals was Starffin, who was subjected to hard labor under armed guard through the remaining months of the war.[67]

The capture of Saipan by the American forces brought the Japanese main islands within the range of aerial bombing by B-29s, and the Japanese military began garrisoning key urban locations in the fall of 1944 to prepare for the anticipated attacks on the Japanese home islands. On September 6, Kōrakuen Stadium was commandeered by the army to use in defense against American air attacks. A regiment of army troops was stationed in its vicinity, and antiaircraft guns were installed at the top of the stadium grandstands. Although the stadium survived the first of the great Tokyo aerial bombings on March 10, part of its scoreboard burned down during the second bombing on April 14, driving home to the Japanese baseball fraternity—or what was left of it—that the Americans would be coming ashore soon.[68] They indeed were. On June 23, 1945, the Battle of Okinawa, one of the bloodiest military engagements of World War II, was officially declared over. The Americans were now on their way to the Japanese main islands—and so was their game.

7 | A FIELD OF NEW DREAMS

The war in the Asia-Pacific ended on August 15, 1945, with Japan's unconditional surrender to the Allied Powers. Within a scant two months, baseball returned to the prostrate nation. The restoration of organized baseball at all levels—professional, semipro, and amateur—began in the early postsurrender months with the full blessings of the Supreme Commander for the Allied Powers (SCAP), the political authority now in control of the country. With the return of organized baseball, the game's attendant institutions, such as national tournaments, national governing bodies, and baseball journalism, also quickly burst back into life in occupied Japan. Despite, or perhaps because of, the paralyzing material shortage and the emotional dislocation wrought by the long, drawn-out state of war, Japanese of all categories—men and women, young and old—devoured baseball in all of its permutations. By the time the Allied occupation formally ended in April 1952, baseball had clearly eclipsed sumo in popular appeal and established itself as the most beloved mass spectator sport in postwar Japan. During the seven years of the Allied occupation, Japanese professional baseball evolved into a successful commercial enterprise in a format resembling, at least in form, the U.S. major leagues, possessing a two-league structure complete with a players' association and the Commissioner's Office. In the meantime, Japan's semipro industrial league virtually became a regional branch of the NBC, the governing body of American semipro professional baseball now encompassing military teams under its umbrella.

In the early postwar years, the American occupation overlord and its Japanese partners worked closely together in crafting baseball into a new national iconography of peace, democracy, and freedom, signifying both continuity with an idealized yesteryear and a clean break from the rejected past. The rhetoric of baseball as America's and Japan's shared pastime and cultural connective tissue was strategically circulated by both parties. In the spate of early postwar baseball magazines, American major-league stars, both old and new—Babe Ruth, Lou Gehrig, Ted Williams, and Bob Feller—became idolized again as models of fair-playing, hard-working, ambitious, and financially successful manhood, fit for emulation by boys and young men of New Japan. In this carefully reconstructed symbolic order, baseball expanded its presence in Japan's cultural landscape, this time as a metaphor for democracy and American-style consumer culture and a symbol of a new partnership between the two nations forged in the darkening shadows of the Cold War.

The almost seven years of the American-led Allied occupation of Japan also meant an opportunity for a new cast of characters to exercise leadership in the reconstructed U.S.-Japanese baseball brotherhood, while leaving room for holdovers from the prewar years to reassert themselves. Front and center in this reconfigured transpacific sporting fraternity were Major General William Marquat, the director of SCAP's Economic and Scientific Section (ESS), and his aide Captain Tsuneo "Cappy" Harada, a California-born Nisei who played liaison between Japan's baseball lobby, SCAP's upper echelons with close personal ties to General Douglas MacArthur, and American organized baseball. Together, they championed baseball as a tool for democratizing the former enemy country and shepherded professional baseball as a remunerative business enterprise during the postwar reconstruction. In every way, the rebirth of organized baseball in Japan after World War II was a binational project, invested with complex political agendas, social purposes, and cultural symbolism. It was also during this early postwar decade that American baseball capitalism conquered its final continental frontier—the U.S. West—and built a bridgehead to Asia.

The Return of Baseball to Occupied Japan

On November 23, 1945, at Tokyo's Jingū Stadium, the Japanese enjoyed a much-awaited opportunity to satisfy their long pent-up craving for baseball, the game that had until a little over two months before been reviled by their militarist government as an "enemy sport" incongruent with the nation's "true spirit." On a crisp autumn day, 6,000 residents of the flattened capital city gathered at Jingū Stadium (which had been commandeered by the U.S. Eighth Army on August 18 and renamed "Stateside Park") and savored the spectacle of an east-west game played by former

Japanese professional ballplayers—including Fujimura Tomio, Tsuruoka Kazuto, and Chiba Shigeru—who had either eluded the draft or just been discharged from military service.[1] Symbolizing the new political realities of the nation under foreign military occupation, the stadium became the site of the Japanese sporting event thanks to the special approval of Lieutenant General Robert Eichelberger, commander of the U.S. Eighth Army in charge of the occupation of the eastern parts of the Japanese home islands. The punishing conditions of the immediate postsurrender months, most viscerally felt through a life-threatening food shortage, did not stop baseball enthusiasts in Tokyo from forking over six yen for a ticket to watch the game they so loved and had furtively missed during the war. The occupation army's General Headquarters even permitted the exhibition game to be broadcast live on radio nationwide. It was the first time the Japanese had heard a baseball game over the airwaves since 1942, the year when their militarist government banned civilian radio programming as part of war mobilization. The resumption of intercollegiate baseball, kept in abeyance since 1943, had preceded the first professional games by a month with a game between the historic rivals Waseda and Keio Universities. Both alumni and enrolled student players played in the game held at "Stateside Park" on October 28. This maiden voyage of postwar Japanese collegiate baseball drew a crowd of 45,000 faithful, a reflection of Tokyo Big 6's superior prewar popularity.[2]

When Japan was placed under United States–led Allied occupation, nearly every element of national activity came to depend on the dictates, sometimes whimsical ones, of the new military ruler. Even such mundane aspects of everyday life as what people could see, hear, or eat became subject to intrusive bureaucratic control, this time not by its militarist state but by a foreign military apparatus executing policies shaped locally by SCAP and also far away in Washington, D.C. It was in this highly engineered social environment that the American military rulers sought to inculcate democracy and freedom in the local populace, often by disarmingly apolitical means—for example, through the sensationalized visual shock therapy of showing romantic kisses between Japanese actors and actresses in movies.[3] By all indications, SCAP strongly endorsed the restoration of organized baseball in Japan. The first postwar professional game on November 23 came only a few weeks after Nippon Yakyū Hōkokukai announced its intent to revert to its pre-1944 name, Nippon Yakyū Renmei (the Japanese Baseball Association, or NBA). Professional baseball also resumed in western Japan in early December with two east-west games at

Nishinomiya Stadium, which had, unlike Kōshien Stadium, been spared SCAP impoundment. Five months later, on April 27, 1946, the first postwar pennant race among eight professional clubs pieced together from the remains of the prewar professional baseball league opened for the postwar inaugural season at Kōrakuen Stadium, another public facility just released from exclusive use by the U.S. Eighth Army. The message sent to Japan's elite and ordinary citizens was loud and clear: the war against *kichiku beiei* (beastly Anglo-Americans) was over and baseball was now back in favor. The game returned triumphantly, and it did so with the occupation army on an avowed mission to remake the collapsing empire of the fallen sun into a peace-loving, democratic nation in terms serviceable to America's strategic objectives in postcolonial East Asia.[4]

Top SCAP officials, chief among them General Eichelberger, whose Eighth Army occupied Japan east of Kobe, indeed looked to sports, most importantly baseball, as an instrument for pacifying and amicably ruling the occupied islands and their populace, just as the American military rulers had done in the Philippines half a century earlier. On numerous occasions, he stated openly that sports, by providing wholesome distraction and healthful recreation, would facilitate the orderly governance of the subdued enemy country and aid U.S. efforts to reeducate the local populace now under its ward in the ways of a self-directed, rule-abiding, and fair-playing democratic citizenry. Officials under Eichelberger's command who were involved in matters of sports and recreation similarly declared that learning the concept of fair play and sportsmanship was key to Japan's reintegration into the "brotherhood of nations," and they announced SCAP's commitment to reintroduce Western competitive sports in "every college and school in the land." Baseball was deemed particularly important in this reeducation project, for America's favorite game had, in the words of SCAP military intelligence officer Major Paul Rusch, already become "Japan's national pastime prior to December 8, 1941."[5]

That theme of transwar continuity mediated by baseball was not without a wartime antecedent in American policy. The U.S. wartime propaganda apparatus was already circulating a spin that was both old and new: Western-style democracy was teachable to the Japanese, and they had the Japanese love of baseball to prove it. Prewar Japan's enthusiastic adoption of baseball had been referenced in Frank Capra's wartime propaganda film *Know Your Enemy: Japan*, which included footage from the rapturous Japanese reception of the 1931 and 1934 major-league baseball tours. In this 1945 production, the assumed connection was made—and not very subtly—between Japan's embrace of "America's Game" and the enemy nation's innate ability to espouse political liberalism compatible with that of the Euro-American world, with an added allusion to the 1935 assault on Shōriki Matsutarō by a crazed ultranationalist who believed the morally depraved Americans were desecrating the sacred ballpark adjacent to the Jingū Shrine. The Japanese wartime state, for its part, sought to restrict but at the same time appropriate recreational activities such as baseball into the symbolic order of militarism.[6] Now with the nation under the new military ruler called SCAP, baseball was again to be enlisted as a means of national representation to the Japanese populace and to the American audience as a metaphor for democratic citizenry, not anti–Anglo-American military mobilization and masculine soldiering. In the state manipulation of sports as a symbolic vehicle, baseball bridged the prewar, wartime, and postwar years.

One avenue through which baseball was deployed for the occupation headquarters' larger reform agenda for Japan was the wholesale overhaul of youth education. The first wave of SCAP directives on school reform issued in the immediate postsurrender months contained many ambiguities regarding individual sports within Japan's postwar education regime, and the direction of reform was not entirely clear. By early 1946, SCAP's administrative guidelines had cohered around the banning of traditional Japanese martial arts from school curricula because of their close link to wartime militarism and soldier training. As a result, *kendō* (bamboo stick fighting), *naginata* (spears), and *kyūdō* (Japanese archery) could not be taught, even in physical education classes or as extracurricular activities.[7] In their place came Western team sports. To help cope with the dearth of sporting equipment, protective gear used in those martial arts was remade into baseball gear. Many of the SCAP officials who became involved in this social-engineering project, such as Major John W. Norviel, head of the Civil Information and Education Section, had prior experience working in community sports programs in the United States. Through their expertise and professional outlook, the idyllic "American" notion of neighborhood and community-based youth sports and recreational play fertilizing the soil of grassroots democracy was infused into the SCAP blueprint for Japan's reorientation through education and leisure activity.[8]

That baseball occupied a central place in the reform of school physical education was also clear from the preferential treatment the sport received in the rationing of scarce goods and materials in occupied Japan. When the Education Mission dispatched from Washington arrived in

Tokyo in March 1946, the delegation noted, along with the acute problem of malnourished school-age children, the total disappearance of sporting equipment and facilities from Japanese schools and civil life in general. Sports promoters within SCAP seized on that mission report to argue for priority allocation of resources for their favored causes, emphasizing the vaunted effects of "wholesome recreations"—particularly team sports such as baseball, basketball, and football—as inoculation against Japan's potential return to militarism. Their rhetorical strategy yielded a number of dividends for baseball boosters, both American and Japanese. Among the benefits was diversion of leather and rubber for the production of baseballs as one of the "emergency priority items" critical to implementing occupation mandates.[9]

Less formal ways of privileging baseball over other sports emerged in the everyday interactions between the Eighth Army's top brass and Japanese concerned with the resurrection of baseball. American officers not infrequently made a "special dispensation" of releasing baseball equipment and playing venues for Japanese civilian use. The number of sets of baseball equipment circulated in Japan by this means was 8,000, according to one SCAP report.[10] The memoirs written by members of Japan's organized baseball contain a plethora of anecdotal evidence of assistance accorded by SCAP officials in obtaining needed baseball equipment and securing playing fields in the early postwar years. Such acts of individual goodwill and favorable discretion ran the gamut: SCAP leaders promoted the building of a new steel-and-concrete stadium in Osaka by approving priority allocations of rationed construction materials; they extended good offices during the review of applications for the use of requisitioned facilities and the organization of sporting events, with resources provided by SCAP; and the patrolling U.S. military police winked at intercity black-market trafficking of baseball equipment.[11]

In using baseball to help the Japanese relearn American-style democracy, SCAP supported both actual play and spectatorship, the latter element being a by-product of its recreational service policy toward its own rank and file. Soon after its arrival in Japan, the Eighth Army's top brass began channeling substantial resources into intramural athletic programs to give U.S. military personnel a "sense of normalcy amid the alien population." The need to turn the territory under occupation into a home away from home for young American servicemen frustrated by not being able to return to the the United States even after the much-awaited V-J Day generated various officially sponsored events. Important among these were

A Field of New Dreams | 203

the Thanksgiving Day football game, dubbed the "Tokyo Rose Bowl," and the U.S. Army's intramural baseball league, which consisted of the North Japan League of six baseball teams and a twelve-team equivalent for southern Japan, capped by the postseason "Japan Series" between the two division champions. These baseball games were customarily open to the Japanese public as free entertainment, even though most U.S. military facilities were off-limits to the locals. With a dearth of public entertainment in war-devastated Japan, free amateur ball games often drew crowds in the thousands. The limited choice of playing partners in the occupied land forced U.S. Army teams to engage Japanese collegiate teams in practice and exhibition games.[12]

Baseball's amazingly swift postwar reinstatement was owed in part to astute lobbying by stalwarts from the prewar Japanese professional baseball league. In the early postsurrender weeks, Shōriki was conspicuously absent from this band of reactivated baseball lobbyists. He was arrested as a suspected Class-A war criminal in December 1945 for his role in wartime media propagandizing and collaboration with the militarist cabinets. The charges would be dropped, and he was released from Sugamo Prison in September 1947, but the prewar newspaper publicist's ban from public offices would not be lifted until August 1951. Instead, Shōriki's mantle was taken over by other founding brothers of Japanese professional baseball. Suzuki Sōtarō and Matsumoto Takizō, both proficient in English, took charge in the postwar transition with as much political entrepreneurship as the big man's. They lobbied SCAP tirelessly in the immediate postsurrender months to keep key ballparks in Tokyo and the greater Osaka area available to Japanese players, with some significant success. It was through their effective lobbying that Kōshien Stadium was released from military impoundment after only a brief period and made available for baseball play in western Japan.[13]

Standing at the forefront of these pro-baseball campaigns, Suzuki and Matsumoto strategically targeted officials in the Eighth Army Special Service Division (SSD) whose partiality toward baseball was a poorly kept secret. It was also the Japanese baseball lobbyists' good fortune that Dick Sisler, the son of the famed George Sisler, now NBC commissioner, was on the SSD staff. The junior Sisler, who would launch his own major-league career in 1946 as a St. Louis Cardinal, did not need to be persuaded that baseball was the best thing that had ever happened to humanity. The manager of the Brooklyn Dodgers, Leo Durocher, accompanied by actor Danny Kaye, also visited Japan in October on a USO mission and lent a sympathetic ear to Suzuki. Visual reminders of Japan's prewar fealty to America's Game, such as photographs of Babe Ruth and Lou Gehrig taken during their 1934 tour, were dutifully presented by Suzuki and his fellow lobbyists to SCAP officials to garner their support or special dispensations.[14] So as not to make its allegiance to the new ruler too subtle, at the end of the inaugural 1946 season, the Japan Baseball Association (NBA) adopted the official slogan: "Follow American Baseball!" The teams' nicknames, switched to Japanese names during the war, reverted to their English originals, such as the Giants and the Tigers. The association also created "from above" a players' association in November 1946 to approximate Japanese organized baseball to the American prototype and to display responsiveness to SCAP's policy of promoting labor unionism in Japan. April 27, the day that the inaugural 1946 season opened, was named Babe Ruth Day.[15]

In ingratiating themselves with SCAP's power structure, the Japanese baseball lobby found a valuable ally in Captain Tsuneo "Cappy" Harada, a twenty-five-year-old Japanese American intelligence officer who joined ESS in April 1946 as Marquat's aide-de-camp. This Nisei officer's life up to that point embodied a circuitous trajectory of U.S.-Japanese baseball exchange in the prewar decades. Born in Santa Maria, California, in 1921, Harada was raised by his widowed father, a native of Wakayama who had, since his migration to the United States in 1904, toiled on vegetable farms in California's Central Valley alongside Filipino and Mexican farmworkers. As a teenager, Harada helped his father with farmwork and played second base for a local semipro team, the Santa Maria Indians—one of the teams that played against the Tokyo Giants during the latter's second U.S. barnstorming tour in 1936. Impressed by Harada's speed and agility, the tour's business manager, Suzuki, had tried to recruit him for the Tokyo Giants, but the laboring teenager declined the offer so that he could stay with his toiling father.

In the late 1930s, Harada continued to play semipro ball, including for a team in Edmonton, Canada, while he labored in a local lumberyard. In the winter of 1941, he was about to be given a chance to try his hand in the majors, having been invited to the St. Louis Cardinals' spring training. His dream was crushed on the "day of infamy" in December 1941. Harada, then twenty, immediately enlisted in the army to prove his loyalty as a U.S. citizen, while his Issei father and sister, an American citizen, were carted off to an internment camp in Bismarck, North Dakota. Since Harada as a teenager had attended a local Japanese-language school, he could speak the "enemy language." After attending the Military Intelligence Service Language School in Minnesota along with about 2,000 other "Nisei linguists," Harada was dispatched to Australia in the summer of 1942. His subsequent career in the military traced the same geographical pathway as MacArthur's army, advancing from Australia to Japan via the recaptured Philippines. Shortly after he was assigned to Marquat's office in Tokyo, Harada was reunited with Suzuki, then busily lobbying SCAP as vice president of the NBA. This reunion marked the beginning of a decade of collaboration between the two baseball boosters.[16]

For the Japanese baseball lobby, Harada was a useful conduit to ESS director Marquat, one of MacArthur's fifteen trusted aides who became known as the Bataan Boys.[17] Marquat was unusual among this coterie of trusted aides who wielded strong influence within SCAP. He was not a career soldier; he was a former reporter for the *Seattle Times* and had played semipro baseball when he was young. Marquat met Harada in the wartime Philippines and, in early 1946, recommended that this Nisei intelligence officer be named his aide in Tokyo. Marquat and Harada bonded around their shared love of baseball, regularly playing together (forming the double-play combination) on the ESS's softball team at Hibiya Park (renamed Doolittle Field) in downtown Tokyo. Both his love of baseball and the obvious usefulness of Japan's favorite pastime as a political tool explain Marquat's enthusiastic endorsement of reinstituting baseball in occupied Japan. At every key moment of Marquat's decision making regarding Japanese baseball, Harada was there, playing forceful advocate for Japanese supplicants.[18]

Marquat's position as ESS director enabled him to shape the future of Japanese baseball in another way. He was the top administrator of U.S. Army baseball teams in occupied Japan and, as such, was named by Ray Dumont in early 1947 as the NBC's "Japanese Commissioner." With this, occupied Japan became Dumont's next enterprise zone. The NBC's most obvious entry point to the newly conquered territory was Japan's highly popular and well-organized semipro industrial baseball, which had resumed its traditional Inter-City Tournament at Kōrakuen Stadium in August 1946 with sixteen industrial teams participating.[19] At the opening ceremony of the 1948 Inter-City Tournament, Marquat, before throwing the ceremonial first pitch, proudly announced to the crowd of 40,000 packed into the ballpark that the tournament's winner would be formally certified by the NBC as Japan's semipro champion. The annual summer ritual of Japanese industrial baseball closed a week later with the presentation of a championship trophy to the Western Japan Railway Club by the chairman of the NBC International Committee, J. G. Taylor Spink, the ubiquitous publisher of the *Sporting News* and Dumont's longtime buddy. Not all Japanese were thrilled by what some perceived to be another American attempt to colonize their beloved cultural institution, but the Americans soldiered forward unencumbered by such local ambivalence. At the end of the 1948 season, Dumont announced that the NBC would sponsor a United States–Japan "semipro world championship series" the following fall.

In February 1949, the Nippon Shakaijin Yakyū Kyōkai (the Japanese Industrial Baseball Association) was founded in Tokyo to prepare for this binational semipro championship tourney in partnership with the NBC Japan office. Housed within ESS, the NBC Japan office's membership consisted of Marquat, Harada, Don Spencer (the Far East chairman of Coca-Cola), and J. J. McSweeney, the head of Chase Manhattan Bank's new Japan Branch. The office's Japanese members included Matsumoto and representatives from the Kōrakuen Stadium Company and *Mainichi* newspaper, all usual suspects of the Japanese baseball fraternity. Overseeing the NBC offices in Japan, the Philippines, the Republic of China (Chiang Kai-shek's Nationalists), and the newly admitted Republic of Korea was NBC Far Eastern commissioner Rear Admiral Giles Stedman (retired), now vice president for Pacific operations of the United States Lines, an ocean-liner company and a major contractor with SCAP. Dumont's landlocked small-town dream of seafaring overseas expansion now appeared ready for fulfillment thanks to the military-industrial complex coalescing and establishing a foothold in postwar Asia.[20]

The Return of Baseball Institutions

In the new postwar baseball world, Japan's sports ideologues, also adapting themselves to the political reality of the Allied occupation, became uneasy bedfellows of the government bureaucracy invested in recasting baseball as a democratic New Japan's officially sanctioned sport. In this kaleidoscopic political milieu, they searched for a new ideology most serviceable to their agenda. On one end of the emerging political coalition was the Physical Education Section of the reorganized Ministry of Education, operating under SCAP's mandate to begin implementing new "democratic" national education guidelines. In an almost synchronized move, baseball commentators such as Tobita Suishū jumped to the forefront of a campaign to "liberate sports" from state control, elegizing baseball as the mainstay of "democratic people's sports." On November 6, 1945, the *Asahi Shinbun* carried an editorial by Tobita titled "Give Sports Back to the Private Sector." In this feature commentary, the fabled baseball writer bemoaned the way sports had been hijacked by regulation-bent government bureaucrats after the Manchurian Incident and baseball's "purity" and "essence" tainted as a consequence. It was a not-so-veiled allusion to the 1932 *Yakyū Tōseirei*. At the same time, Tobita's editorial betrayed a smothering ambivalence, shared by many of Japan's amateur-sports purists, about baseball's commercialization, the trend that had begun indigenously in the interwar period and now threatened to reemerge in the inexorable Americanization of Japanese society under the Allied occupation. Pointing out that the game had been abused as a tool of corporate advertisement and thus made into a vulgar burlesque before the war, Tobita insisted on restoring the "true" Japanese way of baseball.[21]

While some of Japan's sports ideologues remained averse to the seemingly inexorable advent of sports capitalism as an aspect of American-style consumer modernity, the push for resuming student tournaments began as soon as the war ended, and the initiative came from none other than their prewar corporate sponsors. As early as September 1945, the *Asahi Shinbun* and Saeki Tatsuo, an executive of prewar high school baseball, began spinning a scheme to resume its summer tourney. This private-sector gambit was publicly endorsed by Kitazawa Kiyoshi, the Education Ministry's Physical Education Section chief, and his colleagues. By the year's end, private- and public-sector agreement to reinstitute the summer high school tournament received SCAP's blessings. Although all sides agreed on the general goal of relaunching the tournament, there were plenty of particulars to quibble over. One of the contested points, rehashed from the prewar period, concerned the appropriateness of corporate sponsorship of a student "amateur" tournament. In February 1946, Kitazawa, acting on directions by SCAP's school athletic officer, John Norviel, ordered that a new nonprofit national congress of student baseball be chartered to take charge of a reinstated tournament's organization and management. Norviel's objective was to block Asahi's corporate sponsorship, while at the same time freeing high school baseball from state control by rescinding the ministry's 1932 *Yakyū Tōseirei*. Norviel also insisted that student baseball must be refashioned into a truly "privately organized" and "democratic" enterprise run by a decentralized structure consisting of local governing bodies. Amateur purists in the private sector like Tobita also opposed the tournament's sponsorship by *Asahi*, insisting that student baseball should not be mere fun and games and that the playing field should remain a "pure" training ground for physical and moral education of youth. Complex ideological and bureaucratic struggles thus unfolded over definitions of "free," "privately run," and "democratic" baseball among the game's Japanese advocates, the government bureaucracy, and SCAP.[22]

The ideological contestation regarding student baseball also swirled over the dichotomous symbolism of baseball as a sign of continuity versus a new beginning. SCAP officials initially insisted that the twenty-seven national high school tournaments that had taken place prior to 1942 not be counted; that is, the 1946 summer tournament must start with a clean slate and be called the "first" national high school tournament held under the new postwar educational regime. A compromise eventually was reached to call the 1946 summer tourney the twenty-eighth but set its starting date for August 15, 1946 — exactly a year after Japan's unconditional surrender — and include a commemorative element in the opening ceremony. While battling SCAP over these symbolic issues, the newly created National High School Baseball Association labored to cope with the most immediate challenge: a material shortage. Association officials scrounged around for baseballs to be used in the games. Even though the Education Ministry approved the special rationing of materials for manufacturing 1,000 balls, the Ministry of Industry put a stop to what it considered the production of a nonessential luxury item. In the end, the tournament organizers managed to secure about fifty black-marketed sets of a dozen baseballs each. On August 15, 1946, true to the agreed scenario, the twenty-eighth national high school tournament opened at Nishinomiya Stadium, with the U.S. Army brass band playing.[23] Lieutenant General Robert Brown of the U.S. Sixth Army threw the ceremonial first pitch after delivering a stirring opening speech in which he extolled baseball as "a vehicle of peace and democracy." When the tournament closed, the champion nine of Naniwa Commercial High School of Osaka were treated to an unexpected gift from SCAP: a set of brand-new baseballs and equipment. All the other participants gawked at the gift box bearing Spalding's corporate logo, no doubt feeling the visceral sting of defeat.[24]

The contestation between the Japanese school baseball lobby and SCAP also took place over the resumption of the spring national invitational tournament, another pillar of prewar Japan's national high school baseball ritual. SCAP initially pressured the Education Ministry to squash the Japanese plans for resuming the spring tournament on the grounds that one national high school tournament a year was enough. Japanese baseball officials and the *Mainichi* newspaper, the tournament's corporate sponsor, countered that both the summer and spring tourneys comprised time-honored tradition, and as such were parts of an inviolable whole and equally indispensable.[25] The Japanese got around SCAP's stricture by again resorting to subterfuge: the tournament organizers simply eliminated the word "national" from the spring invitational tournament and went ahead with the opening of the first postwar tournament on March 30, 1947. That SCAP's higher echelon tolerated, if not abetted, this Japanese diversionary tactic was evident from the fact that Marquat attended the tournament's opening ceremony and gave a congratulatory speech, speaking approvingly of this "spring harbinger of the amateur sports season" as a learning place for fair play and good citizenship and thanking the *Mainichi Shinbun* for its material support. As in the case of the summer tournament, though, the newspaper's direct sponsorship would not come until after the end of the occupation.[26] Another mainstay of Japanese student baseball, Tokyo Big 6, resumed on May 19, 1946, in a round-robin format at Shimoigusa Stadium. Its traditional playing field, Jingū Stadium, remained under the Eighth Army's control because of its proximity to SCAP's dependent family housing. The ballpark remained unavailable for Tokyo Big 6's annual league play through the occupation period.[27]

Along with these national tournaments, a spate of baseball magazines came back into circulation once the most acute food and material shortages of the postsurrender months had been brought under control. Amid the stringent paper rationing, a boom in the publication of baseball magazines occurred between early 1947 and 1949. Some of the magazines received priority rationing of admittedly low-quality paper to ensure their continued production. The use of black-marketed paper was also commonplace. The printing presses, concentrated in urban areas, had suffered extensive damage from aerial bombing in early 1945, but at the peak, more than thirty magazines of various qualities and duration were in circulation in occupied Japan.[28]

Under U.S. censorship, the systematic conflation of baseball with messages of postwar democracy and New Japan began. The first among prewar baseball magazines to be restored was *Yakyūkai* (renamed *Sumo to Yakyū* in January 1943 and then *Sumōkai* in January 1944). In December 1945, it reappeared as a thirty-two-page magazine for the price of one yen. Closely following *Yakyūkai* was *Nippon Sports* in Osaka. Although the magazine touted itself as "the one and only venue for sports-only journalism," in reality it was no more than a booklet of ten pages issued three times a month for a little over one yen. Then came *Baseball Magazine*, a second baseball-only magazine in April 1946. It blithely proclaimed that "Japan's tomorrow must lift itself up with sports, and this magazine aims to help polish the ball of a heart of New Japan." In one of the editorials, Tobita denounced the wartime militarists and corrupt bureaucrats for having "persecuted baseball out of base emotionalism" and proclaimed that nobody could take away "our national religion (i.e., baseball)." To play baseball was, elegized Tobita, to "honor the souls of those who perished in war." Among a spate of other magazines launched in 1947 and 1948 was *Yakyūjidai*. Suzuki Sōtarō was on its editorial staff, and he often used this venue to float "messages to the Japanese youth" from Marquat.[29]

One of the reasons that baseball grew into a truly mass entertainment in the early postwar years was that all major daily newspapers began to publish pictorial sports magazines, such as *Yomiuri Sports*, *Asahi Sports*, and *Sports Mainichi*. Crowding the competitive field of this new and more specialized sports journalism was the advent of a daily newspaper solely dedicated to reporting on sports and entertainment. The pioneer *Nikkan Supōtsu* was launched in Tokyo in March 1946. In western Japan, *Deirī Supōtsu* (Daily Sports), based in Kobe, began circulation in August 1948, as did *Supōtsu Nippon* (Sports Nippon) in Osaka in February 1949. The *Hōchi Shinbun*, a prewar general daily, switched to a sports-only format in December 1949.[30]

Another notable development in Japan's early postwar baseball journalism was market segmentation along demographic cohorts. In April 1947, backgrounded by the opening of the new school system modeled after U.S. public education (six years of grade school and three years each for junior and senior high school), the first issue of the magazine titled *Yakyū Shōnen* (Baseball Boys) was published. The editorial purpose of the magazine was to "give young boys a dream and hope for a better future." The cover picture featured Babe Ruth, and the issue carried detailed and consciously edifying autobiographical stories of other American major-league stars, such as Lou Gehrig, Ted Williams, and Bob Feller. Feller's hardscrabble boyhood on an Iowa farm and his military service during World War II (!) were held up as a model of ideal manhood. The publication of *Nekkyū* (Power Ball), *Yakyūfan* (Baseball Fans), and *Suraggā* (Sluggers) followed. In March 1949, *Yakyūō* (Baseball King), also targeting young boys, was launched, and its inaugural editorial extolled baseball as a vehicle for a wholesome, upbeat, optimistic, and "fun" life. *Shōnen Ball Friends* (Boys'

Baseball Friends) followed in April. To court juvenile readership, this upstart boys' magazine, published by former Nisei pitcher Tadashi Wakabayashi, now manager of the Hanshin Tigers, even featured a lottery for bats and balls autographed by popular Japanese professional players. In these journalistic venues, commentators relentlessly elegized baseball as the centerpiece of "democratic people's sports," befitting young citizens of the New Japan, but the role of commercialism in "wholesome" student amateur baseball remained an awkwardly unresolved issue in their commentaries.[31]

The 1947 inaugural issue of *Yakyū Shōnen* was also noteworthy in that it was emblematic of a new orthodoxy then strategically being constructed around the benign and "manifestly human" image of a new postwar Imperial Institution. After disavowing his divinity on New Year's Day 1946, Emperor Hirohito launched a carefully choreographed reformulation of his public persona, beginning with cross-country tours to "meet the people." During these highly publicized tours, his attire conspicuously switched from the wartime's military uniform to a dapper business suit and a fedora. Concerted efforts by both SCAP and the imperial household to construct and circulate a new public image of the "people's" emperor continued throughout the occupation period.[32] The emperor's putative love of all sports—and his and his younger brother Prince Mikasanomiya's athletic skills—was a prominent feature of this new invented imperial iconography. More than any other sport, baseball was presented as the imperial family's favorite pastime. In a powerful showcasing of this imperial patronage of the game, on August 3, 1947, the emperor and the empress attended the opening game of the Inter-City Tournament of industrial baseball at Kōrakuen Stadium, cosponsored by the NBC.[33] The imperial couple's friendly waving from the diamond received thunderous applause by 40,000 spectators who were, until only a few years before, their humble imperial subjects.[34]

Again the young generation of Japanese was particularly targeted in this campaign for an imperial makeover, and Crown Prince Akihito, who had just entered high school, was invariably foregrounded in such age-segmented publicities. *Yakyū Shōnen*'s inaugural issue in 1947 featured a photograph of the crown prince swinging a baseball bat, and the accompanying caption read: "His Imperial Highness loves all sports, but particularly baseball. He works hard to perfect his baseball swing while taking a break from his school work."[35] Akihito's attendance at athletic events was pictorially reported in mass-circulating magazines, culminating in a picture of the crown prince shaking hands with manager Lefty O'Doul at the San Francisco Seals' goodwill game in Tokyo, held in the fall of 1949. Embedding itself into the pastime beloved by Americans and Japanese alike, the once-divine Imperial Institution effectively transformed itself through the work of both Japanese and American image makers into a composite icon of the "people's emperor" of New Japan. The imperial household now presented itself as the Americanized, "wholesome" nuclear family in which the husband accompanied his wife to outings, and the father and his son both passionately loved baseball.[36] Baseball was an integral constitutive element of this strategically circulated image of American-style domesticity.

The "Reverse Course" and the Symbolic World of the New U.S.-Japanese Partnership

By early 1949, the political symbolism mediated through baseball had come to include Japan's postwar redemption and reinstatement in the international community, and once again, both the Americans and the Japanese eagerly participated in the process. The culmination of the binational meaning-making efforts came in October 1949 with the SCAP-sanctioned tour of Japan by the San Francisco Seals. The team in the AAA Pacific Coast League played a total of eleven games in Japan between mid-October and late November. By then, it was a whole new ball game, so to speak, for the relationship between the occupier and the occupied. The intensifying Cold War had elevated Japan's status from former enemy to indispensable strategic ally in the Far East. What became known as the "reverse course" in the American occupation policy was well under way by the time of the Seals' arrival in Japan. Mao Zedong's Communist forces had just triumphed in the civil war in China and proclaimed the establishment of the People's Republic of China in Beijing. Little doubt was left in American strategic thinking that Japan's economic reconstruction must be expedited by all means so that the nation might serve as the capitalist West's redoubt in the Far East—or Asia's "bulwark against communism," in the words of Secretary of the Army Kenneth Royall.[37]

Into this shifting political and diplomatic vortex marched organized baseball's old Japan hand, Lefty O'Doul. The end of World War II enabled the self-appointed American baseball ambassador to Japan to return to his adopted country for the first time in twelve years. After finishing the "best ever" 1946 season, when the Seals won both the PCL pennant and the Governor's Cup, O'Doul visited Japan as a member of a USO delegation.

A Field of New Dreams | 213

There, he was devastated to see the immense physical destruction, debilitating material shortage, and spiritual privation the recent war had left in its wake. The generally dispirited state of the populace saddened him, but O'Doul was equally struck by the Japanese people's undying passion for baseball. Children were joyfully playing baseball all over the wreckage of flattened cities, and games played by American service teams were consistently drawing huge local crowds. Baseball must be brought back to Japan as part of the national reconstruction and heeling process, O'Doul believed.[38]

For this native San Franciscan, the visit to Japan in 1946 was not only a sentimental journey but also an incubator of new ambitions. His affection for Japan was undoubtedly genuine and heartfelt, but it was equally true that his connection with the country betokened an opportunity to buoy his career in midlife. After his plan to head a PCL All-Star squad to tour Japan in the fall of 1937 was shattered by the Japanese invasion of north China, O'Doul, by then age forty, continued on as playing manager for the Seals. Beginning in 1943, the team won four consecutive league pennants and made six consecutive playoff appearances. Local San Francisco fans worshiped O'Doul for his jovial personality and hometown upbringing. These impressive exploits notwithstanding, O'Doul's relationship with the team grew ambivalent as years wore on, because he had an ambition, as many retired major leaguers would, to become a big-league manager. The Seals' owner, Paul Fagan, a wealthy businessman who had amassed a fortune through banking, steamships, and Hawaiian pineapple production, managed to keep this enormously popular native son at home by rewarding him with a salary far larger than what he could command in the majors — $45,000 to $50,000 per year. To cement the wavering O'Doul's loyalty, Fagan made him the team's vice president at the end of the 1948 season.[39]

O'Doul's personal ambition for major-league management overlapped with parallel dreams of status enhancement harbored by the PCL itself, a minor league trying aggressively to capitalize on the expansive economy of the postwar years in which, for a time, organized baseball's growth appeared boundless. The tremendous thirst for recreation in postwar America created a huge boost in baseball spectatorship. Major-league attendance jumped by 71 percent in 1946, and the number of minor leagues rose from twelve to forty-two in the first postwar year alone. Riding on the crest of this new golden age of baseball, the PCL, the most independent and financially sound of all the minor leagues, was upgraded to a newly created AAA status, along with the American Association and the International League. But PCL president Clarence "Pants" Rowland was not content to stop there. He began agitating for major-league status. On the surface of it, his campaign had an indisputably solid basis in the nation's demographic shift. Between 1930 and 1950, the populations of San Francisco and Los Angeles had nearly doubled; in the 1950 census, Los Angeles became the nation's third-largest city, and San Francisco was ranked seventh. The National Football League (NFL) lost no time in adding professional teams in these West Coast cities after World War II. The California NFL teams played schedules against teams on the East Coast and in the Midwest. Air travel made such transregional matchups possible and practicable. Baseball's territoriality rule, which had remained unchanged since the National Agreement of 1903 between the two major leagues, seemed archaic to West Coast baseball boosters.[40]

In December 1945, Rowland petitioned other minor leagues regarding the intention of his AAA circuit to attain big-league status and asked the big-league owners to recognize the PCL as a third major league. Major-league owners summarily denied the request but helped Rowland save face by promising to reconsider his proposal "in the future." Not all PCL owners were as sanguine about this attempted elevation of status as Rowland was, since some of the clubs in smaller-market cities could ill afford to break away from the current majors' farm system. Prodded by Fagan, however, the PCL owners joined Rowland in devising a five-year plan during which the league would operate as an independent circuit and expand and improve stadiums to major-league standards. After this five-year period—so the plan went—the PCL would be recognized as a third major league, conceivably one entrusted with all franchises west of St. Louis.[41]

In early 1948, halfway through this five-year enhancement plan, the Seals' management was approached by SCAP about the possibility of organizing a postseason goodwill tour to Japan. The invitation reflected the occupation authorities' own political imperatives. By then, MacArthur had become aware of the political fallout of some of the earliest steps in the "reverse course." When the first election was held under the new constitution in April 1947, the Japan Socialist Party won a plurality, resulting in the formation of a coalition government headed by the Socialist leader Katayama Tetsu. A broad coalition of labor unions spearheaded by public-sector workers planned a nationwide strike in late March 1948. Fearing the strike's destabilizing political effects, the supreme commander ordered its cancellation. The subsequent revision of the postwar Labor Union Law, undertaken with SCAP's encouragement, curtailed public-sector workers' right to strike. The reversal of SCAP's initial prounion stance alienated Japan's leftists and left-of-center elements, who had almost worshiped the American occupier as a heaven-sent executor of democratic reform. In the meantime, confronted by unmistakable signs that socialist rule, and not just power sharing, was a distinct possibility, conservative elements in MacArthur's inner circles searched for a way to win back the hearts and minds of the Japanese masses and to help restore a more benevolent image of the American presence through means that were not so overtly political. Many, including Marquat, believed that an entertainment spectacle organized around baseball might do the trick. Arguably, this was a policy prototype of what would in the 1950s be pursued more systematically as American "cultural diplomacy."[42]

Since the end of the war, SCAP had received nineteen propositions to bring American professional baseball to occupied Japan, including a troupe featuring Bob Feller. Deeming them "non-essential activity," SCAP had approved none of them. Now all the stars were becoming aligned: Marquat and Harada knew O'Doul from his USO visit and were aware of his deep affection for Japan. All parties on the California side — O'Doul, Fagan, and the Seals' president, Charles Graham Jr. — readily agreed that such an undertaking would be most desirable. After all, what better way was there to achieve in one fell swoop O'Doul's personal ambition and the PCL's quest for recognition as a third major league than a high-profile tour to the former enemy country at SCAP's invitation, the first of its kind since Babe Ruth's 1934 tour? Even major-league clubs had not been able to swing that. At the least, the Seals' trip to Japan, if realized, would showcase the PCL's value as a geographical nexus between organized baseball, which was still very much an east-of-the-Mississippi enterprise, and the Far East, which was the only region in the world besides the Western Hemisphere that trade analysts at the Department of Commerce had identified in the late 1930s as hospitable to baseball and thus a promising overseas market for American manufacturers of baseball goods.[43]

There was no way the Seals' tour could materialize in 1948, however. This early in the postwar reconstruction, Western-style lodging was hard to secure in Japan, and there were still multiple exchange rates at which the dollar-yen conversion was calculated. By the spring of 1949, the lodging problem had been resolved with the remodeling of Gajoen Hotel in downtown Tokyo, but the money issue — regarding a guarantee and the tour's other expenses — remained. Fagan and O'Doul decided that no guarantee would be necessary; the team would forswear a profit and go there as a "nonprofit" venture. The only remaining issue, then, was how the Japanese sponsors—the three major newspapers, *Asahi, Yomiuri,* and *Mainichi*—would cover the cost of the team's transpacific flight and expenses while in Japan. More specifically, how were they to secure enough funds in the now-almighty U.S. dollar when their foreign currency reserves were still depleted by war and under SCAP's restrictions? The key to this question was held by Joseph M. Dodge, president of the Detroit Bank, who arrived in Japan in February as SCAP's financial adviser. Having served as a finance adviser to military governor General Lucius Clay in West Germany in 1947 and successfully designed and implemented a deflationary currency reduction, Dodge was charged with the monumental task of reining in Japan's postwar hyperinflation and stabilizing the economy.[44]

In the spring and summer of 1949, sport's value in boosting Japanese morale and impressing upon the world Japan's postwar redemption appeared higher than ever before. In April, Avery Brundage, now the IOC's vice chairman, announced Japan's possible reinstatement in the Olympic movement and participation in the next Olympics (1952) in Helsinki. Acting on this cue from the central governing body of international athletic competition, Japan's sports administrators arranged for the nation's world-class swimmers, Furuhashi Hironoshin and five others, to compete in the U.S. National Championships, to be held in Los Angeles in August. It would be the first overseas tour by Japanese athletes after World War II, but not only that, it would be an opportunity to erase Japan's national chagrin at being excluded from the world of international sport. In the London Olympics held the previous year, Japan had still been barred from the games, but Furuhashi established world records in the 400-meter and 1,500-meter events at the Japanese Nationals held on the same days as the Olympic swimming events in London. Because of his nation's disbarment from the International Swimming Federation, Furuhashi's records were not eligible for official certification.[45]

Marquat and Harada and their Japanese partner Matsumoto worked with Fred Wada, a Japanese American businessman in Los Angeles who played liaison with the Amateur Athletic Union to make it happen. Just before the swimmers' departure for Los Angeles, they competed in the Japanese National Championships, and after the meet, they received well wishes from the emperor and the empress, who were making another strategic public appearance at a nearby athletic event. In Los Angeles, the

Japanese swimmers became an overnight sensation, setting nine world records. Furuhashi alone broke world records in three freestyle events (400, 800, and 1,500 meters) and earned the alliterating nickname "Flying Fish of Fujiyama." Furuhashi's exploits, achieved despite the adversity of the gnawing postwar food shortage and a finger injury sustained during his wartime labor service at a munitions factory, made him Japan's national hero. It was also a moment of vindication for Los Angeles's Japanese American community, still stymied in the harrowing process of resettlement after their World War II internment.[46]

Another potent sports-generated moment of symbolism in the summer of 1949, this one directly related to baseball, was the repatriation of Mizuhara Shigeru from the Soviet Union in July. Mizuhara, a former Tokyo Big 6 star third baseman and member of the Tokyo Giants' 1935 and 1936 U.S. tours, was drafted in September 1942 while he was active on the Giants roster. He served in the Manchurian theater, and along with 2.7 million other Japanese civilians and military personnel in Manchuria, northern Korea, Sakhalin, and the Kuril Islands, he suddenly encountered the invading Red Army at the close of the war. He was one of about 650,000 Japanese men, both military and civilian, who were captured and assigned to forced labor in the Soviet Union. These captives' repatriation to Japan did not begin until 1947. In the spring of 1949, after learning that Mizuhara was in the clearing camp in Nakhotka, Harada flew to the Soviet Far East to expedite Mizuhara's repatriation. When Mizuhara landed in Japan, he was whisked off to a Giants game in Tokyo without going through the debrainwashing program usually required of returnees from the Soviet Union. His sudden appearance on the Kōrakuen diamond and teary greeting over the microphone—"I, Mizuhara, have finally come home"—stunned the crowd and etched into the minds of the Japanese (baseball-loving ones at least) the starkly dichotomous image of the benevolent American occupier and protector and the ruthless Soviets who were still keeping Japanese nationals in captivity in Siberia's frozen wasteland. The significance of the Seals' October tour, billed as the "U.S.-Japanese Friendship Tour," should be understood in this sequence of developments linked to sports, nationalism, and postwar redemption in Japan's collective consciousness.[47]

In June 1949, a joint U.S.-Japanese committee was set up within Marquat's NBC Japan office to work out details with Seals' president Graham, who flew in from San Francisco. They estimated the total cost of the tour to be $36,000, of which only $20,000 could be expected from gate receipts.⁴⁸ The committee successfully garnered the SCAP Foreign Investment Board's determination that the importation of "service" rendered in baseball met the occupation's policy objectives. A few days before heading back to the United States, SCAP's financial adviser, Dodge, endorsed Marquat's plan to use dollar proceeds from ticket sales to U.S. military personnel and expatriates in Japan to help the Japanese hosts cover the costs of the Seals' six-week tour. In order to make the stern gatekeeper of Japan's foreign exchange reserve appreciate how dear baseball was to the Japanese heart, the committee treated Dodge to a game at Kōrakuen. It is anybody's guess whether his personal guide and interpreter that day, Suzuki, explained to this president of the Detroit Bank that one of the teams playing, the Hanshin Tigers, had taken its nickname from the Detroit Tigers.⁴⁹

Even after the money issue was resolved, considerable opposition to the Seals' tour lingered within the Eighth Army and in Washington. A game between an American professional team and Japanese teams implied equality, regarded by some U.S. officials as not appropriate during the occupation. The open endorsement of a commercial event in the nation still under U.S. military rule was also considered undesirable. In the end, MacArthur overruled the opposition, and Washington approved the tour not as a commercial undertaking but as nonprofit public service—a goodwill visit to American troops stationed in Japan. Thus, four games with U.S. military teams were added to the Seals' original schedule of six games against Japanese professional teams.⁵⁰ Once those financial and political arrangements were made, a cascade of reports and commentaries about the Seals' impending Japan tour began to appear in Japanese newspapers and magazines.⁵¹ In one of these previews, Suzuki cited a personal letter he had received from O'Doul, in which "the father of Japanese baseball" underscored to young Japanese baseball fans the wonders of baseball, which taught children the importance of peace, hard work, respect for the rules, and fair play. Suzuki made a point of noting that "Mr. O'Doul had even signed his name in Japanese."⁵²

The Seals delegation arrived in Tokyo on October 13, 1949. There were both familiar and unfamiliar elements to the arrival of the first American pro baseball tour in fifteen years: the players were again treated royally by the Japanese; however, this time, the latest transportation technology—the airplane—brought them. The Seals delegation was welcomed at Tokyo's Haneda Airport by a crowd of adoring fans and thirty top-flight movie actresses, including Tanaka Kinuyo. Like Babe Ruth's 1934 tour, the motorcade to the Ginza was besieged by hundreds of thousands of people cheering the visitors and waving American flags. O'Doul and his team were also treated to a luncheon with MacArthur at the American Embassy.[53]

Two days later, the Japanese public, now anointed in Washington's strategic thinking and official policy as citizens of a Cold War ally in Asia, saw the Rising Sun flag hoisted next to the Stars and Stripes as their national anthem was played publicly and broadcast over the national radio for the first time since Japan's surrender. The crowd of 48,000 at Kōrakuen Stadium reacted rapturously to O'Doul's greeting: *"tadaima"* (I'm home). From the top of the dugout, Mrs. Douglas MacArthur, with the tour's ultimate impresario, Marquat, at her side, threw out the ceremonial first pitch for the tour's opening game, between the Seals and the Tokyo Yomiuri Giants. Only the presence of the supreme commander himself could have further burnished this carefully choreographed public ritual of Japan's postwar redemption and rebirth as a U.S. ally. During the playing of the Japanese anthem, Harada, standing by the sideline and reminiscing over the plight of his Issei father during the war, could not contain his complex emotions about nation and belonging. Reflexively, he saluted the Japanese national flag as it was being hoisted. This honorific act, done by a Nisei officer and before the signing of a peace treaty, outraged many of Harada's military superiors. When Harada replicated the same act at subsequent Seals games, some called for his court-martial. Marquat and MacArthur took no disciplinary action.[54]

The Seals played six games against Japanese pro teams during the cross-country tour and handily won them all. Only a U.S. military team managed to squeeze out a tie (the arrangement called for no extra innings) after losing three games. Still, a total of more than half a million spectators, both Japanese and American, attended the series. The Seals' tour also helped solidify the newly invented imperial "tradition" of patronizing baseball. A "chance" meeting was prearranged between O'Doul and the imperial couple, who were watching a rugby match at a nearby stadium. The crown prince attended a Sunday game at Jingū Stadium, and the imperial household agency made a point of informing the foreign press corps that it was the very first professional baseball game for His Imperial Highness Akihito. The young prince shaking hands with O'Doul created a perfect opportunity to portray visually a new phase in U.S.-Japanese relations. Emperor Hirohito so appreciated what the Seals did in restoring the nation's morale that he invited the team's owner, Fagan, and president, Graham, to the imperial palace to thank them personally.[55]

Besides male bonding with the crown prince through baseball, O'Doul masterfully played the part of avuncular patron saint of Japanese children. He and his team members held free baseball clinics at elementary schools in four major cities. A game in Tokyo against the Far East Air Force team was set aside as a charity event to which Japanese war orphans were invited free. O'Doul also organized an additional game against the Tokyo Big 6 all-stars. Japanese amateur sport purists, including Tobita and Education Ministry officials, objected to the idea of collegians playing against the American pros. O'Doul and his coconspirators in SCAP silenced that opposition by designating the game an "exhibition match" held on "O'Doul Day," to which children under age fifteen (the new upper limit of compulsory education) were admitted free. Fifteen years past retirement, O'Doul pitched in the game and beat the best of the young Tokyo collegiate team 4–2 in a grueling thirteen innings. Amazingly, "Uncle O'Doul" still had energy left after the game to cavort with champion sumo wrestler Maedayama, to the delight of some 4,000 children in the stadium. The entire event was a saturation bombing of a message of optimism: happier and brighter days were in store for Japan's coming generation under America's benevolent tutelage.[56]

The Seals' postseason Japan tour also meant opportunities for American businesses ever keen to cultivate new markets, including but not limited to the former enemy territory. About thirty American organizations operating in Japan, both business and nonprofit, chipped in to help underwrite the Seals tour. Two of them, Coca-Cola and Pepsi-Cola, were permitted to run full-page ads in the tour's official program. Coca-Cola, whose company logo was printed on the program's box-score pages, was a ubiquitous visual presence during the Seals' tour. The beverage company's operation in occupied Japan actually dated back to October 1945, when it opened a bottling factory in Yokohama at SCAP's request to serve American servicemen. It was the fifth bottling facility the company had opened in its Western Pacific operation, following Australia, the Philippines, Hong Kong, and Okinawa. In early 1949, the first manager of the company's Japan office, Ray Spencer, met with Marquat and obtained SCAP's permission for a trial sale of this military-contracted product outside U.S. military facilities and compounds. Coca-Cola was first sold at SCAP's July 4 intramural softball and baseball games at Doolittle Field and Kōrakuen Stadium. The pamphlet for these games carried a Coca-Cola ad saying: "Between innings . . . have a Coke." The drink, however, remained out of the reach of the Japanese who gathered to see these SCAP games

A Field of New Dreams | 221

because they did not have access to the U.S. dollar. At the Seals games in October, however, the American soft drink could be purchased with the Japanese yen—for fifty yen a bottle and half off that price for children on "O'Doul Day."[57]

Coca-Cola was not the only taste of America that the Japanese were allowed to enjoy, if only fleetingly, at the Seals games. SCAP delighted the Japanese baseball fans who could afford the 300-yen ticket (the price of ten kilograms of rice at the time was 393 yen) — or a scalper's price of seven times that—by granting freedom to purchase at the concession stands coveted PX food items, beverages, and American cigarettes, with the Japanese currency at the single exchange rate of 360 yen to the dollar just set by Dodge. A taste of Coca-Cola, hot dogs, and popcorn indulged in by those lucky Japanese taught them in sensory synergy that the benevolent American occupier and its favorite pastime brought to their country something more than peace, freedom, and democracy: it also brought the seductive appeal of consumer abundance and a vision of the good life promised in those American creeds.[58] With the horrors of war and bloodletting across the Pacific behind them, both nations now appeared ready to launch into the popular pursuit of happiness, pleasure, and even now-distant personal dreams enabled by America's and Japan's national pastime. The October lovefest between the Japanese and the Seals' manager who "came home to Japan" brought back to the surface this undercurrent of U.S.-Japanese affective relations that had continued across the war years.

Closely following the Seals' and PCL's transoceanic march west was the NBC. In late December 1949, the NBC's Far Eastern commissioner, Giles Stedman, announced, with Marquat by his side, that the United States and Japan would face each other in a "Semi-Pro World Series" next fall. The following August, Dumont flew in from Kansas—braving his fear of flying—to attend the opening ceremony of the year's Inter-City Industrial Baseball Tournament. Before Marquat's ceremonial first pitch, the visiting NBC chairman informed the loyal supporters of Japanese industrial baseball that their national champion team would challenge its American counterpart in an "Inter-Hemispheric Semi-Pro World Championship Series" in Tokyo and Osaka next month. To assure the Japanese that this was not an attempt to hijack their local baseball tradition, Dumont declared that the motto of this best-of-seven series would be equality: both American and Japanese balls would be used, and umpires would be provided by both sides. Reflecting the radically changed international circumstances after the outbreak of a military conflict across the straits a few months earlier, Dumont and Marquat referred to MacArthur in their speeches as "Supreme Commander of the United Nations Forces."

In September, the year's national champion, Osaka's All-Kanebō Club, squared off against the Fort Wayne Capeharts of Indiana at the inaugural U.S.-Japanese Semi-Pro World Series. The Americans won the series, four games to one. Again, Mrs. MacArthur honored the event by throwing out the ceremonial first pitch from the top of the dugout. All American—or more precisely, "UN"—soldiers wounded in the "police action" in Korea and recuperating in Japan were invited to the series games free of charge. Two years later, in 1952, the second Inter-Hemispheric Semi-Pro World Series, between the All-Kanebō Club and the Fort Myer Colonials, a U.S. Army team, took place in Tokyo and Osaka. Again the United States won the series, four games to none. This time, the American guest of honor at the series was former baseball commissioner Albert "Happy" Chandler. His support of organized baseball's racial integration and his public support of a proposal to halt pro baseball during the Korean War had putatively cost him a contract renewal in 1951. He now had to content himself with his new position: NBC's international chairman.[59] Dumont's organization again furnished a comforting sinecure to baseball men who had seen better days in the big leagues.

8 | THE SEARCH FOR POSTWAR ORDER

In the early postwar seasons, the chaos that often accompanies a new business enterprise afflicted Japanese professional baseball, where codified business rules were almost nonexistent. Player raiding and contract jumping were rampant, just as they had been in American professional baseball until the National Agreement of 1903 etched the rules of enterprise in granite. By 1949, the self-professed guardians of Japanese baseball in SCAP became seriously concerned by the Japanese pro league's unstable business environment and self-destructive internal strife. General Marquat and Cappy Harada firmly believed in the supremacy and universal relevance of the American model and pushed for its application to Japan. In the business of baseball, that meant a two-league structure stabilized by the player "reserve clause" and an independent commissioner to adjudicate disputes among clubs.

It just so happened that their agenda perfectly dovetailed with the personal interests of the stalwart of prewar Japanese professional baseball, Shōriki Matsutarō, who was angling to reinsert himself into the professional baseball enterprise that had dared survive in the early postwar transition without him. On February 23, 1949, the Japanese Baseball Association, under Marquat's instruction, created the office of baseball commissioner and appointed Shōriki, still the owner of the Tokyo Giants, to take up the position. Immediately afterward, however, Marquat encountered an angry protest from the director of SCAP's Government Section, Courtney Whitney. A committed New Dealer and a force behind the drafting of Japan's postwar pacifist constitution, Whitney had frequently locked horns with groups within SCAP that promoted or condoned the backsliding of American reform efforts in the "reverse course." Whitney's determined opposition to the appointment of Shōriki, a man still banned from public offices, was another episode in this internal ideological strife that afflicted SCAP throughout the Allied occupation. Within two months, Shōriki was pressured to resign as commissioner, and the position remained unfilled for almost two years. This zigzagging in American policy reflected something as inveterate as SCAP's internal bureaucratic strife: many Japanese commercial enterprises, including media companies, had a checkered past of wartime collaborationism and war profiteering.[1]

The Rise of a Two-League Structure

The establishment of a two-league system, or the supposedly "respectable" and "stable" industrial structure the U.S. majors had achieved in the last half century, also suited the agenda of the resurgent Shōriki and the SCAP baseball fraternity, which was seeking to introduce "healthy and orderly competition" among Japanese pro teams. During his brief stint as commissioner, Shōriki announced the so-called Shōriki Plan. Along with the construction of a new ballpark in Tokyo and the invitation of a major-league team, the Shōriki Plan called for a two-league structure modeled after the American major leagues. The plan's progenitor argued that competition between rival leagues would be critical to raising the caliber of Japanese professional baseball. The two-league system would also afford additional revenue generators—a midseason all-star game and a postseason "Japanese World Series" between the two league champions, another borrowing from the American model. After their teams had been utterly crushed by the Seals, Shōriki's fellow club owners had to acknowledge the gap that still existed between American and Japanese levels of play. With varying degrees of alacrity, they went along with Shōriki's plan of adding two teams to the existing ten-team league and splitting it into two separate circuits; if all went well, an expansion into six-team leagues would follow.

As was the case during the prewar period, Shōriki exhibited a shrewd business sense by inviting *Yomiuri*'s chief rival newspaper, *Mainichi*, to start a new club. The company, having owned a short-lived pro team, the Daimai Club, in the interwar period, responded positively. The result was the founding of the Mainichi Orions in September 1950. Reflecting the postwar revamping of the Japanese economy, a range of corporations, including Taiyō Fisheries Company, rushed to enter the business of professional baseball during this period of league expansion.[2] The Japanese Baseball Association, however, descended into an uncontrollable spiral of internal strife over the admission of new clubs and continual player raids as teams were being divided into two leagues. The acrimonious situation achieved a modicum of stability by the opening of the 1951 season. By then, two contending leagues, the Pacific League and the Central League, each consisting of seven teams, were in place. Fukui Morita, a former prosecutor general, was finally appointed as baseball commissioner in April 1951.[3]

Institutionalizing U.S.-Japanese Postseason Exchange

Another pillar of the Shōriki Plan was a postseason tour by U.S. major leaguers to reprise his prewar exploit. Again Shōriki found a valuable business partner in Lefty O'Doul. In the fall of 1950, the Seals' manager returned to Japan, this time bringing with him his old protégé on the Seals and a fellow San Franciscan, Joe DiMaggio. They were on their way to visit UN (American) forces in Korea as part of a USO mission. Their activities during the stopover in Japan were purely promotional. The Yankee Clipper engaged a Yomiuri Giants star slugger, Kawakami Tetsuharu, in a home-run derby. DiMaggio and O'Doul held baseball clinics for student players and young boys, including American Boy Scouts drawn from the local expatriate community. The highlight of their stay came in the opening game of the inaugural "Japan World Series" between the two league champions, the Mainichi Orions and the Shōchiku Robins, on November 22. O'Doul threw the first pitch, with DiMaggio at bat and Marquat as catcher. The baseball tourists were again honored with a luncheon with MacArthur before they headed for Korea. Their travel extended all the way to the Yalu River, where UN troops were engaged in a deadly winter battle against Communist forces, including the Chinese "volunteer" troops that had just begun appearing in droves on North Korea's frozen battlefields.[4]

As it turned out, the two ex-Seals' Far Eastern junket in the fall of 1950 marked the beginning of a long string of nearly biannual postseason tours to Japan by U.S. major leaguers. Postseason media spectacles built around major leaguers proved to be a great revenue generator in the winter months. Again, the *Yomiuri Shinbun* was at the forefront of this new type of baseball entertainment. In early 1951, *Yomiuri*'s vice president, Yasuda Shōji, told Marquat about his company's plans to invite a team of major leaguers and let O'Doul and DiMaggio, the two darlings of Japanese baseball fans, choose its members. From SCAP's perspective, with the war raging in Korea, there were plenty of rationales for sponsoring programs to give American troops stationed in the Far East a taste of a stateside holiday through sports and entertainment. The 1951 Far Eastern tour of the

"O'Doul All-Stars" was a brainchild of this new military-sanctioned sports entertainment business that would become a cultural manifestation of the American overseas military presence and a staple of American cultural diplomacy during the Cold War. In this new market for sports capitalism, entrepreneurial brokers who had connections with the U.S. military had an inside track. A prime example was Harada, who left the U.S. Army at the end of 1950 and started his own business in Japan as a civilian sports promoter and travel agent. Harada was also representative of the Nisei linguists who successfully parleyed their military service and connections with SCAP or America itself into personal business opportunities after the end of the Allied occupation.[5]

O'Doul, whose fortunes in the PCL were then falling precipitously, was similarly eager to partake in this transnational sports business. The 1951 season, when the Seals finished twenty-five games out of first place, proved fatal to O'Doul's managerial career. The franchise that only five years earlier had set the all-time minor-league attendance record drew fewer than 200,000 fans that season. More than anything else, this dwindling attendance betokened the structural decline of American minor-league baseball with the advent of television in the 1950s; nevertheless, before the season had even ended, team owner Paul Fagan responded to this disappointment by informing O'Doul that his services were no longer needed.[6] But a humiliated O'Doul still had Tokyo. On October 17, he arrived in Japan with the "O'Doul All-Stars" and baseball acrobat-comedian Joe Brice in tow. Heading the squad as field manager was DiMaggio, who had just retired from the Yankees. The delegation comprised PCL and American League players such as DiMaggio's brother Dom of the Boston Red Sox and a young Yankee named Billy Martin. Again, with a traffic-stopping hero's welcome, the Japanese let O'Doul know that he was still the king of American baseball in that country. After playing seventeen games, the O'Doul All-Stars left Japan on November 20 for their next stop, a Thanksgiving holiday with American soldiers fighting in Korea. The O'Doul All-Stars' 1951 postseason tour also marked a historical milestone for Japanese professional baseball: the Pacific League all-stars managed to win one game, the first victory ever for a Japanese professional team against American professionals.[7]

The business instinct of transnational brokers such as O'Doul and Harada also led them to the idea of luring Japanese professional players to spring training in the United States. The chief objective, from the Japanese perspective, was to learn firsthand organized baseball's cutting-edge techniques and game strategies. This "tradition" of Japanese pro baseball was invented in 1952 when four top players drawn from the Central and Pacific Leagues participated in the Seals' spring training in Modesto, California. Heading the minisquad of baseball apprentices was Konishi Tokurō, field manager of the previous season's pennant winner, the Shōchiku Robins. In the following year, *Yomiuri* sent the entire Tokyo Giants squad to spring training in the United States as part of the newspaper company's commemorative events planned around the centennial of Commodore Matthew Perry's "opening" of Japan in 1853. Not surprisingly, the Giants' first overseas spring camp was arranged through Harada's travel agency; its venue, Elks Field, was in Santa Maria, California—his hometown. The twenty-nine-member Giants squad headed by field manager Mizuhara spent six weeks in California in the spring of 1953. It was during this first U.S. spring camp that the Giants beat PCL's 1952 championship team, the Hollywood Stars, in an exhibition game. A rematch was also won by the Giants.[8] More historically significant than these victories was what the entire undertaking signaled. The commercial success of pro baseball in postwar Japan, the Japanese adoration of things American, and the permanent U.S. military presence in the postwar Far East combined to create new markets for American-led transnational sports and entertainment businesses. In this new realm of capitalist enterprise, individuals such as O'Doul and Harada occupying liminal spaces between nation-states could capitalize on the transnationality of their existence.

Sporting Womanhood
The story of professional baseball's meteoric rise as a popular entertainment in occupied Japan would not be complete without shifting the spotlight to a sideshow performed by its neglected stepdaughters: women's professional baseball. As baseball reemerged as Japan's nationally popular pastime in the early decades of the twentieth century, the game's boosters and organizers sought to draw more women and girls into their gravitational pull. In the prewar years, the Tokyo Big 6 series, for example, issued free admission tickets for a special Women's Day. In southern Manchuria, civic leaders cooperated with popular industrial clubs such as Dairen Jitsugyō in giving free passes to women and girls so that a wholesome familial atmosphere might be fostered in the ballparks—in contrast to another popular entertainment, horse racing. During World War II, ballpark executives, in an attempt to boost sagging attendance, admitted women and children free of charge. For the most part, Japanese girls and women,

like their American sisters, were consigned to the roles of spectators and cheerleaders.[9] Their fundamental marginality in the baseball world did not mean that there were no serious female ballplayers in Japan. In 1917, the nation's first girls' baseball team was organized by an all-girls' high school in western Japan. A local newspaper in Nagoya sponsored a high school baseball tournament exclusively for female players in 1919. During the Philadelphia Bobbies' shoestring tour of Japan in 1925, the visiting American women had only played against Japanese men because that's what people wanted to see: blond, white American women playing Japanese men. But when a barnstorming American women's softball team from Los Angeles played eighteen games in Tokyo, Yokohama, and Osaka in 1938, their opponents were Japanese women trained in softball.[10]

While SCAP's baseball fraternity championed Japanese men's play at all levels, their promotional vision did not extend to the other sex. In the realm of school athletics, American reformers introduced coeducation in high school in the early occupation years, and gender equality in public education became the norm in Japan. A reform of Japanese female education was instituted during the early years of the Allied occupation as a result of collaboration between female SCAP officers headed by Eileen Donovan and Japanese experts on education for girls, most of them United States–educated Christian women, such as Yamamuro Tamiko. Yet their vision of gender equality in educational opportunities was still predicated on contemporary American middle-class domesticity and did not extend as far as equal physical education and athletic resources for girls and young women. Even in that revolutionary postwar regime, female athletics were envisaged only for less physically taxing sports that were deemed "suitable for their athletic abilities," such as dance and table tennis. The officials of the national high school baseball tournaments and their advocates in SCAP only incorporated female students in the postwar renewed enterprise as members of cheerleading squads, never as players in their own right.[11]

In the absence of public encouragement or policy inducements from above, however, some Japanese women decided to take up baseball as serious athletes and even tried to make a career out of playing ball in the early postwar years. Their passion for the sport, coupled with the sport entrepreneurship of some men, produced a brief interlude in the late 1940s and early 1950s during which women's professional baseball leagues existed in Japan, as they did in the contemporary United States. The very first women's baseball tournament where gate fees were collected took place in Yokohama in August 1947. It was part of a municipal carnival co-sponsored by the city government and a local newspaper. Five industrial teams and one local high school team competed at Yokohama Stadium (renamed Gehrig Stadium during the Allied occupation). Extant press reports on the games indicate that the level of play was uneven and some of the players were not quite schooled in fundamentals of the sport. But the novelty of young women in their late teens and early twenties playing baseball "like a man" attracted 20,000 paying spectators. One newspaper report spoke approvingly of the tournament as a harbinger of "New Women with new social purposes and freedoms, and new beginnings for democratic New Japan."[12]

Hyperbolic as it might have been, this press commentary at some level encapsulated the hope and expansive outlook Japanese women were allowed to embrace in the early postwar years. Pushed by a coalition of SCAP officials and a small band of Japanese feminists who had been active since the 1920s, important political reforms were instituted for Japanese women in the immediate wake of Japan's surrender. First came the granting of the vote to women in November 1945, even preceding the proclamation of a new constitution. In the first postwar elections a few months later, thirty-nine women were elected to the Diet, accounting for nearly 10 percent of the parliamentary seats. A statement of social and legal equality for Japanese women was also inserted into the nation's new constitution in 1946 through the work of a remarkable young SCAP staffer by the name of Baete Sirota. The daughter of a Ukrainian Jewish émigré, Sirota grew up in prewar Japan and became fluent in Japanese. She moved to the United States before World War II and graduated from Mills College in California in 1945. She then returned to Japan as a translator for SCAP. When the SCAP committee drafting Japan's new constitution unexpectedly enlisted her to write provisions concerning human rights, she seized the opportunity. The twenty-two-year-old authored the provisions mandating the "essential equality of the sexes" in marriage and all other legal matters concerning inheritance and the family. To be sure, the insertion of these provisions into the postwar constitution alone did not effect a radical change in gender roles or the relationship between the sexes. Nonetheless, Sirota's handiwork, along with the specific measures of political enfranchisement, shaped a new social context in which Japanese girls and women began imagining greater possibilities for their lives in the early postwar years. Many a pioneer in women's professional baseball in Japan later recalled that she lived and breathed that air of hope and change, aspiring to become, as her brothers and male cousins did, a professional baseball player.[13]

In the spring of 1948, three "salaried" women's baseball teams appeared in Tokyo and Yokohama. One of the two Tokyo-based teams, the Marygolds, consisted of "exotic dancers" at a Tokyo cabaret named Marygold. The team's coach and manager, Araki Hachirō, was a former ace pitcher for the prewar semipro Manshū Club. A second team in Tokyo, the Bluebirds, was organized by Koizumi Gorō, a booking agent and former ad man for the Manchurian Film Company. The two pioneer teams toured Hokkaido together for a month, playing twenty games and drawing significant numbers of paying spectators (a crowd of about 8,000 watched their game in Sapporo). In addition to playing baseball, the touring women made appearances in promotional events at movie theaters and community centers. In some cities, they played against local civic leaders, mostly older men, and even entertained them at postgame parties. In part because of such miscellaneous mercantile activities, the tour turned a handsome profit, and the players were paid relatively well: they received 5,000 yen a month at a time when the starting monthly salary of a female high school graduate was about 3,000 yen.

The following spring, the Marygolds and the Bluebirds went on another monthlong barnstorming tour, this time through western and southern Japan. Again, the tour was profitable, but Araki and Koizumi split up after a dispute over money, and the traveling troupe disbanded. Koizumi proceeded to organize a new team, the Romance Bluebirds. He secured a 200,000-yen start-up fund from the publisher of a newly launched women's magazine, *Romance*, and hired as the team's manager Yamamoto Eiichirō, a former player for Japan's first professional club, Shibaura Kyōkai, and the prewar Tokyo Giants. After retiring as a player, Yamamoto had moved to Dalian and took an office job there. He repatriated to the main islands soon after the Japanese surrender.[14] About five hundred girls and young women showed up at the team's tryout. Most of the thirty women hired were high school students or recent graduates, coming from middle-class families in and around Tokyo. Most were also serious athletes, like Ōshima Masako, who would become the team's ace pitcher and was dubbed "Iron Beauty." In January 1950, Sekiura Shinichi, a former employee of the *Manshū Shinbun* newspaper who had just returned home to Tokyo from labor detention in Siberia, organized the Red Sox. His enterprise received modest financial backing from parliamentarian Sakurai Yasuo, an advocate of women's liberation through sports. The team's players, ranging from eighteen to twenty-two years of age, were also recruited through an open tryout that drew more than two hundred hopefuls.[15]

The genealogy of these early teams reveals that this newly launched female sports business was an offshoot of marginal entertainment capital. Not coincidentally, its "founding fathers" were all recent repatriates from the Asian mainland. When the Asia-Pacific War ended, nearly 10 percent of Japan's population lived in "overseas territories"; 3.7 million soldiers and 3.2 million civilians were in Korea, Manchuria, Taiwan, and the Chinese mainland, as well as the far-flung wartime empire and occupied territories to the south. With the exception of about 400,000 who remained prisoners in the Soviet Union and smaller numbers of mostly young children left behind in Manchuria, the demobilization and repatriation of the Japanese populace were completed by the end of 1948.[16] Many among this vast number of recent returnees felt like uprooted strangers in their supposed "homeland." They also tended to be openly pitied or scorned for their abject poverty and their presumed role in the nation's now-bankrupt imperial project. As they struggled to rebuild their lives in New Japan, many were consigned to work in the marginal (and often underground) sectors of the national economy. Women's professional baseball originated as a brand of such war-born, off-mainstream enterprise.[17]

A weak capital base was a theme common to women's professional baseball in the United States and Japan. In the United States, both of the rival women's professional baseball leagues began to decline in the early 1950s. The first signs of trouble were a shrinking fan base and falling revenues. In 1951 Meyerhoff was bought out of the All-American Girls Professional Baseball League, and the league reorganized itself into a conference of independent operations in five midwestern cities. This decentralization of the league structure turned out to be misguided, and the enterprise was further weakened by the absence of reliable financial backing. What was left of the AAGPBL folded in 1954, when the last of its surviving teams disbanded. The AAGPBL'S demise was a casualty of changing times and the absence of effective centralized leadership. It also reflected the limited market in the midcentury United States for women's professional sports in general.[18]

Tenuous financial footing of its constituent teams also characterized the AAGPBL's Japanese equivalent, the Girls' Baseball League (GBL). Formed with four teams (the Romance Bluebirds, the Red Sox, the Nissan Pearls, and the Tokyo Stars) in March 1950, the GBL's leadership characteristically consisted of individuals marginalized in Japanese society at the time. Its inaugural director was a former officer of the Kwantung Army. League chairman Ōkubo Ryūjirō, a former mayor of Tokyo, had been "purged" from public office for his activities during the war. Ichioka Tadao, a former manager of the prewar Giants who served as the GBL's technical adviser, had been blackballed from men's pro baseball after incurring the wrath of Shōriki. Nonetheless, the GBL, like its American equivalent seven years before, got off to a promising start in the spring of 1950 with initial financial backing by an upstart sports daily, the *Nikkan Supōtsu*, and the publisher of a women's magazine, *Shufuto Seikatsu* (meaning "Housewife's Life"). The league's season opener between the Romance Bluebirds and the Red Sox drew a respectable crowd of about 17,000. Through the summer and early fall, a spate of teams burst into existence in other parts of the country. At one point of this boomlet, which was primed by the Korean War, there were twenty-five teams nationwide, and a rival league was organized in the fall. Most of these clubs, however, were simply not financially viable. As the initial novelty wore off, so did fans' interest. Most of the teams folded within a few months. The GBL embarked on its second season in April 1951 with all the trappings of organized baseball, such as a midseason all-star game and postseason playoffs. As the season wore on, the fan base of even the stronger clubs shrank steadily because of the lack of technically strong players, compounded by ambiguities in female pro baseball's social purpose. In 1952, the GBL revised its charter to allow the surviving teams to go semipro. The players thus became advertising arms of their sponsoring companies' products but secured a modicum of financial security in exchange.[19]

Contending philosophies governing women's athletics were another shared thematic thread in American and Japanese women's pro baseball. The situation stemmed from ambivalence regarding gender representation and the expectations entailed in women playing sport and displaying physicality. On the American side, while players variously grappled with the tension between socially accepted femininity in the (traditionally) male sport, Philip Wrigley and Arthur Meyerhoff were quite clear-eyed about how to deal with that disjuncture: they wanted to accentuate and profit from it rather than suppress it. The AAGPBL's founding fathers touted the league as a dramatic but eye-pleasing spectacle of gender contrasts, presenting women's baseball as a seductive and unique combination of feminine beauty and masculine athletic skill. Meyerhoff described the game as a "colorful sports show," in which spectators would revel in the "novelty" of seeing "baseball, traditionally a men's game, played by feminine type girls with masculine skill." Don H. Black, the owner of the Racine Belles, an AAGPBL affiliate, constantly reminded his players that they were selling both baseball and femininity. To make good on their sales pitch that the AAGPBL players were "nice girls" with a "high moral tone," management enrolled players in charm school, imposed an evening curfew, and hired a chaperone while they toured. While insisting on short skirts or tailored tunics, makeup, and physical attractiveness, they peddled an ideal of wholesome, nonsubversive feminine physicality.[20]

Similar philosophical tensions existed in Japanese women's baseball. Koizumi, the Romance Bluebirds' patriarchal owner-manager, ordered players to affect a particular image of feminine attractiveness, with makeup and well-coiffed hair on and off the playing field. Dress and conduct codes regulating off-field behaviors were commonplace among the GBL's constituent teams. Enrollment in a finishing school was also a requirement for some clubs. Midway through the 1950 season, the Japanese clubs abandoned trousers in favor of uniforms modeled after those of the AAGPBL clubs to enact a certain brand of Americanized "athletic but endearing" femininity for what league management determined was its target audience: men, not girls and women. For some teams, the uniform was shorts or split skirts; for others, it was short skirts. For the more athletically inclined players, like the Bluebirds' Ōshima, management-ordered show(wo)manship—such as tidying her makeup while she was on the pitching mound—caused serious anguish and self-doubt. Others, like Shigeko Kōno, an actress-to-be, did not care that much because she "found some common fascinating factors in both baseball and Takarazuka Theater."[21]

Newly emerging specialized sports journalism also participated in the ideological contest over femininity in tandem with manly athleticism and professionalism. The GBL's financial backer, the *Nikkan Supōtsu*, seeking to carve out its own niche opposite industry heavyweights like *Asahi* and *Mainichi*, vigorously promoted women's professional baseball. Along with the league's other financial backer, *Shufuto Seikatsu*, the daily presented the GBL as a serious athletic enterprise engaged in by dedicated professional athletes. Others, however, brutally ridiculed women's pro baseball and dismissed it as a "girly" show or a clownish spectacle. The *Supōtsu Nippon*, the *Nikkan Supōtsu*'s rival upstart sports daily, was particularly brutal. It derisively reported that "90 percent of spectators are middle-aged lechers" and compared fans in front-row seats to gawkers at strip shows.

Its coverage was also loaded with intensely gendered references to players' makeup, fashion, and even anatomy.[22] The roughly parallel tracks followed by American and Japanese women's professional baseball—with their rise and fall in midcentury—reveal these two otherwise disparate societies' underrecognized ideological affinity on the matters of female athleticism, physicality, and sexuality. On both sides of the Pacific, substantial change in the social and cultural realms lagged decades behind the formal political enfranchisement of women. Despite the widely accepted legend—and Americans' self-understanding—of the American occupiers "gifting" benefits of democracy and emancipation to Japanese women during the occupation period,[23] the gender orders of the two countries in the early Cold War era were perhaps much closer together than first believed.

The Age of Transpacific Baseball Business

On April 24, 1952, with the formal ratification of the San Francisco Peace Treaty, Japan regained its national independence. A month earlier, on March 31, the sign "Stateside Park" was taken down and replaced with "Jingū Stadium," and Tokyo Big 6 was finally able to resume its tradition of biannual league play on its home ground. In mid-April, Marquat left the port of Yokohama onboard the USS *Cleveland* to his new assignment at the Pentagon. At the pier, sending off this American guardian of Japanese baseball were grateful brothers in Japan's organized baseball, such as Suzuki and Matsumoto (who was now a parliamentarian). On the other side of the Pacific, O'Doul had just started a fresh season wearing his new cap as manager of the San Diego Padres, the first of three PCL clubs after the Seals he would manage until his retirement. O'Doul would never fulfill his dream of becoming a major-league manager. Nonetheless, his legacy remained palpable in postoccupation Japan. The proceeds left over from the Seals' 1949 "nonprofit" tour—more than $1,000,000—became an endowment known as the Seals Fund. Its administrator, NBC Japan, used it to invite the ethnically mixed semipro Hawaii Red Sox and the Manila Stars in 1951 and 1952. The fund also enabled the Japanese Semi Pro Association to dispatch Japanese all-stars to the first NBC World Championship, held in Milwaukee, Wisconsin, in 1955. Seven countries—the United States (with a separate team from Hawaii), Canada, the Netherlands, Puerto Rico, Colombia, Mexico, and Japan—took part in the apotheosis of Wichita showman Ray Dumont's dream of a semipro "global World Series." In 1957, the Japanese all-stars beat Canada to win the second NBC World Championship, held in Detroit. The Seals Fund also helped finance the construction of the Japanese Baseball Hall of Fame. The facility, housed within Kōrakuen Stadium, opened on June 12, 1959, exactly twenty years after the American original had opened in Cooperstown, New York.

O'Doul was not alone in plodding through the 1950s with an unfulfilled ambition. The PCL failed to achieve its dream of becoming a third major league after all. At the end of the 1950 season, the major-league club owners still refused to grant the PCL big-league status. Fagan threatened to persuade other PCL club owners to pull out of organized baseball and become a "rogue" circuit. Commissioner Chandler rushed to intervene, and the PCL was given a new and exclusive "Open" classification in 1952—a half step above the other AAA leagues, but a half step below the majors. To the PCL executives' chagrin, that half step to the majors proved impossibly difficult to take. By the end of the 1952 season, the idea of transferring existing major-league franchises to West Coast cities was being floated as a serious consideration within the majors' official circles. A telltale signal was the majors' relaxation of requirements for franchise transfers in December 1952, but the PCL, hoping against hope, continued to reach for the stars. In 1958, the major leagues finally colonized their western frontier—not by making PCL one of their own but by moving two National League franchises, the Brooklyn Dodgers and the New York Giants, to Los Angeles and San Francisco, respectively. With the majors' West Coast expansion, the PCL's major-league hopes died, and the league returned to AAA classification.[24] It was Walter O'Malley, having assumed control of the Brooklyn Dodgers from Branch Rickey in 1950, who was instrumental in the big leagues' final push in their transcontinental march west. Not coincidentally, O'Malley would also cultivate his Los Angeles franchise's ties with the Tokyo Giants in the 1960s through joint spring training.

In retrospect, the 1950s stand as a key temporal marker in the transpacific history of baseball. During this decade, professional baseball on both shores of the Pacific underwent a paradigmatic shift, one caused by new technologies and historical forces unleashed in postwar mass consumer society. In the United States, the shape of the enterprise, which had remained remarkably constant since the National Agreement of 1903 between the National and American Leagues, underwent a profound transformation. After the death of Commissioner Kenesaw Mountain Landis in November 1944 and Branch Rickey's successful "experiment" with Jackie Robinson in 1947, Major League Baseball at long last parted ways with its racist tradition and embarked on a path toward racial integration. The advent of a new technology that would become a signal social force in the postwar decades—television—raised the popularity of Major League Baseball to an all-time high in the early 1950s. Television rights became a critical revenue source for the leagues and individual franchises. In the meantime, the majors' dominance in popularity and commercial clout was the inverse of the fortunes of other forms of organized commercial play, including minor-league baseball and the Negro League. The latter finally collapsed in 1962, a casualty of the majors' racial integration. In a parallel historical process, baseball, once the only sport that could claim itself to be the nation's favored pastime, became only one of an expanding array of successful American professional sports that together projected a seductive glare onto the globalizing late twentieth-century world.[25]

Air travel, another technology that became ubiquitous in the 1950s, also planted the seeds of a new order for organized baseball. First, the majors' distribution of franchises, fixed since the first decade of the twentieth century, finally collapsed in this decade. The first set of franchise transfers took place in 1953 and 1954, when the Boston Braves moved to Milwaukee, the St. Louis Browns moved to Baltimore, and the Philadelphia Athletics moved to Kansas City. This first wave of franchise transfers was, as G. Edward White has argued persuasively, undertaken largely within the established structure of major-league baseball, even though they disrupted the existing league itineraries that had been a cornerstone of organized baseball's time-honored territoriality principle. The cities chosen for relocation then—Milwaukee, Baltimore, and Kansas City—were still not located radically outside the existing railroad circuits. The club owners still imagined those cities (or at least Milwaukee and Kansas City) as part of an extended railroad network, or stops on a "western swing." Regular air travel between franchise cities was not yet envisaged as part of the majors' business routine. Further, the locations of the ballparks in these franchise cities had been planned around public transportation, not the automobile.

The second, more tectonic shift came between 1957 and 1960, when the Brooklyn Dodgers moved to Los Angeles; their crosstown rivals, the New York Giants, moved to San Francisco; and the Washington Senators moved to Minneapolis–St. Paul. The moves of the Dodgers and the Giants to the West Coast in 1958 were fundamentally different from the franchise shifts earlier in the decade. These moves, initiated jointly, were calculated to lay first claim to a burgeoning market, a response made rather belatedly by the majors to the shift in national demography. In so relocating, the owners of these New York clubs, the Dodgers' O'Malley and Horace Stoneham of the Giants, braved the constraints of travel that had figured prominently in the earlier franchise transfers. The two new National League cities were half a continent away from any others in the league and could only be conceived to be part of a circuit of regular play with air travel. The two pioneering owners came to believe, as their fellow owners would in the fullness of time, that the first generation of steel-and-concrete ballparks—built in the 1920s within city centers, serviced by public transportation, and drawing upon closely contiguous populations for client base—had become obsolete in the age of the automobile and suburbanization. Theirs was a "new ball game" whose revenues would be drawn primarily from fans who resided in sprawling areas far from the stadium and who arrived at the games by automobile, and also from radio contracts and the even-more-lucrative television broadcasting rights. California, with its extensive network of freeways, growing population, close connections to the entertainment industry, and suburban lifestyles, signaled the future of the baseball business.[26]

The game of baseball also underwent a metamorphosis in 1950s Japan. On that side of the Pacific, too, baseball evolved into a successful mass spectator-sport entertainment, driven in no small part by the unprecedented economic expansion that Japan experienced after the mid-1950s. Sparked initially by the Korean War boom, a dizzying economic ascent segued into Japan's high-speed growth period in the 1960s. With the advent and rapid diffusion of television, professional baseball truly became a mass commercial entertainment like no other in postoccupation Japan. The Tokyo Giants stood to gain most from this new information-dissemination technology, thanks to the connections that its parent company, *Yomiuri Shinbun*, had to a leading TV and radio network, Nippon Television. Again, Shōriki made himself the banner bearer in this new stage of media-propelled sports capitalism. In July 1952, the company he would soon head as president became the first, and at that point only, private corporation to receive a television license from the government of Prime Minister Yoshida Shigeru, thanks to a politically motivated choice made by key conservative politicians. Shōriki's Nippon Television began broadcasting in 1953. Collaborating with agents of American cultural diplomacy of both public and covert sorts, his TV network imported and broadcast many American television programs that depicted a highly idealized life of the American middle-class, mostly the white suburban nuclear family. Along with such programs as *Father Knows Best*, regularly televised pro baseball games and Hollywood movies became a fixture in the cultural landscape and collective consciousness of postwar Japan's growing middle class pursuing the dream of the good life *à la Americaine*.²⁷

As the two nations coalesced into an anticommunist Cold War alliance after the signing of the dual pact of the San Francisco Peace Treaty and the U.S.-Japanese Security Treaty, a structure of regular baseball exchange between American and Japanese "majors" began to take shape. The opening gambit was prompted by none other than the 100th anniversary of Commodore Matthew Perry's visit to Japan. In the fall, *Yomiuri Shinbun*, spicing up its yearlong Perry Centennial festivities, sponsored the Far Eastern tour of its team's American namesake, the New York Giants. Starting on October 17, the New York Giants, field managed by Leo Durocher, played a fourteen-game series mainly against teams in the Central League. The visiting squad impressed upon Japanese fans that U.S. Major League Baseball was now a changed institution; one of the visiting Giants was Monte Irvin, a former Negro Leaguer and a future inductee into the Hall of Fame. Not to be outdone by the spectacles of the historic Perry Centennial, *Mainichi Shinbun* invited its own squad of major leaguers. Called the Lopat All-Stars (headed by Yankee pitcher Ed Lopat), the composite delegation consisting mainly of American Leaguers included six future Hall of Famers, among them Robin Roberts and Yogi Berra. Arriving in Japan a week later than Durocher's New York Giants squad, the Lopat All-Stars played twelve games, mainly against teams in the Pacific League.

The overlapping tours by the two sets of major leaguers had been approved at the owners' meeting in July, but they proved disruptive, as well as awkward, to all parties involved. To accommodate the exhibition games with the visiting major leaguers, the Japan Series between the Tokyo Giants and the Nankai Hawks had to be suspended for two weeks. The anomaly of the situation forced baseball commissioner Ford Frick to acknowledge the need to restrain postseason junkets that fanned the flames of one-upmanship among Japan's rival leagues and sponsors. In late 1953, Commissioner Frick flew to Japan for consultation with the two Japanese newspapers and pieced together an arrangement whereby the Japanese media moguls would henceforth take turns in hosting a biennial postseason tour by American players. This ground rule of business was first applied with Mainichi's sponsorship of the New York Yankees' 1955 postseason tour. The tripartite agreement over the postseason baseball business was a facet of the fledgling structure of U.S.-Japanese bilateral consultation, which was periodically necessary in the postwar era to tame the disruptive elements in these nations' rapidly expanding trade and other forms of commercial exchange. In this newly minted regime of regular U.S.-Japanese baseball exchange, Hawaii, then going through the transition from a plantation-based economy to that of military bases and tourism, remained an important nexus. The major leaguers touring Japan typically played a miniseries during their refueling stop on the island of Oahu, lying midway in the Pacific. Harada, Noda, and other Nisei sports and tourism entrepreneurs claimed a lion's share of Hawaii's growing sports-entertainment-tourism business.[28] The age of the transpacific market for the baseball business was dawning.

EPILOGUE

Japanese American baseball players' field of new dreams after World War II proved as variegated as their wartime experiences, and only a few had a postwar transition as lucrative as Harada's. The Department of the Army lifted its internment order in January 1945, and the War Relocation Authority (WRA) closed all of its camps by the year's end. About 120,000 Japanese and Japanese Americans held in those facilities returned to their "normal" civilian life after almost three years of captivity at the hands of their own government. Ninety percent of those who had owned land and property before the war had lost everything and had to start from scratch. Upon their release, internees received three dollars in meal money and a ticket back to where they came from, if they chose to go back there; the WRA encouraged Japanese Americans to resettle in areas away from the Pacific Coast. Postwar America's mainstream society, however, remained inhospitable to Japanese Americans. The California state legislature's Joint Committee on Un-American Activities, chaired by Jack B. Tenney of Los Angeles, issued a report in 1945 entitled "Japanese Problems in California."[1] Not only officeholders but also some private citizens campaigned to prevent the Japanese internees' return to the West Coast. In 1944 a small Washington State press circulated a pamphlet entitled *The Japs Must Not Come Back!* Its author expressed racialized and gendered fear of Japanese Americans. "Samurai-indoctrinated" Japanese American citizens "will have the right after the war to settle next door to us and consort with our daughters unless something is done to stop them." The pamphlet thus proposed removing all Japanese Americans after the war to "Japanese Mandated Islands" in the Pacific, where they would be free to live under a democratic, American form of government but would be far away from white women; this "resettlement" would be necessary because "sexual contact between races ha[s] to be prohibited because the white race wants to survive."[2]

Kenichi Zehimura chose to return to Fresno with his family. There, he carried on his lifelong dedication to the game he so loved, coaching Little League Baseball and playing semipro well into his fifties. His sons, Harvey and Howard, who had honed their baseball skills in the internment camp's "minor league," grew up to play for the Fresno State University baseball team. After graduation, the Zenimura brothers were recruited to play for the Japanese professional team Hiroshima Carp in the 1950s. After teaching and practicing art at the assembly center in San Bruno and the internment camp in Topaz, Utah, Chiura Obata resumed his life as a professor of art at the University of California, Berkeley, in the fall of 1945. His Nisei son, Gyo, who managed to elude internment in the camp, studied architecture in St. Louis during World War II. As an accomplished architectural designer, he later cofounded the firm of Hellmuth, Obata, and Kassbaum, the company that designed and built some of the most magnificent ballparks in the United States, including Camden Yards in Baltimore, Coors Field in Denver, and AT&T Park and Pacific Bell (now SBC) Park in San Francisco.[3]

In the early postwar decade, a number of Nisei players joined the Zenimura brothers in migrating west to their parents' homeland to fill the rosters of professional baseball in Japan. To cope with the severe talent loss caused by World War II and to introduce new styles of play and techniques from the United States, Japanese pro teams "imported" Nisei players in the early postwar years. One of the pioneers of this mid-twentieth-century replay of *oyatoi* in baseball was Kaname "Wally" Yonamine, son of an Okinawa-born sugar-plantation worker on the island of Maui. He was recruited by the Yomiuri Giants in 1950.[4] Yonamine cut his teeth in professional sports in football, joining the San Francisco 49ers upon his graduation from high school in 1948. A superb athlete, Yonamine overcame an injury that cut short his playing career in football and went on to make a name for himself in professional baseball, playing for Salt Lake City, the San Francisco Seals' farm team. After the 1949 season, Lefty O'Doul, then the Seals' manager and vice president, gave Yonamine free-agent status so the Nisei player from Hawaii could play for the Tokyo Giants. Yonamine made his mark on Japanese pro baseball with his aggressive style of play, particularly in base running. He was followed by Jim Hirota and Dick Kashiwaeda, who joined the Yomiuri Giants in 1951 and 1953, respectively. These recruitments ushered in a boom in the signing of Nisei players by other Japanese pro baseball clubs in the 1950s. America's and Japan's national pastime became a viaduct through which these Nisei traveled and pursued their dreams of "playing majors" in the home country of their parents, if not in the country of their citizenship.[5]

Ever since the initial encounters between the United States and Japan, baseball as a pastime and business created intersecting networks and cultural corridors that together enriched transoceanic civil society and helped temper the often tension-ridden interstate relationship between the two circum-Pacific empires. After World War II, the shared love of baseball assisted postwar reconciliation and formed a cultural underpinning of the alliance, helping it weather the wear and tear of clashing national interests and mutual frustrations in the realm of high politics. In the unified social field traversing the Pacific, both nations embraced the visions of material abundance and the good life refracted in the American Way of Life, gazing down on the world's ideological camp that had sworn hostility to capitalism. Sports (baseball) capitalism was but one aspect of that transpacific mass consumer culture infiltrating the Western "free world" and speaking with an assuredly American accent in the post–World War II era. The making of the U.S.-Japanese baseball fraternity also trekked a historical pathway that took a temporary detour only in the late 1930s and early 1940s.

While political leaders of the United States and Japan were busy fashioning the new orthodoxy of friendship under the awning of the Cold War, people left on the fringes of the empire of the fallen sun picked up the pieces and rebuilt their lives. Some did so through the game of baseball. In Korea, many individuals, after being released from the shackles of Japanese colonial rule, fertilized the soil of baseball in that liberated country and played an important role in building Korea's now-robust baseball enterprise. Their activities mapped the circuitous routes through which the game embedded itself in postcolonial Korea. For example, a Korean national who played on a Japanese college squad in the 1920s later played for the semipro Manchurian Railway club. In 1945, he was among a team of Koreans who played against a U.S. Army team in Seoul.[6] Korean nationals who had spent the prewar years in Japan and repatriated to Korea after liberation—or those who played for prewar Japanese semipro teams in Korea, such as Kim Seong-geun and Kim Young-jak—became architects of Korea's organized baseball after the war. Japanese imperial rule left in the liberated areas overwhelmingly painful inscriptions, but the seeds of baseball planted in its wake—an imprint of Japanese colonial rule nonetheless—promised a new beginning for those who reclaimed their destiny.[7]

Similar cultural footprints of the Japanese empire were left in Taiwan. In the prewar years, the Youshi High School baseball team's paramount goal was to beat its Japanese mainland rivals in the national championship at Kōshien. Some of the Youshi players, such as Wang Feizhang and Hong Jianchuan, became the founding fathers of Taiwanese baseball, imparting their baseball expertise to younger Taiwanese ballplayers after Chiang

Kai-shek's Guomindong took over the island in 1949.[8] In the reconfiguring Asia of the post–World War II era, fields of dreams continued to be built and visited, fostering multiple channels through which the cultural formation Americans like to call "America's Game" circulated and transformed to affect many indigenous faces.

As a manifestation of industrialization, urbanization, the advent of mass consumerism, and the attendant tighter organization and bureaucratization of society on multiple shores of the Pacific, the game of baseball traveled and proliferated in this part of the globe during the period examined in this book. Along the way, the structure of play evolved from a spontaneous and innocent romp to an organized, even commercialized activity with a defined structure, codified rules, invested symbolisms, and articulated social purposes. The organizations that presided over these interactions became more complex, and so did the transnational networks that connected them. Occupying those interlocking spaces, players, organizers, and spectators of baseball formed a supple coalition of visions that often exercised remarkable independence from the dictates of the state. Although this transnational sporting community ultimately was subsidiary to the imperatives and vagaries of interstate relations—as the history of U.S.-Japanese relations in the mid-twentieth century abundantly shows—it devised, time and again, ingenious ways to sustain the autonomy of its visions and practices. Oftentimes, it even became a determinant of interstate relationships in most tangible ways. In some key historical moments, cultural and affective ties forged through the game made a lasting mark on U.S.-Japanese relations and the international relations coterminus with them. It was this mythical and enduring power, generated by the love of the sport, the pursuit of fun and profits, and sometimes base human impulses, that guided the remarkable odyssey of a cultural formation called baseball—"America's Game" or not.

NOTES

Introduction

1. Barzun's quote is from Jules Tygiel, *Past Time: Baseball as History* (New York: Oxford University Press, 2000), ix; Peter C. Bjarkman, *Diamonds around the Globe: The Encyclopedia of International Baseball* (Westport, CT: Greenwood Press, 2005); George Gmelch, ed., *Baseball without Borders: The International Pastime* (Lincoln: University of Nebraska Press, 2006); Joseph A. Reaves, *Taking in a Game: A History of Baseball in Asia* (Lincoln: University of Nebraska Press, 2004); Leonard Cassuto and Stephen Partridge, eds., *The Cambridge Companion to Baseball* (New York: Cambridge University Press, 2011). For early Cuban baseball, see Roberto González Echevarría, *The Pride of Havana: A History of Cuban Baseball* (New York: Oxford University Press, 1999); and Louis A. Pérez Jr., *On Becoming Cuban: Identity, Nationality, and Culture* (Chapel Hill: University of North Carolina Press, 1999), particularly 75–83. For an account of early baseball in Mexico, see Pedro Treto Cisneros, *The Mexican League* (Jefferson, NC: McFarland, 2002). For baseball in the Dominican Republic, Alan M. Klein, *Sugarball: The American Game, the Dominican Dream* (New Haven, CT: Yale University Press, 1991). See also Colin D. Howell, "Baseball and Borders: The Diffusion of Baseball into Mexican and Canadian-American Borderland Regions, 1885–1911," *Nine* 11, no. 2 (Spring 2003): 16–26. Studies of A. G. Spalding's baseball world tour (1888–89) abound. For the most recent works, see Mark Lamster, *Spalding's World Tour: The Epic Adventure That Took Baseball around the Globe—and Made It America's Game* (New York: Public Affairs, 2006); and Thomas W. Zeiler, *Ambassadors in Pinstripes: The Spalding World Baseball Tour and the Birth of the American Empire* (New York: Rowman and Littlefield, 2006).

2. In this book I use the narrow definition of "Americans," meaning the people who reside within the territories of the United States.

3. The study of baseball in Japan has produced a significant accumulation of English-language literature, especially for the post–World War II period. Some of the best-known English-language works written for popular readership include Robert Whiting, *The Chrysanthemum and the Bat: The Game Japanese Play* (Tokyo: Permanent Press, 1977) and *You Gotta Have Wa* (New York: Vintage, 1990); and Robert Obojski, *The Rise of Japanese Baseball Power* (Radnor, PA: Chilton Books, 1975). Ikei Masaru's *Hakkyū Taiheiyōwo Wataru* (Tokyo: Chūo Kōron Shinsha, 1974) is the trailblazing study of the role of baseball in U.S.-Japanese relations. For a more recent study of Japanese baseball, see Sakaue Yasuhiro, *Nippon Yakyū no Keifugaku* (Tokyo: Seikyūsha, 2001). For useful counterpoint to Whiting's notion of "samurai baseball," see William Kelly, "Samurai Baseball: The Vicissitudes of a National Sporting Style," *International Journal of the History of Sport* 26, no. 3 (2009): 429–41; and Thomas Blackwood, "Through Sweat and Tears: High School Baseball and the Socialization of Japanese Boys" (Ph.D. diss., University of Michigan, 2005). For the pre–World War II period, see Donald Roden, "Baseball and the Quest for National Dignity in Meiji Japan," *American Historical Review* 85 (1980): 511–34; Satoshi Shimizu, "The Creation of Professional Sports

Leagues in Japan: A Cultural History of Human Networks," *International Journal of the History of Sport* 27, no. 3 (2010): 553–69; Richard C. Crepeau, "Pearl Harbor: A Failure of Baseball?," *Journal of Popular Culture* 15, no. 4 (1982): 67–74; Robert Sinclair, "Baseball's Rising Sun: American Interwar Baseball Diplomacy and Japan," *Canadian Journal of the History of Sport* 16, no. 2 (1985): 44–53; and Sumner La Croix, "Rule Changes and Competitive Balance in Japanese Professional Baseball," *Economic Inquiry* 37, no. 2 (1999): 353–68. See also chapter 4 of Dennis Frost, *Seeing Stars: Sports Celebrity, Identity, and Body Culture in Modern Japan* (Cambridge, MA: Harvard University Press, 2010). Sayuri Guthrie-Shimizu, "For Love of the Game: Baseball in Early U.S.-Japanese Encounters and the Rise of a Transnational Sporting Fraternity," *Diplomatic History* 28, no. 5 (2004): 637–62; John Gripentrog, "The Transnational Pastime: Baseball and American Perceptions of Japan in the 1930s," *Diplomatic History* 34, no. 2 (2010): 247–73.

4. Timing was crucial in shaping the world geography of sport dissemination. Western team sports in modern, codified, and standardized form emerged at a particular juncture in world history when the British Empire was at the pinnacle of its power. Sports such as soccer, rugby, and cricket were thus spread to many areas of the world in the late nineteenth century by agents of British imperialism. Baseball, a derivation of cricket and the English children's game of rounders, spread only to areas where U.S. influence was strongest. Andrei S. Markovits, "The Other 'American Exceptionalism': Why Is There No Soccer in the United States?," *International Journal of History of Sports* 7, no. 2 (September 1990): 230–64; John Sugden, "USA and the World Cup: American Nativism and the Rejection of the People's Game," in *Hosts and Champions: Soccer Cultures, National Identities and the USA World Cub*, ed. John Sugden and Alan Tomlinson (Aldershot, Hants, UK: Arena, 1994), 222–40.

5. Charles Bright and Michael Geyer, "Where in the World Is America? The History of the United States in a Global Age," in *Rethinking American History in a Global Age*, ed. Thomas Bender (Berkeley: University of California Press, 2002), 67. Equally useful is the definition of globalization by Alfred Eckes Jr. and Thomas W. Zeiler as "the process of integrating nations and peoples into larger communities—expressed in the actions, visions, and self-identities of citizens and government." *Globalization and the American Century* (Cambridge: Cambridge University Press, 2003), 4.

6. For Cooper's astute critique of the concept of globalization, see *Colonialism in Question: Theory, Knowledge, History* (Berkeley: University of California Press, 2005), 91–112. For another thoughtful overview of the difficulties involved in defining the concept, see Adam McKeown, "Periodizing Globalization," *History Workshop Journal* 63, no. 1 (2007): 218–30.

7. Daniel R. Headrick, *The Tools of Empire: Technology and European Imperialism in the Nineteenth Century* (New York: Oxford University Press, 1981); Dwayne R. Winseck and Robert M. Pike, *Communication and Empire* (Durham, NC: Duke University Press, 2007).

8. In this regard, the United States benefited from the transportation and communication infrastructures initially built by the British. Monthly service in the initial northern steamship route from San Francisco to Hong Kong (via Yokohama) began in 1867. The southern transpacific route, connecting San Francisco to Sydney via Hono-

lulu, Fiji, and Auckland, began in 1875. While a transpacific cable was not laid until the early twentieth century, Hong Kong (1871), Yokohama (1874), and other key Pacific port cities were linked to the global telegraph network via India in the 1870s, and intercolonial networks in Australia and New Zealand were harnessed to the outside world in 1875 and 1876, respectively. Matthew W. Wittmann, "Empire of Culture: U.S. Entertainers and the Making of the Pacific Circuit, 1850–1890" (Ph.D. diss., University of Michigan, 2010), 195–98; David Pletcher, *The Diplomacy of Involvement: American Expansion across the Pacific, 1784–1900* (Columbia: University of Missouri Press, 2001); Jimmy M. Skaggs, *The Great Guano Rush: Entrepreneurs and American Overseas Expansion* (New York: St. Martin's Press, 1994).

9. Walter F. LaFeber, "Presidential Address: Technology and U.S. Foreign Relations," *Diplomatic History* 24, no. 1 (2000): 1–7; Furuta Kazuko, *Shanhai Nettowāku to Kindai Higashi Ajia* (Tokyo: Tokyo Daigaku Shuppankai, 2000); Eileen P. Scully, *Bargaining with the State from Afar: Citizenship in Treaty Port China, 1844–1942* (New York: Columbia University Press, 2001); J. E. Hoare, *Japan's Treaty Ports and Foreign Settlements* (Kent, CT: Japan Library, 1994). Brooke L. Blower's recent work on American expatriates in Paris during the interwar period breaks new ground in highlighting the heretofore largely neglected history of Americans living and working overseas. My book resonates with her book in foregrounding offshore Americans. See Brooke L. Blower, *Becoming Americans in Paris: Transatlantic Politics and Culture between the World Wars* (New York: Oxford University Press, 2011).

10. A. G. Hopkins, ed., *Globalization in World History* (New York: Norton, 2002), 13–17.

11. For a thoughtful overview of Americans' expanding geographical knowledge and its implications for global awareness in the nation's emerging international stewardship, see Susan Schulten, *The Geographical Imagination in America, 1880–1950* (Chicago: University of Chicago Press, 2001).

12. Kristin Hoganson, "Cosmopolitan Domesticity: Importing the American Dream, 1865–1920," *American Historical Review* 107 (2002): 55–83; Hoganson, *Consumers' Imperium: The Global Production of American Domesticity, 1865–1920* (Chapel Hill: University of North Carolina Press, 2007); Mona Domosh, *American Commodities in an Age of Empire* (New York: Routledge, 2006); Craig Clunas, "Modernity Global and Local: Consumption and the Rise of the West," *American Historical Review* 104 (1999): 1497–1511; Jane Converse Brown, "'Fine Arts and Fine People': The Japanese Taste in the American Home, 1876–1916," in *Making the American Home: Middle-Class Women and Domestic Material Culture, 1840–1940*, ed. Marilyn Ferris Motz and Pat Browne (Bowling Green, OH: Bowling Green State University Popular Press, 1988), 121–39; Mari Yoshihara, *Embracing the East: White Women and American Orientalism* (New York: Oxford University Press, 2003); Eileen Scully, "Taking the Low Road to Sino-American Relations: 'Open Door' Expansionists and the Two China Markets," *Journal of American History* 82, no. 1 (1995): 62–83; Scully, "Prostitution as Privilege: The 'American Girl' of Treaty-Port Shanghai, 1860–1931," *International History Review* 20, no. 4 (1998): 855–83; Walter LaFeber, *The New Empire: An Interpretation of American Expansionism, 1860–1898* (Ithaca, NY: Cornell University Press, 1963).

13. Eckes and Zeiler, *Globalization*, 1–37; Daniel T. Rodgers, "An Age of Social Politics," in Bender, *Rethinking American History*, 251.

14. Jessica L. Harland-Jacobs, *Builders of Empire: Freemasons and British Imperialism, 1717–1927* (Chapel Hill: University of North Carolina Press, 2007), 11. On economics and globalization, see Kevin H. O'Rourke and Jeffrey G. Williamson, *Globalization and History: The Evolution of a Nineteenth-Century Atlantic Economy* (Cambridge, MA: MIT Press, 1999).

15. On the cultural dimensions of globalization, see Tony Ballantyne, "Empire, Knowledge, and Culture," in Hopkins, *Globalization in World History*; Roland Robertson, *Globalization: Social Theory and Global Culture* (London: Sage, 1992); Arjun Appadurai, *Modernity at Large: Cultural Dimensions of Globalization* (Minneapolis: University of Minnesota Press, 1996); John Tomlinson, *Globalization and Culture* (Chicago: University of Chicago Press, 1999).

16. For an overview of this historical collision course, see Walter F. LaFeber, *The Clash: U.S.-Japanese Relations throughout History* (New York: Norton, 1997), 3–64.

17. Akira Iriye, *Pacific Estrangement: Japanese and American Expansion, 1897–1911* (Cambridge, MA: Harvard University Press, 1972), 1–25; Joseph Henning, *Outposts of Civilization: Race, Religion, and the Formative Years of American-Japanese Relations* (New York: New York University Press, 2000); Tōkai Daigaku Gaikokugo Kyōiku Sentā, ed., *Wakaki Nippon to Sekai: Iwakura Shisetsukara Enomoto Imindan made* (Tokyo: Tokai Daigaku Shuppankai, 1998).

18. For the concept of "contact zones," see Mary Louise Pratt, *Imperial Eyes: Travel Writing and Transculturation*, 2nd ed. (New York: Routledge, 2008).

19. Louis A. Pérez Jr., "We Are the World: Internationalizing the National, Nationalizing the International," *Journal of American History* 89, no. 2 (2002): 558–66.

20. Here I respond to a call for interfacing Asian and Asian American history made by Eiichiro Azuma in his agenda-setting article "'Pioneers of Overseas Japanese Development': Japanese American History and the Making of Expansionist Orthodoxy in Imperial Japan," *Journal of Asian Studies* 67, no. 4 (2008): 1186–1226.

21. Steven A. Riess, ed., *Major Problems in American Sport History* (Boston: Houghton Mifflin, 1997), viii. International political dimensions of sports have been examined chiefly by sports sociologists. For example, see Pierre Arnaud and James Riordan, *Sport and International Politics: The Impact of Fascism and Communism on Sport* (London: Routledge, 1998); Joseph Maguire, *Global Sport: Identities, Societies, Civilizations* (Cambridge, UK: Polity Press, 1999); Maarten Van Bottenburg, *Global Games*, trans. Beverley Jackson (Urbana: University of Illinois Press, 2001); and Gerald Gems, *The Athletic Crusade: Sport and American Cultural Imperialism* (Lincoln: University of Nebraska Press, 2006). Classic historical surveys of the rise and diffusion of modern sports include Allen Guttman, *From Ritual to Record: The Nature of Modern Sports* (New York: Columbia University Press, 1978) and *Games and Empires: Modern Sports and Cultural Imperialism* (New York: Columbia University Press, 1995); and John Hargreaves, *Sport, Power, and Culture: A Social and Historical Analysis of Popular Sports in Britain* (Cambridge, UK: Polity Press, 1986). For recent studies integrating sports history and international history, see Zeiler, *Ambassadors in Pinstripes*, and Barbara J. Keys, *Globalizing Sport: National Rivalry and International Community in the 1930s* (Cambridge, MA: Harvard University Press, 2006).

22. In this book, the designation "Pacific Northwest" includes the states of Washington, Oregon, and California, and the Canadian province of British Columbia.

Chapter 1

1. George Kirsch, *The Creation of American Team Sports: Baseball and Cricket, 1838–72* (Urbana: University of Illinois Press, 1989), 50–53; "A. G. Spalding Requests Formation of a Special Committee to Investigate the Origins of Baseball (1905)," in *Early Innings: A Documentary History of Baseball, 1825–1908*, ed. Dean Sullivan (Lincoln: University of Nebraska Press, 1995), 281; James A. Vlasich, *A Legend for the Legendary: The Origin of the Baseball Hall of Fame* (Bowling Green, OH: Bowling Green State University Press, 1990), 18–23; Peter Levine, *A. G. Spalding and the Rise of Baseball* (New York: Oxford University Press, 1985), 112–15.

2. For the Mills Commission's "invention" of baseball's foundational myth featuring Abner Doubleday and Cooperstown, see Robert W. Henderson, "How Baseball Began," *New York Public Library Bulletin* 41 (April 1937): 287–91; George Kirsch, *Baseball in Blue and Gray: The National Pastime during the Civil War* (Princeton, NJ: Princeton University Press, 2003), ix–xiv; Warren Goldstein, *Playing for Keeps: A History of Early Baseball* (Ithaca, NY: Cornell University Press, 1989), 10–14; and Ian Tyrrell, "The Emergence of Modern American Baseball, c. 1850–1880," in *Sport in History: The Making of Modern Sport History*, ed. Richard Cashman and Michael McKernan (St. Lucia: Queensland University Press, 1979), 205–26.

3. Kanda Junji, *Yakyū Dendō Monogatari* (Tokyo: Bēsubōru Magajinsha, 1992), 42–58; Ikei, *Hakkyū Taiheiyō wo Wataru*; Shimada Akira, *Meiji Ishin to Nichibei Yakyūshi* (Tokyo: Bungeisha, 2001), 32–61; Sakaue, *Nippon Yakyū no Keifugaku*, 7–52; Allen Guttman and Lee Thompson, *Japanese Sports: A History* (Honolulu: University of Hawaii Press, 2000), 81–89. Quibbles over "firsts" included the question of what constituted the first baseball played in Japan; whether it was first played by Japanese nationals; and evidence of first play by Americans living in Japan. See, for example, Nakamura Satoshi, *Yokohama Supōtsu Gaiden* (Yokohama: Yokohama Shinbunsha, 1998), 2–4.

4. Neil Pedlar, *The Imported Pioneers: Westerners Who Helped Build Modern Japan* (New York: St. Martin's Press, 1990), 13; Olive Checkland, *Britain's Encounter with Meiji Japan, 1868–1912* (Basingstoke, Hampshire: Macmillan, 1989); 38–51; Umetai Noboru, *Oyatoi Gaikokujin* (Tokyo: Nippon Keizai Shinbunsha, 1965), 21–23; Miyoshi Nobuhiro, *Nippon Kyōiku no Kaikoku* (Tokyo: Fukumura Shuppan, 1986), 55–56, 115–20. The best English-language survey of the Meiji government's *oyatoi* program is Edward R. Beauchamp and Akira Iriye, eds., *Foreign Employees in Nineteenth-Century Japan* (Boulder, CO: Westview Press, 1990). American Protestant missionaries made indelible marks on private education in Meiji Japan, particularly the education of girls and women. See Kohiyama Rui, *Amerika Fujin Senkyōshi* (Tokyo: Tokyo Daigaku Shuppankai, 1992).

5. Umetani Noboru, *Oyatoi Gaikokujin* (Tokyo: Kodansha, 2007), 111–18. For Denison's and Stevens's activities as foreign policy consultants, see Kohara Junnosuke, "Meijiki nichibei gaikō ni okeru oyatoi gaikokujin: Denison to stebunsu wo chushinni" (M.A. thesis, Keio University, 2009).

6. Fujita Fumiko, *Hokkaidōwo Kaitakushita Amerikajin* (Tokyo: Shinchōsha, 1993);

Tanabe Yauichi, ed., *Oyatoi Gaikokujin Edowin Dan* (Sapporo: Hokkaido Shuppan Kikaku, 1999).

7. W. E. Griffs, *Verbeck of Japan* (New York: Fleming H. Revell, 1900), 188, 198–99, 255–76; Amioka Shirō, "Changes in Educational Ideals and Objective (From Selected Documents, Tokugawa Era to the Meiji Period)," 323–57, and Kaneko Takashi, "Contributions of David Murray to the Modernization of School Administration in Japan," in *The Modernizers: Overseas Students, Foreign Employees, and Meiji Japan*, ed. Ardath Burks (Boulder, CO: Westview Press, 1985), 301–21; Burks, "The Yatoi Phenomenon: An Early Experiment in Technical Assistance," in Beauchamp and Iriye, *Foreign Employees*, 5–15; Sadoya Nobushige, "Mori Arinori no shūkyō jiyūron," in *Amerika Seishin to Kindai Nippon* (Tokyo: Kōbundo, 1974), 14–33; Umetani, *Oyatoi Gaikokujin*, 149–56.

8. Watanabe Masao, *Oyatoi Beikokujin Kagaku Kyōshi*, rev. ed. (Tokyo: Hokusensha, 1996), 39a–d; see also Watanabe Masao, "Meijishokini okeru rokuninno beijin kagakukyoshitachi," *Kagakushikenkūu* 92 (1969): 203–9.

9. Kōkyūsei (pseudonym meaning "ball game lover"), "Yakyū no Raireki," *Nippon*, July 22, 1886; *New York Clipper*, December 23, 1876; Kishimoto Yoshio, "Kyōiku seido no kindaika," in *Meijino Bunmeikaika Kotohajime*, ed. Nishida Bunshirō (Tokyo: Kinensha, 1969), 219–44; Ikei, *Hakkyū*, 24. For student life in Kaisekō, see Hashinami Gyorō, *Daigaku Gakusei Sōgen*, vol. 1 (Tokyo: Nipposha, 1910).

10. Larry Logue, *To Appomattox and Beyond: The Civil War Soldier in War and Peace* (Chicago: IR Dee, 1996), 82–130.

11. "Declaration for Pension," Claimant: Horace Wilson, April 21, 1925, Certificate no. 1108858, Claimant: H. E. Matthews, San Francisco, April 1, 1927, Certificate no. 1577927, Veterans Records, National Archives, College Park, MD; "Family Reunion at Old 'Wilson Palace' White Rock, Gorham," *Portland Evening Express and Advertiser*, December 8, 1909, Philip Block File, Japanese Baseball Hall of Fame Library, Tokyo; *Japan Weekly Mail*, September 2, 1876. Wilson received an honorary degree from Gettysburg College in 1876. Watanabe, *Oyatoi Beikokujin Kagaku Kyōshi*, 39b.

12. Harold Seymour, *Baseball: The People's Game*, vol. 1 (New York: Oxford University Press, 1990), 15; D. Stanley Eitzen and George Sage, *Sociology of American Sport* (Dubuque, IA: Wm. C. Brown, 1978), 28; Kirsch, *Baseball in Blue and Gray*, 1–27; Kirsch, *Creation of American Team Sports*, 56, 68–69, 79–80.

13. Ōshima Masatake, *Kurāku Sensei to Sono Deshitachi* (Tokyo: Shinchi Shobo, 1991), 24–25.

14. Ōshima Masamitsu, *Suisankai no Senku Iōo Kazutaka to Uchimura Kanzō* (Tokyo: Hokusui Kyōkai, 1964), 21–22; Ōshima Masatake, *Kurāku Sensei*, 62–65.

15. For Japanese attempts to integrate Hokkaido firmly into its territorial reach and the parallel development of coastal trading networks between the island's western shore and the Russian Far East, see Brett Walker, *The Conquest of Ainu Land* (Berkeley: University of California Press, 2001).

16. Fujita Fumiko, "Encounters with an Alien Culture: Americans Employed by the *Kaitakushi*," in Beauchamp and Iriye, *Foreign Employees*, 89–119; Emily Rosenberg, *Spreading the American Dream: American Economic and Cultural Expansion, 1890–1945* (New York: Hill and Wang, 1982), 19.

17. For "muscular Christianity," see Clifford Putney, *Muscular Christianity: Man–*

hood and Sports in Protestant America, 1880–1920 (Cambridge, MA: Harvard University Press, 2001), 1–10.

18. Ikei, *Hakkyū*, 7; Ōshima Masatake et al., eds., *Kurāku Sensei to Sono Deshitachi* (Tokyo: Shinkyo Shuppansha, 1948), 26–27, 64–66; Ōshima Masamitsu, *Suisankai no Senku*, 17–23. Yokoi Haruno's *Nippon Yakyūsenshi* (Tokyo: Nittō Shoin, 1932) took the position that the Karigakkō was the first.

19. For Captain Janes's life in Japan, see F. G. Notehelfer, *American Samurai: Captain L. L. Janes and Japan* (Princeton, NJ: Princeton University Press, 1985); Marquis L. Gordon, *An American Missionary in Japan* (Boston: Houghton Mifflin, 1892), 53–56.

20. Kumamoto Ninichi Shinbunsha, *Kumamoto no Tairyoku-Kyōdo Supōtsu no Ayumi* (Kumamoto: Kumamoto Nichinichi Shinbunsha, 1967), 7; Kimijima Ichirō, *Nippon Yakyū Sōseiki* (Tokyo: Bēsubōru Magajinsha, 1972), 18; Hirose Kenzō, ed., *Nippon no Yakyū Hattatsushi* (Kyoto: Yūkan Kyoto Shinbunsha, 1957), 3–5.

21. Kinoshita Hideaki, *Supōtsuno Kindai Nipponshi* (Tokyo: Kyōrin Shoin, 1970), 13–19.

22. Paul C. Phillias, "The Amherst Illustrious: George A. Leland," *Amherst Graduates' Quarterly* 14 (1924–25): 29–33.

23. Kinoshita, *Supōtsuno*, 13–48; Shirahata Yozaburo, "Fukuzawa Yukichi no undokai," in *Undōkaito Nippon Kindai*, ed. Yoshimi Shunya (Tokyo: Seikyūsha, 1999), 61–66.

24. Ikei, *Hakkyū*, 26; Kinoshita Hideaki, "Amāsuto Daigaku Buratto Jimu to Taisō Denshūsho Taiikukantono Kankei," *Studies in Humanities and Social Sciences* 35 (1988): 149–62; Kimura Kichiji, "Amāsuto Daigaku no Kenkō Rongi Shiryō to Taisō Denshūsho no Kyōiku," *Taiikushi Kenkyū* 13 (1997): 15–24; Imamura Yoshio, *Nippon Taiikushi* (Tokyo: Fumaido, 1970), 327–45; Tsuboi Gendō and Tanaka Segyō, *Kogai Yūgihō* (Tokyo: Taisō Denshūsho, 1885), 66–95.

25. Shiozaki Satoshi, *Amerika "Chinichiha" no Kigen* (Tokyo: Heibonsha, 2001), 118; Tōkai, *Wakaki Nippon to Sekai*; Hirose, *Nippon no Yakyū Hattatsushi*, 5–6; Makino Nobuaki, *Kaikoroku*, vol. 2, (Tokyo: Chūōkōronsha, 1978), 115.

26. For Hiraoka's colorful life, see Takahashi Yoshio, *Hiraoka Ginshuouto Tōmeikyoku* (Tokyo: Shuhoen, 1934).

27. Ibid., 10–17; Yamato Kyūshi, *Shinsetsu Nippon Yakyūshi: Meijihen* (Tokyo: Bēsubōru Magajinsha, 1977), 21–31; Suzuki Yasumitsu and Sakai Kenji, *Nipponde Hajimete Kābuwo Nageta Otoko* (Tokyo: Shōgakukan, 2000), 23–25; Levine, *A. G. Spalding*, 13–20.

28. Hiraoka charged a monthly membership fee of one yen, which was an exorbitant sum affordable only for the very wealthy. Dainippontaiiku Kyōkai, *Supōtsu 80nennshi* (Tokyo: Nippon Taiiku Kyōkai, 1958), 484.

29. Suzuki and Sakai, *Nipponde Hajimete*, 96–107.

30. Portuguese lost its status as lingua franca to English in maritime Asia around 1830, and English rose to become the number one global language by the mid-nineteenth century. David Crystal, *English as a Global Language* (Cambridge: Cambridge University Press, 1997), 24–63.

31. Kanda, *Yakyū Dendō Monogatari*, 53–54; Suzuki and Sakai, *Nipponde Hajimete*, 78–80; Ikei, *Hakkyū*, 10–15.

32. Allen Guttman, *Games and Empires: Modern Sports and Cultural Imperialism* (New York: Columbia University Press, 1995), 75–76; Steven J. Ericson, *The Sound of*

the Whistle: Railroad and the State in Meiji Japan (Cambridge, MA: Harvard University Press, 1996), 54.

33. Japan's very first Field Day was held at the navy officer's school in 1874. The key organizers were British language instructors on the faculty. Hirata Takafumi, "Wagakunino undokaino rekishi," in Yoshimi, *Undōkaito Kindainippon*, 88–98, 131.

34. Watanabe Tōru, "F. W. Sturenjikō," *Taiikugakukiyō*, no. 7 (1972); for the charter objectives of the athletic teams, see the text of Kikuchi's speech in *Gakushikai Geppō*, October 1898.

35. Meiji Gakuin, ed., *Meiji Gakuin Hachijūnennshi* (Tokyo: Meiji Gakuin, 1959), 7.

36. Ibid., 17–49, 55; Meiji Gakuin, ed., *Meiji Gakuin Hyakunenshi* (Tokyo: Meiji Gakuin, 1977), 122–23, 153–55, 245, 702–3; Hara Yutaka, *Hebonjukuni Tsuranarubitobito* (Tokyo: Meiji Gakuin Sābisu, 2008), 157–63, 166–71. Young American Christian missionaries teaching at other private colleges in Tokyo, such as Aoyama Gakuin and Rikkyō, also organized a baseball team in the late 1880s and early 1890s, and these college teams soon began to play against each other regularly.

37. Ōshima, *Suisankaino Senku*, 28; Hara, *Hebonjukuni*, 173–83.

38. Hara, *Hebonjuku*, 175–82; Matsumura Shōnen, *Matsumura Shōnen Jiden* (Tokyo: Zokei Bijutsu Kyokai, 1960), 58–63.

39. Seguchi Akira, *Dōshisha Supōtsuno Ayumi, 1891–2000* (Kyoto: Dōshisha Supōtsuyunion, 2002), 11–14.

40. For trouble accruing from Janes's proselytizing and a mass conversion of students at his school, see Notehelfer, *American Samurai*, 195–209. The Kumamoto Band would constitute one of the three mainline Protestant movements in Meiji Japan. For the Kumamoto Band and its connection with Dōshisha, see Tanaka Ryōichi, *Kumamorobandoto Dōshisha* (Kyoto: Kirisutokyōshakaimondai Kenkyūjo, 1960); and Dōshisha Jinbunkagaku Kenkyūjo, ed., *Kumamotobando Kenkyū* (Tokyo: Misuzu Shobō, 1965).

41. Seguchi, *Dōshisha Supōtsuno Ayumi*, 26–27.

42. For an illuminating discussion of the rise of baseball and corresponding decline of cricket in the United States, see Kirsch, *Creation of American Team Sports*, 91–108.

43. Martina Deuchler, *Confucian Gentlemen and Barbarian Envoys: The Opening of Korea, 1875–1885* (Seattle: University of Washington Press, 1977), 109–27.

44. Levine, *A. G. Spalding*, 71–75; Yokoi Haruno, *Nippon Yakyū Hattatsushi* (Tokyo: Mizuno, 1922), 43–45; *Japan Weekly Mail*, May 31, 1902, July 12, 1903; Kinoshita, *Supōtsuno*, 48–49.

45. Ikei, *Hakkyū*, 18–22; The standardized ball weighed five ounces, containing a less than one-ounce rubber nucleus, and was made of yarn and leather. The circumference was nine inches. *Spalding's Official Base Ball Guide: 1884* and *Guide: 1889*. By 1892, the company grew into a million-dollar commercial empire, with about sixty branches across the United States and ten or so overseas sales agents. *Spalding's Official Base Ball Guide: 1992*, advertisement.

46. Kirsch, *Baseball in Blue and Gray*, 131–35.

47. For this point, see Zeiler, *Ambassadors in Pinstripes*, particularly 187–92.

48. *Sporting Life*, March 28, April 11, 1888; Mills to A. G. Spalding, April 9, 1989, Mills Papers, Albert G. Spalding Scrapbooks, New York Public Library; *New York Times*, December 30, 1888; Benjamin G. Rader, *Baseball: A History of America's Game*, 2nd rev.

ed. (Urbana: University of Illinois Press, 2002), 53. For William Cody's Wild West Show touring in Europe and its historical significance, see Robert W. Rydell and Rob Kroes, *Buffalo Bill in Bologna: the Americanization of the World, 1869-1922* (Chicago: University of Chicago Press, 2005).

49. *Chicago Tribune*, July 15, 1888; Tamazawa Keisō, ed., *Tōkyō Undōgu Seizō Hanbai Kumiaishi* (Tokyo: Tōkyō Undōgu Seizō Hanbai Kumiai, 1936), 76.

50. Suzuki and Sakai, *Nipponde Hajimete*, 96-107.

51. Kimijima, *Nippon Yakyū Sōseiki*, 46; *Wilson's First Reader*, lesson 7, 15, Keio University Rare Book Collection, Tokyo.

52. F. W. Strange, *Outdoor Games* (Tokyo, Z. P. Maruya, 1883), 37-47; Tsuboi and Tanaka, *Kogai Yūgihō*.

53. Kiku Kōichi, *Kindai Puro Supōtsuno Rekishi Shakaigaku* (Tokyo: Fumaidō, 1993), 6; Dai Ichi Kōtō Gakkō Kōyōkai, ed., *Kōryōkai Zasshi* (Tokyo: Kōryōkai, 1895), 53-64. Fukuzawa encouraged outdoor play as conducive to learning. Kinoshita, *Supōtsuno*, 13-15.

54. See rules explained in annual issues of *Yakyō Nenpō*, no. 1 (1902) to no. 10 (1911). Watanabe Tōru, "Bēsubōru kara Yakyūye," *Hikakubunka Kenkyū* 21 (1982): 1-53. By 1895, the baseball club of Ichikō further standardized codified rules and published them at the end of each issue of *Kōyukai Zasshi* (Journal of Friends of the School) on the basis of the rules explained in *Spalding's Official Base Ball Guide*.

55. Steven A. Riess, *The City Games: The Evolution of American Urban Society and the Rise of Sports* (Urbana: University of Illinois Press, 1991).

56. Furuta Kazuko, "Shanhai Nettowākuno nakano Kobe," in *Meiji Ishinno Kakushin to Renzoku*, ed. Kindai Nippon Kenkyūkai (Tokyo: Yamakawa Shoten, 1992), 203-26.

57. Yokohama Kaikō Shiryōkan and Yokohamashi Rekishi Hakubutsukan, eds., *Kaikōjō Yokohama Monogatari, 1859-1899* (Yokohama: Yokohama Kaikō Shiryōkan, 1999), 49-50; LaFeber, *The Clash*, 27-29; Seward W. Livermore, "American Naval-Base Policy in the Far East, 1850-1914," *Pacific Historical Review* 13 (June 1944): 106-7; Kokaze Hidemasa, *Teikokushugika no Nippon Kaiun* (Tokyo: Yamakawa Shuppan, 1995), 101-4, 132.

58. Seymour, *Baseball*, 3:310-12.

59. *Japan Weekly Mail*, November 4, 1871. The game was played on October 30 but was called for rain after the fourth inning. The score was 15-11.

60. *New York Clipper*, December 23, 1876; *Japan Gazette*, September 4, October 23, 1876.

61. For the life and career of Durham Stevens, see David Nordmann, "Idealism, Immigration and Imperialism: Durham Stevens and the Rise and Fall of United States Diplomacy with Japan and Korea, 1873-1908" (Ph.D. diss., Indiana University, 2001).

62. Shimada, *Meiji Ishin*, 96; *New York Clipper*, December 23, 1876. Denison's superior at the Treasury Department was also Abraham Mills. Philip Block, *Nippon Keizai Shinbun*, June 2, 2000; clippings of Atarashi Miwako's articles in Nichibei Yakyū scrapbooks, both in Japanese Baseball Hall of Fame Library, Tokyo.

63. Hara, *Hebonjuku*, 173-75.

64. *Yokohama Bōeki Shinbun*, May 6, 1899; *Japan Weekly Mail*, November 4, 1871. Once regular contests among Japanese collegians became routine, their interaction with Yokohama foreigners declined. For the increase in inland travel and appearance

of travel guides, see Maruyama Hiroshi, "Kindai Turizumuno Reimei," in *19-Seiki Nippon no Jōhō to Shakai Hendō*, ed. Yoshida Mitsukuni (Kyoto: Kyōtodaigaku Jinbunkagaku Kenkyūjo, 1985), 89–112.

65. Andrei S. Markovits and Steven L. Hellerman, *Offside: Soccer and American Exceptionalism* (Princeton, NJ: Princeton University Press, 2001), 16–17.

66. For the reorganization of various schools and the establishment of Imperial University, see Nakayama Shigeru, *Teikoku Daigaku no Tanjō* (Tokyo: Chūō Kōronsha, 1978); and Amano Ikuo, *Daigakuno Tanjō*, 2 vols. (Tokyo: Chūō Kōronsha, 2009).

67. For the development of a distinct masculine elite culture at Ichikō, see Donald Roden, *Schoolboys in Imperial Japan: A Study in the Culture of a Student Elite* (Berkeley: University of California Press, 1980), 71–94; Kimijima, *Nippon Yakyū Sōseiki*, 58–61, 94–95; "Bēsubōru buhō," *Dai Ichi Kōtō Gakkō Kōyūkai Zasshi Furoku* 53 (1896): 59–60; Watanabe, "Bēsubōru kara Yakyūye," 6.

68. Dai Ichi Kōtō Gakkō Kishukuryō, *Kōryōshi* (Tokyo, Kōryōkai, 1939), 644–45, 649–51; Roden, "Baseball and the Quest," 521–22.

69. *Nippon*, May 28, 1896; *Japan Weekly Mail*, May 30, 1896; Roden, "Baseball and the Quest," 523–24.

70. Reported in *Nippon*, June 7, 1876; *Kōryōshi*, 651–56, "Itsuwa," *Dai Ichi Kōtō Gakkō Kōyūkai Zasshi Furoku* 58 (1869): 15; *Asahi Shinbun*, June 7, 1896; *Jiji Shinpō*, June 6, 1896; *Japan Weekly Mail*, June 13, 1896.

71. *Kōryōshi*, 656–67; *Jiji Shinpō*, June 30, 1896.

72. *Kōryōshi*, 657–60; *Japan Weekly Mail*, July 11, 1896; Nakamura, *Yokohama Supōtsu Gaiden*, 4–34; Watanabe Tōru, "The Influence of Yokohama Foreigners' Sport Club in the Meiji Era on the Development of Western Sports in Japan," *Taiikugaku Kiyō* 10 (1976): 1–33; Tanaka Shinsuke, "Kyorūgaikokujin ni yoru Kobe Supōtsu Kotohajimekō," *Kōbe Shōka Daigaku Keizai Kenkyūsho* 56 (1996): 141–53; *Yakyūbushi*, February 1895; *Kōyūkai Zaisshi*, special issue, February 1895.

73. Kii Mutsuo, *Masaokashiki* (Tokyo: Kurenaishobō, 1996), 155–161; Ikeuchi Hiroshi, *Shiki Ryōtōhantōno33nichi* (Tokyo: Tankashinbunsha, 1997), 14–15.

74. He would also write Japan's first baseball novel. For Masaoka Shiki and his literary expressions of his love of baseball, see Shimada, *Meiji Ishin*, 61–66; Kanda Junji, *Shiki to Bēsubōru* (Tokyo: Bēsubōru Magajinsha, 1991).

75. *Nippon*, July 19, 23, 27, 1896. Between 1897 and 1904, Ichikō played nine more games against the YCAC and emerged victorious in eight, including a 4–0 shutout and two runaway victories (34–1 and 27–0) over the battleship *Kentucky*, which replaced the *Olympia* in the early 1900s as the U.S. Pacific Fleet's flagship. Roden, "Baseball and the Quest," 529.

76. Watanabe Tōru, "Meijiki no Chugakkō ni okeru supōtsu katsudō," *Taiikugaku Kiyō* 12 (1976): 1–22.

77. Watanabe Tōru, "Nipponni Okeru Supōtsu Kansen no Bunkashi," *Taiikuno Kagaku* 49 (April 1999): 279–83; Putney, *Muscular Christianity*, 49–50; Levine, *A. G. Spalding*, 98–99.

78. Ihara Gaisuke, "Wagakuni Yakyū no Yōnenjidai no Omoide," in *Meiji Bunka Shiryō Sōsho*, ed. Kimura Takeshi, vol. 10 (Tokyo: Kazama Shoten, 1962), 236–46.

79. The best scholarly analysis of Chūman's 1897 manual is Watanabe, "Bēsubōru kara Yakyūye."

80. For a list of modifications, see Watanabe, "Bēsubōru kara Yakyūye," 24–28.

81. Ibid., 17.

Chapter 2

1. Adrian Burgos Jr., *Playing America's Game: Baseball, Latinos, and the Color Line* (Berkeley: University of California Press, 2007), 8; Klein, *Sugarball*, 6, 15–17.

2. Robert Henderson, *Ball, Bat, and Bishop: The Origin of Ball Games* (New York: Rockfort Press, 1947); *New York Times*, June 4, 1953; Steven Pope, *Patriotic Games: Sporting Traditions in the American Imagination, 1876–1926* (New York: Oxford University Press, 1997), 69–71.

3. Harold Peterson, *The Man Who Invented Baseball* (New York: Charles Scribner's Sons, 1973); H. Peterson, "Baseball's Johnny Appleseed," *Sports Illustrated*, April 14, 1969, 56–76. A recent biography by Jay Martin is more rigorously documented than Peterson's work, but it still credits Cartwright with spreading and promoting baseball in Hawaii. Other key works on Hawaiian baseball history also subscribe to this Cartwright mythology. For example, Chinpei Gotō, *Hawaii Hōjin Yakyūshi* (Oahu: Yakyū Ippyakunensai Hawaii Hōjin Yakyū Shuppankai, 1940); Michael Okihiro, *AJA Baseball in Hawaii: Ethnic Pride and Tradition* (Honolulu: Hawai'i Hochi, 1999), 5.

4. Monica Nucciarone, *Alexander Cartwright: The Life Behind the Baseball Legend* (Lincoln: University of Nebraska Press, 2009). For an early history of California baseball well supported by empirical sources, see Kevin Nelson, *The Golden Game: The Story of California Baseball* (Berkeley: California Historical Society, 2004), 2–7.

5. Frank Ardolino, "Missionaries, Cartwright, and Spalding: The Development of Baseball in Nineteenth-Century Hawaii," *Nine* 10, no. 2 (2002): 29; Tom Coffman, *Nation Within: The Story of America's Annexation of the Nation of Hawai'i* (Kane'ohe, Hawaii: EPI Center, 1998), 53–54;

6. Bruce Cumings, *Dominion from Sea to Sea: Pacific Ascendancy and American Power* (New Haven: Yale University Press, 2009), 178–80.

7. Ardolino, "Missionaries," 29; Richard Gama, "National Heritage Has Rich Heritage in the Territory," *Honolulu Star Bulletin*, July 15, 1948.

8. Ardolino, "Missionaries," 27–28.

9. Peterson, *Man Who Invented Baseball*, 172–75; Frank Boardman, "Honolulu Man Who Began the Great National Game," *Pacific Commercial Advertiser*, June 5, 1910; "Park Renamed to Honor Cartwright, Father of Baseball," *Star Bulletin* 7 (September 1938): 9; Edwin McClellan, "Baseball in Hawaii," *Forecast* 13 (September 1954): 8, 22.

10. *Pacific Commercial Advertiser*, August 9, 1884; Ardolino, "Missionaries," 31; Chinpei Goto, "The Early Baseball in Hawaii," 773–74, AJC File, Japanese-American Cultural Center of Hawaii, Honolulu; Dan Cisco, "Baseball," in *Hawai'i Sports: History, Facts, and Statistics* (Honolulu: University of Hawaii Press, 1999), 1–2; Mary C. Alexander and Charlotte P. Dodge, *Punahou, 1841–1941* (Berkeley: University of California Press, 1941), 2, 42, 117, 177–79, 198; *Hawaiian Gazette*, August 28, 1867.

11. Nucciarone, *Alexander Cartwright*, 78–80.

12. Ibid., 194–95; Jay Martin, *Live All You Can: Alexander Joy Cartwright and the Invention of Modern Baseball* (New York: Columbia University Press, 2009), 42–46; William R. Castle, *Reminiscences* (Honolulu: Advertiser Publishing, 1960), 51–52; *Pacific Commercial Advertiser*, July 13, 1892; *Hawaiian Gazette*, July 19, 1892.

13. Cumings, *Dominion from Sea to Sea*, 175.

14. Nakajima Yumiko, *Hawaii Samayoeru Yakuen* (Tokyo: Tokyo Shoseki, 1993), 39–40; Gavan Daws, *Shoal of Time: A History of the Hawaiian Islands* (Honolulu: University of Hawaii Press, 1968), 124–28.

15. Arthur Alexander, "Baseball at Punahou Thirty-Seven Year Ago" *Oahuan* (June 1906), 25–26; Castle, *Reminiscences*, 51–52; *Hawaiian Gazette*, August 27 and 28, 1867; Ardolino, "Missionaries," 33–34; *Hawaiian Gazette*, June 16, 1875. These *Hawaiian Gazette* articles on baseball games make no mention of Alexander Cartwright in attendance or anything of that nature.

16. Ardolino, "Missionaries," 34. As minister of the interior, Charles Gulick was one of the few local white elites who sided with the queen at the time of the overthrow of the Hawaiian monarchy in 1893.

17. Although the United States secured exclusive control of Pearl Harbor, a tight-fisted Congress did not disburse funds needed for dredging and harbor improvements, and the coveted harbor remained unnavigable and practically useless until the eve of annexation. Eric Love, *Race over Empire: Racism & U.S. Imperialism 1865–1900* (Chapel Hill: University of North Carolina Press, 2004), 75.

18. Ardolino, "Missionaries," 35; Pletcher, *Diplomacy of Involvement*, 63–65; Coffman, *Nation Within*, 59–60, 91–92.

19. Under the Bayonet Constitution, suffrage was limited to haole settlers and Hawaiians who pledged allegiance to the new constitution. About two-thirds of Hawaii's population, mostly Asians, was excluded from the electoral process. Under the new constitution adopted by the Republic of Hawaii on July 4, 1894, property requirements and ability to speak and write English counted among requirements for voting, bearing a striking similarity with the Jim Crow disenfranchisement of blacks in the U.S. South. Most of the Hawaiians or Asians were disenfranchised because of these requirements. See also Love, *Race over Empire*, 116–19.

20. Nucciarone, *Alexander Cartwright*, 120.

21. Zeiler, *Ambassadors in Pinstripes*, 67–68; *Hawaiian Gazette*, October 30, 1885; *Daily Bulletin*, November 23 and 26, 1888; A. G. Spalding, *America's National Game* (New York: American Sports Publishing, 1911; reprint, Lincoln: University of Nebraska Press, 1992), 256.

22. Daws, *Shoal of Time*, 72; Ardolino, "Missionaries," 38.

23. Seymour, *Baseball*, 3:291; Pope, *Patriotic Games*, 141.

24. Seymour, *Baseball*, 3:291–95.

25. Pope, *Patriotic Games*, 142; Seymour, *Baseball*, 1:296–300; Elizas, *Empire Strikes Out*, 35–36.

26. Wanda Wakefield, *Playing to Win: Sports and the American Military, 1898–1945* (Albany: State University of New York Press, 1997), 2–9.

27. Pérez, *On Becoming Cuban*; Burgos, *Playing America's Game*, 74–75, 80–84; *Sporting News*, October 1 and 29, 1898; *Sporting Life*, November 1, 1898.

28. Reaves, *Taking in a Game*, 92.

29. Carl Crow, *America and the Philippines* (Garden City, NY: Doubleday and Page, 1914), 119–20; Reaves, *Taking in a Game*, 91–92; Elizas, *Empire Strikes Out*, 45.

30. Gems, *Athletic Crusade*, 48–49; Bell, quoted in Seymour, *Baseball*, 1:324–25; Elias, *Empire Strikes Out*, 44.

31. For Theodore Roosevelt's thinking about race, civilization, imperialism, and bodily fortitude, see Gale Baderman, *Manliness and Civilization* (Chicago: University of Chicago Press, 1996), chap. 5.

32. W. Cameron Forbes, *Philippines Islands*, rev. ed. (Cambridge: Harvard University Press, 1945), 183–85; Gems, *Athletic Crusade*, 48–59. For Forbes's activities as governor-general of the Philippines, see Peter Stanley, "William Cameron Forbes: Proconsul in the Philippines," *Pacific Historical Review* 35, no. 3 (1966): 285–301.

33. Sullivan also gave Spalding & Brothers space for a merchandise exhibit at the St. Louis World Fair. Because of his close ties with Spalding, Sullivan would also be appointed to the Mills Commission later in the decade. For Sullivan, see John Lucas, "The Hegemonic Rule of the American Amateur Athletic Union, 1888–1914: James Edward Sullivan as Prime Mover," *International Journal of the History of Sport* 11 (1994), 355–71.

34. W. J. McGee, "Professor W. J. McGee," *World's Fair Bulletin* 4 (August 1903): 29; Pope, *Patriotic Games*, 41–42; see also Paul Kramer, "Race and Empire Revisited at the Philippines Exposition, St. Louis, 1901–1905," *Radical History Review* 73 (Winter 1999): 75–115.

35. Pope, *Patriotic Games*, 42–43; Mark Dyreson, "The Playing Fields of Progress: American Athletic Nationalism and the 1904 St. Louis Olympics," *Gateway Heritage*, Fall 1993, 9–10. For recent studies of "Anthropology Days" and their historical significance, see Susan Brownell, *The 1904 Anthropology Days and Olympic Games* (Lincoln: University of Nebraska Press, 2008); and Nancy Prezo, *Anthropology Goes to the Fair* (Lincoln: University of Nebraska Press, 2009).

36. Dubbed "the Greatest Annual Event in the Orient," the Manila Carnivals began in 1908 and continued until 1939. This two-week fair was held to showcase "harmonious relationship between the United States and the Philippines" and the cultural, economic, and industrial progress achieved by the American colony. Governor Forbes was one of the original architects of this enterprise and took an initiative in raising funds for the carnivals with proceeds from the crowning of the Manila Carnival Queen.

37. Frederick England, "History of the Far Eastern Athletic Association," *Bulletin Officiel du Comité International Olympique* 3 (July 1926): 18–19; Andrew Morris, *Marrow of the Nation: A History of Sport and Physical Culture in Republican China* (Berkeley: University of California Press, 2004), 22–23.

38. Ian Buchanan, "Elwood S. Brown: Missionary Extraordinary," *Journal of Olympic History* 6, no. 3 (1998): 12–13; Beran, "Americans in the Philippines"; Gems, *The Athletic Crusade*, 45–46. For the history of the Far East Games and their significance, see Ikuo Abe, "Historical Significance of the Far Eastern Championship Games: An International Political Arena," in *Tsukuba Daigaku Taiiku Kagaku-kei kiyō* 27 (2003): 37–68; Takashima Kō, "Kyokutōsenshukenkyōgitaikaito YMCA," in *Chūgoku Higashiajia*

Gaikō Kōryūshino Kenkyū, ed. Fuma Susumu (Kyoto: Kyoto Daigaku Gakujutsu Shuppankai, 2007), 461–505; Ozawa Takato, "Ajiano Orinpikku Tōakyōgitaikai," in *Maboroshino Tokyo Orinpikkuto Sonojidai*, ed. Sakaue Hiroyasu and Takaoka Hiroyuki (Tokyo: Seikyūsha, 2009), 182–84.

39. John McGraw, "Americans in Manila Turned Out in Great Crowds to Welcome Giants and White Sox," *New York Times*, January 25, 1914.

40. Nakajima, *Samayoeru Rakuen*, 63–66, 76–87. By 1933, 96 percent of Hawaiian sugar production was controlled by the Big Five. Daws, *Shoal of Time*, 311–12.

41. Ronald Takaki, *Pau Hana: Plantation Labor and Life in Hawaii* (Honolulu: University of Hawaii Press), 25–40.

42. Aaron Hara, "The Issei Experience," *Hawaii Herald*, May 13, 1990; Hawai Nikkeijin Iminshi (Hawai Nikeijin Rengō Kyōkai, 1963).

43. Gary Okihiro, *Cane Fires: The Anti-Japanese Movement in Hawaii, 1865–1945* (Philadelphia: Temple University Press, 1991), 27; Cummings, *Dominion*, 181.

44. Nakagawa Fusa, *Tosakara Hawaie: Okumura Takieno Kiseki* (Kochi: Kochi Shinbun Kigyo, 2000) 26–29, 64–66.

45. Nakagawa, *Tosakara Hawaie*, 77–81.

46. Elenor C. Nordyke, *Peopling of Hawaii* (Honolulu: University of Hawaii Press, 1989), 65; Dorothy Hazama and Jane Komeiji, *Okage Sama De: The Japanese in Hawaii* (Honolulu: Bess Press, 1986), 26.

47. Kerry Yo Nakagawa, *Through a Diamond: One Hundred Years of Japanese American Baseball* (San Francisco: Rudi, 2001), 3–8; Eiichiro Azuma, "Historical Overview of Japanese Emigration, 1868–2000," in *Encyclopedia of Japanese Descendants in the Americas*, ed. Akemi Kikumura-Yano (Walnut Creek, CA: Alta Mira Press, 2002), 32–33.

48. Okihiro, *AJA Baseball in Hawaii*, 70; Yukiko Kimura, *Issei: Japanese Immigrants in Hawaii* (Honolulu: University of Hawaii Press, 1998), 166–68. Gotō also authored the oft-cited annals (1940) of Japanese American baseball in Hawaii.

49. Takaki, *Pau Hana*, 102–5; Franklin Odo and Kazubo Sinota, *A Pictorial History of the Japanese in Hawaii, 1885–1924* (Honolulu: Bishop Museum Press, 1985), 79.

50. Okihiro, *AJA Baseball in Hawaii*, 52–55.

51. Shimizu Sayuri, "Hawaiino Ekyonipponjin Nikkeijinyakūto Aidentiti," in *Nipponjinno Keikento Kokusaiidō*, ed. Yoneyama Hiroshi and Kawahara Norifumi (Kyoto: Jinbunshoin, 2007), 129–30: Mary Watayama, "Banzai Noda: Japanese American Pioneer," *Hawaii Herald*, August 3, 1984.

52. Andrew Morris, "Taiwan: Baseball, Colonialism and Nationalism," in Gmelch, *Baseball Without Borders*, 66.

53. Yukawa Mitsuo, ed., *Taiwan Yakyūshi* (Taibei: Taiwan Nichinichi Shinposha, 1932); Junwei Yu, *Playing in Isolation* (Lincoln: University of Nebraska Press, 2007), 13.

54. Nishiwaki Noshitomo, *Taiwan Chutogaikko Yakyū shi* (Kakogawa, Kyoto: Nishiwaki Yoshitomo, 1996), 2–9; Andrew Morris, *Colonial Project, National Game: A History of Baseball in Taiwan* (Berkeley: University of California Press, 2011), 10.

55. Yu, *Playing in Isolation*, 11–14; Zhang Like, "Taiwan bangqiu yu rentong" (master's thesis, Qinghua University, 2000), 32.

56. Morris, *Colonial Project*, 11.

57. Yu, *Playing in Isolation*, 15.
58. Takemura Toyotoshi, *Taiwan Taiikushi* (Taipei: Taiwantaiiku Kyōkai, 1933), 8.
59. Morris, "Taiwan," 69.
60. Xie Shiyuan and Xie Jiafen, *Taiwan bangqiu yibai nian* (Taipei: Guoshi chubanshe, 2003), 34–36.
61. *Taiwan Riri Xinbao*, January 9, 1921.
62. Louise Young, *Japan's Total Empire: Manchuria and the Culture of Wartime Imperialism* (Berkeley: University of California Press), 23; Nishiwaki Yoshitomo, *Manshū Kantōshū Chūtō Gakkō Yakyūshi* (Nishinomiya, 1999), 2.
63. Tsukase Susumu, *Mansūukoku* (Tokyo: Yoshikawa Kobunkan, 1998), 16–17; Manshikai, ed., *Manshu Kaihatsu Yonjunenshi*, vol. 1 (Tokyo: Manshukaihatsu Yonjunennshi Kankokai, 1964), 83–86; Tategami Takezō, *Dairenjitsugyōdan Nijūnenshi* (Dalian: Dairen Manshushinposha, 1932), 5–8. That U.S. fleet teams were regular contestants from the early days of Japan's colonial leasing of Dalian is clear from local newspapers. See, for example, *Ryōtō Shinpō*, September 3, 1909; Yamazaki Yūkō, "Mohitotsuno Shutoken to Goraku," in *Toshi to Goraku*, ed. Oku Sumako and Haneda Hhiroaki (Tokyo: Nihon Keizai Hyoronsha, 2004), 159–92.
64. Yamazaki, "Mohitotsuno Shutokento Goraku," 164–69, 173, 184–85.
65. Yanagisawa Asobu, *Nipponjinno Shokiminchi Keiken* (Tokyo: Aoki Shoten, 1999), 84–87.
66. For collusion by the Roosevelt administration, see Akifumi Nagata, *Seodoarūzuberutoto Kankoku* (Tokyo: Miraisha, 1992).
67. Since Gillett's first overseas assignment landed him in Pyongyang in 1901, some baseball chroniclers have considered whether the northern Korean city might be the real birthplace of Korean baseball. See, for example, Reaves, *Taking in a Game*, 114–15.
68. Japan established a dual-track public school system in colonial Korea as well. Between 1911 and 1921, Koreans attended four years of segregated middle school. Schooling was extended to five years after 1922.
69. *Yakyūkai* 2, no. 13 (December 1911): 63–69; Reaves, *Taking in a Game*, 118–19; Bang-Chool Kim, "Professional Baseball in Korea: Origins, Causes, Consequences and Implications," *International Journal of the History of Sport* 25, no. 3 (2008): 372–73.
70. Ōshima Katsutaro, *Chōsen Yakyūshi* (Kyōjō: Chōsenyakyūshi Jakkojo, 1932), 4.
71. Wi Jo Kang, *Christ and Caesar in Modern Korea: A History of Christianity and Politics* (Albany: State University of New York Press, 1997), 38–39; *San Francisco Call*, 21, 23, 24 March 1908.
72. Kang, *Christ and Caesar*, 40; Letter from Gillett to John Mott, 22 May 1912, the Presbyterian Library, New York.
73. Letter from Sharrocks to Komatsu, 16 December 1911, the Presbyterian Library, New York; Ōshima, *Chōsen Yakyūshi*, 1–2; Kang, *Christ and Caesar*, 44–47; Reaves, *Taking in a Game*, 115; Ōshima Hiroshi, *Kankokuyakyūno Genryū* (Tokyo: Shinkansha, 2006), 10–12; *Annual Report on Reforms and Progress in Chosen, 1912–1913* (Keijo: Government General of Chosen, 1914), 56; Jon Thares Davidann, *A World of Crisis and Progress* (Bethlehem, PA: Lehigh University Press, 1998), 144–45.
74. For a superb study of a motley crew of Japanese colonial settlers in Korea who

worked in complex relationships of collaboration and resistance, see Jun Uchida, "Brokers of Empire" Japanese Settler Colonialism in Korea, 1910-1937" (Ph.D. diss., Harvard University, 2005).

75. Nishiwaki Yoshitomo, *Chōsen Chūtōgakkō Yakyūbushi* (Nishinomiya, Nishiwaki Yoshitomo, 2000), 1-4; Ōshima, *Kankokuyakyūno Genryū*, 72.

76. Uchida, "Brokers of Empire," 125.

77. Ōshima, *Kankokuyakyūno Genryū*, 11-12.

78. Takasaki, 141-45.

79. Nishiwaki, *Chōsen Chūtōgakkō Yakyūbushi*, 8; oral history by Hirose Tsuduku, "Kyōshō yakyūbu kotohajime," 1923, in Nishiwaki, *Chōsen Chūtōgakkō*, 240.

80. Young, *Japan's Total Empire*, 434.

81. Sakaue Yasuhiro demonstrates this point through Koreans playing soccer (the sport they distinctly excelled in) during Japanese colonial rule. Sakaue Yasuhiro, "Senzenno supōtsunimiru. Nipponto chōsenchūgoku," *Zenei* 743 (October 2001): 145-53.

82. Nishiwaki, *Chōsen Chūtōgakkō*, 236-37, 274-75.

83. Hakukoku Taiiku Renmei, *Burajiru Yakyūshi*, vol. 1 (Sao Paulo: Sishū Yakyū Renmei, 1985), 24-25. For life in general in the Japanese expatriate community in Shanghai, see Takatsuna Hirofumi, *Kokusaitoshi Shanghainonakano Nipponjin* (Tokyo: Kenbun Shuppan, 2009).

Chapter 3

1. For American political debates over the perceived threats of Japan's annexationist designs toward Hawaii, see Love, *Race over Empire*, 133-58.

2. William Reynolds Braisted, *The United States Navy in the Pacific, 1897-1909* (Austin: University of Texas Press, 1958), 191-232. For the 1906 crisis in San Francisco over the attempted segregation of Japanese children in public schools, see Kagawa Mari, *Sanfuranshisukoniokeru Nipponjingakkō Womeguru Kakurimondai* (Tokyo: Ronsōsha, 1999); *Los Angeles Times*, January 20, 1907. The crux of the U.S.-Japanese deal made under the Gentlemen's Agreement was for Tokyo to "voluntarily" halt issuing passports to laborers seeking to migrate to Hawaii and the U.S. mainland.

3. Kenneth J. Hagan, *This People's Navy: The Making of American Sea Power* (New York: Free Press, 1991), 239; Braisted, *United States Navy*, 223-32.

4. Keio Gijuku Daigaku Taiikukai Yakyūbu, *Keio Gijuku Daigaku Yakyūbushi*, 36-40; *Gakuho*, no. 136 (November 1908); *Yomiuri Shinbun*, October 19, 20, 22, and 24, 1908; *Tokyo Nichinichi Shinbun*, October 20, 21, 22, 25, and 27, 1908. The Great White Fleet also played against the Japanese Asahi and other baseball teams in Hawaii during its anchoring in Honolulu. *Nippu Jiji*, 2 May 1908.

5. Nelson, *The Golden Game*, 63; Fred Lange, *History of Baseball in California and Pacific Coast Leagues 1847-1938* (Oakland, CA: Fred Lange, 1938), 7.

6. William F. McNeil, *The California Winter League: America's Fist Integrated Professional Baseball League* (Jefferson: McFarland & Company, 2002), 9.

7. Bill O'Neal, *The Pacific Coast League, 1903-1988* (Austin, TX: Eakin Press, 1990), 1-5; Joel Franks, *Whose Baseball? The National Pastime and Cultural Diversity in California, 1859-1941* (Lanham, MD: Scarecrow Press, 2001), 74-77, 171, 315.

8. For the details of the "Great Baseball War" and the National Agreement of 1903,

see Rader, *Baseball*, 86–91. For Johnson's role in the Great Baseball War, see Eugene C. Murdock, *Ban Johnson: Czar of Baseball* (Westport: Greenwood Press, 1982), 43–66.

9. Robert Obojski, *Bush League: A History of Minor League Baseball* (New York: MacMillan, 1975), 13–16, 142–45.

10. Nelson, *The Golden Game*, 60–64; O'Neal, *The Pacific Coast League*, 1–10, 55–56; Lloyd Johnson and Miles Wolff, eds., *The Encyclopedia of Minor League Baseball* (Durham, NC: Baseball America, 1993), 101: David G. Rowe, ed., *Pacific Coast League Official Record Book, 1903–1955* (San Francisco: Pacific Coast League of Professional Baseball Clubs, 1956), 4; *San Francisco Chronicle*, November 10, 1903, January 13, 1905, April 5, 1905.

11. McNeil, *The California Winter League*, 12; Quintard Taylor, *In Search of the Racial Frontier: African Americans in the American West, 1528–1990* (New York: W. W. Norton, 1998), 222–25.

12. In the 1880s, Spalding's balls were sold in three grades: 8 sen, 15 sen, and 20 sen. For comparison, a *shō* (about 1.8 liter) of rice cost 7 to 8 sen at the time. Baseballs were definitely a luxury item. Hirose Kenzō, *Nippon Yakyūshi* (Tokyo: Nipponyakyūshikankōkai, 1963), 1–2, 155.

13. "Komeissho 17 sen mitto ichien nari," in Dainippon Taiiku Kyōkai, *Supōtsu 80nenshi* (Tokyo: Dainippon Taiiku Kyokai, 1959), n.p.

14. Mizuno Kenjirō, "Watashino Rirekisho," *Nippon Keizai Shinbun*, March 2, 1987; Mizuno Kenjirō, *Supōtsuwa Rikukara Umikara Ōzorae* (Tokyo: Mizuno, 1973), 116–18.

15. Tamazawa, *Tōkyō Undōgu*, 113–18; Sugihara Kaoru, *Ajiakan Boeki no Keisei to Kozo* (Kyoto: Mineruva Shoten, 1996), 32–33, 69, 88–90; Kōtsu Masaru, *Nippon Kindai Supōtsushi no Teiryū* (Tokyo: Sobun Kikaku, 1994), 302–3; Mizuno, *Supōtsuwa*, 126.

16. Mizuno, *Supōtsuwa*, 117–18.

17. In 1935, Japan's sporting goods exports reached 16 million yen. Ito Takuo, ed., Yakyū Shiai Kinen, July 1903, Japanese Baseball Hall of Fame Library; advertising in Nagatsuka Junjiro, Beijin Edowado Shi cho, Diikkou Nakatsuka Junjiro Jutsu, *Makyuujutsu*, n.p.; Mizuno Rihachi, *Kouri Shoten no Keieini Tsuite* (Nagoya: Nagoya Kōkokukyōkai, 1938); Mizuno, *Supōtsuwa*, 114–26; Kanda, *Yakyū Dendō Monogatari*, 135; Tamazawa, *Tōkyō Undōgu*, 113–21, 279; Mizuno, *Supōtsuwa*, 138–39.

18. Mizuno, *Supōtsuwa*, 138–67.

19. Zennippon Nanshiki Yakyūrenmei, ed., *Nanshiki Yakyūshi* (Tokyo: Bēsubōru Magajinsha, 1978), 14–17.

20. Ibid., 25–28.

21. Ikei Masaru, "Meijiki Nipponniokeru Dairigu Joho," *Besubōroji* 4 (2003): 50–64.

22. Before it folded in March 1900, it published a total of thirty-three issues.

23. Ito Akira, "Nipponni Okeru Taiiku Supōtsuzasshi no Rekishi," *Jochidaigaku Taiiku* 2 (1968): 18–20.

24. Ito, "Nipponni," 27–28; Ikei, "Meijiki Nipponniokeru Dairigu Joho," 52. In 1911, *Gekkan Bēsubōru* renamed itself *Yakyūkai*. *Gekkan Bēsubōru* 1, no. 1 (1908); Ikei Masaru, "Nippon ni Okeru Yakyūzasshi no shocho-1", *Besubōroji* 5 (2004): 110–12; Dainippon Taiiku Kyokai, *Supōtsu 80nennshi* (Tokyo: Dainippon Taiiku Kyokai, 1959), n.p.

25. Ito Akira, "Nipponni," 31–33.

26. Ito, "Undokai Kaisetsu," 8–11, information sheet available at the Japanese Base-

ball Hall of Fame Library; Ito, "Nipponni," 44–45; *Asahi Supōtsu* was a pictorial sports magazine and the pioneer in its genre. From its inception in 1923 it continued until November 1956, except for six years during the war; 931 issues were published, and always the back cover was a full-page ad from Mizuno. Mizuno, *Supōtsuwa*, 167–68.

27. Nagamine Shigetoshi, *"Dokusho Kokumin" no Tanjo* (Tokyo: Nippon Editasu Sukuru Shuppan, 2004), i–viii, chap. 1.

28. Ronald A. Smith, *Pay for Play: A History of Big-Time College Athletic Reform* (Urbana: University of Illinois Press, 2011), 8–9; John R. Betts, *America's Sporting Heritage, 1850–1950* (Reading, MA: Addison-Wesley, 1974), 111; John R. Betts, "The Technological Revolution and the Rise of Sport," *Mississippi Valley Historical Review* 45 (1953): 231–56; Guttman and Thompson, *Japanese Sports*, 183.

29. Watanabe, "Nippon no Daigaku Suptsu Shoshi," *Gendai Supōtsu Hyoron* 14 (2005) (5), 132.

30. Hirose Kenzō, *Sōkeiyakyūshi* (Tokyo: Sanseido, 1828), 1–5; *Yorozuchōbo*, November 22, 1903, *Jiji Shinpō*, November 11, 1906.

31. Bēsubōru Magajinsha, *Tokyo Rokudaigaku 80nennshi* (Tokyo: Baseball Magazinesha, 2005), 26.

32. Ericson, *Sound of the Whistle*, 45–46, 82–84, 311–22; Harada Katsumasa et al., eds., *Tetsudo to Bunka* (Tokyo: Nippon Keizai Hyoronsha, 1986), 8–10, 115–32, 192; Takechi Kyozo, *Toshikinkotetsudo no shitekitenkai* (Tokyo: Nippon Keizai Hyoronsha, 1986), 16–17.

33. Yamato, *Shinsetsu Nippon Yakyūshi*, 125–29; John R. Betts, "Sporting Journalism in Nineteenth Century America," *American Quarterly* 5 (1953): 39–56. For a discussion of incremental drops in domestic and United States–Japan mail and telegraph rates, see Kokaze, *Teikokushukiga no Nippon Kaiun*, 34–35; Sugiyama Shinya, "Joho nettowaku no keisei to chiho keizai," in *Meiji Ishin no Kakushinto Renzoku*, ed. Kindai Nippon Kenkyukai (Tokyo: Yamakawa Shoten, 1992), 238–48.

34. Sonoda Hidehiro, *Seiyoka no Kozo* (Kyoto: Shibunkaku, 1993), 17–52; Kokaze, *Teikokushukiga No Nippon Kaiun*, 208–25; Kimura Masato, *Nichibei Minkan Keizai Gaiko, 1905–1911* (Tokyo: Keio Tsushin, 1989), 34–35; Asahara Bunpei, *Nippon Kaiun Hattatsushi* (Tokyo: Shinshosha, 1978), 79–80; William D. Wray, *Mitsubishi and the N. Y. K., 1870–1914* (Cambridge: Harvard University Press, 1984), 263–65, 400–405. The first challenge from an American college in fact came only a few months after Ichikō's rousing 1896 victories over the Americans. Yale College invited the Ichikō nine to an all-expenses-paid trip to play against its baseball squad. Although the travel would have forced the team members to miss a whole semester of school, they believed that it was a price worth paying to visit the proverbial land of opportunity. The Ichikō student dorm assembly voted to accept the challenge. The Education Ministry, however, decreed that the invitation must be declined because it was "not appropriate for students to miss school." Ichikō being a government-chartered school, its administration had no choice but to follow this order from above. Hirose, *Nippon Yakyūshi*, 146–54; Roden, "Baseball," 528.

35. LaFeber, *The Clash*, 84–98.

36. For an excellent sociological study of Japanese baseball ideologies that led to professionalization, see Kiku, *Kindai Puro Supōtsu*.

37. Ibid., 110–12; Ikei, *Hakkyū*, 68–70.

38. The concept of charging admission fees was not widespread in Japan prior to Waseda's 1905 U.S. tour. For example, notices of Ichikō games with the battleship *Kentucky* in 1903 and 1904 did not mention gate charges. *Kōryōshi*, 806.

39. *Jiji Shinpō*, October 28, 1907; Keio Gijyuku Taiikukai Yakyūbu, ed., *Keiou Gijyuku Daigaku Yakyūbishi* (Tokyo: Keiou Gijuku Yakyūbu, 1960), 20; *Jiji Shinpō*, September 6, 1906, October 28, 1907; Kiku, *Kindai Puro Supōtsu*, 113–14; Yamato, *Shinsetsu Nippon Yakyūshi*, 198–202; Shimada Akira, *Meiji 44nen Keiō Yakyūbu Amerika Ōdanjikki* (Tokyo: Bēsubōru Magajinsha, 1993).

40. Keio Daigaku Yakyūbu, *Keio Yakyūbushi*, 48.

41. Sundaikurabu, *Meijidaigaku Yakyūbushi*, vol. 1 (Tokyo: Sundaikurrabu, 1974), 233–38.

42. Minutes, May 28, June 18, October 29, 1910, May 13, 1915, January 24, 1920, May 9, 1924, April 29, 1925, Board of Physical Culture and Athletics, Amos Stagg Papers, University of Chicago Library; Aida Yoichi, *Aa Abekyūjō Konpekino Soranikiyu* (Tokyo: Bēsubōru Magajinsha, 1987), 10–11.

43. Robin Lester, *Stagg's University* (Urbana: University of Illinois Press, 1995), 12–13.

44. Smith, *Pay for Play*, 38.

45. Lester, *Stagg's University*, 28–31; Hal A. Lawson and Alan G. Ingham, "Conflicting Ideologies Concerning the University and Intercollegiate Athletics: Harper and Hutchins at Chicago, 1892–1940," *Journal of Sport History* 7, no. 3 (Winter 1980), 37–46. For Stagg's early life and his athletic entrepreneurship at the University of Chicago, see Peter I. Berg, "A Mission on the Midway: Amos Alonzo Stagg and the Gospel of Football" (Ph.D. diss., Michigan State University, 1996).

46. Stagg to Isoo Abe, 20 June 1910; Stagg to Alfred W. Place, 20 June 1910; Stagg to White, 10 July 1910; Stagg to Riley Allen, 28 July 1910, Box 63, Amos Stagg Papers, University of Chicago Library.

47. "Pat" to Stagg, 13 August 1910; Douglas Knight to Board of Athletics, 29 December 1910; Box 63, Stagg Papers.

48. *Special Souvenir Issue, Eighth Annual National Interscholastic Basketball Tournament*, (n.p., n.d.), 23–26.

49. Lester, *Stagg's University*, 118; Stagg to Frank Crowell, Jr., December 22, 1928, Box 13; Minutes, Board of Trustees, May 4, 1936, Box 13, Amos Stagg Papers.

50. Mizuno, *Supōtsuwa*, 146–48.

51. *Osaka Asahi Shinbun*, August 16, 1915.

52. Chikanesawa Toshihiro, *Takarazuka Senryaku* (Tokyo: Kodansha, 1994), 13.

53. Ariyama Teruo, *Kōshienyakyū to Nipponjin* (Tokyo: Yoshikawa Kvbunkan, 1997), 71–76; For Asahi's corporate strategies, see also Ariyama Teruo, *Kindai Nippon Janarizumuno Kōzō* (Tokyo: Tokyōshuppan, 1995), x; Tsuganesawa Toshihiro, Yamamoto Taketoshi, et al., eds., *Kindai Nipponno Shinbun Kōkokuto Keiei* (Tokyo: Asahi Shinbunsha, 1979), xx; Nakao Tadashi, "taikai 26nen no kaiko, zenkoku chūtōgakkō yūshō yakyū taikaishi," 31–32.

54. Hanshin Denki Tetsudo, *Yūsō Hōshino 50nen* (Osaka: Hanshin Denki Tetsudo, 1955), 23–25; Tamaki Michio, *Kōshienkyūjō Monogatari* (Tokyo: Bungeishunju, 2004), 24.

55. *Zenkoku Chūtogakkō Yakyūtaikaishi*, 63; Ariyama, *Kōshienyakyū*, 120–21, 144–48; Osaka Asahi, August 15, 1926.

56. Nishiwaki, *Taiwan Chutogakkō*, 13–16; Nishiwaki, *Chōsen Chūtōgakkō*, 4–5; Ōshima, *Kankokuyakyūno Genryū*, 12–14.

57. Nishiwaki, *Taiwan Chūtōgakkō Yakyūshi*, 144–145.

58. Morris, "Taiwan," 67. For an illuminating analysis of the role Taiwanese' baseball exploit played in the Japanese colonial state's assimilationist policy in the 1930s, see Morris, *Colonial Project*, 30–50. Wu Bo, who starred in Jiayi's 1935 and 1936 championship teams, was signed by the Tokyo Giants in 1937 for a successful seven-year career in Japanese professional baseball.

59. Ishii Kanji, *Nippon Keizaishi* (Tokyo: Tokyodaigaku Shuppankai, 1976), 78.

60. *Tokyo Nichinichi Shinbun*, July 15, 1927; Bēsubōru Magajinsha, *Gekidōno Showa Supōtsushi*, vol. 5, Shakaijin Yakyū (Tokyo: Bēsubōru Magajinsha, 1989), 12–13; Suzuki Toshihiko, "Nippon Sangyo no Seisui to Shakaijin Yakyū," *Besubōroji*, 174–76.

61. *Gekidōno Showa Supōtsushi*, 52. In the last prewar intercity tournament held in 1940, the final was fought between the All Seoul and the Dairen Jitsugyō.

62. *Dairenjitsugyōdan Nijūnenshi*, passim; Kubota Takayuki, *Kōkōyakyū 50nen* (Tokyo: Jijitsushinsha, 1956), 131; Nagata Yoichi, *Besubōruno Shakaishi* (Tokyo: Toho Shuppan, 1994), 328–32.

63. Tobe Yoshiya, "Taiwan Yakyūno Rutsu: Nokodan ni Hajimatte Nippon wo Sekkenshita Bokyushi" *Besubōroji* 5 (2004): 169–83.

64. Nakagawa, *Through a Diamond*, 31–32; Nelson, *The Golden Game*, 65–66; Nomura, "Beyond," 18.

65. The concept of cultural citizenship emerges from the work of Latino/Latina scholars such as Renato Rosaldo, Rina Benmayor, and William Flores. In examining the experiences of Latino/a Americans in cities such as San Jose and Fresno. It refers "to the right to be different (in terms of race, ethnicity, or native language) with respect to the norms of the dominant national community, without compromising one's right to belong, in the sense of the nation-state's democratic processes." Renato Rosaldo and William V. Flores, "Ideology, Conflict, and Evolving Latino Communities: Cultural Citizenship in San Jose, California," in *Latino Cultural Citizenship: Claiming Identity, Space, and Rights*, ed. William V. Flores and Rina Benmayor (Boston: Beacon Press, 1997), 57.

66. Nakagawa, *Through a Diamond*, 31–32; Nelson, *The Golden Game*, 65–66.

67. Nelson, *The Golden Game*, 73; Ralph M. Pearce, *From Asahi to Zebras: Japanese American Baseball in San Jose, California* (San Jose: Japanese American Museum of San Jose, 2005), 2–8.

68. *Sacramento Bee*, June 15, 1925; *San Francisco Chronicle*, October 5, 1926.

69. Sakaguchi Mitsuhiro, *Nipponjin Amerikaiminshi* (Tokyo: Fujishuppan, 2001), 22–24; Miura Akio, *Kitataiheiyō Teikikyakusenshi* (Tokyo: Shuppankyodosha, 1994), 36.

70. Samuel O. Regalado, "'Play Ball!' Baseball and Seattle's Japanese-American Courier League, 1928–1941," *Pacific Northwest Quarterly* 87, no. 1 (Winter 1995): 29–37. For the Seattle Japanese-American Courier League, see also, Shelley Sang-Hee Lee, *Claiming the Oriental Gateway: Prewar Seattle and Japanese America* (Philadelphia: Temple University Press, 2010), 143–77.

71. Gail Nomura, "Beyond the Playing Field: The Significance of Pre–World War II Japanese American Baseball in the Yakima Valley," in *Bearing Dreams, Shaping Visions:*

Asian Pacific American Perspectives, ed. Linda A. Revilla, Gail M. Nomura, Shawn Wong, and Shirley Hune (Pullman: Washington State University Press, 1993), 16–17.

72. Goto Norio, *Densetsuno Yakyūchīmu: Bankūbā Asahimonogatari* (Tokyo: Iwanami Shoten, 2010), 15–16.

73. Goto, *Densetsuno*, 28; *Tairiku Nippo*, March 26, 1907, June 6, 1910, August 27, 1935.

74. Goto, *Densetsuno*, 34–35.

75. Pat Adachi, *Asahi: A Legend in Baseball* (Etobicoke, Ontario: Asahi Baseball Organization, 1992), 11–14, 32, 45–46, 125; Louis Fiset and Gail Nomura, eds., *Nikkei in the Pacific Northwest* (Seattle: University of Washington Press, 2005), 4.

76. Nakagawa, *Through a Diamond*, 38–52.

77. Ibid., 38–40.

78. For the *kengakudan*, see Yuji Ichioka, "Kengakudan: The Origin of Nisei Study Tours of Japan," in *Before Internment: Essays in Prewar Japanese American History*, ed. Gordon Chang and Eiichiro Azuma (Stanford: Stanford University Press, 2006), 53–74.

79. Goto, *Densetsuno*, 49; *Tairiku Nippo*, July 19, 1927.

80. Nelson, *The Golden Game*, 145–46.

81. For the life and career of Henry Tadashi "Bozo" Wakabayashi, see Yamamoto Shigeru, *Nanairono Makyū: Kaisōno Wakabayashitadashi* (Tokyo: Bēsubōru Magajinsha, 1994).

82. Nakagawa, *Through a Diamond*, 34–42.

83. David Voigt, *American Baseball: From Gentleman's Sport to the Commissioner System* (Norman: University of Oklahoma Press, 1966), 12–22.

84. Yoshimi Shunya, *Shinbei to Hanbei* (Tokyo: Iwanami Shoten, 2007), 27–61.

Chapter 4

1. Focusing on the diffusion of the American entertainment industry, such as circuses and black minstrel performances in Australia and New York in the mid 1850s, Matthew Wittmann has identified the emergence of a "Pacific circuit" linking the U.S. West Coast and Australia and New Zealand. I argue that the diffusion of baseball to East Asia later in the nineteenth century is an extension of this "Pacific circuit." For the concept of the "Pacific circuit," see Wittmann, "Empire of Culture."

2. Kiku, *Kindai Puro Supōtsu*, 113.

3. Bruce Kuklick, *To Every Thing a Season: Shibe Park and Urban Philadelphia 1909–1976* (Princeton: Princeton University Press, 1991), 15–16; Stephen Hardy, "Adopted by All the Leading Clubs": Sporting Goods and the Shaping of the Leisure, 1800–1900," in *For Fun and Profit: The Transformation of Leisure into Consumption*, ed. Richard Butsch (Philadelphia: Temple University Press, 1990), 79–80.

4. *New York Clipper*, February 2, 1878; March 26 and June 25, 1881; March 8 and November 4, 1882; April 13, 1886; *Sporting Life*, September 4, 1889; Voigt, *American Baseball*, 217–18; Hardy, "Adopted," 82–85; Sayama Kazuo, *Nichibei Yakyū Uramenshi* (Tokyo: NHK Shuppan 2005), 20–25.

5. Reach & Co., *The Reach 1909 Base Ball Guide* (Philadelphia, 1909), 582–85; Tamazawa, *Tōkyō Undōgu*, 76.

6. *Undōsekai*, no. 9 (December 1908) clippings of the special 1910 New Year issue in *Nichibei Yakyū* scrapbook, Japanese Baseball Hall of Fame Library.

7. Contemporary newspapers and baseball magazines did not use the term "perfect game," but an *Undōsekai* article says, "It was a disgraceful no-hitter . . . no one could reach first base." Kabushiki Kaisha Hanshintaigasu, ed., *Hanshintaigasu Showanoayumi* (Osaka: Hanshintaigasu, 1991), 116.

8. *Bēsubōru*, vol. 1 no. 2 (1908), 13–21.

9. *Undōsekai*, no. 9. American League President Ban John did his best to recruit Theodore Roosevelt, known for his athletic inclination, to this invention of a tradition, but he was unsuccessful in this endeavor. Murdock, *Ban Johnson*, 87.

10. James Elfers, *The Tour to End All Tours: The Story of Major League Baseball's 1913–1914 World Tour* (Lincoln: University of Nebraska Press, 2003), 1–2; Charles Alexander, *John McGraw* (New York: Viking, 1988), 173–74.

11. Frank Farrel, M. Dick Bunnell, and Lee Magee, *World Tour, National and American League Base Ball Teams: October 1913–March 1914* (Chicago: S. Blake Willsden, 1914), 3; Timothy Paul Sullivan, *History of World's Tour: Chicago White Sox and New York giants* (Chicago: M. A. Donohue, 1914), 9–10; *Sporting Life*, July 26, 1913, November 7, 1913; Elfers, *Tour*, 3–9.

12. Elfers, *Tour*, 10–12; G. W. Axelson, *"Commy": The Life Story of Charles A. Comiskey* (Chicago: Reilly & Lea, 1919), 221; *Sporting Life*, November 7, 1913.

13. Elfers, *Tour*, 108–12; *Jiji Shinpō*, December 6, 7, and 8, 1913; *Tokyo Nichinichi Shinbun*, December 6 and 7, 1913; *Tokyo Nichinichi Shinbun*, November 5, 6, 7, 1913.

14. Keiōgijuku Yakyūbushi Henshuiinkai, *Keiōgijuku Yakyūbu Hyakunenshi*, vol. 1, 53–55, 60–61, 70–71; *Yakyū Nenpō*, 1914; *Yakyūkai* 4, no. 1 (1914); *Japan Times*, November 30, December 6 and 7, 1914; newspaper clippings in Nichibei Yakyū File, Japanese Baseball Hall of Fame Library; Sullivan, *History of World's Tour*, 14–16.

15. Bill Crawford, *All American: The Rise and Fall of Jim Thorpe* (New York: John Wiley, 2005), 197–238; Donald Osinski, "Baseball in the Olympics," in *Total Baseball*, ed. John Thorn and Pete Palmer (New York: Warner Books, 1995), 582.

16. Smith, *Pay for Play*, 54–58. For the origin of British amateurism, see David C. Young, "The Modern Origins of Amateurism," in *The Olympic Myth of Greek Amateur Athletics* (Chicago: Ares, 1985), 15–27. Ronald A. Smith, *Sports and Freedom*, 165–74.

17. Crawford, *All American*, 197–238; Elfers, *Tour*, 16–21.

18. *New York Times*, June 26 and 30, 1913; *Yakyūkai* 4, no. 1 (1908): 26–35; *Tokyo Nichinichi Shinbun*, June 26 and 28, 1913; November 5 and 6, 1913; *Kokumin Shinbun*, November 8, 1913. For the tour's Shanghai and Hong Kong legs, see Elfers, *The Tour to End All Tours*, 122–34.

19. For a superb analysis of the transnational politics of race, gender, sports, nationalism, and empire, see Theresa Runstedtler, "Journeymen: Race, Boxing, and the Transnational World of Jack Johnson" (Ph.D. diss., Yale University, 2007), 1–57.

20. Elfers, *Tour*, 245; *Library Digest* 74 (August 5, 1933), 62–63; *Library Digest* 84 (February 14, 1925), 66–69.

21. Clippings in Herb Hunter Player File, Baseball Hall of Fame Museum and Library, Cooperstown, NY (hereafter cited as BHFML).

22. *Yakyūkai* 11, no. 1 (January 1920).

23. *Yakyūkai* 11, no. 2 (February 1920); clippings in Herb Hunter Player File, BHFML.

24. *Yakyūkai* 13, no. 1 (1923), 50–51.

25. Suzuki Sōtarō, *Nippon Yakyūshi* (Tokyo: Nipponhōsō Shuppankyōkai, 2005), 3; *Yakyū Nippon*, vol. 2, no. 2 (February 1949); *Yakyūkai*; *Sporting News*, February 16, 1922.

26. Elias, *Empire Strikes Out*, 99.

27. G. Edward White, *Creating the National Pastime* (Princeton: Princeton University Press, 1996), 104–15.

28. Reaves, *Taking in a Game*, 64; Sayama, *Nichibeiyakyū*, 129.

29. Some Japanese observers felt that Hunter's team went deliberately easy on its Japanese challengers. *Yakyūkai* 13, no. 1 (1923): 52–53.

30. Various letters in the Japan Tour files in the collection of the Baseball Hall of Fame Library in Cooperstown reveal this hesitation on the part of Commissioner Landis. See "Tours: Japan 1934" File, BHFML. For years, Landis suspected that Hunter threw the game in 1922 based on a report that probably came from George Moriarty, an American League umpire assigned to the tour. Fred Lieb, *Baseball As I Have Known It* (New York: Coward, McCann & Geoghegan, 1977), 198.

31. For the Bloomer Girls, see Gai Ingham Berlage, *Women in Baseball* (Westport, CT: Praeger, 1994), 34–42.

32. Sayama, *Nichibeiyakyū*, 75–77; *Yakyūkai* 13, no. 50.

33. *Yakyūkai* 15, no. 15 (1927): 99.

34. Ibid., 100; Mizuno Co. flyer for Bobbies games, October 31 and November 1 and 2, 1927, in author's possession.

35. Barbara Gregorich, "Stranded," *North American Review* (May–August 1998): 3–9.

36. Sayama, *Nichibeiyakyū*, 91–92.

37. Ainsmith, too, stayed in the baseball business, coaching, umpiring, and scouting for major-league teams. Incredibly, for a short time in 1947, he even fielded another all-women's professional baseball squad, the Rockford (Illinois) Peaches.

38. Despite this dreadful experience, O'Gara stayed in the business of women's professional baseball until the Great Depression sapped life out of her club and many others like it. The scare of being stranded penniless in an unfamiliar foreign country did not keep the Bobbies' most junior member, Edith Houghton, from making baseball her lifelong vocation. She continued to play semipro ball through her young adulthood. In 1946, she became a scout for the Philadelphia Phillies, the first female major-league scout. Sayama, *Nichibeiyakyū*, 90–98.

39. Sayama, *Kuroki Yasashiki Jaiantsu* (Tokyo: Bēsubōru Magajinsha, 1986), 24–26. For the Negro League, see Neil Lanctot, *Negro League Baseball: The Rise and Ruin of a Black Institution* (Philadelphia: University of Pennsylvania Press, 2004).

40. McNeil, *The California Winter League*, 114–20.

41. *Japan Times and Mail*, March 30, 1927.

42. *Yakyūkai* 17, no. 6 (1927); *Undōkai*, May 1927; *Asahi Supōtsu*, April 15, 1927.

43. *Japan Times and Mail*, March 30, 1927; *Yakyūkai* 17, no. 6 (1927); *Undokai*, May 1927; *Asahi Supōtsu*, April 15, 1927; *Hawaii Hōchi*, June 6, 1922.

44. *Honolulu Star Bulletin*, June 4 and 14, 1927; *Hawaii Hochi*, June 6, 1927. These Negro Leaguers who ventured to colonial Japan and Hawaii for three months in the spring and early summer of 1927 left lasting legacies in African American baseball. Mackey, in particular, made his mark as a coach and manager after finishing his splendid playing career. After his Hilldale club folded, Mackey struggled on a series

of ephemeral clubs until he partnered with Effa Manley, "the Queen of the Negro League," and managed her Newark Eagles. He led that team to the Negro World Championship in 1946. Among Mackey's disciples on the diamond was Monte Irvin, who would tour Japan after World War II as the first African American major leaguer to do so. The American League's first black player, Larry Doby, and Don Newcome, another future black major leaguer, also began their pro career under Mackey, and both played for a Japanese professional team, the Chūnichi Dragons, in the 1960s. The legendary Dodger Roy Campanella, a three-time National League MVP in the 1950s, played for the Baltimore Elites under Mackey's field management and revered Mackey as his lifelong mentor. After the tour of Japan and its continental colonies, Rap Dixson joined the Pittsburgh Crawfords, the Negro League's powerhouse in the 1930s, where he was a teammate of legendary Satchel Paige and Josh Gibson, "the black Babe Ruth." Dixson played in the 1933 Negro League All-Star Game alongside them. Frank Duncan later became the manager of the indomitable Kansas City Monarchs. One of the players he managed there was Jackie Robinson, the pioneer who would finally break through the major leagues' color barrier in 1947. Sayama, *Nichibeiyakyū*, 118–19.

45. Nakagawa, *Through a Diamond*, 68–72.

46. Nelson, *The Golden Game*, 144–46.

47. Sayama, *Nichibeiyakyū*, 120–21.

48. Sawayanagi Masayoshi, *Yakyūjōkensetsu no Kenkyū* (Tokyo: Yakyūjōkensetsuno Kenkyūkankōkai, 1951), 39–44; Sugiyama Hisatsugu, *Beēsubōrushitī* (Tokyo: Fukutake Shoten, 1990), 169–70; Irie Katsumi, "Kindaino tennoōseito Meijijingūkyōgitaikai," in *Undōkaito Nipponkindai*, ed. Yoshimi Shunya (Tokyo: Seikyūsha, 1999), 173–74.

49. *Sporting News*, January 1 and November 5, 1931; Lieb, *Baseball As I Have Known It*, 191–92; Reaves, *Taking in a Game*, 64–65.

50. Ikei, *Hakkyū*, 108–11; Shoriki Matsutaro, "Beidairigu Shoheihiwa," *Yomiuri Supōtsu*, November 1931; telegram from Foreign Minister Shidehara Kijuro to Consul General Sawada Setsuzo in NY, November 20, 1930, Foreign Ministry Telegram, Foreign Ministry Archives, Tokyo.

51. Suzuki Sōtarō, *Nippon Puro Yakyū Gaishi* (Tokyo: Bēsubōru Magajinsha, 1980), 45; Yomiurishinbun 100nennshi Henshuiinkai, ed., *Yomiuri Shinbun 100nenshi* (Tokyo: Yomiuri Shinbunsha, 1976), 358; Hatano Masaru, *Nichibeiyakyūshi* (Tokyo: PHP Shinsho, 2001), 28–29.

52. Shōriki Matsutarō, "Beidairīgu daiikkai, dainikai shōhei hiwa," in *Nippon Puroytakyū 30nen no Rekishi*, ed. Noguchi Tsutomu (Tokyo: Press Tokyo, 1964), 54–55.

53. Lieb, *Baseball As I Have Known It*, 198–99; *Yomiuri Shinbun*, October 4, 1931.

54. Lieb, *Baseball As I Have Known It*, 203–4; *New York Times*, October 29 and 30, 1931; *Sporting News*, November 5 and December 3, 1931; clippings from *Spalding Official Base Ball Guide, 1931*, in "Tours: 1931 Japan" file, BHFML; Reaves, *Taking in a Game*, 65.

55. *San Francisco Chronicle*, October 12, 1931; *Los Angeles Times*, October 12, 1931.

56. *Sporting News*, December 3 and 7, 1931: *New York Times*, December 21 and 23, 1931.

57. For Lefty O'Doul's life, see Richard Leutzinger, *Lefty O'Doul: The Legend That Baseball Nearly Forgot* (Carmel, CA: Carmel Bay Publishing Group, 1997).

58. O'Neil, *Pacific Coast League*, 90; Nelson, *The Golden Game*, 166–68.

59. Leutzinger, *Lefty O'Doul*, 58; Nelson, *The Golden Game*, 170.

60. *Japan Times and Mail*, September 10, 1932.

61. *Yakyūkai* 22, no. 15 (1927).

62. For the 1932 Los Angeles Olympics and its impact on both Issei and Nisei in the local Japanese American community, see Eriko Yamamoto's excellent article "Cheers for Japanese Athletes: The 1932 Los Angeles Olympics and the Japanese American Community," *Pacific Historical Review* 69, no. 3 (2000): 399–431.

63. *Yomiuri Shinbun*, September 8, 1932. For Miura Tamaki's career, see Mari Yoshihara, "The Flight of the Japanese Butterfly: Orientalism, Nationalism, and Performance of Japanese Womanhood," *American Quarterly* 56, no. 4 (2004): 975–1001.

64. Sayama, *Kuroki Yasashiki Jaiantsu*, 215.

Chapter 5

1. Inoue Toshikazu, *Kikinonakano Kyōchōgaikō* (Tokyo: Iwanami Shoten, 1994), 2–8.

2. Leutzinger, *Lefty O'Doul*, 62; Suzuki Sōtarō, *Fumetsuno Daitōshu Sawamura Eiji* (Tokyo: Bēsubōru Magajinsha, 1982), 297.

3. For formation on this first professional baseball club in Japan, see Sato Mitsufusa, *Mouhitotsuno Puroyakyū* (Tokyo: Asahishinbunsha, 1986), 11–26.

4. Kiku, *Kindai Puro Supōtsu*, 123–45; Bēsubōru Magajinsha, ed., *Nippon Puroyakyū 50nenshi* (Tokyo: Bēsubōru Magajinsha, 1984), 43–44; Azumada Issaku, *Puroyakyū Tanjōzenya* (Tokyo: Tokai Daigaku Shuppankai, 1989), 4–23, 40–54.

5. Zennippon Nanshiki Yakyū Renmei, ed., *Nanshiki Yakyūshi* (Tokyo: Bēsubōru Magajinsha, 1976), 32.

6. John Thelin, *Games Colleges Play: Scandal and Reform in Intercollegiate Athletics* (Baltimore: Johns Hopkins University Press, 1994), 25–26; Andrew Zimbalist, *Unpaid Professionals: Commercialism and Conflict in Big-Time College Sports* (Princeton: Princeton University Press, 1999), 6–7.

7. White, *Creating the National Pastime*, 113–14; J. G. Taylor Spink, *Judge Landis and Twenty-Five Years of Baseball* (New York: Thomas Y. Crowell Company, 1947), 97–98. Since the coaching of Japanese collegiate players by American major leaguers took place in the off-season, it never posed a problem like the one faced by Ray Fisher.

8. For example, *Hawaii Hōchi*, April 25, 1925. For a problem of amateurism in American collegiate athletics, see also Ronald Smith, *Sports and Freedom: The Rise of Big-Time College Athletics* (New York: Oxford University Press, 1988), 165–74.

9. Nakamura Tetsuya, "Yakyū Tōseirei to Gakusei Yakyū no Jichi," *Supōtsushi Kenkyu* 20 (2007): 90–91.

10. For this point, see Takaoka Hiroyuki, "Dainippon Taiikukaino Seiritsu," in Sakaue and Takaoka, *Maboroshino Tokyo Orinpikkuto Sonojidai*, 200–234.

11. Katō Kitsuo, "Yakyū Tōseino Mondai," *Taiikuno Kagaku* 25, no. 9 (September 1975): 613–15. For representatives works on government control of student baseball in this era, see Nakajima Takeshi, "Showashoki Monbushono Kokumintaiiku Seisakuno Tenkaikateini Tuite," *Taiikushikenkyū* 10 (1993): 43–61; Tashiro Masayuki, "Yakyūtōseireiga Gakuseiyakyū ni Ataeta Eikyō," *Supōtsushikenkyu* 9 (1996): 11–26.

12. Nakamura, "Yakyū Tōseirei," 83–84; Kagawa Hideo, "Wagakuniiokeru 1932nenno Gakuseiyakyūno Tōseinituite," *Hokkaidōdaigaku Kyōikugakubukiyō* 51 (1988): 1–16.

13. For an illuminating view of the government use of *shingikai* (advisory coun-

cil) in Japan's modern social management, see Sheldan Garon, *Molding Japanese Minds* (Princeton: Princeton University Press, 1997).

14. Yamakawa Ken, *Yakyū Tōsei no Hanashi* (Tokyo: Monbushō Taiiku Kachō), 6–8, 187–201; Ariyama, *Kōshienyakyū*, 163–65; *Tokyo Asahi Shinbun*, February 2 and 27, 1932.

15. The pelagic contest between the Caucasian French and the Japanese boxers were often cast in press commentaries in racial terms. It bears an intriguing thematic resemblance of boxing matches between Max Schmeling, an "Aryan" German, and African American Joe Louis later in the decade. For an excellent analysis of the racial politics of the Schmeling-Louis contests, see Lewis Erenberg, *The Greatest Fight of Our Generation* (New York: Oxford University Press, 2006).

16. *Sporting News*, October 12, 1933, and January 4, 1934.

17. Sano Shinichi, *Kyokaiden* (Tokyo: Beungei Shunjū, 1994), 178.

18. *Yomiuri Shinbun*, January 1, 1934.

19. Yamato, *Shinsetsu Nippon Yakyūshi*, 105–6; Hatano, *Nichibeiyakyūshi*, 64–69; *Yomiuri Shinbun*, July 18, 1934.

20. Charles C. Alexander, *Breaking the Slump: Baseball in the Depression Era* (New York: Columbia University Press, 2002), 79.

21. Suzuki, *Nippon Puroyakyū Gaiden*, 34, 161–2.

22. Ōe Shinkichi, *Yakyūo Bēburūsu* (Tokyo: Bonjinsha, 1931).

23. *Sporting News*, October 18, 1934.

24. The conventional interpretation of the Amau Doctrine considers it an incendiary remark that signified an aggressive intent toward China. A close examination of Amau's actual statement and the context in which the statement was made indicates a much more nuanced circumstance. For this point, see Inoue, *Kikinonakano*; *Yomiuri Shinbun*, 16 November 1934.

25. *New York Times*, November 3, 1934; *Sporting News*, November 8, 1934; Joseph Grew, *Ten Years in Japan* (New York: Simon and Schuster, 1944), 193.

26. Suzuki Ryūji, *Suzukiryūji Kaikoroku* (Tokyo: Bēsubōru Magajinsha, 1980), 101; Azumada, *Puroyakyū*, 96.

27. *New York Times*, November 5, 1934; *Washington Post*, November 13 and 14, 1934; *Sporting News*, November 22, 1934; *Yomiuri Shinbun*, November 9, 1934. Mac said there was no chance that the baseball-loving Japanese would ever become America's enemy. *Sporting News*, January 7 and February 14, 1935; *New York Times*, February 24, 1935; Grew, *Ten Years in Japan*, 193.

28. Nicholas Dawidoff, *The Catcher Was a Spy: The Mysterious Life of Moe Berg* (New York: Vintage, 1994); Nippon Hōsō Kyōkai, ed. *Moe Berg, Nipponwo Aishita Supai* (Tokyo: NHK Shuppan Kyōkai, 1979).

29. Dawidoff, *Catcher Was a Spy*, 92–95. Berg's fondness for Japan and its people also appears genuine. Throughout the 1930s, he maintained a close personal friendship with those Japanese he met through baseball, including Matsumoto Takizō, then a professor at Meiji University. Berg would later help Matsumoto with his graduate-school application to Harvard. A few months after the Pearl Harbor attack, Berg sent a shortwave radio message to the Japanese people, urging them to stand up to the militarists and reminding them of the friendship the two countries had built through

baseball, referring to his experiences during his two visits to the country. Hatano, *Nichibeiyakyūshi*, 125–32.

30. *Yomiuri Shinbun*, November 21, 1934; Suzuki, *Fumetsuno*, 106.

31. For Starffin's early life, see Richard Puff, "The Amazing Story of Victor Starffin," *National Pastime* 12 (1992): 17–18; and Natasha Starffin, *Roshiakarakitaēsu* (Tokyo: PHP, 1986).

32. Because of *Yakyū Tōseirei*, both Sawamura and Starffin had to quit high school in 1934 to play against the visiting major leaguers. By playing against the professionals, they were also forced to forfeit their future college eligibility, which, in Sawamura's case, opened the way for his multiple military inductions during World War II.

33. Azumada, *Puroyakyū*, 102–4.

34. For the actual text of the founding vision statement of the club, see Date Masao, *Watashino Shōwa Yakyūshi* (Tokyo: Bēsubōru Magajinsha, 1988), 213–29. On the fact that pre–World War II Japanese professional baseball was mostly oriented toward future regular competition with the Pacific Coast League, see remarks by Kono Atsushi, who became the manager of the Nagoya Eagles. Roudtable, "Shokugōyakyūno Yakushinwokataru," *Yakyūkai* 30, no. 11 (June 1940): 209–10.

35. Sano, *Kyokaiden*, 178.

36. Suzuki, *Kaikoroku*, 30–31; Shōriki, "Beidairīgu," 53; Yamato, *Shinsetsu Nippon Yakyūshi: Shōwahen: Sono2* (Tokyo: Bēsubōru Magajinsha, 1977), 194–95.

37. Hanshindenki Kabushiki Kaisha, *Yusōhōshino Gojūnen* (Osaka: Hanshindenki Co, 1955), 126–28.

38. Azumada, *Puroyakyū*, 116–18. The NPBA was later renamed Nippon Yakyū Renmei, or the Nippon Baseball Association (NBA). It continued in this form—except for a one-year wartime interlude—until it was reorganized in 1949 under the direction of the American occupation authorities.

39. The vast majority of the existing literature on Japanese baseball calls Shōriki's Dai Nippon Tokyo Bēsubōru Kurabu Japan's first professional baseball club (as claimed by Shōriki and company), but that is not accurate. The generation of clubs that came into being in the mid-1930s was the *first to survive* for an extended period, but not the first to be organized.

40. For a superb empirical analysis of the link between the industrial development, capital accumulation, (s)urbanization, and target markets of these industries, see Kiku, *Kindai Puro Supōtsu*, 189–230.

41. Ikei Masaru, "Puroyakyū Keieibotai no Kenkyū," *Bēsubōrojī* 3 (2002): 82–87; Kiku, *Kindai Puro Supōtsu*, 189–90. For Kobayashi Ichizō and the Takarazuka Strategy, see Tsuganezawa Satohiro, *Takarazukasenryaku* (Tokyo: Kōdansha, 1991); *Yakyūkai* 27, no. 11 (August 1937): 103; *Yakyūkai* 27, no. 12 (September 1937): 253; and *Yakyūkai* 27, no. 14 (November 1937): 226, 252.

42. In the year the Dai Nippon Tokyo Bēsubōru Kurabu was formed, approximately 20 percent of the households across the nation owned a radio. By 1944 the figure would exceed 50 percent. Kikkawa Takeo and Nara Takashi, *Fankaramita Puroyakyūno Rekishi* (Tokyo: Nippon Keizai Hyōronsha, 2009), 35–36.

43. Nippon Hōsōkyōkai Hōsōshi Henshūshitsu, ed., *Nipponbōsōshi*, vol. 1 (Tokyo:

Nipponhōsōkyōkai, 1965), 608; Hashimoto Kazuo, *Nippon Supōtsu Hōsōshi* (Tokyo: Taishūkan, 1992), 17–34; Wakuda Yasuo, *Nipponno Shitetsu* (Tokyo: Iwanami Shoten, 1981), 62; Koshimoto Hitoshi, *Watashino Yakyū* (Tokyo: Sanseido, 1928), 17; *Yomiuri Shinbun*, November 13, 1925.

44. *Kibei*, meaning "returning to America," referred to Japanese Americans who traveled to Japan to receive an education and then came back to the United States.

45. For Wakabayashi's early life, see Yamamoto, *Nanairono Makyū*.

46. Nakagawa, *Through a Diamond*, 55; For a comprehensive account of the circuitous life of this remarkable Nisei pitcher, see Nagata Yoichi, *Bēsubōruno Shakaishi* (Osaka: Toho Shuppan, 1997).

47. Kōno Atsushi, "Harisuhoshuron," *Yakyūkai* 28, no. 11 (July 1938): 192; Ikei Masaru, *Harō Stanka Genkikai* (Tokyo: Sōryūsha, 1983), 11–14.

48. For a thoroughly researched account of this North American tour, see Nagata Yoichi, *Tokyō Jaiants Hokubeitairiku Enseiki 1935* (Osaka: Tōhō Shuppan, 2007).

49. Ibid., 320–26.

50. Ibid., 36.

51. Martin Jacobs and Jack McGuire, *San Francisco Seals* (Charleston, SC: Arcadia, 2005), 59.

52. Suzuki, *Fumetsuno*, 108–14.

53. Pacific Coast League president Allen T. Baum barred blacks from playing in the league's parks in April 1914. McNeil, *The California Winter League*, 13. In January 1915, Walter McCredie, the owner of the Portland Beavers, canceled a contract he had signed with a Chinese Hawaiian on the grounds that signing this nonwhite player would risk a wholesale boycott by his players. *Chicago Defender*, January 4, 1915. Kenso Nushida of the Fresno Athletic Club became the first Japanese American to play (briefly) in the PCL in 1932. Jimmy Horio became the second Nisei Pacific Coast Leaguer in 1935.

54. *San Francisco Chronicle*, February 27, 1935; *Sacramento Union*, March 1, 1935; *San Francisco Examiner*, March 2, 1935. Memories of the participants in the 1935 tour invariably referred to the support of *Nikkei* communities as a critical element in the successful legs of the tour. For example, see Mizuhara Shigeru, *Watashinoayunda Yakyūseikatsu* (Osaka: Zenkoku Shobō, 1962), 105–8.

55. Suzuki, *Fumetsuno*; Miyake Daisuke, "Amerika Enseiki," in Suzuki, *Nippon Puro Yakyū Gaishi*, 48–49.

56. Nagata, *Tokyō Jaiants*, 150–53.

57. Suzuki, *Fumetsuno*, 149–50; Nagata, *Tokyō Jaiants*, 343–47; *Detroit Free Press*, June 8 and 9, 1935.

58. Spalding, *America's National Game*, 395–96.

59. Nagata, *Tokyō Jaiants*, 289–91; Miyake, "Amerikaenseiki," 48.

60. For a painstaking survey of local newspaper coverage of the tour, see Nagata, *Tokyō Jaiants*.

61. Yamatokyūshi, "Shokugyouyakyūno Ninshikiwo Aratameyo," *Yakyūkai* 29, no. 11 (June 1939): 231.

62. Nagata, *Tokyō Jaiants*, 62–65, 262–64, 273–82; *Shinsekai Nichinichi*, March 26, 1935; *San Jose Mercury Herald*, June 18, 1935; *Los Angeles Times*, March 31, 1935; *San Fran-*

cisco News, March 7, 1935; Adria Imada, "Hawaiians on Tour: Hula Circuits through the American Empire," *American Quarterly* 56, no. 1 (2004): 111–49.

63. The would-be assassin's reasons for attacking Shōriki also included the *Yomiuri Shinbun*'s recent syndication contract with the anti-Japanese Hearst papers.

64. Tobita, *Tokyo Asahi Shinbun*, March 15, 16, 17, and 18, 1936; *Yomiuri Shinbun*, March 28 and 29, 1936.

65. *Nippu Jiji*, June 30, July 5 and 8, 1935.

66. Suzuki, *Fumetsuno*, 217–25.

67. Alexander, *Breaking the Slump*, 80.

68. Ibid., 208.

69. Bob Broeg, *Baseball's Barnum: Ray "Hap" Dumont* (Wichita, KS: Center for Entrepreneurship, Wichita State University, 1989), 2–5, 9, 34, 38; Travis Larsen, "Satchel Paige and Hap Dumont: The Dynamic Duo of the National Baseball Congress Tournament," in *Satchel Paige and Company*, ed. Leslie A. Heaphy (Jefferson, NC: McFarland, 2007); Seymour, *Baseball*, 3:283–84.

70. Larsen, "Satchel Paige," 93–94; Broeg, *Baseball's Barnum*, 42–44.

71. Broeg, *Baseball's Barnum*, 6–7, 61, 84.

72. *Yomiuri Shinbun*, November 3, 1934.

73. M. E. Travaglini, "Olympic Baseball 1936: Was es Das?," *National Pastime* (1985): 46–55.

74. At the Berlin Olympics, the Japanese soccer team beat one of the Gold Medal hopefuls, Sweden, 3–2. This surprise victory was called "the Miracle in Berlin." This unexpected feat in Europeans' favorite sport gave an added boost to Japan's Olympics bid at the IOC. Nippon Shūkyūkyōkai, *Nippon Sakkāno Ayumi* (Tokyo: Kōdansha, 1974), 108–9.

75. Meeting minutes, 4th meeting of the Olympic Preparation Committee, September 26, 1935, in Dainippon Taiikukyōkai, ed. *Daijukkai Orinpikku Hōkokusho* (Tokyo: Dainippon Taiikukyōkai, 1937), 5; Leslie Mann, "Demonstration Events: Report of Manager of Baseball Team," *American Olympic Committee Report* (Colorado Springs, CO, 1936), 302–5; Seymour, *Baseball*, 3:287–88; Sundaikurabu, ed., *Meijidaigaku Yakyūbushi*, vol 1. (Tokyo: Sundaikurabu, 1974); *Orinpikku* 13, no. 12 (December 1935): 14–16; *Undōnenkan* 21 (November 1936): 79–80; Carlos Garcia, *Baseball Forever*, trans. Suzuki Mirei (Tokyo: Bēsumōru Magajinsha, 1979), 67–72. See Tobita's scathing commentary on the caliber of the Wheaties All-Stars in *Undōnenkan*, 21 (November 1936): 3–4.

76. Mann, "Demonstration Events," 301; Sano, *Kyokaiden*, 383–87.

77. Keys, *Globalizing Sport*, 65.

Chapter 6

1. Seymour, *Baseball*, 3:289–90; Bjarkman, *Diamond around the Globe*, 416–17; *New York Times*, August 11, 13, 16, 18, 20, 21, 25, and 27, 1939. Mann joined the USO during World War II. *New York Times*, February 1, 1943.

2. Telegram from Saitō to Arita, November 16, 1938, Taiikunarabini undōkyōgikankei zakken, vol. 5, Honpō daigakuchīmuno beikokuyakyū hyakunensai sankakankei, Japanese Foreign Ministry Archives.

3. The deployment of renowned athletes for constructing the iconography of war-

time athlete-soldiers was not limited to baseball. The wartime military service of both Schmeling and Joe Louis were showcased by their governments in similar ways. For this point, see Erenberg, *The Greatest Fight*, chapter 6. Dennis Frost's *Seeing Stars* gives an excellent summation of this theme built around Sawamura in chapter 4.

    4. Sandra Collins, *The 1940 Tokyo Games* (London: Routledge, 2008), 12–14; Sakaue Hiroshi, *Kenryokusōchi toshiteno Supōtsu* (Tokyo: Kōdansha, 1998); Kawashima Torao, *Nippon Taiikushi Kenkyū* (Nagoya: Reimei Shobo, 1982), 147–59.

    5. *Osaka Asahi*, August 10, 1936, and August 12, 1937; Ariyama, *Koshienyakyū*, 171–76.

    6. November 11, 1936, was calculated to be the 2,600th anniversary of this supposed founding moment of imperial rule based on obscure references in oral tales compiled in A.D. 720, the *Nihon Shoki*. The 2,600th imperial anniversary has been commonly understood as a signal event of Japanese ultranationalism and totalitarian mobilization, but Furukawa Takahisa has argued convincingly that the enterprise, initially featuring the Tokyo Olympics and a World Expo, was an amalgamation of much more complex historical forces that pointed to rising tides of consumerism in prewar Japan. For this perspective, see Furukawa Takahisa, *Kōki, Banpaku, Orinpikku* (Tokyo: Shuko Shinsho, 1998) and "'Kigen 2600nen Hōshuku' to Taigaibunkakōryu," in *Kindai Nipponto Jōhō* (Tokyo: Yamakawa, 1990). For a recent English-language study of this historical event, see Kenneth J. Ruoff, *Imperial Japan at Its Zenith: The Wartime Celebration of the Empire's 2,6000th Anniversary* (Ithaca, NY: Cornell University Press, 2010). Contrary to claims made by recent historians that Japan was forced to cancel the 1940 Olympic Games, Tokyo voluntarily relinquished them after intense debates between elite political groups. The history behind the decision to cancel the 1940 Tokyo Games reveals the complex and intricate negotiations required by Japanese imperial politics of the late 1930s. The decision was not unilaterally made by the military; rather it was a complex compromise between the military, factional political groups, elite bureaucrats, and members of the Japanese Olympic Organizing Committee (OOC). On June 23, 1938, Prime Minister Konoe announced his "New Austerity," calling for severe restrictions in the national budget, and this decision bore directly on the funds available for the Tokyo Games. Because of a reduction in the allocation of steel for the purposes of Olympic Games (12,000 tons originally), the scale of the games had to be reduced to respect the reduction in resources available. After negotiations with the IOC, the OOC unanimously voted to respectfully decline both the Tokyo and Sapporo Olympic Games in July 1938. Collins, *The 1940 Tokyo Games*, 4.

    7. Collins, *The 1940 Tokyo Games*, 143–76.

    8. *Yomiuri Shinbun*, May 6, 1936.

    9. *Yomiuri Shinbun*, January 1, 1939; *Nippon Yakyūrenmei Nyūsu*, January 25, 1939; Yamato, *Shinsetsu Yakyūshi*, 289–94. For the 1939 San Francisco International Exposition's "Pacific Rim" orientation, see Robert W. Rydell, "The 1939 San Francisco Golden Gate International Exposition and the Empire of the West," *European Contributions to American Studies* 16, (1989): 342–59.

    10. Yamato, *Shinsetsu Yakyūshi*, 295.

    11. Mizuhara, *Watashinoayunda*, 124; *Nanshiki Yakyūshi*, 37–42; *Kōrakuenstajiamu 50nenshi* (Tokyo: Kōrakuenstajiamu, 1990), 37–38.

12. Kubota Takayuki, *Kaiteishinban Kōkōyakyū Hyakunen* (Tokyo: Jijitsūshin, 1976), 206; Asahi Shinbunsha, ed., *Zenkoku Kōtōgakkō Yakyū Senshuken Taikaishi* (Tokyo: Asahi Shinbunsha, 1958), 124-27.

13. Ikei Masaru, "Nippon ni Okeru Yakyūzasshi no Shincho-1," *Bēsubōrojī* 5 (2004): 115-16.

14. *Hawaii Hōchi*, June 5-9, 1940; *Nippu Jiji*, April 17, 24, 25, 1940; *Yakyūkai* 27, no. 14 (November 1937): 80-81; *Yakyūkai* 30, no. 14 (July 1940); 64-78; *Yakyūkai* 30, no. 24 (December 1940): 68-69.

15. Nakamura Tetsuya and Kunugi Toshio, "Gakuseiyakyūno Kokkatoseito Jichi," in Sakaue and Takaoka, *Maboroshino Tokyo Orinpikkuto Sonojidai*, 354-78; Bēsubōru Magajinsha, *Tokyorokudaigakuyakyū 8onenshi* (Tokyo: Bēsubōru Magajinsha, 2005), 29. *Yomiuri Shinbun*, June 5 and 10, 1940; *Asahi Supōtsu*, Tōa Kyogitaikai Special Issue, July 1940; Furukawa, *Kōki Banpaku*, 180-83.

16. For example, *Yakyūkai* 27, no. 14 (November 1937): 158-59; *Yakyūkai* 27, no. 15 (November 1937): 228-9; *Yakyūkai* 28, no. 1 (January 1938): 56-62.

17. Suzuki, *Fumetsuno*, 313-20, 341-44.

18. *Yomiuri Shinbun*, June 15, 1941.

19. *Yakyūkai* 29, no. 18 (December 1939): 164.

20. Suzuki, *Kaikoroku*, 107-10; Hirohata Seiji, *Shūsenno Rasutogēmu* (Tokyo: Honnoizumisha, 2005), 74-86; Starffin, *Roshiakarakitaēsu*, 112-28.

21. *Yakyūkai* 30, no. 11 (June 1940): 212; *Yakyūkai* 30, no. 23 (December 1940): 104-5; *Yakyūkai* 31, no. 15 (July 1941): 78.

22. Suzuki, *Kaikoroku*, 103-6.

23. *Yakyūkai* 30, no. 1 (January 1940): 229; *Yakyūkai* 30, no. 6 (March 1940): 193-200, 218; *Yakyūkai* 30, no. 7 (April 1940): 213-16. Revera played for the Giants only one season (1939) and returned to the Philippines in early 1940. Rivera is the only Filipino player to date to play Japanese professional baseball. During World War II, he became an anti-Japanese guerrilla and was killed in action.

24. For Filipino-Japanese cultural exchanges during the commonwealth period, see Terami Motoe, "1930nendaino Nipponn-Firipin Shinzenjigyō," in *Kingendai Nipponfiripin Kankeishi*, ed. Ikehata Setsuho and Lydia N. Yu Jose (Tokyo: Iwanami Shoten, 2004), 159-98.

25. Bēsubōru Magajinsha, ed., *Puroyakyū 7onenshi: Rekishihen* (Tokyo: Bēsubōru Magajinsha, 2004), 57.

26. *Korakuenno 25nen*, 149.

27. *Kōrakuenstajiamu 5onenshi*, 39.

28. Steven Bullock, *Playing for Their Nation: Baseball and the American Military during World War II* (Lincoln: University of Nebraska Press, 2004), 29-30.

29. David Finoli, *For the Good of the Country: World War II Baseball in the Major and Minor Leagues* (Jefferson, NC: McFarland, 2002), 1-2; Nelson, *The Golden Game*, 206.

30. W. C. Madden, *The Women of the All-American Girls Professional Baseball League* (Jefferson, NC: McFarland, 1997), 3.

31. Susan Cahn, *Coming on Strong: Gender and Sexuality in Twentieth-Century Women's Sport* (Cambridge: Harvard University Press, 1994), 147-49; Jean Hastings Ardell,

Breaking into Baseball (Carbondale: Southern Illinois University Press, 2005), 113–15, 118; Lois Browne, *Girls of Summer: In Their Own League* (Toronto: HarperCollins, 1993), 18–29.

32. Browne, *Girls of Summer*, 92–93; Jimmy Skaggs, "Wichita, Kansas: Economic Origins of Metropolitan Development, 1870–1960," in *Metropolitan Wichita: Past, Present, and Future*, ed. Glenn W. Miller and Jimmy M. Skaggs (Lawrence: Regents Press of Kansas, 1978), 14–15.

33. *Sporting News*, April 30 and May 21, 1942.

34. Ibid., December 11 and 18, 1941; Ibid., March 9, 1942.

35. Letter from FDR to Kenesaw M. Landis, January 15, 1942. A copy of Roosevelt's "green light" letter is available at the Sporting News Archive, St. Louis, MO; Richard Goldstein, *Spartan Seasons: How Baseball Survived the Second World War* (New York: Macmillan, 1980), 3–28.

36. Bullock, *Playing for Their Nation*, 12–14; *Sporting News*, April 16 and 23, 1942; *Sporting News*, July 30 and November 9, 1944; *Baseball Magazine*, January 1942; all news clippings in World War II file, BHFML.

37. Wakefield, *Playing to Win*, 68–71.

38. Bullock, *Playing for Their Nation*, xi.

39. *Sporting News*, January 8, 1942. Steven W. Pope has shown the U.S. military's systematic integration, in corporation with the YMCA, of athletics into its training and recreation programs as a result of World War I. Steven W. Pope, "An Army of Athletes: Playing Fields, Battlefields, and the American Military Sporting Experience, 1890–1920," *Journal of Military History* 59 (July 1995): 435–56; Elias, *Empire Strikes Out*, 79–90.

40. *Sporting News*, May 14, 1942; Goldstein, *Spartan Seasons*, 31–39.

41. Bullock, *Playing for Their Nation*, 49; Goldstein, *Spartan Seasons*, 63–93.

42. Ted Williams, who had a draft exemption, played one final season to help support his widowed mother before he enlisted. Leigh Montville, *Ted Williams: The Biography of an American Hero* (New York: Doubleday, 2004), 99–105.

43. *Sporting News*, February 24, 1943. For DiMaggio's reaction to fans' criticism, see David Jones, *Joe DiMaggio* (Westport, CT: Greenwood, 2004), 75–76, 79–78; and Richard Ben Cramer, *Joe DiMaggio: The Hero's Life* (New York: Touchstone, 2000), 198–208. For the erasure of ethnic association as a result of professional ball players' military service, see Peter Levine, *Ellis Island to Ebbets Field: Sport and the American Jewish Experience* (New York: Oxford University Press, 1992), 141–43; White, *Creating the National Pastime*, chap. 8; and Lawrence Baldassaro, "Before Joe D: Early Italian Americans in the Major Leagues," in *The American Game: Baseball and Ethnicity*, ed. Lawrence Baldassaro and Richard A. Johnson (Carbondale and Edwardsville: Southern Illinois University Press, 2002), 112–13.

44. Bullock, *Playing for Their Nation*, 77.

45. Wakefield, *Playing to Win*, 95.

46. Yoshida Yutaka, *Nipponno Guntai* (Tokyo: Iwanami Shoten, 2002), 216–17; Kawasaki Tokuji, *Sensōto Yakyū* (Tokyo: Bēsubōru Magajinsha, 1997), 171–72.

47. Kawasaki, *Sensōto Yakyū*, 41.

48. *Sporting News*, July 23 and 27, 1944.

49. Bullock, *Playing for Their Nation*, 23–25, 95.

50. *Sporting News*, April 20 and June 22, 1944; William Mead, *Baseball Goes to War* (Washington, D.C.: Farragut, 1985), 199.

51. Bullock, *Playing for Their Nation*, 73; *Sporting News*, March 15, 1945.

52. *Sporting News*, July 19, 1945.

53. Nelson, *The Golden Game*, 207–8. For a superb overview of the Roosevelt administration's decision to initiate the wholesale removal of Japanese Americans from the West Coast, see Greg Robinson, *A Tragedy of Democracy: Japanese Confinement in North America* (New York: Columbia University Press, 2009), 59–103.

54. Nelson, *The Golden Game*, 209.

55. Adachi, *Asahi*, 6.

56. Okihiro, *Cane Fires*, 131–61, 173–75. See also Gary Okihiro, *The Columbia Guide to Asian American History* (New York: Columbia University Press, 2001), 120–25.

57. Okihiro, *Cane Fires*, 163–91; Chiyo Yanagida, "The Nippu Uiui and the Japanese Language School Issue in Hawaii, 1919–1927" (M.A. thesis, University of Hawaii at Manoa, 1996), 158–60.

58. Joel Franks, *Hawaiian Sports in the Twentieth Century* (Lewiston, NY: Edwin Mellen Press, 2002), 12–13.

59. Okihiro, *AJA Baseball in Hawaii*, 33; Nagata, *Bēsubōruno*, 280, 302; Franks, *Hawaiian Sports*, 120.

60. Jack B. Moore, *Joe DiMaggio: A Bio-Bibliography* (Westport, CT: Greenwood, 1986), 129–30; Robinson, *A Tragedy of Democracy*, 180–81; Nakagawa, *Through a Diamond*, 76; Nelson, *The Golden Game*, 208.

61. Nakagawa, *Through a Diamond*, 82–86.

62. Otto Friedrich, *City of Nets: A Portrait of Hollywood in the 1940s* (New York: Harper & Row, 1986), 102.

63. *Baseball: Tule Lake Center 1944*, published by Newell Star Sports Department in December 1944; in author's possession.

64. Samuel Regalado, "Sport and Community in California's Japanese American Yamato Colony, 1930–1945," *Journal of Sport History* 19 (Summer 1992): 130; Jay Feldman, "Baseball behind Barbed Wire," *National Pastime* 12 (1992): 38–39; Nelson, *The Golden Game*, 212.

65. *San Francisco Chronicle*, May 3, 1944.

66. Feldman, "Baseball behind Barbed Wire," 37–41; Adachi, *Asahi*, 126.

67. Ushijima Hidehiko, *Kieta Haru* (Tokyo: Kawaide Shobō, 1994); Yamaoka Sōhachi, "Saigono Jūgun," *Asahi Shinbun*, August 8, 1962; Hata Ikuhiko, *Taiheiyōusenso Kōkūshiwa*, vol. 2 (Tokyo: Chūō Koron, 1994), 221–44.

68. Hashimoto Kazuo, *Nippon Supōtsu Hōsōshi*, 160–61; *Kōrakuenstajiamu 50nenshi*, 40–412.

Chapter 7

1. Kōrakuen Stadium was commandeered by the Eighth Army on September 15, 1945, but was released from impoundment on February 6, 1946, just in time for the opening of professional baseball's postwar inaugural season. Kōrakuen Stajiamu, *Kōrakuen no 25nen* (Tokyo: Kōrakuen Stadium Co., 1963), 159–60; Ikei, *Hakkyū*, 198–200.

The Tokyo Big 6's home ground, Jingū Stadium, was commandeered by the occupation army on September 6, 1945, and remained under SCAP control until a month before the end of the Allied occupation. The Yokohama Stadium, another key steel and concrete stadium in the Greater Tokyo area, was also commandeered and renamed Lou Gehrig Stadium and kept off-limits to the Japanese through much of the occupation period. Kōshien Stadium was commandeered on October 3, 1945. Yanagimoto Motoharu, ed., *Tokyo Rokudaigakuyakyū 80nennshi* (Tokyo: Bēsubōru Magajinsha, 2005), 32.

2. Suzuki Ryūji, *Puro Yakyū to Tomoni 50-nen* (Tokyo, 1984), 239–42; Hashimoto, *Nippon Supōtsu Hōsōshi*, 171–72; Suzuki Akira, *Showa 20nen 11 gatsu 23 nichi no purēbōru* (Tokyo, 1978), 211–12; *Pacific Stars and Stripes*, November 22, 1945; *Yakyūkai* 36, no. 1 (January 1946): 2–7.

3. Hirano Kyoko, *Tennō to Seppun: Amerika senyōkano nipponeiga kenetsu* (Tokyo: Soshisha, 1998), 236–60.

4. Baseball play in Korea resumed in early November. The U.S. Army team in Seoul played against a squad selected from the Korean Amateur Baseball Association. The game drew 10,000 spectators. *Pacific Stars and Stripes*, November 4, 1945. In the first year of professional baseball's 105-game season, a total of 1.56 million people, thirsty for peacetime entertainment, attended. Amid the harsh realities of food shortages, breakdown of transportation networks, and equipment shortages, it was quite an astounding figure.

5. *Pacific Stars and Stripes*, November 2 and 22, 1945.

6. For an examination of Capra's propaganda film, see John Dower, *War without Mercy: Race and Power in the Pacific War* (New York: Pantheon, 1986), 18–19; William J. Blakefield, "A War Within: The Making of *Know Your Enemy—Japan*," *Sight and Sound: International Film Quarterly* 52, no. 2 (1983): 128–33.

7. Foreign Ministry Directive, "Shakaitaiikuno jisshinikansuruken," directive no. 95, August 25, 1946, in Nakamura Tamio, *Shiryō Kindaikendōshi* (Tokyo: Shimazu Shobō, 1985), 121.

8. Kusafuka Naoomi, "Taiiku supōtsuno sengokaikakuni kansuru daiichiji beikoku kyōikushisetsudan hōkokusho no sakuseikatei," *Taiikugaku Kenkyu* 41 (1996): 59–67; John Noviel statement, "Nippon supōtsuno hattenno tameni," *Supōtsu* 1 (June 1946): 9; Takemae Eiji and Nakamura Takafusa, eds., *GHQ Nippon Senryōshi*, vol. 20, *Kyōiku* (Tokyo: Nippon Tosho Center, 1996), 160–67.

9. "Nippon no Taiiku," "Physical Education Projects," September 26, 1946, Box 5445, CIE Records, CIE Special Report (166-SR-A), National Archives, College Park, MD; "Conference on the Production of Athletic Equipments," Box 5727, CIE Records, National Archives, College Park, MD.

10. "Physical Education Officer: Conference Reports," Box 5734, CIA Records.

11. Examples of such anecdotal evidence are included in Suzuki, *Puroyakyū*; and Saeki Tatsuo, *Saeki Tatsuojiden* (Tokyo: Bēsubōru Magajinsha, 1980).

12. The earliest reported case of a U.S. service team playing against a combined Japanese college-news agency squad was on October 5, 1945. *Pacific Stars and Stripes*, October 8, 1945, and February 17, 1946.

13. Tamaki, *Kōshienkyūjō Monogatari*, 130–40.

14. Hatano, *Nichibeiyakūshi*, 177–88.

15. "Puroyakyū Kōshikaigi Gijiroku," in Furoku 2 of Suzuki, *Kaikoroku*, 382–85.

16. Sano Shinichi, *Kyokaiden*, 272–73, 376–80; Cappy Harada, *Taiheiyō no Kakehashi* (Tokyo: Bēsubōru Magajinsha, 1980), 58–77; Robert Fitts, *Remembering Japanese Baseball: An Oral History of the Game* (Carbondale: Southern Illinois University Press, 2005), 1–5.

17. The Bataan Boys are fifteen officers who narrowly escaped the Japanese attack on the Bataan Peninsula with MacArthur in December 1942. For detailed biographical information on this group of MacArthur's close aides, see Masuda Hiroshi, *Makkāsā* (Tokyo: Shuokoronshinsha, 2009), 28–31.

18. Harada, *Taiheiyō*, 72–73; Hatano, *Nichibeiyakyūshi*, 194–96.

19. In the inaugural postwar Inter-City Tournament, the Black Lion Flag, the tournament's prestigious champion flag, was returned by the representative of the now-defunct prewar championship team, the Seoul All Star Club. The flag, once reported lost, came back to the Japanese mainland in October 1945, when Akiyama Mitsuo, shortstop for the Seoul All Star Club, repatriated from the Korean peninsula with the Black Lion Flag wrapped around his torso. It was indeed the symbolic return home of Japan's colonial baseball. Suzuki Toshihiko, "Nippon Sangyō no Seisui to Shakaijin Yakyū," 178.

20. Nippon Shakaijin Yakyū Kyōkai, *Jūnennoayumi* (Tokyo: Nippon Shakaijinyakyū Kyōkaihō, 1959), 41–42; Bēsubōru Magajinsha, *Shakaijinyakyū*, 60–61; Suzuki Sōtarō, "Taibono nichibeiyakyū jitsugen," *Yakyūjidai* 2, no. 9 (September 1949): n.p. NBC's Philippines commissioner was Chic Parson, an American businessman living in Manila. The NBC commissioner for the Republic of China was Claire Chennault.

21. *Asahi Shinbun*, November 6, 1945.

22. *Zenkoku Kōtōgakkō Yakyū Senshuken Taikaishi*, 109–11. For Tobita Suishū, see Ariyama Teruo, "Sengo koshienyakyūtaikai no fukkatsu," in Tsuganesawa Toshihiro, *Sengo Nipponno Media Ibento* (Kyoto: Sekai Shisosha, 2002), 29–33; and Saeki, *Saeki Tatsuojiden*, 112–14, 143–48.

23. The conflation of the date of surrender and the opening of the summer high school tournament at the insistence of SCAP in 1946 indicates that what media historian Sato Takumi brilliantly conceptualizes as "the August 15 Mythology" was being crafted through high school baseball this early in the postwar period. Sato Takumi, *Hachigatsu jūgonichino shinwa* (Tokyo: Chikuma Shobō, 2005), 161.

24. In 1947, the high school baseball association tried again to reinstate Asahi's corporate sponsorship, only to be blocked again by the Education Ministry, which passed down a "no-go" order from SCAP. In the end, another tenuous compromise was forged whereby the *Asahi Shinbun*'s material support of the summer tournament would be called *kyōsan* (coendorsement). This merely semantic solution remained in place until Asahi's frontal cosponsorship (*kyōsai*) would resume after the end of the Allied occupation. *Zenkoku Kōtōgakkō Yakyū Senshuken Taikaishi*, 34–35, 111.

25. Harada, *Taiheiyō*, 74–76; Tamaki, *Kōshienkyūjō Monogatari*, 135–37.

26. Saeki, *Saeki Tatsuojiden*, 189–91. As in the case of the summer tournament, the newspaper's formal sponsorship would not come until the end of the occupation.

27. Bēsubōru Magajinsha, *Tokyo Rokudaigakuyakyū 80nenshi* (Tokyo: Bēsubōru Magajinsha, 2006), 32.

28. Minichi Shinbusha, *Bessatsu Ichiokunin no Shōwashi: Nippon Puroyakyūshi* (Tokyo, 1980), 3.

29. Ikei Masaru, "Nippon ni Okeru Yakyū Zasshi no Shōchō 2," *Besubōroji* 6 (2005): 179–86. The Prange Collection of Japanese print publication during the Allied occupation (housed at the University of Maryland's McKelden Library) includes at least thirty-five magazine titles devoted to baseball. Although most of these magazines lasted for a very short time, the sheer number of baseball magazines catering to all age groups reflects the mass appeal of the game among Japanese at the time.

30. Tsuchiya Reiko, "Sōseikino supōtsushito yakyū ibento," in Tsuganesawa Toshihiro, *Sengo Nipponno Media Ibento* (Kyoto: Sekaishisosha, 2002), 50.

31. Ikei, "Nippon ni Okeru Yakyū Zasshi no Shōchō 2," 179–86.

32. For the reformulation of Emperor Hirohito's public image in the early postwar months, see John Dower, *Embracing Defeat: Japan in the Wake of World War II* (New York: Norton, 1999), 330–39.

33. Emperor Hirohito and Empress Nagako's first appearance at a sporting event in the postwar period was at an east-west soccer match at the Meiji Jingu Outdoor Filed on April 3, 1947. Sakamoto Kojiro, *Shōchōtennoseiheno Pafōmansu* (Tokyo: Yamakawa Shuppan, 1989), 162–65. Sakaue Yasuhiro has noted the deployment of sports by the Imperial Household during the Taisho Democracy period. In this sense, the theme of using sports in imperial image making constituted transwar continuity. During this historical antecedence, more "aristocratic" sports such as skiing, tennis, and horseback riding were highlighted. For his insightful analysis, see Sakaue Yasuhiro, "Supōtsuto tennōseino myakuraku," *Rekishi Hyōron* 602 (June 2000): 29–44.

34. Kenneth J. Ruoff, *The People's Emperor: Democracy and the Japanese Monarchy, 1945–1995* (Cambridge: Harvard University Asia Center, 2003), chap. 4; Kasai Hideya, *Shōchōtennō no sengoshi* (Tokyo: Kōdansha, 2010), 44–56, 81–82; *Mainichi Shinbun*, August 2 and 4, 1947; *Shakaijinyakyū*, 59.

35. *YaKyū Shōnen* 1, no. 1 (April 1947 and August 3, 1947); *Yakyū Shōnen*, October special edition (September 1947).

36. "Shinzen," *Agahi Gurafu* 52, no. 20 (November 1949).

37. Sayuri Guthrie-Shimizu, "The United States, Japan, and the Cold War, 1945–1960," in *The Cambridge History of the Cold War*, vol. 1, ed. Melvin Leffler and Odd Arne Westad (Cambridge: Cambridge University Press, 2010), 249–51.

38. Ikei, *Hakkyū*, 210.

39. O'Neal, *The Pacific Coast League*, 90–91; Brent P. Kelley, *The San Francisco Seals, 1946–1957: Interviews with 25 Former Baseballers* (Jefferson, NC: McFarland, 2002), 99; Leutzinger, *Lefty O'Doul*, 101, 109–11.

40. White, *Creating the National Pastime*, 298.

41. Kelley, *The San Francisco Seals*, 99; O'Neal, *The Pacific Coast League*, 89–90; Leutzinger, *Lefty O'Doul*, 92, 98–100; Suzuki Sōtarō, "America no yakyū," *Yakyūkai* 39, no. 9 (September 1949); *Pacific Stars and Stripes*, July 12, 1949.

42. Kelley, *The San Francisco Seals*, 114; Harada, *Taiheiyō*, 87–88; Masuda Hiroshi, *MacArthur* (Tokyo: Chūō Kōronsha, 2009), 388–89. For U.S. cultural diplomacy in the 1950s, see Laura Belmonte, *Selling the American Way* (Philadelphia: University of Penn-

sylvania Press, 2008); and Nicholas J. Cull, *The Cold War and the United States Information Agency* (Cambridge: Cambridge University Press, 2009).

43. Suzuki, "America no yakyū." For an extensive market survey on baseball commerce conducted by the Department of Commerce's Bureau of Foreign and Domestic Commerce in the 1920s and 1930s, see Mark Dyreson, "Mapping an Empire of Baseball: American Visions of National Pastimes and Global Influence, 1919 to 1941," in *Baseball in America and America in Baseball*, ed. Donald G. Kyle and Robert B. Fairbanks (College Station: Texas A&M University Press, 2008), particularly 163, 167–69.

44. Ikei, *Hakkyū*, 210–11. For Dodge's role in the stabilization of the Japanese economy, see Howard Shonberger, *Aftermath of War: Americans and the Remaking of Japan, 1945–1952* (Kent, OH: Kent State University Press, 1989), 198–235.

45. For Furuhashi Hironoshin's life and career, see Furuhashi Hironoshin, *Rikiei 30nen* (Tokyo: Nippontoshosentā, 1997).

46. Harada, *Taiheiyō*, 85–87. Fred Wada also acted as a liaison between Los Angeles's Japanese American community and the AAU during the 1932 Los Angeles Olympics. Since the Japanese Swimming Association did not have enough foreign currency (U.S. dollar) reserves, the 1949 tour by Furuhashi and others was partially financed by donations ($3,000) by Japanese Americans in California. For the Los Angeles Japanese American community's involvement in the 1932 Olympics, see Eriko Yamamoto, "Cheers for Japanese Athletes." The Japanese American community's support of the Japanese swimmers was also part of their larger enterprise to help the homeland Japanese through financial, food, and material-aid packages in the early postwar period. For this point, see Iino Masako, *Mouhitotsuno Nichibeikankeishi* (Tokyo: Yūhikaku, 2000), 148–61.

47. Harada, *Taiheiyō*, 82–84; Mizuhara Shigeru, *Watashino Ayunda*, 131–53; *Yomiuri Shinbun*, July 25, 1949; Mizuhara Shigeru, "Kokyoni kaerite omou," *Hōmuran* 4, no. 10 (October 1949); In one Soviet labor camp where about 10,000 Japanese men were interned, there were enough former Tokyo Big 6 players in the contingent that Waseda-Keio matchups were held. Ikei, *Hakkyū*, 202–8.

48. No. 300 San Francisco Seals Folder, June 1949–October 1949, Box 1031, Legal Section, GHQ/SCAP Records, RG 331, National Archives; Memorandum, Foreign Investment Board, October 5, 1040, contained in above.

49. *Shūkan Nippon Yakyū*, no. 24 (April 1949); Suzuki Sōtarō, "Taibōno nichibeiyakyū jitsugen," *Yakyūjidai* 2, no. 9 (1949).

50. Harada, *Taiheiyō*, 110–13; No. 300 San Francisco Seals Folder, 1946.6–10, SCAP Legal Section Records, LS 17496, Microfilm Collection at the Japanese Diet Library; Ikei, *Hakkyū*, 212.

51. A number of baseball magazines ran a special issue of the Seals' visit. For example, *Baseball News* 638 (October 1949); *Baseball*, no. 27 (October 1949); *Ball Friend*, September and November 1949; *Baseball Magazine*, September and November 1949; *Hōmuran*, August-November 1949; *Kindai Yakyū*, September and October 1949; and *All Yakyū*, October 1949. I thank Ms. Eiko Sakaguchi at the Prange Collection for her help in the bibliographical search.

52. In the Prange Collection, many baseball magazines feature this story after June

1949. For example: Suzuki Sōtarō's essay conveying O'Doul's personal regards to Japanese baseball boys appeared in *Shonen no Yakyū* 2, no. 11 (1949); *Homuran* 4, no. 10 (1949); and *Basuboru Magajin* 4, no. 14 (1949).

53. Nelson, *The Golden Game*, 114.

54. *Pacific Stars and Stripes*, October 14 and 17, 1949; Ikei, *Hakkyū*; Harada, *Taiheiyō*, 90–91.

55. The photography was featured in *Asahi Gurafu* 52, no. 20 (November 9, 1949); Nakagawa, *Through a Diamond*, 102.

56. *Asahi Gurafu* 52, no. 19 (November 2, 1949); *Kindai Yakyū*, August 1949; *Pacific Stars and Stripes*, October 21 and 31, 1949.

57. Tanikawa Takeshi, "Senryokino Tainichi Supōtsu Seisaku," *Intelligence*, no. 3, 38; *Baseball News*, no. 640 (November 1949); *Yakyū News*, no. 40 (December 1949); Morooka Tatsuichi, "Sanfuranshiko siruzuto fuminsho," *Bēsuboroji* 2 (2001): 340; Coca-Cola Export Corporation Folder, January 1949, Box 1040, Legal Section, GHQ/SCAP, RG 331; Miyamoto Atsuo, *Kokakōraeno Michi* (Tokyo: Kano Shobo, 1994), 92–93.

58. *Pacific Stars and Stripes*, September 26 and October 17, 1949; *Yomiuri Shinbun*, October 16, 1949.

59. Harada, *Taiheiyō*, 97–109.

Chapter 8

1. Suzuki, *Suzuki Ryūji Jiden*, 447; Harada, *Taiheiyō*, 79–81; Sano, *Kyokaiden*.

2. Mainichi Shinbun, September 22, 1949; Bēsubōru Magajinsha, *Nippon Puroyakyū 40nenshi* (Tokyo: Bēsubōru Magajinsha, 1976), 130–47; Hanshintaigasu, *Showano Ayumi* (Osaka: Hanshin Tigers, 1991), 165–68.

3. *Nikkan Supōtsu*, January 28, 1950; Harada, *Taiheiyō*, 92–95.

4. *Pacific Stars and Stripes*, November 24, 1950.

5. Harada, *Taiheiyō*, 110–11; Eiichiro Azuma's recent work on the complex cultural brokerage undertaken by Nisei linguists in SCAP is highly useful in placing Harada's activities in a larger historical context. Eiichiro Azuma, "Brokering Race, Culture, and Citizenship: Japanese Americans in Occupied Japan and Post National Inclusion," *Journal of American-East Asian Relations* 16, no. 3 (2009): 1–29.

6. Jacobs and McGuire, *The San Francisco Seals*, 103; Leutzinger, *Lefty O'Doul*, 112.

7. Nelson, *The Golden Game*, 133. As more major-league clubs began to televise their games, its impact on the minor leagues was especially acute. Minor-league attendance declined from 49 million fans in 1949 to 15.5 million in 1957. White, *Creating the National Pastime*, 279.

8. *Yomiuri Kyojingun 20nenshi*.

9. Kōrakuen Sutajiamu, *Kōrakuenno 25nen* (Tokyo: Korakuen Stadium, 1963), 122. For American women and baseball, see Ardell, *Breaking into Baseball*, 1–78.

10. Kōrakuen Sutajiamu, *Korakuennno 25nen*, 135; Tsuchiya, "Sōseikino supōtsushito yakyū ibento," 51; telegram from the Consul General in Los Angeles to Foreign Minister Hirota, 21 May 1938, Taiiku narabini undōkyōgikankei zakken, vol. 5, Beikoku joshiyakyūdan kankei, Japanese Foreign Ministry Archives.

11. *Zenkoku Kōtōgakko Yakyū Senshuken Taikaishi*, 37; Takemae and Nakamura, *GHQ Nippon Senryōshi*, 163–64; Seki Harumi, "Sengoniokeru 'Shintaiiku' norinen," *Ikkyō*

Ronso 67, no. 3, 312–13; Tsuchiya Yuka, *Shinbei Nippon no Kōchiku* (Tokyo: Akashi Shoten, 2009), 207–21; Kawashima, *Nippon Taiikushi Kenkyū*, 184–201.

12. Tsuchiya, "Soseikino," 52–53.

13. Andrew Gordon, *A Modern History of Japan*, 2nd ed. (New York: Oxford University Press, 2009), 234. For a collection of oral history interviews of the pioneer Japanese women pro baseball players, see Tsunekage Junichi, *Watashino Aozora* (Tokyo: Michishobo, 1995).

14. Satō Mitsufusa, *Mouhitotsuno Puroyakyū* (Tokyo: Asahi Shinbunsha, 1986), 202–3.

15. Kuwabara Ietoshi, *Onnatachino Purēbōru* (Tokyo: Fujinsha, 1993), 21–68.

16. Wakatsuki Yasuo, *Sengo Hikiageno Kiroku* (Tokyo: Jijitsushinsha, 1991).

17. Gordon, *Modern History of Japan*, 228, Lori Watt, *When Empire Comes Home* (Cambridge: Harvard University Press, 2009), 1–18.

18. Susan Cahn, *Coming on Strong: Gender and Sexuality in Twentieth-Century Women's Sport* (Cambridge: Harvard University Press, 1994), 147–49; Ardell, *Breaking into Baseball*, 113–15, 118; Browne, *Girls of Summer*, 18–29.

19. Tsuchiya, "Sōseikino," 55–63; Kuwabara, *Onnatachino*, 104–211.

20. Cahn, *Coming on Strong*, 148–53; Ardell, *Breaking into Baseball*, 114–16.

21. Kuwabara, *Onnatachino*, 104–8, 138, 212; "Japan Female Baseball League Formed," *Sankei Shinbun*, March 2, 1993.

22. Tsuchiya, "Sōseikino," 59–60; Ogawa Takeshi, "Jingūkyujohatsuno joshiyakyūsen," *Bēsubōru Magajin* 3, no. 1 (October 1948).

23. For problems of the essentially binary formulation of American "liberators" saving Japanese women from centuries of gender oppression, see Mire Koikari, *Pedagogy of Democracy: Feminism and the Cold War in the U.S. Occupation of Japan* (Philadelphia: Temple University Press, 2008).

24. Nelson, *The Golden Game*, 116, 129; White, *Creating the National Pastime*, 296–315; Obojski, *Bush League*, 132; *Sporting News*, December 17, 1952; James Edward Miller, *The Baseball Business: Pursuing Pennants and Profits in Baltimore* (Chapel Hill: University of North Carolina Press, 1990), 14–15. For political, economic, and social factors leading to Dodgers owner Walter O'Malley's decision to move his New York franchise to Los Angeles, see Neil Sullivan, *The Dodgers Move West* (New York: Oxford University Press, 1987).

25. The word "experiment" was borrowed from Jules Tygiel, *Baseball's Great Experiment: Jackie Robinson and His Legacy* (London: Oxford University Press, 1983). For the allure of American professional sports on the global market, see Walter LaFeber, *Michael Jordan and the New Global Capitalism* (New York: Norton, 1999).

26. White, *Creating the National Pastime*, 306–15.

27. Arima Tetsuo, *Nipponterebito CIA* (Tokyo: Shinchosha, 2006), 124–29, 275–305. For the role of television and American cultural influences during the Cold War, see James Schwoch, *Global TV: New Media and the Cold War, 1946–69* (Baltimore: Johns Hopkins University Press, 2009). For an illuminating study of the role of SCAP-distributed movies in postwar Japan as a case of early U.S. cultural diplomacy, see Tsuchiya Yuka, *Shinbei Nipponno Kōchiku*, particularly chapter 5.

28. Bēsubōru Magajinsha, *Nichibeiyakyūkōryūshi* (Tokyo: Bēsubōru Magajinsha, 2004), 24–28, 89–90. For early prototypes of U.S.-Japanese consultation on "orderly"

bilateral trade, see Sayuri Shimizu, *Creating People of Plenty: The United States and Japan's Economic Alternatives, 1950–1960* (Kent, OH: Kent State University Press, 2001), 102–5.

Epilogue

1. California State Senate, *Journal of the Senate*, 56th sess., 1461; quoted in Kevin Allen Leonard, "'Is That What We Fought For?' Japanese Americans and Racism in California, the Impact of World War II," *Western Historical Quarterly* 21, no. 4 (November 1990): 466; Robinson, *A Tragedy of Democracy*, 254–59.

2. Lambert Schuyler, *The Japs Must Not Come Back!* (Winslow, WA: n.p., 1944), 608; quoted in Leonard, "Is That What We Fought For?," 467.

3. Nelson, *The Golden Game*, 212–14; Nakagawa, *Through a Diamond*, 98–99; Iino Masako, *Mouhitotsuno Nichibeikankei* (Tokyo: Yūhikaku, 2000), 138–42.

4. Yonamine was not the first Nisei to play in Japan's postwar professional baseball. There were three previous players (Jyo Kotani at the Nankai club; Isoo Odate, a Hawaii-born *kibei* who played for the Hanshin club; and Isamu Uchino, a California-born Nisei who got recruited by the Hankyu club in 1949). Robert K. Fitts, *Wally Yonamine: The Man Who Changed Japanese Baseball* (Lincoln: University of Nebraska Press, 2008), 80.

5. Fitts, *Remembering Japanese Baseball*, 21–31, 51–66; Fitts, *Wally Yonamine*, 63–116.

6. Norifumi Kawahara, "Ritsumeikandaigaku Yakyūbuno Taiwan Ensei," *Ritsumeikan Hyakunenshi Kiyō* 15 (2007): 98.

7. Ōshima, *Kankokuyakyūno Genryū*, 55–97.

8. Yu, *Playing in Isolation*, 20–21.

SELECTED BIBLIOGRAPHY

Archives and Manuscript Collections

JAPAN
Japanese Baseball Hall of Fame Library, Tokyo
    Philip Block Clippings File
    Nichibei Yakyū scrapbooks
Japanese Foreign Ministry Archives, Tokyo
    Taiikunarabini Undōkyōgikankei Zakken
Keio University Rare Book Collection, Tokyo
    Wilson's First Reader
Waseda University Archives, Tokyo
    Abe Isoo Papers

UNITED STATES
Baseball Hall of Fame Library, Cooperstown, NY
    Newspaper Clippings File
    Player Files
        Edward Ainsmith
        Herbert Hunter
        Frank O'Doul
    Tour Files
Japanese-American Cultural Center of Hawaii, Honolulu
    AJC File
National Archives, College Park, MD
    GHQ/SCAP Records, RG 331
New York Public Library
    Henry Chadwick Scrapbooks
    Albert G. Spalding Scrapbooks
University of Chicago Library
    Amos Alonzo Stagg Papers
University of Illinois Library, Champaign-Urbana
    Avery Brundage Collection
University of Maryland McKelden Library
    Gordon Prange Collection
University of Michigan Library
    Fielding Yost Papers

Periodicals

CHINESE LANGUAGE
Taiwan Riri Xinbao

ENGLISH LANGUAGE
Army and Navy Journal
Baseball Magazine
Brooklyn Daily Eagle
California Eagle
Chicago Daily News
Chicago Daily Tribune
Chicago Defender
Detroit Free Press
Fresno Bee
Hawaii Herald
Honolulu Advertiser
Honolulu Star-Bulletin
Japanese-American Courier
Japan Times and Mail
Japan Weekly Mail
Life
Los Angeles Daily News
Los Angeles Examiner
Los Angeles Times
New York Clipper
New York Times
Oakland Post-Enquirer
Oakland Tribune
Outing
Pacific Stars and Stripes
Reach Official Base Ball Guide
Sacramento Bee
San Francisco Call-Bulletin
San Francisco Chronicle
San Francisco Examiner
San Jose Mercury Herald
Santa Maria Daily Times
Seattle Daily Times
Seattle Post-Intelligencer
Spalding's Official Base Ball Guide
Sporting Life
Sporting News
Tacoma News Tribune
Time
Vancouver Sun
Washington Post

JAPANESE LANGUAGE (INCLUDING JAPANESE AMERICAN PERIODICALS)
Asahi Shinbun
Bēsubōru
Daihoku Nippō
Deirī Supōtsu
Hawaii Hōchi
Hōchi Shinbun
Hokubei Asahi Shinbun
Kashū Mainichi Shinbun
Kokumin Shinbun
Kyōjō Nippō
Jiji Shinpō
Mainichi Shinbun
Manshū Nichinichi Shinbun
Nagoya Shinbun
Nichibei Shinbun
Nippon
Nippon Keizai Shinbun
Nippu Jiji
Rafu Shinpō
Supōtsu Nippon
Tairiku Nippō
Tokyo Asahi Shinbun
Tokyo Nichinichi Shinbun
Undōkai
Undōsekai
Yakyūkai
Yomiuri Shinbun
Yorozu Chōhō

Books, Articles, and Unpublished Works

Abe, Ikuo. "Historical Significance of the Far Eastern Championship Games: An International Political Arena." *Tsukuba Daigaku Taiiku Kagaku-kei kiyō* 27 (2003): 37–68.

Adachi, Pat. *Asahi: A Legend in Baseball*. Etobicoke, ON: Coronex, 1992.

———. *Road to the Pinnacle: Sequel to Asahi: A Legend in Baseball*. Etobicoke, ON: Coronex, 2004.

Aida, Yōichi, *Aa Abekyūjō Konpekino Soranikiyu*. Tokyo: Bēsubōru Magajinsha, 1987.

Alexander, Charles C. *Breaking the Slump: Baseball in the Depression Era*. New York: Columbia University Press, 2002.

———. *John McGraw*. New York: Viking, 1988.

———. *Ty Cobb*. New York: Oxford University Press, 1984.

Alexander, Mary C., and Charlotte P. Dodge. *Punahou, 1841–1841*. Berkeley: University Of California Press, 1941.

Appadurai, Arjun. *Modern at Large: Cultural Dimensions of Globalization*. Minneapolis: University of Minnesota Press, 1996.

Ardolino, Frank. "Missionaries, Cartwright, and Spalding: The Development of Baseball in Nineteenth-Century Hawaii." *Nine* 10, no. 2 (2002): 27–45.

———. "Sluggers in Paradise: Major League Visits to Hawaii, 1888–1934." *National Pastime* 12 (1992): 20–22.

Ariyama, Teruo. *Kōshienyakyū to Nipponjin*. Tokyo: Yoshikawa Kōbunkan, 1997.

Arnaud, Pierre, and James Riordan. *Sport and International Politics: The Impact of Fascism and Communism on Sport*. London: Routledge, 1998.

Asahara, Bunpei. *Nippon Kaiun Hattatsushi*. Tokyo: Shichōsha, 1978.

Auslin, Michael R. *Negotiating with Imperialism: The Unequal Treaties and the Culture of Japanese Diplomacy*. Cambridge, MA: Harvard University Press, 2004.

———. *Pacific Cosmopolitans: A Cultural History of U.S.-Japan Relations*. Cambridge, MA: Harvard University Press, 2011.

Axelson, G. W. *"Commy": The Life Story of Charles A. Comiskey*. Chicago: Reilly and Lea, 1919.

Azuma, Eiichiro. *Between Two Empires: Race, History, and Transnationalism in Japanese America*. New York: Oxford University Press, 2005.

———. "Brokering Race, Culture, and Citizenship: Japanese Americans in Occupied Japan and Post National Inclusion." *Journal of American–East Asian Relations* 16, no. 3 (2009): 1–29.

———. "'Pioneers of Overseas Japanese Development': Japanese American History and the Making of Expansionist Orthodoxy in Imperial Japan." *Journal of Asian Studies* 67, no. 4 (2008): 1186–1226.

Baderman, Gale. *Manliness and Civilization*. Chicago: University of Chicago Press, 1996.

Baldassaro, Lawrence, and Richard A. Johnson, eds. *The American Game: Baseball and Ethnicity*. Carbondale: Southern Illinois University Press, 2002.

Bankers, James. *The Pittsburgh Crawfords*. Dubuque, IA: Wm. C. Brown, 1991.

Beauchamp, Edward R., and Akira Iriye, eds. *Foreign Employees in Nineteenth-Century Japan*. Boulder, CO: Westview Press, 1990.

Belamonte, Laura A. *Selling the American Way: U.S. Propaganda and the Cold War.* Philadelphia: University of Pennsylvania Press, 2010.
Bender, Thomas, ed. *Rethinking American History in a Global Age.* Berkeley: University of California Press, 2003.
Berg, Peter I. "A Mission on the Midway: Amos Alonzo Stagg and the Gospel of Football." Ph.D. diss., Michigan State University, 1996.
Berlage, Gai Ingham. *Women in Baseball.* Westport, CT: Praeger, 1994.
Betts, John R. *America's Sporting Heritage, 1850–1950.* Reading, MA: Addison-Wesley, 1947.
———. "Sporting Journalism in Nineteenth Century America." *American Quarterly* 5 (1953): 39–56.
———. "The Technological Revolution and the Rise of Sport." *Mississippi Valley Historical Review* 45 (1953): 231–56.
Beverage, Richard E. *Hollywood Stars: Baseball in Movieland 1926–57.* Placentia, CA: Deacon Press, 1984.
Bjarkman, Peter C. *Diamonds around the Globe: The Encyclopedia of International Baseball.* Westport, CT: Greenwood Press, 2005.
Blackfield, William J. "A War Within: The Making of *Know Your Enemy—Japan.*" *Sight and Sound: International Film Quarterly* 52, no. 2 (1983): 128–33.
Blackwood, Thomas. "Through Sweat and Tears: High School Baseball and the Socialization of Japanese Boys." Ph.D. diss., University of Michigan, 2005.
Block, David. *Baseball before We Knew It: A Search for the Roots of the Game.* Lincoln: University of Nebraska Press, 2006.
Blower, Brooke L. *Becoming Americans in Paris: Transatlantic Politics and Culture between the World Wars.* New York: Oxford University Press, 2011.
Braisted, William Reynolds. *The United States Navy in the Pacific, 1897–1909.* Austin: University of Texas Press, 1958.
Broe, Bob. *Baseball's Barnum: Ray "Hap" Dumont.* Wichita: Center for Entrepreneurship, Wichita State University, 1989.
Browne, Lois. *Girls of Summer: In Their Own League.* Toronto: HarperCollins, 1993.
Brownell, Susan. *The 1904 Anthropology Days and Olympic Games.* Lincoln: University of Nebraska Press, 2009.
Bruce, Janet. *The Kansas City Monarchs: Champions of Black Baseball.* Lawrence: University Press of Kansas, 1984.
Buchanan, Ian. "Elwood S. Brown: Missionary Extraordinary." *Journal of Olympic History* 6, no. 3 (1998): 12–15.
Bullock, Steven R. *Playing for Their Nation: Baseball and the American Military during World War II.* Lincoln: University of Nebraska Press, 2004.
Burgos, Adrian, Jr. *Playing America's Game: Baseball, Latinos, and the Color Line.* Berkeley: University of California Press, 2007.
Butch, Richard, ed. *For Fun and Profit: The Transformation of Leisure into Consumption.* Philadelphia: Temple University Press, 1990.
Cahn, Susan. *Coming on Strong: Gender and Sexuality in Twentieth-Century Women's Sport.* Cambridge, MA: Harvard University Press, 1994.

Cassuto, Leonard, and Stephen Partridge, eds. *The Cambridge Companion to Baseball.* New York: Cambridge University Press, 2011.

Chang, Gordon, and Eiichiro Azuma, eds. *Before Internment: Essays in Prewar Japanese American History.* Stanford, CA: Stanford University Press, 2006.

Checkland, Olive. *Britain's Encounter with Meiji Japan, 1868–1912.* Basingstoke, Hampshire: Macmillan, 1989.

Chikanesawa, Toshihiro. *Takaruzuka Senryaku.* Tokyo: Kōdansha, 1994.

Cisneros, Pedro Treto. *The Mexican League.* Jefferson, NC: McFarland, 2002.

Clark, Daniel A. *Creating the College Man: American Mass Magazines and Middle-Class Manhood, 1890–1915.* Madison, WI: University of Wisconsin Press, 2000.

Clunas, Craig. "Modernity Global and Local: Consumption and the Rise of the West." *American Historical Review* 104 (1999): 1497–1511.

Coffman, Tom. *Nation Within: The Story of America's Annexation of the Nation of Hawai'i.* Kane'ohe, HI: EPI Center, 1998.

Coke, Robert. "Ersatz Octobers: Baseball Barnstorming." *Baseball History* 4 (1999): 75–103.

Collins, Sandra. *The 1940 Tokyo Games.* London: Routledge, 2008.

Cooper, Frederick. *Colonialism in Question: Theory, Knowledge, History.* Berkeley: University of California Press, 2005.

Cramer, Richard Ben. *Joe DiMaggio: The Hero's Life.* New York: Touchstone, 2000.

Crawford, Bill. *All American: The Rise and Fall of Jim Thorpe.* New York: John Wiley and Sons, 2005.

Crepeau, Richard C. *Baseball: America's Diamond Mind, 1919–1941.* Orlando: University Presses of Florida, 1980.

———. "Pearl Harbor: A Failure of Baseball?" *Journal of Popular Culture* 15, no. 4 (1982): 67–74.

Cull, Nicholas J. *The Cold War and the United States Information Agency.* Cambridge: Cambridge University Press, 2008.

Cumings, Bruce: *Dominion from Sea to Sea: Pacific Ascendancy and American Power.* New Haven, CT: Yale University Press, 2009.

Date, Masao. *Watashino Shōwa Yakyūshi.* Tokyo: Bēsubōru Magajinsha, 1988.

Davidann, Jon Thares. *A World of Crisis and Progress.* Bethlehem, PA: Lehigh University Press, 1993.

Dawidoff, Nicholas. *The Catcher Was a Spy: The Mysterious Life of Moe Berg.* New York: Vintage, 1994.

Daws, Gavan. *Shoal of Time: A History of the Hawaiian Islands.* Honolulu: University Of Hawaii Press, 1968.

De-Hart, Evelyn, ed. *Across the Pacific: Asian American and Globalization.* Philadelphia: Temple University Press, 1999.

Derby, Richard E., Jr., and Jim Coleman. "House of David Baseball." *National Pastime* 14 (1994): 7–10.

Deuchler, Martina. *Confucian Gentlemen and Barbarian Envoys: The Opening of Korea, 1875–1885.* Seattle: University of Washington Press, 1977.

Dobbins, Dick, and Jon Twichell. *Nuggets on the Diamond: Professional Baseball in the Bay Area from the Gold Rush to the Present.* San Francisco: Woodford Press, 1994.

Domosh, Mona. *American Commodities in an Age of Empire*. New York: Routledge, 2006.
Dower, John W. *Embracing Defeat: Japan in the Wake of World War II*. New York: Norton, 1999.
———. *War without Mercy: Race and Power in the Pacific War*. New York: Pantheon, 1986.
Dubois, Lauren. *Soccer Empire: The World Cup and the Future of France*. Berkeley: University of California Press, 2011.
Duus, Peter. *The Abacus and the Sword: The Japanese Penetration of Korea, 1895–1910*. Berkeley: University of California Press, 1998.
Duus, Peter, Ramon H. Myers, and Mark R. Peattie. *The Japanese Wartime Empire, 1931–1945*. Princeton, NJ: Princeton University Press, 1996.
Dyreson, Mark. "The Emergence of Consumer Culture and the Transformation of Physical Culture: American Sport in the 1920s." *Journal of Sports History* 16 (Fall 1989): 261–81.
———. "The Endless Olympic Bid: Los Angeles and the Making of the American West." *Journal of the West* 47 (Fall 2008): 26–39.
———. *Making the American Team: Sport, Culture, and the Olympic Experience*. Urbana: University of Illinois Press, 1997.
———. "Nature by Design: Modern American Ideas about Sport, Energy, Evolution, and Republics, 1865–1920." *Journal of Sport History* 26, no. 3 (Fall 1999): 447–69.
———. "The Playing Fields of Progress: American Athletic Nationalism and the 1904 St. Louis Olympics." *Gateway Heritage* 16, no. 2 (Fall 1993): 4–23.
Echevarría, Roberto González. *The Pride of Havana: A History of Cuban Baseball*. New York: Oxford University Press, 1999.
Eckert, Carter. *Offspring of Empire: The Koch'ang Kims and the Colonial Origins of Korean Capitalism, 1876–1945*. Seattle: University of Washington Press, 1991.
Eckes, Alfred, Jr., and Thomas W. Zeiler, eds. *Globalization and the American Century*. Cambridge: Cambridge University Press, 2003.
Elfers, James E. *The Tour to End All Tours: The Story of Major League Baseball's 1913–1914 World Tour*. Lincoln: University of Nebraska Press, 2003.
Elias, Robert, ed. *Baseball and the American Dream: Race, Class, Gender and the National Pastime*. Armonk, NY: M. E. Sharpe, 2001.
———. *The Empire Strikes Out: How Baseball Sold U.S. Foreign Policy and Promoted the American Way Abroad*. New York: New Press, 2010.
Erenberg, Lewis. *The Greatest Fight of Our Generation: Louis vs. Schmeling*. New York: Oxford University Press, 2005.
Ericson, Steven J. *The Sound of the Whistle: Railroad and the State in Meiji Japan*. Cambridge, MA: Harvard University Press, 1996.
Espinosa, Mariola. *Epidemic Invasions: Yellow Fever and the Limits of Cuban Independence, 1878–1930*. Chicago: University of Chicago Press, 2009.
Farrel, Frank, and M. Dick Bunnell. *World Tour, National and American League Base Ball Teams: October 1913–March 1914*. Chicago: S. Blake Willsden, 1914.
Feldman, Fay. "Baseball behind Barbed Wire." *National Pastime* 12 (1992): 38–39.

Finoli, David. *For the Good of the Country: World War II Baseball in the Major and Minor Leagues*. Jefferson, NC: McFarland, 2002.
Fiset, Louis, and Gail Nomura, eds. *Nikkei in the Pacific Northwest*. Seattle: University of Washington Press, 2005.
Fitts, Robert K. *Remembering Japanese Baseball: An Oral History of the Game*. Carbondale: Southern Illinois University Press, 2005.
———. *Wally Yonamine: The Man Who Changed Japanese Baseball*. Lincoln: University of Nebraska Press, 2008.
Forbes, W. Cameron. *The Philippine Islands*. Rev. ed. Cambridge, MA: Harvard University Press, 1945.
Franks, Joel S. *Crossing Sidelines, Crossing Cultures*. Lanham, MD: University Press of America, 2000.
———. *Hawaiian Sports in the Twentieth Century*. Lewiston, NY: Edwin Mellen Press, 2002.
———. *Whose Baseball? The National Pastime and Cultural Diversity in California, 1859–1941*. Lanham, MD: Scarecrow Press, 2001.
Friedrich, Otto. *City of Nets: A Portrait of Hollywood in the 1940*. New York: Harper and Row, 1986.
Frost, Dennis. *Seeing Stars: Sports Celebrity, Identity, and Body Culture in Modern Japan*. Cambridge, MA: Harvard University Press, 2010.
Fujita, Fumiko. *Hokkaidōwo Kaitakushita Amerikajin*. Tokyo: Shinchōsha, 1993.
Furuhashi, Hironoshin, *Rikiei 30nen*. Tokyo: Nippontoshosentā, 1997.
Furukawa, Takahisa. *Kōki, Banbapku, Orinpikku*. Tokyo: Chūkōshinsho, 1998.
Furuta, Kazuko. "Shanhai Nettowākuno nakano Kobe." In *Meiji Ishinno Kakushin to Renzoku*, edited by Kindai Nippon Kenkyūkai, 203–26. Tokyo: Yamakawa Shoten, 1992.
———. *Shanhai Nettowāku to Kindai Higashi Ajia*. Tokyo: Tokyo Daigaku Shuppankai, 2000.
Gallicchio, Marc. *The African American Encounter with Japan and China: Black Internationalism in Asia, 1895–1945*. Chapel Hill: University of North Carolina Press, 2000.
Gems, Gerald. *The Athletic Crusade: Sport and American Cultural Imperialism*. Lincoln: University of Nebraska Press, 2006.
Gilbert, Daniel A. "Expanding the Strike Zone: Baseball in the Age of Free Agency." Ph.D. diss., Yale University, 2003.
Gmelch, George, ed. *Baseball without Borders: The International Pastime*. Lincoln: University of Nebraska Press, 2006.
Goldstein, Richard. *Spartan Seasons: How Baseball Survived the Second World War*. New York: Macmillan, 1980.
Goldstein, Warren. *Playing for Keeps: A History of Early Baseball*. Ithaca, NY: Cornell University Press, 1989.
Gordon, Andrew. *A Modern History of Japan*. New York: Oxford University Press, 2009.
Gordon, Marquis L. *An American Missionary in Japan*. Boston: Houghton Mifflin, 1892.

Goto, Chinpei. *Yakyū Hyakunen Kinen Hawaii Hōjin Yakyūshi*. Honolulu: Yakyūhyakunensai-hōjinyakyūshi Shuppankai, 1940.
Gotō, Norio. *Sensetsuno Yakyūchīmu: Bankūbā Asahimonogatari*. Tokyo: Iwanami Shoten, 2010.
Gregorich, Barbara. "Stranded." *North American Review* 283, no. 3/4 (May/August 1998): 6–9.
———. "Blues, Bloomers, and Bobbies." *Pennsylvania Heritage* 19, no. 3 (September 1993): 32–37.
———. *Women at Play: The Story of Women in Baseball*. New York: Harcourt, 1993.
Grew, Joseph C. *Ten Years in Japan*. New York: Simon and Schuster, 1944.
Gripentrog, John. "The Transnational Pastime: Baseball and American Perceptions of Japan in the 1930s." *Diplomatic History* 34, no. 2 (2010): 247–73.
Guschov, Stephen D. *The Red Stockings of Cincinnati*. Jefferson, NC: McFarland, 1998.
Guttman, Allen. *From Ritual to Record: The Nature of Modern Sports*. New York: Columbia University Press, 1978.
———. *Games and Empires: Modern Sports and Cultural Imperialism*. New York: Columbia University Press, 1995.
Guttman, Allen, and Lee Thompson. *Japanese Sports: A History*. Honolulu: University of Hawaii Press, 2000.
Gyorō, Hashinami. *Daigaku Gakusei Sōgen*. Tokyo: Nipponsha, 1910.
Hanshindenki Kabushiki Kaisha. *Yusōbōshino Gojūnen*. Osaka: Hanshindenki Co., 1955.
Hara, Takeshi. *Minto Ōsakato Teito Tōkyo*. Tokyo: Kōdansha, 1998.
Hara, Yutaka. *Hebonjukuni Tsuranaruhitobito*. Tokyo: Meiji Gakuin Sābisu, 2008.
Harada, Cappy (Tsuneo). *Taiheiyōno Kakehashi: Sengoyakyūfukkatsuno Uramenshi*. Tokyo: Bēsubōru Magajinsha, 1980.
Hargreaves, John. *Sport, Power, and Culture: A Social and Historical Analysis of Popular Sports in Britain*. Cambridge, UK: Polity Press, 1986.
Harland-Jacobs, Jessica L. *Builders of Empire: Freemasons and British Imperialism, 1717–1927*. Chapel Hill: University of North Carolina Press, 2007.
Hashimoto, Kazuo. *Nippon Supōtsu Hōsōshi*. Tokyo: Taishūkan, 1992.
Hatano, Masaru. *Nichibeiyakyūshi*. Tokyo: PHP Shinsho, 2001.
Headrick, Daniel R. *The Tools of Empire: Technology and European Imperialism in the Nineteenth Century*. New York: Oxford University Press, 1981.
Heaphy, Leslie A., ed. *Satchel Paige and Company*. Jefferson, NC: McFarland, 2007.
Henderson, Robert W. "How Baseball Began." *New York Public Library Bulletin* 41 (April 1937): 287–91.
Henning, Joseph. *Outposts of Civilization: Race, Religion, and the Formative Years of American-Japanese Relations*. New York: New York University Press, 2000.
Hirahara, Naomi. *An American Son: The Story of George Aratani, Founder of Mikasa and Kenwood*. Los Angeles: Japanese American National Museum, 2001.
Hirano, Kyoko. *Mr. Smith Goes to Tokyo: Japanese Cinema under the American Occupation, 1945–1952*. Washington, D.C., and London: Smithsonian Institution Press, 1992.
Hirobe, Izumi. *Gurū: Shinno Nipponno Tomo*. Kyoto: Minerva Shobō, 2011.

———. *Japanese Pride, American Prejudice: Modifying the Exclusion Clause of the 1924 Immigration Act*. Stanford: Stanford University Press, 2001.
Hirohata, Seiji. *Shūsenno Rasutogēmu*. Tokyo: Honnoizumisha, 2005.
Hirose, Kenzō. *Nippon Yakyūshi*. Tokyo: Nippon yakyūshi kankōkai, 1963.
———. *Sōkeiyakyūshi*. Tokyo: Sanseidō, 1928.
Hoare, J. E. *Japan's Treaty Ports and Foreign Settlements*. Kent, CT: Japan Library, 1994.
Hoganson, Kristin. *Consumers' Imperium: The Global Production of American Domesticity, 1865–1920*. Chapel Hill: University of North Carolina Press, 2007.
Holtzman, Jerome. *Commissioners: Baseball's Midlife Crisis*. New York: Total Sports, 1998.
Hopkins, A. G., ed. *Globalization in World History*. New York: Norton, 2002.
Howell, Colin D. "Baseball and Borders: The Diffusion of Baseball into Mexican and Canadian-American Borderland Regions, 1885–1811." *Nine* 11, no. 2 (2003): 16–26.
Humber, William. *Cheering for the Home Team: The Story of Baseball in Canada*. Erin, ON: Boston Mills Press, 1983.
———. *Diamonds of the North: A Concise History of Baseball in Canada*. Toronto: Oxford University Press, 1995.
Ichioka, Hiroshige, and Ami Fukunaga. *Puroyakyūwosukuttaotoko Cappy Harada*. Tokyo: Soft Bank Creative, 2009.
Iino, Masako. *Mouhitotsuno Nichibeikankeishi*. Tokyo: Yūhikaku, 2000.
Ikehata, Setsuho, and Lydia N. Yu Jose, eds. *Kingendai Nipponfiripin Kankeishi*. Tokyo: Iwanami Shoten 2004.
Ikei, Masaru. *Hakkyū Taiheiyōwo Wataru*. Tokyo: Chūo Kōron Shinsha, 1974.
———. *Harō Sutanka Genkikai*. Tokyo: Sōryūsha, 1983.
Imada, Adria. "Hawaiians on Tour: Hula Circuits through the American Empire." *American Quarterly* 56, no. 1 (2004): 111–49.
Inoue, Toshikazu. *Kikinonakano Kyōchōgaikō*. Tokyo: Iwanami Shoten, 1994.
Iriye, Akira. *Cultural Internationalism and World Order*. Baltimore: Johns Hopkins University Press, 1997.
———. *Global Community: The Role of International Organizations in the Making of the Contemporary World*. Berkeley: University of California Press, 2004.
———. *Pacific Estrangement: Japanese and American Expansion, 1897–1911*. Cambridge, MA: Harvard University Press, 1972.
———. *Power and Culture: The Japanese-American War, 1941–1945*. Cambridge, MA: Harvard University Press, 1982.
Ishii, Kanji. *Jōbōtsushinnoshakaishi*. Tokyo: Yūhikaku, 1994.
———. *Nippon Keizaishi*. Tokyo: Tōyōdaigaku Shuppankai, 1976.
Jacobs, Martin, and Jack McGuire. *San Francisco Seals*. Charleston, SC: Arcadia, 2005.
Johnson, Lloyd, and Miles Wolff. *The Encyclopedia of Minor League Baseball*. 2nd rev. ed. Durham, NC: Baseball America, 1997.
Johnson, Susan Lee. *Roaring Camp: The Social World of the California Gold Rush*. New York: W. W. Norton, 2000.
Jones, David. *Joe DiMaggio*. Westport CT: Greenwood Press, 2004.
Kabushiki Kaisha Hanshintaigāsu, ed. *Hanshintaigasu Showanoayumi*. Osaka: Hanshintaigāsu, 1991.

Kagawa, Mari. *Sanfuranshikoniokeru Nipponjingakudō Kakurimondai*. Tokyo: Ronsōsha, 1994.
Kanda, Junji, *Yakyū Dendō Monogatari*. Tokyo: Bēsubōru Magajinsha, 1992.
———. *Shiki to Bēsubōru*. Tokyo: Bēsubōru Magajinsha, 1991.
Kang, Wi Jo. *Christ and Caesar in Modern Korea: A History of Christianity and Politics*. Albany: State University of New York Press, 1997.
Kaufman, Louis, Barbara Fitzgerald, and Tom Sewell. *Moe Berg: Athlete, Scholar, Spy*. Boston: Little Brown, 1974.
Kawasaki, Tokuji. *Sensōto Yakyū*. Tokyo: Bēsubōru Magajinsha, 1997.
Keiōgijuku Taiikukai Yakyūbu Hensaniinkai. *Keiōgijuku Yakyūbushi*. Tokyo: Keiogijuku-yakyūbu, 1960.
Kelly, William. "Is Baseball a Global Sport? America's 'National Pastime' as Global Field and International Sport." *Global Networks: A Journal of Transnational Affairs* 7, no. 2 (2007): 187–201.
———. "Kōshien Stadium: Performing National Virtues and Regional Rivalries in a 'Theater of Sport.'" *Sport in Society* 14, no. 4 (2011): 481–93.
———. "Samurai Baseball: The Vicissitudes of a National Sporting Style." *International Journal of the History of Sport* 26, no. 3 (2009): 429–41.
———, ed. *Fanning the Flames: Fans and Consumer Culture in Contemporary Japan*. Albany: State University of New York Press, 2004.
Keys, Barbara J. *Globalizing Sport: National Rivalry and International Community in the 1930s*. Cambridge, MA: Harvard University Press, 2006.
Kikkawa, Takeo, and Nara Takashi. *Fankaramita Puroyakūuno Rekishi*. Tokyo: Nippon Keizai Hyōronsha, 2009.
Kiku, Kōichi. *Kindai Puro Supōtsuno Rekishi Shakaigaku*. Tokyo: Fumaidō, 1993.
Kim, Bang-Chool. "Professional Baseball in Korea: Origins, Causes, Consequences and Implications." *International Journal of the History of Sport* 25, no. 3 (2008): 372–85.
Kimijima, Ichirō, *Nippon Yakyū Sōseiki*. Tokyo: Bēsubōru Magajinsha, 1972.
Kinoshita, Hideaki. *Supōtsuno Kindai Nipponshi*. Tokyo: Kyōrin Shoin, 1970.
Kirsch, George. *Baseball in Blue and Gray: The National Pastime during the Civil War*. Princeton, NJ: Princeton University Press, 2003.
———. *The Creation of American Team Sports: Baseball and Cricket, 1938–72*. Urbana: University of Illinois Press, 1989.
Kishi, Toshihiko, and Yuka Tsuchiya, eds. *Bunkareisennojidai: Amerikatoajia*. Tokyo: Kokusai Shoin, 2009.
Kitamura, Hiroshi. *Screening Enlightenment: Hollywood and the Cultural Reconstruction of Defeated Japan*. Ithaca, NY: Cornell University Press, 2010.
Klein, Alan M. *Growing the Game: The Globalization of Major League Baseball*. New Haven, CT: Yale University Press, 2006.
———. *Sugarball: The American Game, the Dominican Dream*. New Haven, CT: Yale University Press, 1991.
Kohara, Junnosuke. "Meijiki nichibei gaikō ni okeru oyatoi gaikokujin: Denison to stebunsu wo chūshinni." M.A. thesis, Keio University, 2009.

Koikari, Mire, *Pedagogy of Democracy: Feminism and the Cold War in the U.S. Occupation of Japan*. Philadelphia: Temple University Press, 2008.

Kokaze, Hidemasa. *Teikokushugika no Nippon Kaiun*. Tokyo: Yamakawa Shuppan, 1995.

Kōrakuen Stajiamu. *Kōrakuen no 25nen*. Tokyo: Kōrakuen Stadium Co., 1963.

Koshimoto, Hitoshi. *Beikokuenseiki*. Tokyo: Tsudakikurō, 1929.

———. *Watashino Yakyū*. Tokyo: Sanseidō, 1928.

Kōtsu, Masaru. *Nippon Kindai Supōtsushino Teiryū*. Tokyo: Sōbun Kikaku, 1994.

Kramer, Paul. *The Blood of Government: Race, Empire, the United States, and the Philippines*. Chapel Hill: University of North Carolina Press, 2006.

———. "Race and Empire Revisited at the Philippines Exposition, St. Louis, 1901–1905." *Radical History Review* 73 (Winter 1999): 75–115.

Kuklick, Bruce. *To Every Thing a Season: Shibe Park and Urban Philadelphia, 1909–1976*. Princeton, NJ: Princeton University Press, 1991.

Kurashige, Lon. *Japanese American Celebration and Conflict: A History of Ethnic Identity and Festival in Los Angeles, 1934–1990*. Berkeley: University of California Press, 2002.

Kurashige, Scott. *The Shifting Grounds of Race: Black and Japanese Americans in the Making of Multiethnic Los Angeles*. Princeton: Princeton University Press, 2010.

Kussuth, Robert. "Boondoggling, Baseball, and the WPA." *Nine* 9, nos. 1 and 2 (2001): 56–71.

Kuwabara, Ietoshi. *Onnatachino Purēbōru*. Tokyo: Fūjinsha, 1993.

Kyle, Donald G., and Robert B. Fairbanks, eds. *Baseball in America and America in Baseball*. College Station: Texas A&M University Press, 2008.

LaFeber, Walter F. *The Clash: A History of U.S.-Japanese Relations throughout History*. New York: Norton, 1997.

———. *Michael Jordan and the New Global Capitalism*. New York: Norton, 2002.

———. *The New Empire: An Interpretation of American Expansionism, 1860–1898*. Ithaca, NY: Cornell University Press, 1963.

———. "Presidential Address: Technology and U.S. Foreign Relations." *Diplomatic History* 24, no. 1 (2000): 1–7.

Lamster, Mark. *Spalding's World Tour: The Epic Adventure That Took Baseball around the Globe—and Made It America's Game*. New York: Public Affairs, 2006.

Lanctot, Neil. *Negro League Baseball: The Rise and Ruin of a Black Institution*. Philadelphia: University of Pennsylvania Press, 2004.

Lange, Fred W. *History of Baseball in California and Pacific Coast Leagues, 1847–1938*. Oakland, CA: Fred Lange, 1938.

Lawson, Hal A., and Alan G. Ingham. "Conflicting Ideologies Concerning the University and Intercollegiate Athletics: Harper and Hutchins at Chicago, 1892–1940." *Journal of Sport History* 7, no. 3 (1930): 37–46.

Lee, Shelley Sang-Hee. *Claiming the Oriental Gateway: Prewar Seattle and Japanese America*. Philadelphia: Temple University Press, 2010.

Leonard, Kevin Allen. "'Is That What We Fought For?' Japanese Americans and Racism in California, the Impact of World War II." *Western Historical Quarterly* 21, no. 4 (1990): 463–82.

Lester, Robin. *Stagg's University*. Urbana: University of Illinois Press, 1995.
Leutzinger, Richard. *Lefty O'Doul: The Legend That Baseball Nearly Forgot*. Carmel, CA: Carmel Bay Publishing Group, 1997.
Levine, Peter. *A. G. Spalding and the Rise of Baseball*. New York: Oxford University Press, 1985.
———. *Ellis Island to Ebbets Field: Sport and the American Jewish Experience*. New York: Oxford University Press, 1993.
Lieb, Fred. *Baseball As I Have Known It*. New York: Coward, McCann and Geoghegan, 1977.
Love, Eric. *Race over Empire: Racism and U.S. Imperialism, 1865–1900*. Chapel Hill: University of North Carolina Press, 2004.
Mackey, R. Scott. *Barbary Baseball: The Pacific Coast League of the 1920s*. Jefferson, NC: McFarland, 1995.
Madden, W. C. *The Women of the All-American Girls Professional Baseball League*. Jefferson, NC: McFarland, 1997.
Mangan, J. A., ed. *The Cultural Bond: Sport, Empire, Society*. London: Frank Cass, 1992.
Markovits, Andrei S. "The Other 'American Exceptionalism': Why Is There No Soccer in the United States?" *International Journal of History of Sports* 7, no. 2 (1990): 230–64.
Markovits, Andrei S., and Steven L. Hellerman. *Offside: Soccer and American Exceptionalism*. Princeton, NJ: Princeton University Press, 2001.
Marshall, William. *Baseball's Pivotal Era, 1945–1951*. Lexington: University of Kentucky Press, 1999.
Martin, Jay. *Live All You Can: Alexander Joy Cartwright and the Invention of Modern Baseball*. New York: Columbia University Press, 2009.
Masuda, Hiroshi. *MacArthur*. Tokyo: Chūō Kōronsha, 2009.
Maguire, Joseph. *Global Sport: Identities, Societies, Civilizations*. Cambridge, UK: Polity Press, 1999.
McKeown, Adam. *Chinese Migrant Networks and Cultural Change: Peru, China and Hawaii, 1900–1936*. Chicago: University of Chicago Press, 2001.
———. *Melancholy Order: Asian Migration and the Globalization of Borders*. New York: Columbia University Press, 2010.
———. "Periodizing Globalization." *History Workshop Journal* 63, no. 1 (2007): 218–30.
McNeil, William F. *The California Winter League*. Jefferson, NC: McFarland, 2002.
Meiji Gakuin, ed. *Meiji Gakuin Hachijunenshi*. Tokyo: Meiji Gakuin, 1959.
———, ed. *Meiji Gakuin Hyakunenshi*. Tokyo: Meiji Gakuin, 1977.
Miller, Glenn W., and Jimmy M. Skaggs, eds. *Metropolitan Wichita: Past, Present, and Future*. Lawrence: Regents Press of Kansas, 1978.
Miller, James Edward. *The Baseball Business: Pursuing Pennants and Profits in Baltimore*. Chapel Hill: University of North Carolina Press, 1990.
Miura, Akio. *Kitataiheiyo Teikikyakusenshi*. Tokyo: Shuppankyodosha, 1994.
Miyamoto, Atsuo, *Kokakōraenomichi*. Tokyo: Kanō Shobō, 1994.
Miyoshi, Nobuhiro. *Nippon Kyōiku no Kaikoku*. Tokyo: Fukumura Shuppan, 1986.
Mizuhara, Shigeru. *Watashinoayunda Yakyūseikatsu*. Tokyo: Bēsubōru Magajinsha, 1962.

Mizuno, Kenjirō, *Supōtsuwa Rikukara Umikara Ōzorae*. Tokyo: Mizuno, 1973.
Moffi, Larry. *The Conscience of the Game: Baseball's Commissioners from Landis to Selig*. Lincoln, NE: University of Nebraska Press, 2006.
Montville, Leigh. *Ted Williams: The Biography of an American Hero*. New York: Doubleday, 2004.
Moore, Jack B. *Joe DiMaggio: A Biography*. Westport, CT: Greenwood, 1986.
Morgan, William Michael. *Pacific Gibraltar: U.S.-Japanese Rivalry over the Annexation of Hawai'i, 1885–1898*. Annapolis, MD: Naval Institute Press, 2011.
Morris, Andrew. *Colonial Project, National Game: A History of Baseball in Taiwan*. Berkeley: University of California Press, 2011.
———. *Marrow of the Nation: A History of Sport and Physical Culture in Republican China*. Berkeley: University of California Press, 2004.
Morris, Peter. *But Didn't We Have Fun? An Informal History of Baseball's Pioneer Era, 1843–1870*. Chicago: Ivan R. Dee, 2008.
Motz, Marilyn Ferris, and Pat Browne, eds. *Making the American Home: Middle-Class Women and Domestic Material Culture, 1840–1940*. Bowling Green, OH: Bowling Green State University Popular Press, 1988.
Murdock, Eugene C. *Ban Johnson: Czar of Baseball*. Westport, CT: Greenwood Press, 1982.
Nagamine, Shigetoshi. *"Dokushokokumin" no Tanj*. Tokyo: Nippon Editor School Shuppanbu, 2004.
Nagata, Akifumi. *Seodoarūzuberutoto Kankoku*. Tokyo: Miraisha, 1992.
Nagata, Yoichi. *Bēsubōruno Shakaishi: Jimīhoriotonichibeiyakyū*. Osaka: Tōhōshuppan, 1994.
———. "The First All-Asian Pitching Duel in Organized Baseball." *Baseball Research Journal* 21 (1992): 13–14.
———. *Tōkyō Jaiants Hokubeitairiku Enseiki 1935*. Osaka: Tōhōshuppan, 2007.
Nakagawa, Fusa, *Tosakara Hawaie: Okumura Takieno Kiseki*. Kōchi: Kōchi Shinbun Kigyō, 2000.
Nakagawa, Kerry-Yo. *Through a Diamond: 100 Years of Japanese American Baseball*. Los Angeles: Rudi Press, 2001.
Nakajima, Yumiko. *Hawaii: Samayoeru Rakuen*. Tokyo: Tokyo Shoseki, 1993.
Nelson, Kevin. *The Golden Game: The Story of California Baseball*. Berkeley: California Historical Society, 2004.
Niiya, Brian, ed. *More Than a Game: Sport in Japanese American Community*. Los Angeles: Japanese American National Museum, 2000.
Nippon Hōsōkyōkai Hōsōshi Henshūshitsu, ed. *Nippon Hōsōshi*. Tokyo: Nipponhōsōkyōkai, 1965.
Nippon Yūsen Kabushiki Kaisha. *Nippon Yūsen Kabushiki Kaisha 70nenshi*. Tokyo: Tokyo Yūsen Kabushiki Kaisha, 1956.
Nishida, Bunshirō, ed. *Meijino Bunmeikaika Kotahajime*. Tokyo: Kinensha, 1969.
Nishiwaki, Yoshitomo. *Manshu Kantoshu Chutogakko Yakyūshi*. Kakogawa, Kyoto: Nishiwaki Yoshimoto, 1999.
———. *Taiwan Chuūtōgakō Yakyūshi*. Kakogawa, Kyoto: Nishiwaki Yoshimoto, 1996.
Noguchi, Tsutomu, ed. *Nippon Puroyakyū 30nen no Rekishi*. Tokyo: Press Tokyo, 1964.

Nordmann, David. "Idealism, Immigration and Imperialism: Durham Stevens and the Rise and Fall of United States Diplomacy with Japan and Korea, 1873–1908." Ph.D. diss., Indiana University, 2001.
Notehelfer, F. G. *American Samurai: Captain L. L. Janes and Japan*. Princeton, NJ: Princeton University Press, 1985.
Nucciarone, Monica. *Alexander Cartwright: The Life behind the Baseball Legend*. Lincoln: University of Nebraska Press, 2009.
Obojski, Robert. *Bush League: A History of Minor League Baseball*. New York: Macmillan, 1975.
———. *The Rise of Japanese Baseball Power*. Radnor, PA: Chilton Books, 1975.
Odo, Franklin. *No Swords to Bury: Japanese Americans in Hawai'i during World War II*. Philadelphia: Temple University Press, 2004.
Okano, Toshishige. *Yomiurishinbun 80nenshi*. Tokyo: Yomiurishinbunsha, 1955.
Okihiro, Gary. *Cane Fires: The Anti-Japanese Movement in Hawaii, 1865–1945*. Philadelphia: Temple University Press, 1991.
———. *The Columbia Guide to Asian American History*. New York: Columbia University Press, 2001.
Okihiro, Michael. *AJA Baseball in Hawaii: Ethnic Pride and Tradition*. Honolulu: Hawai'i Hochi, 1999.
Oku, Sumako, and Haneda Hiroaki, eds. *Toshi to Goraku*. Tokyo: Nihon Keizai Hyōronsha, 2004.
O'Neal, Bill. *The Pacific Coast League, 1903–1988*. Austin, TX: Eakin Press, 1990.
O'Rourke, Kevin H., and Jeffrey G. Williamson. *Globalization and History: The Evolution of a Nineteenth-Century Atlantic Economic*. Cambridge, MA: MIT Press, 1999.
Ōshima, Hiroshi. *Kankokuyakyūno Genryū*. Tokyo: Shinkasha, 2006.
Ōshima, Katsutarō. *Chōsen Yakyūshi*. Kyōjō: Chōsenyakyūshi Hakkōjo, 1932.
Ōshima Masamitsu. *Suisankai no Senku Iōo Kazutaka to Uchimura Kanzō*. Tokyo: Hokusui Kyōkai, 1964.
Ōshima Masatake. *Kurāku Sensei to Sono Deshitachi*. Tokyo: Shinchi Shobō, 1991.
Parrott, Harold. *The Lords of Baseball*. New York: Praeger, 1976.
Patterson, Wayne. *The Korean Frontier in America: Immigration to Hawaii, 1896–1910*. Honolulu: University of Hawaii Press, 1988.
Pearce, Ralph M. *From Asahi to Zebras: Japanese American Baseball in San Jose, California*. San Jose: Japanese American Museum of San Jose, 2005.
Pedlar, Neil. *The Imported Pioneers: Westerners Who Helped Build Modern Japan*. New York: St. Martin's Press, 1990.
Pérez, Louis A., Jr. *On Becoming Cuban: Identity, Nationality, and Culture*. Chapel Hill: University of North Carolina Press, 1999.
———. "We Are the World: Internationalizing the National, Nationalizing the International." *Journal of American History* 89, no. 2 (2002): 558–66.
Peterson, Harold. *The Man Who Invented Baseball*. New York: Charles Scribner's Sons, 1973.
Pietrusza, David. *Baseball's Canadian-American League*. Jefferson, NC: McFarland, 1990.

———. *Judge and Jury: The Life and Times of Judge Kenesaw Mountain Landis.* South Bend, IN: Diamond Communications, 1998.
Pletcher, David. *The Diplomacy of Involvement: American Expansion across the Pacific, 1784–1900.* Columbia: University of Missouri Press, 2001.
Pope, Steven W. "An Army of Athletes: Playing Fields, Battlefields, and the American Military Sporting Experience, 1890–1920." *Journal of Military History* 59 (July 1995): 435–56.
———. "God, Games, and National Glory: Thanksgiving and the Ritual of Sport in American Culture." *International Journal of History of Sport* 10, no. 2 (1993): 242–49.
———. *Patriotic Games: Sporting Traditions in the American Imagination, 1876–1926.* New York: Oxford University Press, 1997.
———. "Rethinking Sport, Empire, and American Exceptionalism. *Sport History Review* 37, no. 2 (2007): 92–120.
Pratt, Mary Louise. *Imperial Eyes: Travel Writing and Transculturation.* 2nd ed. New York: Routledge, 2008.
Puff, Richard. "The Amazing Story of Victor Starffin." *National Pastime* 12 (1992): 17–20.
Putney, Clifford. *Muscular Christianity: Manhood and Sports in Protestant America, 1880–1920.* Cambridge, MA: Harvard University Press, 2001.
Rader, Benjamin G. *Baseball: A History of America's Game.* 2nd rev. ed. Urbana: University of Illinois Press, 2002.
Reaves, Joseph A. *Taking in a Game: A History of Baseball in Asia.* Lincoln: University of Nebraska Press, 2002.
Regalado, Samuel O. "'Play Ball!' Baseball and Seattle's Japanese-American Courier League, 1928–1941." *Pacific Northwest Quarterly* 87, no. 1 (1995): 29–37.
———. "Sport and Community in California's Japanese American Yamato Colony, 1930–1945." *Journal of Sport History* 19 (Summer 1992): 130–43.
———. "Incarcerated Sport: Nisei Women's Softball and Athletics during Japanese American Internment." *Journal of Sport History* 27 (Fall 2000): 431–44.
Revilla, Linda A., Gail N. Nomura, Shawn Wong, and Shirley Hune, eds. *Bearing Dreams, Shaping Visions: Asian Pacific American Perspectives.* Pullman: Washington State University Press, 1993.
Ribowsky, Mark. *Don't Look Back: Satchel Paige in the Shadows of Baseball.* New York: Simon and Shuster, 1994.
Riess, Steven A. *The City Games: The Evolution of American Urban Society and the Rise of Sports.* Urbana: University of Illinois Press, 1991.
———. "Sport and the Redefinition of Middle-Class Masculinity in Victorian America." In *The New American Sport History: Recent Approaches and Perspectives,* edited by Steven W. Pope, 173–97. Urbana: University of Illinois Press, 1997.
———. *Touching Base: Professional Baseball and American Culture in the Progressive Era.* Westport, CT: Greenwood Press, 1980.
Rober, Scott. "Uncovering Satchel Paige's 1935 Season: A Summer in North Dakota." *Baseball Research Journal* 23 (1994): 51–54.
Robertson, Roland. *Globalization: Social Theory and Global Culture.* London: Sage, 1992.

Robinson, Greg. *A Tragedy of Democracy: Japanese Confinement in North America*. New York: Columbia University Press, 2009.
Roden, Donald. "Baseball and the Quest for National Dignity in Meiji Japan." *American Historical Review* 85 (1980): 511–34.
———. *Schoolboys in Imperial Japan: A Study in the Culture of a Student Elite*. Berkeley: University of California Press, 1980.
Rodgers, Daniel T. *Atlantic Crossings: Social Politics in a Progressive Age*. Cambridge, MA: Harvard University Press, 2000.
Rosenberg, Emily. *Spreading the American Dream: American Economic and Cultural Expansion, 1890–1945*. New York: Hill and Wang, 1982.
Ruck, Rob. *Raceball: How the Major Leagues Colonized the Black and Latin Game*. Boston: Beacon Press, 2011.
Runstedtler, Theresa. "Journeymen: Race, Boxing, and the Transnational World of Jack Johnson." Ph.D. diss., Yale University, 2007.
Ruoff, Kenneth J. *Imperial Japan at Its Zenith: The Wartime Celebration of the Empire's 2,600th Anniversary*. Ithaca, NY: Cornell University Press, 2010.
———. *The People's Emperor: Democracy and the Japanese Monarchy, 1945–1995*. Cambridge, MA: Harvard University Press, 2003.
Rydell, Robert W. "The 1939 San Francisco Golden Gate International Rare Book Exposition and the Empire of the West." *European Contributions to American Studies* 16 (1989): 342–59.
Rydell, Robert W., and Rob Kroes. *Buffalo Bill in Bologna: The Americanization of the World, 1869–1922*. Chicago: University of Chicago Press, 2005.
Sakaguchi, Mitsuhiro. *Nipponjin Amerikaiminshi*. Tokyo: Fujishuppan, 2001.
Sakaue, Yasuhiro. *Kenryokusōchitoshiteno Supōtsu*. Tokyo: Kōdansha, 1998.
———. *Nippon Yakyū no Keifugaku*. Tokyo: Seikyūsha, 2001.
Sakaue, Yasuhiro, and Takaoka Hiroyuki, eds. *Maboroshino Tokyo Orinpikkuto Sonojidai*. Tokyo: Seikyūsha, 2009.
Sakurai, Kiyoshi. *Senzenno Nichibeijidōshamasatsu*. Tokyo: Hakutōshobō, 1978.
Sano, Shinichi, *Kyokaiden*. Tokyo: Bungei Shunjūsha, 1994.
Satō, Mitsufusa. *Mouhitotsuno Puroyakyū: Yamamotoeiichirōno Sūkinashōgai*. Tokyo: Asahi Shinbunsha, 1986.
Sayama, Kazuo. *Kuroki Yasashiki Jaiantsu*. Tokyo: Bēsubōru Magajinsha, 1986.
———. *Nichibei Yakyū Uramenshi*. Tokyo: Nipponhōsō Shuppankyōkai, 2005.
Schaller, Michael. *The American Occupation of Japan: The Origins of the Cold War in Asia*. New York: Oxford University Press, 1987.
———. *Douglas MacArthur: The Far Eastern General*. New York: Replica Books, 2001.
Schonberger, Howard B. *Aftermath of War: Americans and the Remaking of Japan, 1945–1952*. Kent, OH: Kent University Press, 1989.
Schulten, Susan. *The Geographical Imagination in America, 1880–1950*. Chicago: University of Chicago Press, 2001.
Schwoch, James. *Global TV: New Media and the Cold War, 1946–69*. Baltimore: Johns Hopkins University Press, 2009.
Scully, Eileen P. *Bargaining with the State from Afar: Citizenship in Treaty Port China, 1844–1942*. New York: Columbia University Press, 2001.

Seguchi, Akira. *Dōshisha supōtsuno ayumi, 1891–2000*. Kyoto: Dōshisha Supōtsuyunion, 2002.
Seymour, Harold, *Baseball: The People's Game*. 3 vols. New York: Oxford University Press, 1990.
Shimada, Akira. *Meiji Ishin to Nichibei Yakyūshi*. Tokyo: Bungeisha, 2001.
Shimizu, Satoshi. "The Creation of Professional Sports Leagues in Japan: A Cultural History of Human Networks." *International Journal of the History of Sport* 27, no. 3 (2010): 553–69.
Sinclair, Robert. "Baseball's Rising Sun: American Interwar Baseball Diplomacy and Japan." *Canadian Journal of the History of Sport* 16, no. 2 (1985): 44–53.
Skaggs, Jimmy M. *The Great Guano Rush: Entrepreneurs and American Overseas Expansion*. New York: St. Martin's Press, 1994.
Smith, Ronald. *Pay for Play: A History of Big-Time College Athletic Reform*. Urbana: University of Illinois Press, 2011.
———. *Sports and Freedom: The Rise of Big-Time College Athletics*. New York: Oxford University Press, 1990.
Snelling, Dennis. *The Pacific Coast League: A Statistical History, 1903–1957*. Jefferson, NC: McFarland, 1995.
Spink, J. G. Taylor. *Judge Landis and Twenty-Five Years of Baseball*. New York: Thomas Y. Crowell, 1947.
Stanley, Peter. "William Cameron Forbes: Proconsul in the Philippines." *Pacific Historical Review* 35, no. 3 (1966): 285–301.
Starffin, Natasha. *Roshiakarakitaēsu*. Tokyo: PHP Kenkyūjo, 1986.
Starr, Kevin. *Americans and the California Dream, 1850–1915*. New York: Oxford University Press, 1986.
———. *Embattled Dreams: California in War and Peace, 1940–1950*. New York: Oxford University Press, 2003.
———. *Golden Dreams: California in an Age of Abundance, 1950–1963*. New York: Oxford University Press, 2011.
———. *Material Dreams: Southern California through the 1920s*. New York: Oxford University Press, 1991.
Sugden, John, and Alan Tomlinson, eds. *Hosts and Champions: Soccer Cultures, National Identities and the USA World Cup*. Aldershot, Hants, UK: Arena, 1994.
Sugiyama, Hisatsugu. *Bēsubōrushitī*. Tokyo: Fukutake Shoten, 1990.
Sullivan, Dean, ed. *Early Innings: A Documentary History of Baseball, 1825–1908*. Lincoln: University of Nebraska Press, 1995.
Sullivan, Neil J. *The Dodgers Move West*. New York: Oxford University Press, 1987.
Sullivan, Timothy Paul. *History of World's Tour: Chicago White Sox and New York Giants*. Chicago: M. A. Donohue, 1914.
Suzuki, Ryūji. *Puroyakyū totomoni 50-nen*. Tokyo: Bēsubōru Magajinsha, 1984.
———. *Suzukiry Shugo ūji Kaikoroku*. Tokyo: Bēsubōru Magajinsha, 1980.
Suzuki, Sōtarō. *Fumetsuno Daitōshu Sawamura Eiji*. Tokyo: Bēsubōru Magajinsha, 1982.
———. *Nippon Puro Yakyū Gaishi*. Tokyo: Bēsubōru Magajinsha, 1976.
Suzuki, Yasumitsu, and Dainippontaiku Kenji. *Nipponde Hajimete Kābuwo Nageta Otoko*. Tokyo: Shōgakukan, 2000.

Takahashi, Yoshio. *Hiraoka Ginshuouto Tōmeikyoku*. Tokyo: Shuhōen, 1934.
Takaki, Ronald. *Pau Hana: Plantation Labor and Life in Hawaii, 1835–1920*. Honolulu: University of Hawaii Press, 1983.
Takegami, Takezō, *Dairenjitsuyōdan Nijūnenshi*. Dalian: Dairen Manshūshinpōsha, 1932.
Takemura, Toyotoshi. *Taiwan Taiikushi*. Taipei: Taiwantaiiku Kyōkai, 1933.
Tanikawa, Takeshi. "Senryokino tainichi supōtsu seisaku." *Intelligence*, 3 (2003): 6–18.
Tanioka, Masaki. *Joshipuroyakyūseishunfu 1950*. Tokyo: Kōdansha, 2007.
Taylor, Quintard. *In Search of the Racial Frontier: African Americans in the West, 1852–1990*. New York: Norton, 1999.
Thelin, John. *Games Colleges Play: Scandal and Reform in Intercollegiate Athletics*. Baltimore: Johns Hopkins University Press, 1994.
Thorn, John, and Peter Palmer, eds. *Total Baseball*. New York: Warner Books, 1995.
Tobita, Suishū. Kyūdōhansenki. Tokyo: Hakuyūsha, 1951.
———. *Yakyūseidan*. Tokyo: Tōkaishuppan, 1940.
Tomlinson, John. *Globalization and Culture*. Chicago: University of Chicago Press, 1999.
Travaglini, M. E. "Olympic Baseball 1936: Was Es Das?" *National Pastime* 5 (1985): 108–12.
Tsuboi, Gendō, and Tanak Seigyō. *Kogai Yugihō*. Tokyo: Taisō Denshūsho, 1885.
Tsuchiya, Yuka. *Shinbeinippon no Kōchiku*. Tokyo: Akashi Shoten, 2009.
Tsuganezawa, Toshihiro. *Sengo Nipponno Mediaibento*. Kyoto: Sekaishisōsha, 2002.
———. *Takarazukasenryaku*. Tokyo: Kōdansha, 1991.
Tsukase, Susumu. *Manshūkoku*. Tokyo: Yoshikawa Kōbunkan, 1998.
Tsunekage, Junichi. *Watashino Aozora*. Tokyo: Michishobō, 1995.
Tygiel, Jules. *Past Time: Baseball as History*. New York: Oxford University Press, 2000.
Tyrrell, Ian. "The Emergence of Modern American Baseball, c. 1850–1880." In *Sport in History: The Making of Modern Sport History*, edited by Richard Cashman and Michael McKernan, 205–26. St. Lucia, AU: Queensland University Press, 1979.
———. *The Gardens of the Gods: Canadian-Australian Environmental Reform, 1860–1930*. Berkeley: University of California Press, 1999.
———. "Looking Eastward: Pacific and Global Perspectives on American History in the Nineteenth and Early Twentieth Centuries." *Japanese Journal of American Studies*, no. 18 (2007): 41–57.
———. *Reforming the World: The Creation of America's Moral Empire*. Princeton, NJ: Princeton University Press, 2010.
———. *Women's World/Women's Empire: The Women's Christian Temperance Union in International Perspectives, 1830–1930*. Chapel Hill: University of North Carolina Press, 1991.
Uchida, Jun. "Brokers of Empire: Japanese Settler Colonialism in Korea, 1910–1937." Ph.D. diss., Harvard University, 2005.
Umetani, Noboru. *Oyatoi Gaikokujin*. Tokyo: Nippon Keizai Shinbunsha, 1965.
Ushijima, Hidehiko. *Fūun Nipponyakyū: V. Sutarubin*. Tokyo: Mainichishinbunsha, 1978.

Van den Heuvel, Cor, and Nanae Tamura. *Baseball Haiku: The Best Haiku Ever Written about the Game.* New York: W. W. Norton, 2007.

Vlasich, James A. *A Legend for the Legendary: The Origin of the Baseball Hall of Fame.* Bowling Green, OH: Bowling Green State University Press, 1990.

Voigt, David A. *American Baseball: From Gentleman's Sport to the Commissioner System.* Norman: University of Oklahoma Press, 1966.

———. *America through Baseball.* Chicago: Nelson-Hall, 1976.

———. "Serfs versus Magnates: A Century of Labor Strife in Major League Baseball." In *The Business of Professional Sports*, edited by Paul D. Staudohar and James A. Manga, 95–114. Urbana: University of Illinois Press, 1991.

Wakatsuki, Yasuo. *Sengohikiageno Kiroku.* Tokyo: Jijitsūshinsha, 1991.

Wakefield, Wanda. *Playing to Win: Sports and the American Military, 1898–1945.* Albany: State University of New York Press, 1997.

Wakuda, Yasuo. *Nipponno Shitetsu.* Tokyo: Iwanami Shoten, 1981.

Wasedadaigaku Yakyūbu, ed. *Beikokuyakyūensei.* Tokyo: Yakyūkaisha, 1921.

Watanabe, Masao. *Oyatoi Beikokujin Kagaku Kyōshi.* Rev. ed. Tokyo: Hokusensha, 1996.

Watt, Lori. *When Empire Comes Home.* Cambridge, MA: Harvard University Press, 2009.

White, G. Edward. *Creating the National Pastime: Baseball Transforms Itself, 1903–1958.* Princeton, NJ: Princeton University Press, 1996.

White, Richard. "Information, Markets, and Corruption: Transcontinental Railroads in the Gilded Age." *Journal of American History* 90 (June 2003): 19–43.

Whiting, Robert. *The Chrysanthemum and the Bat: The Game Japanese Play.* Tokyo: Permanent Press, 1977.

———. *The Meaning of Ichiro: The New Wave from Japan and the Transformation of Our National Pastime.* New York: Grand Central Publishing, 2004.

———. *You Gotta Have Wa.* New York: Vintage, 1990.

Winseck, Dwayne R., and Robert M. Pike. *Communication and Empire.* Durham, NC: Duke University Press, 2007.

Winter, Thomas. *Making Men, Making Class: The YMCA and Workingmen, 1877–1920.* Chicago: University of Chicago Press, 2002.

Wittmann, Matthew W. "Empire of Culture: U.S. Entertainers and the Making of the Pacific Circuit, 1850–1890." Ph.D. diss., University Of Michigan, 2010.

Wong, Scott. *Americans First: Chinese Americans and the Second World War.* Philadelphia: Temple University Press, 2008.

Wray, William D. *Mitsubishi and the N.Y.K., 1870–1914.* Cambridge, MA: Harvard University Press, 1984.

Xie, Shiyuan, and Wie Jiafen. *Taiwan bangqiu yibai nian.* Taibei: Guoshi chubanshe, 2003.

Yamakawa, Ken. *Yakyū Tōsei no Hanashi.* Tokyo: Monbushō Taiiku Kachō, 1932.

Yamamoto, Eriko. "Cheers for Japanese Athletes: The 1932 Los Angeles Olympics and the Japanese American Community." *Pacific Historical Review* 69, no. 3 (2000): 399–431.

Yamamoto, Shigeru. *Nanairono Makyū: Kaisōno Wakabayashitadashi*. Tokyo: Bēsubōru Magajinsha, 1994.
Yamashita, Samuel. *Child of War: A Memoir of WWII Internment in the Philippines*. Honolulu: University of Hawaii Press, 2011.
Yanagida, Chiyo. "The Nippu Jiji and the Japanese Language School Issue in Hawaii, 1919–1927." M.A. thesis, University of Hawaii at Manoa, 1996.
Yearley, Steven. *Science Technology and Social Change*. London: Unwin Hyman, 1988.
Yokoi, Haruno. *Nippon Yakūusenshi*. Tokyo: Nittō Shoin, 1932.
Yoneyama, Hiroshi, and Norifumi Kawahara, eds. *Nipponjinno Keikento Kokusaiidō*. Kyoto: Jinbunshoin, 2007.
Yoshida Mitsukuni, ed. *19-Seiki Nippon no Jōhō to Shaki Hendō*. Kyoto: Kyotodaigaku Jinbunkagaku Kenkyūjo, 1985.
Yoshihara, Mari. *Embracing the East: White Women and American Orientalism*. New York: Oxford University Press, 2003.
———. "The Flight of the Japanese Butterfly: Orientalism, Nationalism, and Performance of Japanese Womanhood." *American Quarterly* 56, no. 4 (2004): 975–1001.
Yoshimi, Shunya. *Shinbei to Hanbei*. Tokyo: Iwanami Shoten, 2007.
———, ed. *Undōkaito Nipponkindai*. Tokyo: Seikyūsha, 1999.
Young, David. *The Olympic Myth of Greek Amateur Athletics*. Chicago: Ares, 1985.
Young, Louise. *Japan's Total Empire: Manchuria and the Culture of Wartime Imperialism*. Berkeley: University of California Press, 1999.
Yu, Junwei. *Playing in Isolation: A History of Baseball in Taiwan*. Lincoln: University of Nebraska Press, 2007.
Yukawa, Mitsuo, ed. *Taiwan Yakyūshi*. Taibei: Taiwan Nichinichi Shinpōsha, 1932.
Yutaka, Yoshida. *Nipponno Guntai*. Tokyo: Iwanami Shoten, 1997.
Zeiler, Thomas W. *Ambassadors in Pinstripes: The Spalding World Baseball Tour and the Birth of the American Empire*. New York: Rowman and Littlefield, 2006.
Zennippon Nanshiki Yakyū Renmei, ed. *Nanshiki Yakyūshi*. Tokyo: Bēsubōru Magajinsha, 1976.
Zhang, Like. "Taiwan bangqiu yu rentong." M.A. thesis, Qinghua University, 2000.
Zimbalist, Andrew. *Unpaid Professionals: Commercialism and Conflict in Big-Time College Sports*. Princeton, NJ: Princeton University Press, 1999.
———. *May the Best Team Win: Baseball Economics and Public Policy*. Washington, D.C.: Brookings Institution Press, 2003.
Zingg, Paul J., and Mark D. Medeiros. *Runs, Hits, and an Era: The Pacific Coast League, 1903–58*. Urbana: University of Illinois Press, 1994.

INDEX

Abe, Isoo, 87, 89–91, 94, 112, 115, 120, 134, 147, 149
Advertising, 4, 81–83, 158
African Americans, 123, 128–30, 139
Ainsmith, Eddie, 125–27
Allied occupation of Japan, 7, 198–200, 207–8, 225, 227, 229–30
Amateur baseball: IABF (International Amateur Baseball Federation), 170, 171–72; players, 169; student baseball, 142, 147, 164; USA Baseball Congress, 168
Amateurism, 117–18, 143
American baseball, 15, 116, 121, 129–30, 181, 227; players, 36, 83, 109, 124; collegiate, 90, 144; teams, 36, 73, 103
American Baseball entrepreneurs, 92–94, 99, 119–20, 125–27, 137, 153, 158–59, 166–70, 171, 183, 206–7, 222–23
American League, 79, 84, 111, 121, 236; all-stars, 141, 149; players, 160, 227
American Negro Leagues, 128–29, 139, 167, 237
American professional baseball, 1, 11, 20, 55, 65, 84, 90, 98, 112, 115–16, 120–21, 123, 136, 138, 148, 181, 216, 219, 221, 224, 227
Americans, 2–15 passim, 19, 22, 31–33, 35–37, 50–55, 65, 69, 73, 110–21 passim, 140–41, 151–53, 162, 168–70, 171, 197, 199, 201–2, 207–8, 213
America's Game, 1, 21, 26, 32–33, 38, 41, 43, 59, 94, 119, 130, 189, 195, 202, 205, 244
Amherst College, 18, 25, 86. *See also* Collegiate baseball
Armed forces, 186–87, 193, 195
Army, 48–49, 179, 187–89, 191, 196, 205–6, 227, 241
Asahi, 58, 60, 147, 176, 191–92, 208

Asahi Shinbun, 85, 95–96, 98, 164, 208, 217, 234. *See also* Japanese press
Asian Americans in Southern California, 130; ballplayers, 123; barnstorming tour, 129; colonial subjects, 158; colony, 53, 55; empire, 77; imperium, 180; mainland, 65, 177, 232; markets, 88, 162; modernizing country, 56; nation, 13, 27, 75, 112, 118, 169
Asians, 9, 118
Athletics, 48, 50, 54, 92. *See also* Collegiate baseball
Atsushi, Kōno, 159

Ball games, 2, 14, 19, 26, 43, 46, 51
Ballplayers, professional, 144, 172, 177, 188
Baseball: ascendancy of, 7, 26, 33; boosters, 69, 134, 183, 203, 206; clinics, 132, 226; clubs, 24, 37, 157; commentators, 154, 207; commercialized, 107–8, 164, 208; diffusion of, 6–7, 60, 63, 67, 72; entertainment, 121, 226; establishment, 184–86; fans, 184, 211; fever, 8, 16, 65, 77, 80, 98, 108, 120, 159; fields, 1, 44, 49–50, 62, 109, 173, 189, 193, 195; genesis of, 12, 15; local enthusiasts, 47, 115; matches, 21, 92; networks, 72, 106; professional enterprise, 8, 224; rhetoric of, 152, 199; teams, 23–24, 37, 62, 83, 195, 204, 229; transpacific, 9, 72, 77, 82, 84, 88, 92, 106, 109, 130–31, 135, 145, 189, 199, 217, 235–36, 240, 243; youth, 51, 59, 142. *See also* American baseball; Japanese baseball; Major League Baseball; Professional baseball; Semipro baseball
Baseball journalism: annual baseball guides, 81, 111, 194; baseball writers, 126, 164; magazines, 4, 84–86, 121, 152, 210–12, 219

Baseball journalism, American: *Baseball Magazine*, 184; *Reach Baseball Guide*, 136; *Spalding's Official Base Ball Guide*, 28–29, 38, 81, 85, 110; *Sporting Life*, 50, 54; *Sporting News*, 50

Baseball journalism, Japanese: *Asahi Supōtsu*, 83, 85; *Deirī Supōtsu*, 211; *Japan Weekly Mail*, 31; *Kogai Yūgihō*, 29; *Nekkyū* (Power Ball), 211; *Nikkan Supōtsu*, 211, 233–34; *Shōnen Ball Friends* (Boys' Baseball Friends), 211; *Sumo to Yakyū* (Sumo and Baseball), 176; *Supōtsu Nippon*, 211; *Suraggā* (Sluggers), 211; *Undōsekai*, 85; *Yakyūfan* (Baseball Fans), 211; *Yakyūkai* (Baseball World), 83, 176, 210; *Yakyūō* (Baseball King), 211; *Yakyū Shōnen* (Baseball Boys), 211–12

Baseball leagues: Japanese, 145, 156, 177, 226; major, 130, 150, 159, 195; minor, 160, 236; relocation camp, 193; San Francisco city, 137; U.S. military, 189; Women's professional, 232–34. *See also* Major League Baseball; Minor leagues

Baseball players, 8, 76; drafting of, 78; former celebrities, 67; Japanese, 22, 24, 32, 34, 37, 71, 99–100, 107, 112, 116, 121, 129, 132, 137, 141, 147–48, 154, 163, 173, 178, 180, 196, 205, 231; major-league, 115, 120, 122–23, 132–33, 135, 150–51, 181, 186; minor-league, 78–80, 219

Boston, 11, 20–21, 25, 27

Boston Red Sox, 64, 114, 119–20, 227, 231–33, 235

British Columbia, 102, 115, 191

Brooklyn Dodgers, 204, 236–37

Brundage, Avery, 168, 174–75, 217

Business of baseball: baseball equipment, 15, 19–20, 26, 31, 38, 41, 81, 185, 203; in Japan, 156, 224–25; legitimizing the game, 108; postseason, 239; radio, 107; tour support, 221, 239; transpacific, 235, 240, 242; West Coast, 77, 238. *See also* Sporting goods; Baseball: transpacific

California, 42, 47, 77–79, 89, 101–2, 104, 106, 110, 128, 131, 136–37, 155, 160, 165, 167, 186, 190, 192–93, 199, 205, 216, 228, 238, 241. *See also* California Winter League; Pacific Coast League

California National Baseball Convention's rules, 45

California Winter League, 76–77, 80. *See also* Pacific Coast League

Canadian Pacific Railroad, 109, 114–15, 149

Carnegie Commission, 144, 146–47

Cartwright, Alexander, 42–44, 77

China, 9, 42, 54, 56, 69, 88, 95, 107, 114, 165, 170, 172, 174–75, 177, 207, 213

Cities, 50, 62, 66, 68–71, 77, 94, 98, 101–3, 115, 120, 126, 131, 137, 153–54, 166, 175, 182, 231, 237

Civilian Conservation Corps (CCC), 165–66

Civilians, 14, 48–49, 52, 61, 63, 65, 73, 119, 165, 174, 176, 179, 184–87, 200, 203, 218, 227, 232, 241

Civil War, U.S., 11–15, 17, 48, 55, 213

Club owners, 20, 79, 122–25, 130–31, 133, 141, 149, 237

Clubs, 22, 29, 32, 58, 60, 77–78, 98, 102, 107, 115, 118, 142, 155–56, 160, 164, 169, 178–79, 191–92, 215, 224, 233–34

Cold War, 9, 199, 220, 227, 243

Colleges, 13, 19, 23, 25, 93–94, 99, 106, 143, 148, 201; private, 24, 33, 86–87, 90–91

Collegiate baseball, 92, 145, 148, 176–77; players, 66, 172

Collegiate baseball, Japanese, 24, 86, 88, 200; ballplayers, 94–95, 112, 116, 132; barnstormers, 91, 163; collegiate teams, 2, 33, 68, 76, 89–90, 92, 112, 204; in Meiji Japan, 22

Colonial baseball, American: Australia, 28, 114, 144, 206; Cuba, 1, 40, 49–50, 109, 130, 170, 171; Puerto Rico, 40, 49, 171, 235

Colonial baseball, Japanese, 61, 66–67, 92, 106; Korea, 8, 26, 31–32, 63, 67–72, 84, 94–95, 97–99, 105–6, 122, 124, 127, 129–30, 142, 154–55, 207, 223, 226, 232, 243; Korean baseball, 68, 70; Manchuria, 75, 105–6, 135, 140, 179, 218, 232; Southern Manchuria, 65–67, 71, 84, 97–99, 122, 155, 228; Taiwan, 8, 54, 61–65, 71, 95, 97–99, 122, 140, 196, 232, 243; Taiwanese youth, 62–64

Comiskey, Charles, 55, 113–14, 118–19

Commissioner: Japanese Baseball Association, 224–25; Major League Baseball, 122–23, 144, 149, 184; National Baseball Congress, 167. *See also* Landis, Kenesaw Mountain

Cricket, 7, 19, 26, 28, 33, 39, 43

Dalian, 65–67, 72, 98–99, 106, 127, 129–30, 142, 179, 231

Democracy, 119, 183, 187, 198–99, 209, 222, 235

DiMaggio, Joe, 161, 181, 186, 226–27

Dōshisha, 24–25, 57, 81. *See also* Collegiate baseball

Education: as blueprint for Japan's reorientation, 202; for colonial subjects, 62; for girls in Japan, 25, 229; higher, 22, 86, 93; for missionary children, 43

Eiji, Sawamura, 154, 172, 177, 179, 188, 196

Executive Order 9066, 190, 192

Fans, 108, 126, 130–31, 136, 181–82, 227, 233–34, 238

Field of dreams, 9, 173

Fisher, John, 77, 79

Fisher, Ray, 144

Forbes, William Cameron, 51–52, 135

Foreign settlement, 14, 23–24, 26, 30–32, 34, 73, 81

France, 13, 28, 34, 114, 119

Franchises, 77, 110, 227, 237

Franchise transfers, 236–38

Gate receipts, 89–91, 99, 142, 145–46, 148, 186

Gehrig, Lou, 131, 134, 136, 141, 150, 154, 199, 205, 211

Gillett, Phillip L., 68–70, 94

Globalization, 3–5

Government: Japanese, 12–13, 18–19, 23, 29, 32–33, 35, 57, 63, 75–6, 87–89, 134, 140, 151–52, 157, 169, 174–77, 195–96, 238; Japanese militarist, 178, 199–200; U.S., 53, 140, 153, 172, 183, 193, 195, 241

Graham, Charlie, 160, 220

Great Baseball War, 78

Great Depression, 8, 139, 149, 159–60, 166–67, 183

Hamilton, Earl, 125–27

Hankyū Railroad Company, 156–57

Hanshin Railroad Company, 152, 156, 158

Harada, Tsuneo "Cappy," 205–7, 216–17, 220, 227–28, 240–41. *See also* Japanese baseball: lobbyists

Harper, William Rainey, 93

Hawaii, 3, 8, 28, 40–48, 55–61, 75–76, 91, 95, 99–100, 103, 105–6, 109, 111, 140, 144, 150, 155, 158, 164–65, 170, 171–72, 176, 188–89, 191, 240; Hawaiian monarchy, 44–46; Hawaiians, 43–45, 55–56, 60; Japanese labor migration to, 74; Japanese population in, 57–58

Hawaiian baseball, 44–47, 56–58, 60, 88, 111, 126, 129, 136, 150, 165, 171, 189, 192; baseball missionary, 42, 44; early, 41, 43, 45; Hawaiian Baseball Association, 47; Hawaiian Sugar Plantation Association (HSPA), 59; Hawaii Baseball League, 192; Honolulu Asahi, 104–6; Nisshin Club, 58, 60; Pacifics, 45; players, 45, 60

Hironoshin, Furuhashi, 217–18

Ichikō, 14; baseball, 34, 38, 107; students, 21, 26, 34, 36

Identities, 41, 100, 131

Index | 307

Immigration, Japanese: to Hawaii, 56; to Brazil, 74
Imperialism, 5, 33, 69, 72
Industrial baseball, 206, 212; clubs and teams, 65–67, 71, 98, 105–6, 126, 165, 206
Inter-City Industrial Baseball Tournament, 212, 222
International Amateur Baseball Federation (IABF), 170, 171–72
Internees, 193–94, 241
Internment camps, U.S., 191, 196, 205, 241–42
Issei, 9, 60, 85, 89, 100–102, 131, 161, 173, 192, 195; teams, 101–2. *See also* Japan: Japanese nationals

Janes, Leroy Lansing, 17–18, 25
Japan: agricultural laborers in, 101–2; amateur sports in, 91, 123, 169, 171, 221; athletes in, 60, 217; campaigns of, 89, 160, 163; children in, 58, 75, 221; colonial rule of, 62–63, 70–72, 97, 243; Education Ministry, 18, 145–48, 169, 173, 176–77, 207–9, 221; empire of, 61, 66, 72, 96, 106, 155, 243; Foreign Ministry, 13, 32, 149; Japanese expatriates, 66, 68, 97, 154, 179; Japanese imperium, 8, 63, 76, 106; Japanese migration, 56–57, 60, 67; Japanese nationals, 30–32, 35, 57, 103, 173, 217–18; Japanese state, 63, 88, 145, 173; military of, 13, 61, 63, 67, 70–71, 171, 174–75, 177–78, 180, 187–89, 196, 218; New Japan, 199, 207, 210–13, 230, 232; postoccupation, 235, 238; postwar, 198, 239; prewar, 201, 209, 230; southern, 204, 231; sports in, 8, 82, 84–85, 108, 112, 118, 174, 217; students in, 16–17, 19, 24, 32, 35, 99; western, 17, 24–25, 30, 57, 71–72, 83, 95, 99, 105, 115, 126, 156, 200, 204, 211, 229; women in, 126, 229–30, 235
Japan Amateur Sports Association, 169
Japanese American baseball: Fresno Athletic Club (FAC), 104–5, 130–31, 161; Japanese-American Courier baseball league, 102; L.A. Nippons, 102, 106, 158–59, 161, 190; Nikkei teams, 101, 103–4; North American Pacific Northwest Japanese Baseball Championship, 103; Northern California Japanese Baseball League, 104
Japanese American relocation camps, 173, 190, 192–95, 241–42; Tule Lake, 194–95. *See also* Internment camps, U.S.
Japanese Americans, 7, 9, 55, 76, 100–106, 130–31, 155, 160–61, 165, 172–73, 190–92, 217–18, 241; local communities, 89, 161
Japanese ancestry, 60, 191. *See also* Nikkei
Japanese baseball, 12, 14, 19, 26–27, 29, 61, 95, 103, 109, 138, 146, 154, 162, 173, 180, 206, 224; ballplayers, 36, 83, 97, 116, 148, 160–65, 204; celebrity culture, 87; east-west games, 199–200; entrepreneurs, 20–21, 26, 28, 80, 138; fans, 112–13, 115–16, 126, 135–36, 151, 154, 219, 222, 226, 239; fraternity, 120, 132, 141, 147, 153, 169, 197, 207, 243; industrial baseball, 206, 222; industrial league clubs, 98; intraimperial baseball, 97; Japan Baseball Society, 180; Japanese Baseball Association, 200, 205, 224–25; Japanese Baseball Hall of Fame, 236; Japanese Industrial Baseball Association, 207; Japanese World Series, 161, 225; Japan Series, 204, 239; Kōshien Stadium, 96, 129, 133, 152, 156, 180, 201, 204; lobbyists, 199, 204–6; officials, 129, 137, 210; Pacific League, 226–28, 239; pre–World War II, 145; student athletes, 34–35; student baseball, 97, 208, 210
Japanese baseball clubs and teams, 22, 26, 64, 69, 71, 74, 88, 97, 103, 106, 148, 156–58, 176, 192, 219–20, 225, 227, 242; All-Japan team, 155, 158; All-Kyōjō Club, 71; All-Osaka Club, 99; Dai Nippon Tokyo Yakyū Kurabu (All-Nippon Tokyo Baseball Club), 148, 155–56,

158–60; Fuji Athletic Club, 101, 192; Greater Japan Tokyo Baseball Club, 155; Kōrakuen Eagles, 159; Nagoya Club, 106, 158–59, 196; Nippon Tokyo Baseball Club, 148; Osaka's AllKanebō Club, 223; Shibaura Kyōkai (Nippon Undōkai), 141, 231; Shinbashi Athletic Club (SAC), 21, 26–29; Tokyo Giants, 159–65, 172, 178–80, 189, 192, 205, 218, 224, 228, 231, 236, 238–39, 242

Japanese press, 121, 152, 219, 239. *See also* Newspapers

Japanese professional baseball, 157–60, 172, 188, 196, 198, 200, 204, 224–25, 227–28, 242; league, 175, 204; players, 212; prewar, 158, 180, 201, 204

Johnson, Ban, 78, 111, 114

Kaitakushi (Hokkaido Development Agency), 15–16

Kaitakushi Karigakkō, 15–16. *See also* Collegiate baseball

Kanoe, Chūma, 37–39, 90

Keio, 23, 87, 90–91, 112–13, 119–20. *See also* Collegiate baseball

Koreans, 10, 69, 71–72, 243

Kōshien, 96–97, 176, 243

Kumamoto, 17, 25

Kyōjō Shinbun, 71. *See also* Japanese press

Kyoto, 24–25, 81, 87, 100, 126, 154, 157

Laborers, 56, 59

Landis, Kenesaw Mountain, 122–24, 132–33, 144, 149, 184

League of Nations, 140, 155

Lieb, Fred, 132–33, 135–36

Little Tokyo, 102, 190

Los Angeles, 80, 89, 129, 138, 161, 192, 215, 217, 229, 236–37, 241

MacArthur, Douglas, 206, 215–16, 219–20, 223, 226

Mackey, Biz, 128–29

Major League Baseball, 8, 64, 91, 123, 133, 144, 184, 236–37, 239; major leaguers, 64, 80, 84, 91, 110, 119–20, 123–26, 132, 135–37, 141, 148, 152–56, 158, 160, 167, 172, 181, 184, 186–87, 190, 226, 239; leagues and teams, 40, 78–80, 84–85, 98, 107, 110–11, 113–14, 118–24, 128–33, 135–37, 141, 144, 147, 149–51, 154–55, 167–68, 172, 175, 181–82, 185–88, 193, 204–5, 214–16, 225, 235–37; owners, 185, 193, 215; postseason play, 122–23, 137, 204, 225. *See also* Tours, team

Major-league status, 215, 236

Makoto, Hashido, 90, 98, 147

Manchukuo, 54, 152, 176, 178–79

Marquat, William, 199, 205–7, 210–11, 216–24, 226, 235. *See also* SCAP

Massachusetts Agricultural College, 16–17

Matsutarō, Shōriki, 133–34, 136, 147–50, 154–56, 165, 204, 224–26, 233, 238

McGraw, John, 55, 84, 91, 113–16, 118–20, 122

Meiji Japan, 7, 12, 15, 19, 21–22, 25–26, 33, 84: early, 7, 12, 14; late, 36, 86; Meiji Gakuin, 23–24, 32

Middle schools, 18, 37, 64–65, 84, 95, 99–100

Midwest, 92–93, 144, 182–83, 215

Military, 14, 21, 48, 51–52, 71, 172, 174, 177–78, 180–81, 183–87, 189, 206–7, 218, 221, 227–28; military-industrial complex, 207; Nisei service in the United States, 206; police, 21; teams, 198, 219–20; training, 14

Minor leagues, 76, 79, 117, 155, 165, 214–15, 241

Missionaries, 23, 43–45, 145–47, 208

Missionaries, American, 43, 69–70

Mizuno Company, 72, 81–83, 85, 95. *See also* Sporting goods: Japanese sporting equipment

Nation, 3–7, 9, 14, 16, 19–20, 27, 33–34, 36–37, 39, 48, 55, 60, 69, 80, 85, 92, 96, 107–8, 140–41, 157, 185–86, 199–200, 219–20, 228–30, 239–40

National Agreement: of 1892, 78; of 1903, 78, 215, 224, 236
National Association of Professional Baseball Leagues, 78–79. *See also* Minor leagues
National Association of Professional Base Ball Players, 1
National game, 36–37, 111, 162, 183
National High School Baseball Association, 209
National League (NL), 11, 27–29, 78–79, 84, 86, 110–11, 114–16, 132, 151, 167, 181, 185, 236, 238
National pastime, 11–12, 17, 39–40, 54, 60, 64, 72, 201, 222, 242
Navy, 12, 26, 31, 36, 40, 46, 119, 176, 184, 188–89, 196
NCAA (National Collegiate Athletic Association), 117, 143–45, 148, 168
Newspapers, 22, 35–36, 86, 95, 102, 121, 142, 146, 151–52, 156, 158, 163, 176, 191, 210–11; English-language, 35; Japanese-language, 103, 161; Korean-language, 72; local Japanese-language, 66, 71, 100, 165
New York Giants, 55, 84, 91, 113–14, 116, 118–19, 121–22, 134, 137, 151, 160, 236–39
Nikkei, 60, 190–91, 196; and America's Game, 195; baseball in Hawaii and North America, 60, 100, 104, 191, 193–95; baseball in the Pacific Northwest, 103; baseball teams in California, 101–2, 104; in California, 190; in Canada, 190–91; communities, 100–101, 105, 194; internment, 191–95; spectators, 138, 165
Nippon Professional Baseball Association (NPBA), 156, 175, 177
Nippon Yūsen Company, 88, 102
Nisei, 58, 100, 105, 158, 173, 242; players, 103, 105, 158, 177, 190–91, 242; teams, 60, 104–5, 191

Occupied Japan, 198–99, 202, 206, 210, 216, 221, 228

O'Doul, Lefty, 131, 136–38, 141, 149, 151, 155, 160–61, 163–64, 213–14, 216, 219–21, 226–28, 235–36, 242
Okumura, Takie, 57–58, 60
Olympics, 117, 146, 168–70, 173–74, 217; American Olympic Committee (AOC), 168, 174; Olympic Organizing Committee (OOC), 168, 174; United States Olympic Committee (USOC), 117–18
Organized baseball, 8–9, 78–79, 104, 111, 113, 121–24, 132, 136, 138, 144, 149, 167, 172, 186, 198–99, 203, 216, 223, 227, 233, 235–37, 243; American, 8, 109, 199; Japanese, 198, 200, 205
Organized sports, 30, 48–49, 52, 54, 93
Osaka, 72, 81–83, 95, 100, 115, 126, 158, 176, 180, 203, 211, 222–23, 229
Osaka Asahi Shinbun, 95–96, 98
Owners, team, 79, 85, 101, 113, 133, 142, 149, 160, 185, 214, 224, 234, 236–37, 239
Oyatoi, 12–13, 17, 32, 242

Pacific Coast League, 64, 76, 79, 84, 110, 119–20, 131–32, 160–61, 171, 192, 215, 227, 236
Pacific crossings, 103
Pacific Northwest League, 78
Pacific Ocean, 1, 7–8, 75, 88, 114–15, 119, 132–33, 136, 159, 172, 183, 188–89, 222, 235, 238, 241, 243–44; Asia-Pacific, 183, 188, 198; crossing the, 12, 15, 95, 104–6, 109, 128, 133; diffusion of baseball across the, 72, 236; mid-Pacific, 2, 43, 144, 240
Paige, Satchel, 167
Passenger liners, transpacific, 88
Pastime, shared, 73–74, 76, 199
Pearl Harbor attack, 175, 181, 183, 191
Philadelphia, 11, 19–21, 50, 110, 125, 128–29
Philadelphia Athletics, 21, 27, 110, 114, 132, 149, 237
Philadelphia Bobbies, 124–28, 229
Philadelphia Royal Giants, 129–30, 138–39
Philippines, 8, 40, 48, 50–52, 54–55, 61,

310 | Index

64, 69, 75–76, 95, 99, 109, 111–12, 114, 116, 135, 139–41, 144, 170, 172, 176–77, 179, 189, 196, 201; Filipino amateur baseball teams, 109; Filipinos, 50–51, 53, 55, 59–60, 69, 179; Manila, 51–55, 91, 94, 111, 122, 154, 179–80, 189, 235. *See also* Colonial baseball, Japanese

Physical education, 17–18, 25, 85, 146, 202

Princeton University, 24, 51, 137

Professional baseball, 2, 78, 80, 82, 86, 98, 128, 141, 144, 154, 158, 164, 177, 180–82, 184, 198, 200, 225, 228, 230, 232–36, 238, 242; leagues, 78, 106, 165, 201, 229, 232; National Association of Professional Baseball Leagues, 78; players, 144, 172, 231

Public schools, 18, 51–52, 62–63

Punahou School, 43–47

Race, 118, 130, 161–62, 241

Radio, 107, 152, 157–58

Reach, Albert, 110–11

Reach All-Americans, 85, 110–13, 115

Rosters, team, 32, 36, 69, 97, 105, 116, 119, 121, 124–25, 131, 134, 136, 148, 158, 172, 178, 192, 242

Rules, baseball, 29, 38, 41, 45, 123, 178, 187, 201, 219, 224

Russo-Japanese War, 13, 65, 75, 82, 88–89

Ruth, Babe, 130–31, 133–34, 141, 148–52, 154, 168, 181, 183, 189, 199, 205, 216, 219

Sacramento: California League, 77; Nikkei baseball teams in, 101; Nikkei population of, 195; Pacific Coast League, 106, 159, 161, 192

Sailors, 50–51, 184, 188

Saipan, 188–89, 196

Sakuma, Samata, 61–64

San Francisco, 101, 136–37, 164, 192, 215, 218; as the hub of regional baseball, 77; city leagues in, 137; Fuji Athletic Club, 101; homegrown major leaguers from, 186; Issei teams in, 101; Japanese Consular Office in, 15; Japanese consul general in, 69; King Kalakaua in, 47; New York Giants move to, 236–37; and 1906 earthquake, 101; 1927 Yankees postseason tour of, 13, 15, 20, 40, 42, 69; 1931 Japan tour, 136–37; PCL president in, 79; rapid population growth of, 215; seasonal play in, 80; Tokyo Giants in, 159, 192; United States–Japan intercollegiate baseball in, 88–89

San Francisco Seals, 132, 137–38, 160, 213–16, 218–22, 225–28, 235, 242

San Jose, 77, 101–2; Issei teams in, 102; Nikkei population in, 190; San Jose Asahi, 104–5, 161

Sapporo Agricultural College, 16–17, 24. *See also* Collegiate baseball

SCAP (Supreme Commander for the Allied Powers), 198–200, 202–3, 206–7, 209–10, 212–13, 215–17, 219, 221–22, 224–25, 227, 229–30; Economic and Scientific Section (ESS), 199, 205, 207; and Japanese school baseball lobby, 209; officials, 202–3, 205, 209, 230

Schools, 14, 16, 18, 20, 22, 24–25, 34, 37, 43, 61, 63, 65, 68, 75, 92–94, 96–97, 99, 115, 142–3, 145–46, 157, 201–2

Seattle, 88–89, 102, 125, 128, 192

Seattle Asahi, 103, 105

Semipro baseball, 9, 60, 89, 98–99, 102, 104–6, 131, 141, 158–60, 165, 176, 193, 198, 206, 233, 235; industrial, 107, 177; teams, 161, 183

Semi-Pro World Series, 222–23

Servicemen, 187–88

Service teams, 51, 172, 183, 185

Shigeru, Mizuhara, 218

Shinbashi Railroad Bureau, 20–22

SinoJapanese War, 34, 36, 65

Second Sino-Japanese War, 171

Soccer, 68, 168–69

Soldiers, 14–15, 48–49, 51, 172, 184–85, 187, 223, 232

Sōtarō, Suzuki, 134, 159–61, 204–6, 211, 219, 235

Index | 311

Spalding, Albert G., 11, 26–29, 38, 41, 46–47, 82, 110–11, 114, 162
Spartan league (pre–World War II Japan), 173, 175, 177, 179, 181, 183, 185, 187, 189, 193, 195, 197
Spectators, 14, 22, 32, 66, 71, 96, 100, 107, 112, 116, 126, 130–31, 136, 148, 152, 161, 166–67, 170, 173, 186, 195, 212, 220, 229, 233–34
Spectator sport, 8, 36–37
Sporting equipment, 18, 48, 202–3
Sporting goods, 110, 167, 194; A. J. Reach Company, 110–12; Japanese sporting equipment, 72, 81–83, 85, 95; Spalding & Brothers, 27, 53, 81–82, 110–11, 114, 209
Sports, 7, 9, 12, 16, 21, 23–24, 28, 33–34, 39, 41, 49–50, 52, 55, 59, 63, 83–85, 90, 117–18, 121–23, 146–48, 184–85, 201–3, 210–12, 229–31, 243–44; college, 143; international, 168, 170, 217; national, 117, 136; upstart, 233–34
Starffin, Victor, 154–55, 161, 163, 178, 196
Star players, 28, 35, 51, 73, 76, 84–85, 92, 99, 105–7, 112, 114–15, 121, 132, 141, 145, 149–50, 152, 169, 171–72, 176–77, 188–89, 220–21, 227, 235–36, 239
State control, 6, 146–47, 207–8
Student baseball, 38, 143, 145–47, 173, 177, 208–9
Students, 14, 17–19, 23, 25, 37, 43, 62, 68–69, 76, 91, 95, 107, 142, 144, 160, 208
Suishū, Tobita, 147, 164, 208, 211
Supporters, 34–36, 86, 143

Tatsuo, Saeki, 208
Teachers, 16–17, 45, 102; American teacher in Japan, 17–18, 34
Teams, 1, 21, 32, 58, 87, 97–98, 100–103, 105–7, 125–26, 130–31, 146–48, 154–55, 160–62, 166–69, 171–72, 178–79, 181, 190, 193–95, 204–5, 213–15, 225–26, 232–35, 239, 243; ethnic, 59–60; national, 117, 168; surviving, 232–33

Thorpe, Jim, 116–18
Tokyo, 12, 15–16, 18, 20–24, 26, 32–33, 63, 68, 80, 87, 94–95, 101, 105, 120, 126, 135, 142, 152–53, 169–70, 171, 173–76, 203–4, 206–7, 221–23, 231; downtown, 21, 153, 157, 206, 216; metropolitan area, 87
Tokyo Big 6 League, 87, 91–92, 99, 106, 121, 132, 134, 136–37, 144, 148–49, 154, 157, 169, 172, 174, 176–77, 196, 200, 210, 218, 221, 228, 235. *See also* Collegiate baseball
Tokyo Imperial University, 14–15, 21–23, 36, 38, 87. *See also* Collegiate baseball
Tokyo Nichinichi Shinbun, 98, 105. *See also* Japanese press
Tokyo Olympics, 174, 176
Tournaments, 65, 71, 73, 87, 95–96, 98–99, 145–46, 166–67, 208–10, 230; All-Korea Middle School, 71; high school baseball, 67, 146, 209–10, 229; multination baseball, 172; national, 96–98, 145, 157, 198, 210; national championship, 84, 97; national finals, 96–97; sponsor youth baseball, 145; summer tournament, 209–10; tournament organizers, 209–10; very first women's baseball, 229
Tours, team, 28, 40, 89, 94–95, 99, 105, 111, 113–16, 118, 120–26, 129, 131, 133, 135–38, 141, 144–45, 147, 149–56, 159–65, 188, 194, 205, 216, 218–21, 231; "All-American National Team," 119–20; booking agents for, 102, 125–26, 231; expenses of, 70, 91, 95, 125, 134, 144–45, 149, 169, 174, 176, 216–17; to Japan, 85, 91–92, 94–95, 100, 105, 120, 122, 125, 127, 129, 131, 133, 136–38, 144, 149–50, 152–53, 159, 171, 214; Japanese collegiate baseball, 91; Japanese sponsors of, 150, 169, 217; 1934 All-Americans tour, 148; overseas baseball, 91, 94, 99, 142, 144; postseason baseball, 121–23, 132, 148–49, 226–27, 239; student baseball, 100; world, 28, 46, 55–56, 91, 113–14, 122, 141, 149

Town teams, 15, 32, 44, 48, 125, 166
Transnational interactions, 2, 4–5, 100, 109, 148, 227–28, 244
Transnational sports, 227–28
Transpacific world, 3, 6, 8–9, 25, 41, 72, 77, 82, 84, 88, 92, 106, 109, 118, 130–31, 135, 145, 189, 199, 217, 235–36, 240, 243. *See also* Baseball: transpacific
Two-league structure, 198, 224–25, 232

United States, 1–2, 5, 8, 12–14, 16, 19, 26, 28, 30, 39–40, 46, 50, 69, 73, 76, 78, 81–82, 84, 86–87, 89, 91, 94, 140–41, 171–72, 174–75; amateur coaching regulations in, 144; American expatriates in Tokyo, 15, 112; American visitors to Japan, 120, 123, 136, 169; ballparks in, 242; barnstorming in, 159, 165; baseball boosters in, 152; baseball in, 1, 12, 36, 40, 78, 90, 124, 236; bat-and-ball games in, 26; citizenship in, 60; college sports in, 143; commercialized baseball's origins in, 108; community sports programs in, 202; engagement with the wider world, 2, 4; intercollegiate baseball in, 86; Japanese labor migration to, 90, 104, 205; Japanese professional players in, 227–28; Japanese students educated in, 16, 19–20; Japan's first business mission to, 84; military leaders of, 200–201; as a multiracial empire, 53; "muscular Christianity" movement in, 17–18, 68; power of, 4–5; sports in, 7, 54, 92, 113, 175; sports pedagogy in, 146; sports stakeholders in, 143; war against Japan, 177, 188
United States and Japan, relations between, 6, 8, 29, 75, 140, 172, 222, 232, 242–43
U.S. Commissioner of Education, 94
U.S. Eighth Army, 200–201, 210, 219
United States–Japan Commerce and Navigation Treaty, 175
U.S.-Japanese baseball exchange, 7, 9, 73, 85, 92, 135, 140, 148, 170, 172, 175, 205, 207, 240; amateur "World Series," 170, 171; baseball brotherhood, 92, 122, 163, 199; baseball fraternalism, 76; baseball interaction, 55, 172; compatibility, 148, 152; friendship, 134–35, 151; relations, 3, 6, 9, 65, 75, 118, 135, 140–41, 153, 170, 220, 244
U.S. military, 48, 51–52, 172, 181, 183–87, 189, 227–28; naval capabilities of, 76
University of Chicago, 92–93; baseball team, 83, 91, 94–95, 102, 149; Board of Physical Culture and Athletics, 94. *See also* Collegiate baseball

Vancouver, 103–4, 109, 125, 127

West Coast, 109, 125, 160, 184, 192; baseball boosters, 215; Hawaiian all-star tour, 106; internment camps, 173, 190; Japanese pro ballplayer tours, 160–61; Major League Baseball expansion to, 236–37; military installations, 188; newspapers, 163; NFL expansion to, 215; professional baseball, 80; returning Japanese internees, 241; Waseda tour of, 89, 140–41, 155
West Point, 11, 17, 48
Wilson, Horace E., 13–15, 29
Women, 4, 45, 67, 74, 181–82, 191, 194, 198, 228–32, 234–35
Women's baseball: first Japanese team, 229; players, 229–31, 233–35
Women's professional baseball, 181, 228–30, 232, 234–35; All-American Girls Professional Baseball League (AAGPBL), 182, 232; American and Japanese women, 233, 235; American Girls Professional Baseball League, 182, 232; femininity and, 233–34; Japanese women's, 233–34; National Girls Baseball League, 182; pioneer female baseball players, 124; salaried women's teams, 231
World Baseball Tournament, 170, 171
World championships, 166–67, 171–72

Index | 313

World Series, 185–86; United States–Japanese amateur, 170, 171, 175
World War II, 2, 7–9, 87, 95, 106, 135, 147–48, 151, 153, 165, 180–84, 186, 190–91, 196–97, 199, 211, 213, 215, 217, 228, 230, 241–43
WRA (War Relocation Authority), 241

Yakyū Tōseirei, 141, 145, 147–48, 154, 208
Yale University, 24, 86, 92–93
Yamato, 60, 159
YMCA (Young Men's Christian Association), 25, 54, 68

Yokohama, 14, 19, 22–24, 26, 30–32, 34–35, 51, 56, 76, 100, 112, 115, 126, 134–35, 138, 151, 159, 221, 229–31
Yokohama Baseball Club (YBC), 31, 33
Yokohama Cricket and Athletic Club (YCAC), 33–35
Yokohama Cricket Club (YCC), 31, 33
Yomiuri Shinbun, 133–34, 136, 148–52, 156, 158, 164, 211, 217, 220, 225–26, 228, 238–39, 242

Zenimura, Kenichi, 105, 193–94